Migration, Multi and Education

NEW PERSPECTIVES ON LANGUAGE AND EDUCATION

Founding Editor: **Viv Edwards**, *University of Reading, UK*
Series Editors: **Phan Le Ha**, *University of Hawaii at Manoa, USA* and Joel Windle, *Monash University, Australia.*

Two decades of research and development in language and literacy education have yielded a broad, multidisciplinary focus. Yet education systems face constant economic and technological change, with attendant issues of identity and power, community and culture. What are the implications for language education of new 'semiotic economies' and communications technologies? Of complex blendings of cultural and linguistic diversity in communities and institutions? Of new cultural, regional and national identities and practices? The New Perspectives on Language and Education series will feature critical and interpretive, disciplinary and multidisciplinary perspectives on teaching and learning, language and literacy in new times. New proposals, particularly for edited volumes, are expected to acknowledge and include perspectives from the Global South. Contributions from scholars from the Global South will be particularly sought out and welcomed, as well as those from marginalized communities within the Global North.

All books in this series are externally peer-reviewed.

Full details of all the books in this series and of all our other publications can be found on http://www.multilingual-matters.com, or by writing to Multilingual Matters, St Nicholas House, 31–34 High Street, Bristol BS1 2AW, UK.

NEW PERSPECTIVES ON LANGUAGE AND EDUCATION: 91

Migration, Multilingualism and Education

Critical Perspectives on Inclusion

Edited by
Latisha Mary, Ann-Birte Krüger and Andrea S. Young

MULTILINGUAL MATTERS
Bristol • Blue Ridge Summit

DOI https://doi.org/10.21832/MARY2941
Library of Congress Cataloging in Publication Data
A catalog record for this book is available from the Library of Congress.
Names: Mary, Latisha - editor. | Krüger, Ann-Birte - editor. |
   Young, Andrea S. - editor.
Title: Migration, Multilingualism and Education: Critical Perspectives on
   Inclusion/Edited by Latisha Mary, Ann-Birte Krüger and Andrea S. Young.
Description: Bristol, UK; Blue Ridge Summit, PA: Multilingual Matters,
   2021. | Series: New Perspectives on Language and Education: 91 |
   Includes bibliographical references and index. | Summary: "This book
   addresses the question of how equitable and inclusive education can be
   implemented in heterogeneous classes where learners' languages and
   cultures reflect the social reality of mass migration and everyday
   plurilingualism. The book brings together researchers and practitioners
   to address language policy and pedagogy"—Provided by publisher.
Identifiers: LCCN 2021004705 (print) | LCCN 2021004706 (ebook) | ISBN
   9781800412934 (paperback) | ISBN 9781800412941 (hardback) | ISBN
   9781800412958 (pdf) | ISBN 9781800412965 (epub) | ISBN 9781800412972
(kindle edition) Subjects: LCSH: Immigrant children—Education. | Language and
education.| Multilingualism in children. | Multicultural education.
Classification: LCC LC3715 .M533 2021 (print) | LCC LC3715 (ebook) | DDC
370.117—dc23
LC record available at https://lccn.loc.gov/2021004705
LC ebook record available at https://lccn.loc.gov/2021004706

British Library Cataloguing in Publication Data
A catalogue entry for this book is available from the British Library.

ISBN-13: 978-1-80041-294-1 (hbk)
ISBN-13: 978-1-80041-293-4 (pbk)

Multilingual Matters
UK: St Nicholas House, 31–34 High Street, Bristol BS1 2AW, UK.
USA: NBN, Blue Ridge Summit, PA, USA.

Website: www.multilingual-matters.com
Twitter: Multi_Ling_Mat
Facebook: https://www.facebook.com/multilingualmatters
Blog: www.channelviewpublications.wordpress.com

Copyright © 2021 Latisha Mary, Ann-Birte Krüger, Andrea S. Young and the authors of individual chapters.

All rights reserved. No part of this work may be reproduced in any form or by any means without permission in writing from the publisher.

The policy of Multilingual Matters/Channel View Publications is to use papers that are natural, renewable and recyclable products, made from wood grown in sustainable forests. In the manufacturing process of our books, and to further support our policy, preference is given to printers that have FSC and PEFC Chain of Custody certification. The FSC and/or PEFC logos will appear on those books where full certification has been granted to the printer concerned.

Typeset by SAN Publishing Services.
Printed and bound in the UK by the CPI Books Group Ltd.
Printed and bound in the US by NBN.

Contents

	Contributors	ix
	Acknowledgements	xix
	Part 1 Ideology Drives Policy: Rethinking Inclusion	
1	Pushing Back Monoglossic Ideologies of Language: Towards Transformative and Inclusive Pedagogies for 21st Century Multilingual Classrooms *Christine Hélot*	3
2	Lines of Exclusion and Possibilities of Inclusion: A Tale of Two Schools in Austria *Judith Purkarthofer*	16
	The Value of Languages in a Multilingual Classroom, *Renata Emilsson Peskova*	33
3	Multilingual Teachers Meet Recently Arrived Students: Language Ideologies and Practices in Preparatory Classes in Germany *Julie A. Panagiotopoulou, Lisa Rosen and Jenna Strzykala*	35
	Supporting Plurilingual Students by Building Professional Educational Networks, *Maryse Adam-Maillet*	52
4	Parents Speaking *Other* Languages in Early Childhood Settings: A 'Language Barrier' for Building an Inclusive Partnership of Education Between Practitioners and Parents? *Nathalie Thomauske*	54
	Establishing a Relationship of Trust between Parents and School, *Marie-Claire Simonin*	68
5	'Dutch if Possible, and Also When It's Not': The Inclusion of Multilingualism in Declared, Perceived and Practiced Language Policies in a Brussels Secondary School *Kirsten Rosiers*	70
	The Importance of Supporting Students' First Languages: Avoiding Unintended Consequences, *Jordan Foster*	91

6	A Longitudinal Study of Emergent Bilinguals among Chinese Pupils at a Japanese Public School: A Focus on Language Policies and Inclusion *Junko Majima and Chiho Sakurai* Inclusive Practices in Multilingual Schools, *Andy Hancock*	93 110
7	'To Make Headway You Have to Go Against the Flow': Resisting Dominant Discourses and Supporting Emergent Bilinguals in a Multilingual Pre-School in France *Latisha Mary and Andrea S. Young* From a Monolingual to a Multilingual Approach in Primary Schools in the Netherlands, *Frederike Groothoff*	112 130
8	Rethinking Inclusion: A Case Study of an Innovative University Diploma Programme for Refugee Students in Grenoble (France) *Stéphanie Galligani and Diana-Lee Simon* The Empowering Role of Teachers, *Samúel Lefever*	131 146

Part 2 'Actuality Implies Possibility': New Practices of Inclusion

9	Experiences, Challenges and Potential of Implementing a Participatory Approach to Designing Educational Material For and With Refugee Women in Greece *Roula Kitsiou, Sofia Tsioli, George Androulakis and Inaam Alibrahim* Recognizing Parents as Resources, *Sylvie Birot-Freyburger*	149 168
10	Transforming Our Classrooms to Embrace Students' Multilingualism Through Translanguaging Pedagogy *Maite T. Sánchez and Ivana Espinet* Monolingualism as a Cure for Language Disorder?, *Joy Pénard*	169 184
11	'Spaces of Power, Spaces of Resistance': Identity Negotiation Through Autobiography with Newcomer Immigrant Students *Timea Kádas Pickel* Understanding, Adapting and Being Noticed in a New School Context, *Kia Kimhag*	185 200
12	Framing Critical Perspectives on Migration, Fairness and Belonging Through the Lens of Young People's Multilingual Digital Stories *Vicky Macleroy* A Non-Traditional Approach to Listening to Students' Voices, *Marie-Paule Lory*	202 220

13	Inclusion Strategies for Emergent Bilingual Pupils in Pre-School in France: The Importance of the Home-School Relationship *Ann-Birte Krüger and Nathalie Thamin*	222
	Funds of Knowledge in Home, School and Research, *Jean Conteh*	241
14	Teacher Language Awareness: A Personal and Pedagogical Journey *Ondine Gage*	242
	Awakening to Languages for Japanese Primary Schools, *Mayo Oyama*	259
15	Fostering More Inclusive Linguistic Practices in Portuguese Classrooms: Is Teacher Education the Key for Integrating Heritage Languages? *Rosa Maria Faneca, Maria Helena Araújo e Sá and Sílvia Melo-Pfeifer*	261
	Suitably Equipped: Towards Confidently Handling a Multicultural Class, *Kathelijne Jordens*	282
16	Pedagogies of Powerful Communication: Enabling Minoritized Students to Express, Expand and Project Identities of Competence *Jim Cummins*	284
	Glossary	298
	Index	300

Contributors

Maryse Adam-Maillet studied French language and literature, psychology, history and philosophy. She has taught French language and literature for 20 years to various student groups ranging from lower secondary school to university. Maryse became a school inspector 19 years ago and has since developed a strong interest in teaching and learning French as a second language and language of schooling. Her writing focuses on French literature, equity in education through language policies, inclusive schooling policies and French as a second schooling language.

Inaam Alibrahim has an Art Diploma from the National College of Syria and has also studied marketing and advertising at the Technological Educational Institute (TEI) of Central Greece. She has completed an MA in 'Language education for refugees and migrants' (2020) and has worked as an interpreter for Arabic, a facilitator and a researcher in various research and educational projects concerning women's and men's educational empowerment and integration. Inaam's research interests include language education for bilinguals, multilingualism, women's rights, arts-based methodologies and religious identities.

George Androulakis studied linguistics and sociolinguistics at the Universities of Athens and Paris 7. He has taught as Adjunct or Visiting Professor at several universities in Greece, France, Switzerland, Canada and the UK. He is now Professor of Sociolinguistics and Language Teaching and Head of the Greek Language and Multilingualism Lab at the University of Thessaly. George's research focuses on migrant and refugee communities, language policy, task-based language teaching and open and distance education. He has been the academic coordinator of many European projects, and he is an expert on language issues for the European Commission and the Council of Europe.

Maria Helena Araújo e Sá is Full Professor in the Department of Education and Psychology (DEP) at the University of Aveiro, Portugal, where she teaches and supervises masters, doctoral and postdoctoral students in the area of language teacher education. She obtained her PhD in didactics in 1994 at the University of Aveiro (UA). Maria has been the Coordinator of the Research Centre on Didactics and Technology in the Education of

Trainers – CIDTFF (since 2016) and the Director of the Doctoral Programme in Education of the UA (since 2014). She is one of the founding members of the Open Laboratory for Foreign Language Learning. She has been involved in several research projects and has published on issues related to intercomprehension, plurilingualism and interculturality.

Sylvie Birot-Freyburger taught in primary schools for 40 years and in nursery school classes that were part of educational priority areas. She worked mainly with children from immigrant backgrounds of the first and second generations. Through this experience, Sylvie gradually realized that recognizing and taking into account the mother tongue and culture led to much better results at school. Meeting academics Andrea Young and Latisha Mary provided a theoretical basis to her observations and real-life practices.

Jean Conteh worked in multilingual contexts for her whole career, first as a primary teacher and teacher educator in different countries and then as an academic. She was a Senior Lecturer at the University of Leeds from 2007 to 2018, where she developed and taught a successful part-time master's course for teachers. Jean has published many books, chapters and articles for different audiences, including *The Multilingual Turn in Languages Education* (Multilingual Matters, 2014) and *The EAL Teaching Book* (3rd edn, Sage, 2019). Her edited book, *Researching Education for Social Justice in Multilingual Settings* (Bloomsbury, 2017), was written in collaboration with her former PhD students.

Jim Cummins is a Professor Emeritus at the Ontario Institute for Studies in Education of the University of Toronto. His research focuses on literacy development in educational contexts characterized by linguistic diversity. In exploring ways in which students' multilingual repertoires can be mobilized for learning within the classroom, Cummins has worked actively and collaboratively with educators to document promising instructional initiatives. A central theme running through his scholarly work has been that educators, individually and collectively, who aspire to reverse patterns of underachievement among minoritized students must be prepared to challenge patterns of coercive power relations operating both in the wider society and in schools.

Ivana Espinet is an Assistant Professor at Kingsborough Community College, USA. She holds a PhD in urban education from the CUNY Graduate Center and an MA in instructional technology and education from Teachers College, Columbia University. She is a former project director for the CUNY-New York State Initiative on Emergent Bilinguals (CUNY-NYSIEB). Ivana is interested in the use of multimodal and collaborative methodologies to learn about emergent bilinguals in school and in out-of-school programmes.

Rosa Maria Faneca is a researcher at the Centre for Didactics and Technology in the Education of Trainers at the University of Aveiro, Portugal. She concluded her PhD in didactics (in 2011) at the University of Aveiro, Portugal. She holds a masters in language didactics from Sorbonne University, France and a degree in French and Portuguese teacher education. She is a member of the Open Laboratory for Foreign Language Learning. Rosa Maria's research interests centre on pedagogy for linguistic and cultural diversity, didactic resources to work on linguistic and intercultural diversity in educational contexts and heritage languages in schools. She is the national coordinator of the KAMILALA project (ERASMUS+) and coordinator of the Multilingual Kamishibai Competition, Portugal.

Jordan Foster is a language educator from Edmonton, Canada. In addition to teaching English, French and Spanish as second languages in a variety of settings in Canada, France and South America, Jordan has also worked as a languages curriculum developer in his home province of Alberta, supporting programming in international languages and English as a second language. As part of his master's degree in applied linguistics at Concordia University (Montréal), Jordan's research focused on topics such as corpus linguistics and written corrective feedback in additional language learning contexts.

Ondine Gage is an Assistant Professor of Education at California State Monterey Bay, USA, whose area of research is language awareness and pre-service teacher language awareness through reflection in writing, training in linguistics and languages, intercultural communication and international virtual exchange. Ondine was perhaps the last graduate student of the late Leo van Lier. Her interest in language awareness follows van Lier's ecological account by exploring pre-service teacher language awareness and opportunities for initiating a generative understanding of language and culture, which enhances language awareness in pedagogical practice.

Stéphanie Galligani is a senior lecturer in language science and French as a foreign language and a member of the Lidilem Laboratory at Grenoble Alpes University, France. Her research into sociolinguistics and language teaching focuses on the phenomena of language contacts – language representations and practices – in a migratory context and on the teaching/learning of French in different academic and social contexts. Stéphanie has developed work on language biographies and plural approaches to languages and culture in teacher education with a special interest in the research methodology undertaken for each of the fields invested.

Frederike Groothoff is a linguist with a background in primary education. She completed her PhD on the Dutch language development of young newly arrived migrant pupils in January 2020 at Utrecht University, the

Netherlands. She currently works as a peripatetic language support advisor in primary education in Amstelveen, the Netherlands, where she coaches and trains teachers on the subject of teaching multilingual students. She also helps schools to make their language policy more inclusive towards home languages. As the founder of LangWhich, Frederike gives lectures and workshops and she develops educational materials about multilingualism and language awareness.

Andy Hancock is Head of the Graduate School of Education & Sport at the University of Edinburgh, UK. He has a background as a teacher working in multilingual schools in London, Zimbabwe and Glasgow. Andy has researched and published extensively on a range of issues including complementary schools and language policy in Scotland. In 2014 he co-edited a volume with Xiao Lan Curdt-Christiansen, *Learning Chinese in Diasporic Communities* (John Benjamins). This book stems from an interest that relates to his PhD study exploring children's biliteracy practices in multilingual settings in Scotland.

Christine Hélot is Emeritus Professor of English at the University of Strasbourg, France. As a sociolinguist, her research focuses on language in education policies in France and in Europe, bi-multilingual education, intercultural education, language awareness, early childhood education and children's literature and multiliteracy. In 1988 Christine obtained her PhD from Trinity College Dublin, Ireland, with a thesis on bilingualism in the family, and in 2005 she was awarded an *Habilitation* (University of Strasbourg) for her research on bi/plurilingualism at school. Christine was a lecturer at the University of Ireland before returning to France and since then has been a guest professor in Spain, Germany, Japan and the USA. She has published widely in French and English, and co-edited several volumes on bilingual and multilingual education. Her research on critical language awareness was the subject of a documentary film entitled *Raconte-moi ta langue/Tell me how you talk*: https://vimeo.com/402284515.

Kathelijne Jordens is passionate about language learning. After she graduated as a speech and language therapist, she started working as a teacher in a school for children with learning disorders. From 2003 to 2016 she worked at the University of Leuven (Belgium) as a developer of language learning resources, teacher trainer and researcher on language acquisition, language testing and multilingualism. Her PhD thesis dealt with the use of multilingual repertoires during children's learning processes. In 2016 she returned to the classroom and now teaches low-literate adults.

Timea Kádas Pickel is an Associate Professor at the University of Paris 8 Vincennes-Saint-Denis, France. Previously she was a postdoctoral fellow at the University of Luxembourg and she has worked as a teacher with 10–16 year-old students of French as a second language in Mulhouse, France, for more than 10 years. Timea holds a PhD from the Universities of Strasbourg and Luxembourg on the successful integration of newcomer students into the French education system. Her research interests include second language learning and teaching, identity (re)construction, empowerment and newcomer students.

Kia Kimhag holds a Fil. Mag in pedagogy/education and works as a senior lecturer in the Department of Education at the University of Gävle, Sweden. Kimhag educates students in teacher education programs and courses for teachers and mother-tongue tutors from the field. She has been involved in international relations for over 23 years and has participated in several national and international projects in the field of uniting humanity, ethnic minorities, culture encounters, interculturalism, migration, refugee pupils, communicating with parents of newly migrated children and early years education. She is also involved in research in the field of education with an interest in internationalisation, interculturalism, migration, values attitudes, learning strategies, early years, and special needs.

Roula Kitsiou holds a PhD in sociolinguistics from the University of Thessaly, Greece, and is a member of the Greek Language and Multilingualism Laboratory at the University of Thessaly. Currently she is working as a tutor of critical pedagogy in the postgraduate programme on language education for refugees and migrants (Hellenic Open University), and has been recently appointed as an Assistant Professor of Sociolinguistics in the Department of Linguistic and Intercultural Studies at the University of Thessaly. Roula's ongoing postdoctoral research is about conventional and alternative literacies of young Arabic-speaking refugees (University of the Aegean, state scholarship). Her research interests include the sociolinguistics of immigration, the sociolinguistics of writing, multiliteracies, multimodality and critical research methodologies.

Ann-Birte Krüger is an Associate Professor of Language Education in the Faculty of Education and member of the Center for Interdisciplinary and Transcultural Research (CRIT) at the University of Bourgogne Franche-Comté, France. Her research in sociolinguistics and language teaching focuses on language contacts – language representations and practices – in a migratory context and on the teaching/learning of the school language for different ages (kindergarten to secondary school) and for different national contexts (France, Germany, Switzerland). Ann-Birte has developed work on home/school relationships and on the subject of Turkish migrants.

Samúel Lefever is an Associate Professor at the University of Iceland and teaches language teaching methodology at the School of Education. He holds a BA degree in Sociology and an MA in Education with emphasis on Teaching English as a Second Language. His research interests include early childhood multilingualism and he is co-editor of *Icelandic Studies on Diversity and Social Justice in Education* (Cambridge Scholars

Publishing) and *Multicultural Voices: Stories from the Classroom* (University of Iceland: Educational Research Institute). His recent publications include articles and chapters which focus on immigrants' language use and participation in Icelandic schools and society.

Marie-Paule Lory is an Assistant Professor in the Department of Language Studies at the University of Toronto Mississauga, Canada. Her main research interests focus on linguistic social representation and beliefs among language learners and teachers. Marie-Paule has extensive experience in training teachers on innovative plurilingual pedagogical practices (in Quebec and Ontario). She is also part of two innovative research projects that support second language development through creative expression: theatre and language awareness activities and plurilingual Kamishibaï. She has been the President of EDILIC (the International *Awakening to Languages* Association, www.edilic.org) since 2017.

Vicky Macleroy is a Reader in Education and Head of the Research Centre for Language, Culture and Learning at Goldsmiths, University of London. Her research focuses on language development, creative writing practices, poetry, multiliteracies and transformative pedagogy. Vicky was principal investigator with Jim Anderson of a global literacy project funded by the Paul Hamlyn Foundation, 'Critical Connections: Multilingual Digital Storytelling' (2012–2017), which uses digital storytelling to support engagement with language learning and digital literacy. Vicky continues to lead multilingual digital storytelling projects funded by the Language Acts and Worldmaking AHRC project and a public engagement grant from Goldsmiths (2018–2021).

Junko Majima is Professor Emerita of Japanese Language Education in the Graduate School of Language and Culture at Osaka University, Japan. She received her BEd from Kyoto University of Education, Japan, in 1982, her MEd in 1990 and her EdD in 1994 from the University of Georgia, Athens, USA, in foreign language education. Junko's research and teaching interests include teaching Japanese as a second language (JSL) to international students, JSL teacher education, second language acquisition, bi/plurilingual education, especially of culturally linguistically diverse (CLD) children raised in Japan, and language policy.

Latisha Mary is an Associate Professor of English and Language Education in the Faculty of Education and Lifelong Learning (INSPE) at the University of Strasbourg, France, where she is involved in initial primary teacher education. A member of the LiLPa Research Group (UR1339), her research focuses on teacher knowledge, attitudes and beliefs about languages, teacher education for the support of second language acquisition, teacher language awareness and the identity construction of multilingual children. Latisha is committed to fostering critical teacher language awareness, developing collaborative home–school relationships and helping teachers support bilingual learners in the classroom. She has been involved in several national and international research and teacher education projects focusing on language awareness, multilingualism and intercultural education.

Sílvia Melo-Pfeifer is an Associate Professor in the Faculty of Education at the Universität Hamburg, Germany. She obtained her degree in French and Portuguese teacher education (in 2000) and her PhD (in 2006) at the University of Aveiro (Portugal). She coordinated the Department of Education at the Portuguese Embassy in Berlin between 2010 and 2013. Sílvia is the coordinator of the Erasmus-Plus Project LoCALL (Local Linguistic Landscapes for Global Language Education in the School Context) and has been publishing about issues related to pluralistic approaches to foreign language learning and teaching, and language teacher education.

Mayo Oyama is a Lecturer in the College of Letters at Ritsumeikan University, Kyoto, Japan. She teaches both French and English as well as teacher training for pre-service elementary school teachers. Mayo's current research interests include plurilingual education for elementary learners, specifically with the *Éveil aux Langues* methodology, for which she has developed materials for the Japanese elementary school context, and teacher training.

Julie A. Panagiotopoulou is a Professor in the Department of Education and Social Sciences at the University of Cologne, Germany. Her research interests include social justice education and inclusion/exclusion in migration societies, multilingualism and literacy, multilingual education and translanguaging, language policy in families, day-care centres and schools and the methodology of multi-sited ethnography.

Joy Pénard is a speech language pathologist in Basel, Switzerland, where she provides assessment and intervention for families, and advocates for multilingualism via presentations and consultations. Joy has presented internationally for the Comité Permanent de Liaison des Orthophonistes-Logopèdes (CPLOL) conference as well as locally for professionals at Novartis, for example. Fluent in French, she has also presented for the Université de Strasbourg as a guest lecturer on multilingualism for future teachers.

Renata Emilsson Peskova is a PhD candidate in the School of Education, Faculty of Education and Diversity at the University of Iceland. Her dissertation, 'School experience of plurilingual students: Multiple case study from Iceland', explores the interplay of linguistic repertoires and school experience of five students in an elementary school, who attend heritage language classes in a non-formal setting. Renata's academic interests span across heritage language education in informal, non-formal and formal settings, plurilingualism and linguistically responsive pedagogies. Renata is a co-founder and teacher at the Czech heritage school in Iceland and a board member of Móðurmál – the Association on Bilingualism.

Judith Purkarthofer is a Junior Professor in the German Studies Department at the University Duisburg-Essen, Germany. She holds a PhD from the University of Vienna, Austria, and has completed postdoctoral work at the Center for Multilingualism in Society across the Lifespan of the University of Oslo, Norway, and at Humboldt-University Berlin, Germany. Judith has published on multilingual speakers in families, teacher education, school language profiles and community media and is currently most interested in language and the construction of multilingual social spaces, particularly in the connection to family language policy and foster care. She carries out ethnographic and biographic research in families, schools and kindergartens.

Lisa Rosen is Professor of Education with a focus on intercultural education at the University of Koblenz-Landau, Department of Educational Science (Campus Landau, Germany). She is the Link Convenor of Network 07 of the European Educational Research Association (EERA) and co-speaker of the special interest group 'Inclusion Research' for the German Educational Research Association (GERA). Lisa's research areas include social justice and intercultural education, multilingual education, inclusive education, pedagogical professionalism, subjectivation and identities in migration societies, forced migration and refugee studies, and intersectional and international comparative educational research.

Kirsten Rosiers is a postdoctoral assistant at Ghent University, Belgium. As a former language teacher, she is interested in multilingual teacher–pupil interaction. Her research interests include language policy, education and multilingualism. Within the research project 'Between the devil and the deep blue sea' (PI Jürgen Jaspers, Université Libre de Bruxelles), she investigated how teachers in secondary education reconcile a monolingual policy with a multilingual reality. For her PhD at Ghent University, Kirsten analysed pupils' and teachers' translanguaging in multilingual primary classrooms in Belgium.

Chiho Sakurai is Associate Professor of Japanese Language Education in the Graduate School of Language and Culture at Osaka University, Japan. She received her BA and MA from former Osaka University of Foreign Studies (which merged into Osaka University in 2007), and her PhD from Osaka University in 2013. Chiho's interests are in teaching Japanese as a second language to children, bilingual education and bilingualism.

Maite T. Sánchez is an Assistant Professor of Bilingual Education at Hunter College of the City University of New York (CUNY). Her research focuses on language education policy and practice for minoritized bi/multilinguals, translanguaging pedagogy and the experiences of novice bilingual education teachers entering the profession. Maite has published in journals such as *Bilingual Research Journal*, *International Journal of Bilingual Education and Bilingualism* and *TESOL Quarterly*. She holds a PhD in education from Boston College. Further information can be found on her website: www.maitesanchez.org.

Diana-Lee Simon is Senior Lecturer in Language Science and French as a Foreign Language and a member of the Lidilem Laboratory, Grenoble Alpes University, France. Her research in the field of language didactics focuses on foreign language teaching and learning within both school and university contexts. Fieldwork in different countries has led Diana-Lee to explore intercultural dimensions, mediation and the role of language repertoires in developing plurilingual competence for both adult and child learners within the scope of pluralistic societies.

Marie-Claire Simonin has been a primary school teacher since 1992. She has worked in a variety of positions, including that of coordinator for the education of Travellers' children from 2006 to 2014. She currently teaches in a multilingual nursery school in a priority education zone in the east of France. Marie-Claire obtained a master's degree in educational research in 2018, with a thesis focused on learning French as a second language in kindergarten. She is currently preparing a doctoral thesis in language sciences; this practical research aims to understand language acquisition by young emergent bilinguals.

Jenna Strzykala is a research fellow and PhD candidate at the University of Cologne, Germany. Her ongoing doctoral dissertation focuses on multilingual teachers' views on language(s) and everyday multilingual practices of staff and students in German schools in the USA and Canada. Jenna's research interests include (forced) migration and multilingualism, educational language policies, translanguaging and internationally comparative educational research.

Nathalie Thamin has been an Associate Professor and Researcher in Linguistics and Language Pedagogy at the University of Bourgogne Franche-Comté, France, since 2011, within the French as a Foreign Language Department. She is a member of the Center for Interdisciplinary and Transcultural Research (CRIT) and an associate researcher at LIDILEM (Center for Research on Linguistics and Native and Foreign Language Teaching) at the University of Grenoble Alpes. Part of Nathalie's current research focuses on language socialization and the schooling of bilingual children within the context of kindergarten; this work concentrates on home/school relationships, support networks and professional training.

Nathalie Thomauske is a French-German researcher and has always been interested in plurilingualism and language education. She has conducted research in this field through her collaboration in a broader international research project, in which she compared language policies in early childhood settings and families in Germany and France. Nathalie is concerned with a deeper understanding of and change in discriminatory practices contributing to an exclusion of plurilingual children from the educational system. She is also interested in translanguaging, (inclusive) plurilingual language education in day-care centres and with families. She works as a consultant, a counsellor and a lecturer.

Sofia Tsioli holds a PhD in applied linguistics and research methodology from the National and Kapodistrian University of Athens, Greece. She is a member of the Greek Language and Multilingualism Laboratory (University of Thessaly), where she has participated in several research programmes concerning immigrants' and refugees' language education. During the previous academic year, she taught courses in 'Issues of Bilingual Education' (University of Patras), 'Sociolinguistic theories of language and teaching' and 'Language didactics' (University of Thessaly). Sofia is currently a postdoctoral researcher in sociolinguistics (University of Thessaly) and is interested in language didactics, research methodology, language policies, arts-based approaches, posthumanism, human rights and political theory. She believes that utopias could come true.

Andrea S. Young is Professor of English and Language Education in the Faculty of Education and Lifelong Learning (INSPÉ) at the University of Strasbourg, France. Throughout her career in the French education sector and within the framework of a variety of initial and continuing professional development programmes, she has sought to raise language awareness among education professionals working in multilingual environments. As a member of the LiLPa Research Group (UR1339), Andrea's research interests include teacher knowledge, attitudes and beliefs about languages and language, home–school educational partnerships and plurilingual and intercultural education in the school context. She has published in a variety of international journals and contributed to a number of edited books specializing in these areas and has also participated in several European projects, notably with the ECML (European Centre for Modern Languages).

Acknowledgements

This edited volume is the fruit of many discussions and exchanges that have taken place over the years among treasured friends, family and colleagues. We thank all of you for your support and for nurturing our reflections and scholarship along the way. We are greatly indebted to you.

We are tremendously grateful to the authors of the chapters and personal perspectives for their valuable contributions, incredible patience and enthusiasm throughout the publication process. It has been an immense pleasure to collaborate with you.

We would like to thank our external reviewers who gave their time and invaluable feedback on the chapters: Mehmet-Ali Akinci, Anne-Sophie Calinon, Antoinette Camilleri Grima, Jean Conteh, Marc Deneire, Joke Dewilde, Anne Durr, Andy Hancock, Christine Hélot, BethAnne Paulsrud, Gail Prasad, Ingrid Smette, Jeanette Toth, Luk Van Mensel, Kutlay Yağmur and Maria Zerva.

Special thanks are also extended to the Université Franco-Allemande for their support of the conference *Migration, multilingualism and education in France and Germany* which was the catalyst for this project. We would also like to thank the Faculty of Education and Lifelong Learning (INSPE) and the research group *Linguistique, Langue, Parole* (LiLPa-UR1339) of the University of Strasbourg for their continued support during this process.

We would like to extend a personal thank you to our families and in particular to our children who continue to be a central source of inspiration. We are particularly grateful to Luc Mary for sharing his time and artistic talent.

Finally, a sincere thank you to the team at Multilingual Matters for their encouragement, patience and editorial assistance.

Part 1
Ideology Drives Policy: Rethinking Inclusion

1 Pushing Back Monoglossic Ideologies of Language: Towards Transformative and Inclusive Pedagogies for 21st Century Multilingual Classrooms

Christine Hélot

In a report published in 2008 by UNESCO, inclusive education is described in the following terms:

> Inclusive education is central to the achievement of high quality education for all learners and the development of more inclusive societies. Inclusion is still thought of in some countries as an approach to serving children with disabilities within general educational settings. Internationally however, it is increasingly seen more broadly as a reform that supports and welcomes diversity amongst all learners. (UNESCO, 2008: 5)

Inclusion is the central notion explored in the 14 chapters that compose this engaging book – a book that takes us on an inspiring journey inside linguistically and culturally diverse classrooms across Europe, North America and Japan. The researchers and practitioners who contributed to the volume all address one crucial question: How can we achieve a more inclusive and equitable education for all learners in 21st century multilingual settings? Indeed, most education systems in the world still educate children through one dominant language, and continue to hold on to the belief that this is the best way towards social integration (Van Avermaet *et al.*, 2018). However, in the process, learners lose their own previously acquired languages and, whether these languages are referred to as 'heritage' or 'family' or 'languages of origin', they end up disappearing or, worse, being forbidden. Why, in our multilingual times, should schools remain bastions of monolingualism, ignore the very resources students need to acquire in the age of a knowledge-based society and waste the opportunity to understand that social cohesion can only be born out of inclusive education?

This book is about inclusion and multilingual education and it links the research and practice of new pedagogical approaches that tackle the relationships between language education and exclusion, language use in school and discrimination (Escudé, 2018), language practices and subordination, and the disempowerment and voicelessness of children who are prevented from using their full linguistic repertoires to learn. In the face of the growing inequalities pervading our contemporary societies and affecting our education systems (see Lahire, 2019, for the latest research in France on inequality, for example), the present volume offers a wealth of examples of 'pedagogies of the possible' (Hélot & Ó Laoire, 2011), pedagogies that conceive of new practices of inclusion based on the following principles: acceptance of all learners, respect for their singularities and pluralities, and curricula in which they see their physical linguistic and cultural environment as well as their identity reflected.

Alongside such an understanding of inclusion, many of the chapters refer to the notion of equity. Equity is different from equality, a central principle of many education systems. Equity means a fair, inclusive and respectful treatment of all people. It is important to insist that, contrary to equality, an equitable approach to education does not imply disregard for individual differences, but that it acknowledges the individual needs of students who, as social actors, have their own learning biographies and their own plurilingual repertoires linked to their socialization and experiences of mobility. In other words, the many children growing up today in families where various languages are spoken display individual linguistic repertoires including multiple cultural experiences that play a crucial role in their learning journeys, and thus demand individual attention. This point is central for many of the educational contexts under study, where the principle of equality supersedes the notion of equity and makes it difficult for teachers to understand that the specific needs of their multilingual students are a matter of equity and not just equality.

As we have written elsewhere (Hélot et al., 2018; Mary & Young, 2018; Young, 2018), and as clearly illustrated in this volume, all classrooms today across the world are multilingual, not because multilingual education is widespread, but because many children come to school speaking a great diversity of languages. An inclusive approach to education therefore means that teachers are educated to understand what it means to grow up with several languages, and that whether these languages are allowed or forbidden in the classroom, they are an integral part of students' learning experiences, of acquiring knowledge in all school subjects, including the language of instruction and the languages taught in schools. In other words, multilingual children should no longer be asked to censor some of their languages, because all their linguistic and cultural experiences are part of their identity, part of their understanding of the world around them and therefore part of the acquisition process of new knowledge.

All the classrooms described in this volume, whether in France, Germany, Austria, England, Cyprus, Portugal, Greece, Palestine, Japan, New York or California, and all the settings presented in the interesting personal testimonies illustrate that linguistic and cultural diversity is now the norm in 21st century classrooms. Previous publications refer to similar research in terms of 'the multilingual turn' (Conteh & Meier, 2014; May, 2013). The multilingual turn not only calls for a profound rethink of our pedagogies, but it demands that we challenge the conceptualization of language and language education as it was formulated in the 20th century, that is, with the main objective of serving the nation-state. Research on language education and language policy in the 21st century has questioned such ideological borders and reframed our understanding of the role of language and languages in our personal lives and for societal goals. Based on poststructuralist approaches to research, the multilingual turn in sociolinguistic and educational research focuses on the language practices rather than on a monolithic vision of language, and on language speakers being social actors who act on their environment through their own way of languaging and translanguaging when they are plurilingual. This implies that, in educational contexts, professionals should understand what it means to language, in and out of school and in and out of different languages, in order to give all learners a chance to understand the role of language(s) in their lives and in society, and to access knowledge through their own individual linguistic repertoires, plurilingual or pluridialectal.

Clearly, as the many studies in this volume show, once learners enter schools, they come into contact with different languages and language varieties and they reconfigure their linguistic repertoires through new communicative experiences in academic settings: they learn the so-called language of instruction even when it is not their first language, they learn foreign or second languages and they acquire the academic register of different school subjects. Furthermore, an impressive body of research has now shown convincingly that there is no need to censor home languages in schools because such policies are not efficient for the acquisition of the dominant language. On the contrary, excluding learners' languaging experiences developed outside school has been shown to be discriminatory, stigmatizing, a form of exclusion and of symbolic violence, an erasure of their linguistic capital, a silencing of minoritized language speakers, a disqualification of students' linguistic resources, a denial of children's voices and one of the main ways through which schools reproduce societal inequalities (Blommaert *et al.*, 2016; Flores & García, 2013; Jaspers, 2011; Martin-Rojo, 2010; Van Avermaet *et al.*, 2018; etc.). As aptly explained by Blommaert *et al.* (2016: 36) in relation to a primary school class for newcomers in Antwerp, 'the home linguistic resources disqualified by teachers are perfectly valuable as resources per se; but they do not qualify symbolically as language'.

What qualifies as a legitimate language in schools or not, and why, is the central question of the first part of the book, which investigates the power of ideologies at work in language education, issues of language inequalities and their impact on speakers of minoritized languages in and out of schools. For example, why is it that, despite the voluminous and evidence-based research that has come out in the past 20 years showing that the maintenance of heritage languages and cultures has benefits on affective, cognitive and social levels and on the acquisition of the school language, it is still so difficult for minoritized language speakers to maintain their family languages (Ferreira et al., 2019)? The second part of the book then concentrates on examples of new conceptualizations of language education with a social justice paradigm in mind, that is, analysing how such inequalities between languages and their speakers can be redressed, how persistent monoglossic ideologies can be contested and how classrooms can become spaces of emancipatory and inclusive practices.

The contexts described can all be considered as monolingual polities. From Austria to Germany, Belgium, France and Japan, we are offered analyses of educational settings where researchers and practitioners struggle against a dominant monolingual ideology which pervades teachers' representations of language and multilingualism, and then impacts their pedagogy and produces different dimensions of exclusion, more specifically when it comes to so-called 'immigrant' or refugee children. The reader will even be exposed to shocking discriminatory practices, for example in a school in Germany, where Arabic speaking children are asked to denounce other children speaking Arabic. This reminds us of the language policies enforced in European countries at the beginning of the 20th century regarding the eradication of regional languages, France being the often-quoted example of the very successful eradication of its many indigenous languages. It also illustrates how a teacher puts the responsibility of her language policy on the shoulders of young learners, destroying any form of solidarity and forcing them to integrate a practice of denunciation, which is highly questionable ethically. Beyond the (im)moral and ideological dimension of such a policy, this example highlights the symbolic violence exercised in educational settings through the practised language policy of some teachers (Bonacina Pugh, 2012), who have had no education about multilingualism and thus remain imprisoned within a monoglossic ideology that constrains the pedagogical affordances of multilingualism in schools. This begs the following question: How does one analyse the persistence of such violent and racist language practices and how does one conceptualize a shift from exclusionary pedagogical practices to inclusive ones?

The chapter by **Purkarthofer** provides us with an illuminating example of mechanisms of inclusion and exclusion through the comparison of the way in which multilingual education is understood in two schools in Austria. Thus a first important point is made: bilingual and multilingual education does not necessarily imply inclusive practices; for example, some languages remain absent from the curriculum and teachers are not aware of their contradictory discourses regarding the languages other than the language of schooling. On the one hand, the teachers express frustration about the lack of Croatian language use at home, but on the other hand, when minoritized migration languages are present in homes, they do not support them at school.

Moving to a classroom for newcomers in Germany, **Panagiotopoulou, Rosen and Strzykala** analyse the pertaining ideology of assimilation in place for refugee students and the delegitimation of Arabic by a teacher with a migrant background in a reception class. I have already mentioned above the denunciation policy put in place in this school regarding Arabic, but other dimensions of the policy are relevant to the discussion on inclusion. For example, in this so-called 'preparatory class', the students never have joint lessons together with mainstream students and the language policy enforced is a telling example of an exclusionary language regime: students are only allowed to whisper in Arabic during recess! While this could be seen by the teachers as a concession or a form of opening towards this minoritized language, what we see here is an example of Othering and exclusion. Arabic speakers are made to silence their language for the benefit of dominant language speakers. In other words, the message is clear: Arabic is not legitimate in the school. Interestingly, the shouting of a teacher when hearing Arabic used by children on the way to the toilets – 'you'll never learn German' – reveals yet again the belief that the use of a home language is a hindrance to the acquisition of the school language, except that not all home languages are subjected to the same negative representations, as indeed in this German school English, for example, is always valued. We are reminded here how some ethnic groups are more vulnerable to social exclusion than others, and how frequent it is for migrant youths speaking Arabic to be marginalized in schools in Europe.

Thomauske, in her chapter on language policies and practices in preschools in Germany, aptly uses the term 'Othered languages' to describe the monolingual hegemonic language order implemented in kitas. She explains how integration and inclusion are always discussed with reference to minoritized language speakers and not to dominant language speakers, and that for most early childhood educators the key to integration in society and to achievement in school remains the mastery of the national language. This then leads to a deficit perspective regarding competence in the national language by minoritized speakers and to Othered languages being seen as a barrier to integration. Furthermore, this deficit perspective often extends from language practices to the educational choices made by minoritized speakers for their children at home. Through focus group interviews with parents and teachers in an early education setting where she compared their de facto language policy, Thomauske shows how parents are made responsible for laying the foundations in the children's home languages and how this leads to Othered languages being banned to the home sphere. She then argues that parents should be equal partners in the education of their children through collaboration with educators and that this could lead to inclusive education being aimed at all children, rather than only to Othered language speakers.

Language policy is the focus of analysis in the next chapter which takes us to a secondary Dutch-medium school in Brussels and to contradictory policy discourses about multilingualism and integration. Here again the prevailing ideology of monolingualism lies at the heart of the institutional language policy and not surprisingly it trickles down into the policy of the school where the research took place. A strict Dutch-only policy was enforced which meant that students speaking Othered languages should be punished. **Rosiers** analyses another example of discriminatory practices towards Othered language speakers: when they speak a language other than Dutch they get a ticket synonymous with a fine. Even if this policy is not written down and has not been seen put into practice during the time of the study, it is still part of the school policy, implying that it could legally be implemented. Yet, at the same time, the school claims to 'want to prepare pupils to respectfully live together in a multilingual city', illustrating how schools are caught in a complex web of token discourses around integration and inclusion that are in fact synonymous with assimilation. This chapter is an excellent example of how difficult it can be in some contexts for teachers to openly choose a positive stance towards multilingualism and then to develop a multilingual pedagogy based on the plurilingual competence of their students. Even if the vagueness of the top-down policy leaves some spaces for interpretation, the teachers have to develop their agency and creativity within such constraints that it seems unlikely that any strategies they implement in their classrooms could ground new policies at the institutional level.

The longitudinal research presented by **Majima and Sakurai** gives some insight into the time it took (10 years) for a school in Japan to move away from a monolingual habitus and to develop an inclusive pedagogy, which led to the high performance of the 20% of Chinese speaking students attending an Osaka school. The authors outline the eight factors that were instrumental in the elaboration of an inclusive policy of multilingualism: support in the Chinese language through the appointment of a very engaged bilingual teacher and specific classes in which this teacher drew on both languages for instruction; improved relationships with Chinese parents through translation; visualization of multilingualism in the school; valuing of the Chinese students' bilingual language practices; an intercultural approach to different cultures including Chinese; a literacy project engaging students to write in both their languages; and an understanding of the relationship between language and identity by encouraging students to express themselves in public in both their languages. According to the authors, it is the combination of all these measures that led to the students' academic success. Followed over five years by Majima and Sakurai, the students became proficient bilingual speakers with high self-esteem and positive attitudes towards their identity; moreover, the school's ethos was transformed as well as the attitudes of students, teachers and people in the local community towards different cultures and languages.

The next chapter takes us to a kindergarten classroom in France where **Mary and Young** analyse how one experienced teacher managed to develop an inclusive pedagogy with very young multilingual children (three years old) speaking languages of which she had very little knowledge. Through this case study, the authors describe in detail the longitudinal reflexive journey this one teacher took to embrace multilingualism, to devise inclusive strategies to support her students' identity and bi/multilingual language development and to involve parents in her classroom. Mary and Young argue that this in-depth understanding of the teacher's critical reflections on her own professional identity helps to understand how and why some teachers are able to become agents of change even within very constrained monoglossic policies. Drawing on this biographical journey, they propose new directions for teacher education, arguing that the multilingual classrooms of the 21st century demand a shift in values, an increased engagement for social justice and a new understanding of critical teacher cognition.

Mary and Young's chapter is all the more relevant when the reader is reminded, in the next chapter by **Galligani and Simon**, that the UNESCO (2005) report on inclusion stresses the importance of attitudes towards inclusion. In this chapter we are given examples of what teachers' attitudes mean in a university context in Grenoble (France), where a course was designed for refugee students which delivered a special diploma. In this case, the context studied by the two researchers is a university known for its humanitarian values towards migrant students; in other words, it not only welcomes diversity, but aims to respond to it by removing barriers and providing equal access to education to all. Galligani and Simon focus on the challenges faced by the teachers involved in teaching French to refugees and how their roles and functions had to change in order for them to implement a process of social and academic inclusion. Using García *et al.*'s (2017) notion of stance and their model for the new roles teachers must endorse as activists if they wish to depart from an authoritative and transmission stance, they show, as in the previous chapter, that inclusive pedagogies imply a shift in teachers' perception of their roles and functions. Furthermore, in the case of adult migrants, as was argued in the Council of Europe report on the education of adult migrants (Beacco *et al.*, 2017), social inclusion is necessary to nourish the motivation to learn the societal language, rather than the traditional belief that language competence is a prerequisite for social integration.

The second part of this volume, entitled 'Actuality Implies Possibility: New Practices of Inclusion', includes another seven chapters that focus on innovative pedagogical practices of inclusion in a further variety of educational contexts, spanning from Greece to New York to California, France and Portugal, and in the chapter by Macleroy three schools in Cyprus, England and Palestine are compared.

Like Galligani and Simon in the first part of the volume, **Kitsiou, Tsoli, Androulakis and Alibrahim** discuss the education of adult refugees, in this case women refugees on two islands in Greece, and a project initiated, as in Grenoble, by a university (The Hellenic Open University). The chapter deals with one part of a wider initiative to develop education and support for refugees. Entitled 'Languages without Borders', this initiative gives a truly inspiring example of transformative and emancipatory education designed by, with and for refugee women. Based on critical pedagogy, on participatory research and on translanguaging theory, the project involved a group of women with different experiences of migration and varied language repertoires who, together, elaborated educational materials which they then exchanged with 80 refugee women. Starting from a reflection on the emergency context in which refugee women live, a context characterized by lack of freedom of movement, no opportunities to improve their lives, and many experiences of exclusion, the research participants imagined their project as offering a new dynamic space of transformation and empowerment. Compared to the constraints described in traditional educational spaces such as schools, the affordances of a context such as refugee camps seemed far more challenging, yet the participatory approach combined with the translanguaging framework produced the most creative and innovative educational materials to answer refugee women's future aspirations.

A further understanding of translanguaging pedagogy as a transformative and transgressive practice is presented in the next chapter by **Sánchez and Espinet**, who analyse two highly diverse classrooms in New York City where English is the main language of instruction. A translanguaging pedagogy was introduced in these two classrooms in order, as in the previous chapter, to transform the students' learning space. Thus we discover the transformative practices of two educators who managed to leverage the students' cultural and linguistic home practices in the classroom. The notion of translanguaging is central to the concept of inclusion because it allows students to language using their plurilingual competence as befits the communicative situation and context of exchange. Indeed, the notion of translanguaging has reframed the understanding of multilingual practices in education, because it does not involve only the language of instruction but concerns all the languaging resources that are considered essential components of the students' lives and learning. Here again, we understand that it is a matter of teachers' stance for diverse linguistic and cultural practices to flow through classrooms and therefore to give a voice to disempowered students.

In the following chapter, the same issues are at stake: How can one support young adolescent students to draw on their plurilingual competence in order to investigate complex issues of identity, integration and inclusion? **Pickel**'s context is a reception class for newcomer adolescent students in France, where she challenged the institutional language policy focusing predominantly on the rapid acquisition of the French language and questioned the erasure of her students' linguistic and cultural capital. Based on a pluridisciplinary theoretical investigation of the notion of identity, declined as narrative identity, autobiographical self, identity texts and silenced dialogue, she implemented a transformative pedagogical space which gave her students a new voice and confidence to rebuild their lives in France. In other words, through a multilingual multimodal literacy project on autobiography, and through the photo-voice approach, her so-called 'beginner learners of French' developed competences that went way beyond acquiring the school language: they became authors of their own lives through the writing of autobiographical texts and like professional photographers they showcased their portraits in an art gallery, modelling to the public through this process that they were well able to reconstruct their identities and make sense of their new lives through the powerful use of the dominant societal language.

Looking at three schools in Cyprus, England and Palestine, **Macleroy**'s chapter also deals with innovative approaches to teaching literacy within a social justice framework. Like Pickel, she argues for young people to be allowed to draw on their full plurilingual repertoires in order to become storytellers of their own lives. Only through this process could they investigate complex questions of identity, integration and inclusion. And again, just like Pickel in France, Macleroy was inspired by the desire of her students to be seen in a different light and to express strong messages of resistance and hope. These two illuminating chapters point to the need to reframe literacy teaching, to understand that a single fixed literacy approach cannot be inclusive of the diverse students' experiences and voices, and that students are well able to define inclusion on their own terms. Therefore we need to listen to these students' voices if we want to challenge the dominant discourses on migration and displacement.

Krüger and Thamin take a different angle on schools as spaces for social transformation by looking at the role of parents in a multilingual pre-school in France where parents became legitimate partners of the institution. Parents acted as translators, read stories to children in class and participated in 'parents' cafés' where they could exchange on their role in and out of school. The analysis shows how the project had two main consequences: the so-called 'migrant' parents felt empowered through the legitimation of their languages in the school, and the teachers became aware of the way their young students' languages had been invisibilized and the children silenced in class. One teacher is even reported as having stopped repeating the often-heard school message, 'here we speak French'.

Researching a low-income rural English classroom in California, **Gage** describes yet another context that is hostile to multilingualism but where one highly multilingual teacher makes a difference for her Spanish speaking students and their families. Reminiscent of Mary and Young's chapter in the first part of the book, we are given further proof that it is possible for one individual teacher working in a restrictive monolingual context to develop an inclusive learning environment. In this case inclusion comes in three dimensions: the support of the students' multiple identities (through having them value their heritage languages); the development of an empathetic perspective towards them (through a home-school connection); and a focus on moments of affordances for language awareness (drawing out metalinguistic comments through the comparison of Spanish with English). Interestingly, Gage makes the point that this was all due to the teacher's personal experiences of diversity and her engagement in language learning throughout her life, two factors that shaped her views on teaching multilingual students. In other words, because she was linguistically aware herself, she could implement a metalinguistic awareness approach with her students, and engage them cognitively, emotionally, and socially.

Moving from one teacher's language awareness to teacher education programs in Portugal, **Faneca, Araújo e Sá and Melo-Pfeifer** discuss the reasons why we need to include an emancipatory perspective in the education of teachers today if we expect them to transform their professional context, i.e. to understand the pedagogical value of integrating the students' heritage languages in their learning experiences. They examine ten follow-up didactic implementations by trainee teachers who had attended a course on the integration of linguistic and cultural diversity in Portuguese schools. The analysis shows how the teachers became aware that they could actually negotiate their constraining curriculum and open new spaces in their teaching of Portuguese or other languages for their students' heritage languages, for some language awareness activities and to develop motivation to learn new languages. This said, the chapter points to the difficulty for teachers to rethink their stance regarding their role as actors of change in an education system that has still not abandoned its monolingual habitus and that does not encourage collaboration between individual teachers. Another strong point is made in relation to the notion of power: teachers need to legitimate the students' knowledge of their heritage languages, and to let go of their own control, if such knowledge is to be shared in the classroom. This is still seen as risk taking by many teachers such as those in these Portuguese classrooms who are ready to support their multilingual students affectively but less sure about actually making space for their plurilingual repertoires to be an integral part of the teaching culture.

All in all, the 15 chapters of this book tell a fascinating story of how researchers and teachers throughout the world are grappling with the barriers that prevent them from including the languaging of multilingual learners in today's classrooms while at the same time creatively opening new transgressive spaces where they will lead them to achieve academic success. Through the numerous examples of teachers adopting a new stance in their professional identities based on values such as engagement for social justice, we are given convincing evidence that inclusion is no longer a tokenistic notion figuring only in international reports (European Parliament, 2009) or official policy documents. Inclusive educational practices can become a reality when relationships of power, language subordination, voicelessness and lack of agency are scrutinized in everyday interactions in multilingual classrooms as we are given to read in this volume. This said, none of the chapters avoids the complexity involved in the implementation of inclusive educational practices and of adopting an emancipatory philosophy of education in contexts that remain hostile to multilingualism.

As an added bonus to the 15 chapters, the book also includes 15 corresponding vignettes of personal testimonies from a great variety of educational actors (a speech pathologist, parents, teachers, a teacher educator, a school inspector, second language coordinators, etc.) who also tell us their own stories of inclusive practices as they have seen them implemented or have researched them. All these testimonies take us to further contexts such as Iceland, Switzerland, Scotland, Sweden, Canada, Japan, the UK, the Netherlands, etc., and provide us with extra evidence that teachers can be major agents of change, on an individual basis or through a reconceptualization of teacher education curricula. Again, what we see at work are various forms of engagement at policy and practice levels, examples of how to contest monoglossic policies in place, arguments for equitable practices that are sensitive to the individual learning needs of multilingual students, and imagination to innovate pedagogically when, for example, working with a multiplicity of languages one does not know, or transgressing traditional literacy practices for newcomers.

This book offers many inspiring examples of classrooms as sites of transformative and transgressive pedagogies, where collaborative approaches to language education show convincingly that it is possible to make multilingualism the new norm in 21st century classrooms, where the language subordination of minoritized language speakers can be challenged and where students with migration experiences can become accomplished storytellers and authors of their own lives and learning paths. Many students' and teachers' voices are heard in the wealth of data presented. They tell stories of resistance and hope, of reflective journeys through lived experiences of multiple languages and of the creativity of educators who believe it is up to schools to adapt to the new realities of the 21st century and not up to students to adapt to constraining learning contexts that rob them of their potential as creative thinkers.

For researchers, the similarity of issues across contexts such as the remaining dominant ideology of monolingualism in our language education policies gives food for thought for future research into how best to challenge the dominant negative discourses on migration and displacement and on the relationship between linguistic diversity and social justice (Piller, 2016). Most importantly, the empirical evidence running through the 15 chapters of this book pushes back monoglossic and diglossic ideologies of language that position multilingualism as a challenge to be overcome, rather than as the very resource we need to educate children in the 21st century. This should convince policymakers and international institutions dealing with multilingualism that it is high time that inclusive education is taken seriously, because in our knowledge-based societies, social cohesion starts with inclusive educational practices (see also Flecha, 2015). There are still too many school systems in the world that are failing children through exclusionary practices and robbing them of the benefits that should be available to all. This book gives ample proof that this situation can be reversed because, as expressed by Dei (2006), a Canadian anti-racism advocate, 'inclusion is not bringing people into what already exists; it is creating a new space that is better for everyone'.

References

Beacco, J.C., Krumm, H.J., Little, D. and Thalgott, P. (eds) (2017) *The Linguistic Integration of Adult Migrants/L'intégration linguistique des migrants adultes. Some Lessons from Research/Les enseignements de la recherche*. Berlin and Boston, MA: Conseil de l'Europe, De Gruyter Mouton.
Blommaert, J., Spotti, M., Arnaut, K. and Rampton, B. (2016) Introduction. In K. Arnaut, J. Blommaert, B. Rampton and M. Spotti (eds) *Language and Superdiversity* (pp. 1–17). New York: Routledge.
Bonacina Pugh, F. (2012) Researching 'practiced language policies': Insights from conversation analysis. *Language Policy* 11 (3), 213–234.
Conteh, J. and Meier, G. (eds) (2014) *The Multilingual Turn in Languages Education: Opportunities and Challenges*. Bristol: Multilingual Matters.
Dei, G.S.N. (2006) Meeting equity fair and square. Keynote address to the Leadership Conference of the Elementary Teachers' Federation of Ontario, 28 September 2006, Mississauga, Ontario.
Escudé, P. (2018) *Langues et discriminations*. Les cahiers de la lutte contre les discriminations 7. Paris: L'Harmattan.
European Parliament (2009) *Educating the Children of Migrants (2008/2328(INI))*. Brussels: European Parliament.
Ferreira, A., Viola, G. and Schwieter, J.W. (2019) Minority languages at home and abroad: Education and acculturation. In J. Schwieter and A. Benati (eds) *The Cambridge Handbook of Language Learning* (pp. 696–726). Cambridge: Cambridge University Press.
Flecha, R. (ed.) (2015) *Successful Educational Actions for Inclusion and Social Cohesion in Europe*. Cham: Springer.

Flores, N. and García, O. (2013) Linguistic third spaces in education: Teachers' translanguaging across the bilingual continuum. In D. Little, C. Leung and P. Van Avermaet (eds) *Managing Diversity in Education: Languages, Policies, Pedagogies* (pp. 243–256). Bristol: Multilingual Matters.

García, O. and Leiva, C. (2014) Theorizing and enacting translanguaging for social justice. In A. Blackledge and A. Creese (eds) *Heteroglossia as Practice and Pedagogy* (pp. 199–216). New York: Springer.

García, O., Johnson, S. and Seltzer, K. (2017) *The Translanguaging Classroom: Leveraging Student Bilingualism for Learning*. Philadelphia, PA: Caslon.

Hélot, C. and Ó Laoire, M. (eds) (2011) *Language Policy for the Multilingual Classroom: Pedagogies of the Possible*. Bristol: Multilingual Matters.

Hélot, C., Frijns, C., Gorp, K. and Sierens, S. (eds) (2018) *Language Awareness in Multilingual Classrooms in Europe*. Amsterdam: De Gruyter Mouton.

Jaspers, J. (2011) Managing globalization at school: A review of constructing inequality in multilingual classrooms. *Journal of Multicultural Discourses* 6 (1), 93–97.

Lahire, B. (ed.) (2019) *Enfances de classe: De l'inégalité parmi les enfants*. Paris: Editions du Seuil.

Martin Rojo, L. (2010) *Constructing Inequality in Multilingual Classrooms*. New York: De Mouton Gruyter.

Mary, L. and Young, A. (2018) 'Black, blanc, beur': The challenges and opportunities for developing teacher language awareness in the French educational context. In C. Hélot, C. Frijns, K. Van Gorp and S. Sierens (eds) *Language Awareness in Multilingual Classrooms in Europe: From Theory to Practice* (pp. 275–299). Contributions to the Sociology of Language 109. Berlin: De Gruyter Mouton.

May, S. (2013) *The Multilingual Turn: Implications for SLA, TESOL and Bilingual Education*. London: Routledge.

Piller, I. (2016) *Linguistic Diversity and Social Justice: An Introduction to Applied Sociolinguistics*. Oxford: Oxford University Press.

UNESCO (2005) *Guidelines for Inclusion: Ensuring Access for Education for All*. Paris: UNESCO. See https://unesdoc.unesco.org/ark:/48223/pf0000140224 (accessed 13 January 2020).

UNESCO (2008) *Inclusive Education: The Way of the Future*. Reference document, International Conference on Education, 48th session, 25–28 November 2008, International Conference Centre, Geneva. See http://www.ibe.unesco.org/fileadmin/user_upload/Policy_Dialogue/48th_ICE/CONFINTED_48-3_English.pdf (accessed 13 January 2020).

UNESCO (2017) *A Guide for Ensuring Inclusion and Equity in Education*. Paris: UNESCO. See http://unesdoc.unesco.org/images/0024/002482/248254e.pdf.

Van Avermaet, P., Slembrouck, S., Van Gorp, K., Sierens, S. and Maryns, K. (eds) (2018) *The Multilingual Edge of Education*. London: Palgrave Macmillan.

Young, A. (2018) Language awareness, language diversity and migrant languages in the primary school. In P. Garrett and J.M. Cots (eds) *The Routledge Handbook of Language Awareness* (pp. 23–39). New York: Routledge.

2 Lines of Exclusion and Possibilities of Inclusion: A Tale of Two Schools in Austria

Judith Purkarthofer

Introduction

Multilingual education (ME) can take many different forms (Cenoz, 2009) but is understood here to cover educational contexts where learning and teaching are conducted in more than one language. ME takes place in classrooms with heterogeneous groups of learners and it ranges from highly structured trilingual teaching programmes to ad hoc responses to the communicative needs that students may bring to class. In light of the European Union's goals to enhance individual multilingualism among its citizens, ME is considered an appropriate response and is assumed to be generally beneficial in policy documents, e.g. by the Barcelona European Council (European Commission, 2002). Research on multilingual language biographies (Busch, 2017) underlines the importance of multilingual learning opportunities in order for speakers to be able to successfully build their multilingual repertoires. Hornberger (2009) speaks of ideological and implementational spaces for multilingual learning, thereby highlighting the influence of ideologies on education as well as the need to implement policy and thus create spaces where exchange and learning can occur. Still, as language is a socially contested field, it is linked to language hierarchies of minoritized languages and marginalized speakers, and there is the risk that ME produces and enforces new lines of exclusion. In this chapter, I present the case of two schools, each multilingual in its own way, to understand how ideologies, policies and organization contribute to the possibilities of inclusion or exclusion of certain languages and speakers. I will start with a closer look at the triad of ideology, policy and organization in ME, before I introduce the two schools and my methodological and analytical framework. Inclusion and exclusion, serving as analytical concepts, will be discussed thereafter. In the following section, the triad of ideology, policy and organization will serve as the lens of the analysis, before arriving at the concluding discussion.

Ideology, Policy and Organization in Multilingual Education

ME is an organizational issue that requires policies and planning to take communicative resources into account and make them work together for the benefit of speakers and learners. It draws on international and national resources (i.e. curricula), on multilingual teachers with their respective learning biographies and trajectories and on communities of parents and children deeming this type of schooling relevant for them. Decisions concerning ME are guided by language ideologies and lived language experiences, and they are put into practice by taking the availability of teachers, students and other resources into account. Language ideologies can be understood as 'speakers' consciousness of their language and discourse as well as their positionality [...] in shaping beliefs, proclamations, and evaluations of linguistic forms and discursive practices' (Kroskrity, 2010: 192). Teachers in educational institutions as well as parents and children may act on contradictory ideologies at times: they favour certain language uses over others, express whether and which languages are regarded as valuable or imagine multilingual futures for children and the means by which they should be achieved. Pavlenko and Blackledge speak of the power relations between languages and language ideologies which they consider anything but neutral, and where 'negotiation is a logical outcome of this inequality: it may take place between individuals, between majority and minority groups, and, most importantly, between institutions and those they are supposed to serve' (Pavlenko & Blackledge, 2004: 3).

Ideologies can translate into policies and influence language organization. But teaching and learning practices also challenge ideologies, leading to potential changes over time. Canagarajah (2013) calls for the recognition of translingual practices in opposition to a monolingual orientation that draws simplified connections between territories, speakers and languages as separable entities. He writes that 'users negotiate both the diverse semiotic resources in their repertoire and the context to [be ...] most appropriate [...] and effective for this situation' (Canagarajah, 2013: 8). Speakers, as well as researchers, are thus always positioned at a certain point in time and space, and need to be aware of their partiality. ME takes many different shapes, and Hornberger (2009) summarizes in the following three points how, at its best, ME is:

> (1) multilingual in that it uses and values more than one language [...], (2) intercultural in that it recognizes and values understanding and dialogue across different lived experiences [...], and (3) education that draws out,

taking [...] the knowledge students bring to the classroom and moving toward their participation as full and indispensable actors in society – locally, nationally, and globally. (Hornberger, 2009: 198)

To understand ME in any given school, a perspective on macro, meso and micro levels is needed. Musk (2010) argues that schools take on an important role at the meso level of society and should thus be at the centre of attention. Both individuals and social connections are relevant. hooks reminds us that 'the classroom itself needs to be a space where each person can be confident that their voice will be recognized and valued' (hooks, 1994: 186), while Dewey highlights the role of structure and connections, stating that 'organization is nothing but getting things into connection with one another, so that they work easily, flexibly, and fully' (Dewey, 1990 [1915]: 64). As educators and researchers, we need to see both the macro level of ideology and policy as well as the micro level of individuals who interact with each other on a regular basis. At the same time, we have to be aware of both the manifest and the hidden curricula, the latter being learned by all students despite no teacher ever having explicitly taught it (Banks, 2001).

In the next section, I will describe two very specific schools, and they will serve as examples to highlight how ideologies, policies and forms of language organization can contribute to the normalization of multilingualism but also to the normalization of hierarchies and exclusion within institutions.

Data Collection, Methodological and Analytical Framework

A tale of two schools

The analysis in this chapter builds on research conducted in two schools between 2010 and 2015, and their example is used to draw attention to the 'close detail of local action and interaction [...] embedded in a consideration of the wider social world' (Creese, 2011: 44). The results are not only specific to Austria, but are also transferable to other locations where multilingual students meet national public education.1 Both schools voiced interest in developing their potential of ME and both present themselves as bi- or multilingual. The size of the schools is comparable, despite their respective locations in a small town and a rather large city. I have named them School A and School B, and in this section I will give a brief description of their language set-up, as described by the teachers and the school leadership (see also Table 2.1).

School A is situated in a region where Burgenland-Croatian2 is recognized as a minority language but is now infrequently used with the exception of older speakers. This school is located on the eastern border of Austria, in a region that has flourished economically, with an increase in migrants from the neighbouring countries as well as Turkey due to

Table 2.1 Overview of language education in the two schools

	School A	School B
Surroundings	Small town, bilingual area with recognized minority languages	Capital city, no recognized minority languages in schools
Age of students	6–10 years	6–10 years
Types of classes (according to the schools)		
'Bilingual classes'	Unstructured bilingual instruction (German, Burgenland-Croatian)	Team teaching in the English/ German classes
'Spanish classes'		30 minutes of Spanish per day
'Multilingual classes'		Turkish, Bosnian-Croatian-Serbian (12 hours per week, in team teaching
'Foreign languages'	English for all students (one hour per week)	English for all students (one hour per week)
'Mother tongue education'	Turkish (two hours per week, in the afternoon, as a voluntary subject for home language speakers)	Prior to multilingual classes: Bosnian-Croatian-Serbian and Turkish (two hours per week, in the afternoon, as a voluntary subject for home language speakers)
Teaching staff	German and Burgenland-Croatian speaking classroom teachers Mother tongue education teacher (Turkish)	German speaking classroom teachers English speaking native speakers (bilingual classes) Spanish speakers (Spanish classes) Mother tongue education teachers (Turkish, Bosnian-Croatian-Serbian) (multilingual classes)
Other languages (of students and their families)	Croatian, Hungarian, Slovak, …	Polish, Arabic, Chechen, Romanian, Albanian, …

employment opportunities. Hungarian and Slovak, along with Turkish, have thus become more frequent home languages. The school is officially bilingual in German and Burgenland-Croatian and offers English for all students as a foreign language. Students with Turkish as a home language have the option of signing up for Turkish mother tongue education.

School B is situated in a residential district in Vienna, the capital city of Austria. A traditional working-class neighbourhood, with an above average population of residents with migrant backgrounds, the area has recently seen effects of gentrification with noticeable demographic changes in the student population. The school offers one 'bilingual' class per grade with team teaching of one German speaking teacher and one 'native speaker' teacher for English (I will elaborate on the term 'native speaker' further below). Students in all other classes receive tuition in

English as a foreign language. In addition, the school offers one class per grade where Spanish is taught. One class per grade is taught in German as the language of instruction, with inclusion of trilingual literacy in recent years in Bosnian-Croatian-Serbian and Turkish.

Methodological and analytical framework

School language profiles (SLP) consist of a series of activities and research modules aimed at involving teachers, students and parents in joint research of their language experiences (for a more complete picture, see Busch, 2010; Purkarthofer, 2017). The focus is on the speakers' biographical and situational experiences, taking into account their emotions, motivations and imaginations. The research process is driven by the aim to uncover language attitudes and motivations, to collaborate with participants in and around the school and to finally bring the results and findings to the attention of policymakers. This research is situated in a framework of biographic approaches (Busch, 2017) and has close links to the ethnography of language policy and planning research and ethnographic monitoring (De Korne & Hornberger, 2017).

In this specific case, the data collection in both schools was done over a period of several months which included repeated visits to the schools. Within a larger project on language experiences in minority language schools that included several bilingual schools in the region, I was present in School A as a participant observer, collected linguistic landscapes and held workshops with students from different classes. In addition, about one-third of the school's teachers were interviewed, with a focus on the third and fourth grades, and one group discussion with parents was organized with the help of the school. Interestingly enough, many multilingual parents took part in the discussion, which was reportedly not so often the case in regular parent activities. In School B, I was contacted by one of the school teachers and joined their school development efforts: I carried out participant observations in several classes, collected linguistic landscapes and held one biographic workshop in a bilingual class. Group discussions with teachers and feedback sessions with the school team were organized as part of the consultations. Field notes and recordings were then analysed. For dissemination purposes, a presentation for the school community in School A was organized. In School B, bi-monthly consultations with the teachers on ME and multilingualism were part of the collaboration agreement during one school year.

To present the analysis of mechanisms of inclusion or exclusion here, I am drawing on the observed practices, on linguistic landscapes and also on interviews with teachers and parents. In the next subsection, I will discuss the concepts and how they are relevant with regard to ideology, policy and organization.

Inclusion/exclusion in the school context

Inclusion is defined broadly in the UNESCO documents about equity and inclusion in schools as a 'process that helps to overcome barriers limiting the presence, participation and achievement of learners' (UNESCO, 2017: 7). While aiming for an understanding that focuses on the process instead of a specific group of learners who are constructed as being 'in need of special treatment', this definition conveniently renders actors invisible and leaves the responsibility for inclusion relatively unclear. The social set-up of society is 'not an unchangeable order beyond human control but a pattern of human action' (Rawls, 1972: 102) and, as such, inclusion and exclusion are produced through policy and organizational practices, and their underlying ideologies. However, it is necessary to see that inclusion and exclusion do not work as binary oppositions, let alone as static concepts. In an observation of social circumstances, the construction of such a distinction can only serve as an artifice constructed for instrumental purposes (Mascareño & Carvajal, 2015: 127). Scholars agree that inclusion and exclusion are cumulative, and can form exclusionary chains (Luhmann, 1995). Let us look at the example of a student's background. They can experience disadvantages from having a language other than the language of instruction as their main home language (as they might only be learning the language of instruction), but they might also experience exclusionary effects of lower social status, lower household income and so forth, that are not in direct connection to their home language but are also not completely independent from it (as their parents might be perceived differently in society, resulting in lesser paid jobs, for example). The same language need not necessarily be a limitation for another student who might have a different background or possesses more economic resources. However, languages are not neutral and some are more likely to be negatively evaluated or are more closely linked to the discursive construction as the 'Other' within a society (Norton, 2013). Differentiating speakers, for instance, according to their languages, constructing their belonging to certain imagined groups and linking expectations to this belonging is what produces social exclusion or inclusion.

Hillmert (2009: 85) identifies education as one of the fields of exclusion and he describes its strong effects on both individuals and collective groups: on the one hand, each individual can benefit from or be hindered through lack of education; on the other hand, education is seen as collectively relevant for social cohesion and integration. Who can join certain schools, who gets offers for educational opportunities and in which languages those offers are available are some questions whose answers cater to specific individuals, but their collective effects produce the durable exclusion of some (speakers and languages) in society (Hillmert, 2009: 97).

Gibson (2009: 12) highlights the need to evaluate teacher roles in light of mixed-ability groups and, as I would add, in groups of multilingual students. 'Education communities need to create "safe spaces" for departures from normative practice to be discussed: space and time devoted to accessing, listening to and understanding the voices and therefore ideas of that deemed "other"' (Gibson, 2009: 17). Giroux (1992: 32) addresses this when he writes about the 'ways in which difference is constructed through various representations and practices that name, legitimate, marginalize, and exclude the voices of subordinate groups'. Both Gibson and Giroux highlight the role of educational institutions and teachers in particular in creating opportunities to de-learn hegemonic discourses and to open up spaces of interaction. In the following examples, I will draw on those ideas to see how two Austrian primary schools create spaces for ME and how they take into consideration the background of their multilingual students.

Ideology, Policy and Organization of Languages and Speakers

ME caters to different students, from international schools with a highly mobile and rather elite student body to bilingual schools whose aim is a well-balanced education in two or more national languages or schools that want to support minoritized languages or even revitalize them. Within European countries, we see a distinction between migrant and minority languages, with proponents of the latter sometimes being among the strongest opponents of inclusive ME. But we also see examples of minority language schooling serving as a model to integrate more than one or two languages into the language policy of a school, as well as minority language teachers drawing on their experiences to deal with multilingual practices. In the following analysis, I demonstrate how ideology, policy and organization open up ideological and implementational spaces for different languages and how this contributes to the inclusion or exclusion of certain (groups of) speakers.

Languages included: Ideologies of languages and speakers

Austria's school system is for the most part monolingual, despite one-quarter of its student population speaking another language in addition to German at home (BMB, 2018). In contrast, both schools in this study understand themselves to be part of ME, and they express strong beliefs in its value, by adopting national and local policies and contributing to multilingual practices through their organization and their teachers and students.

In School A, both German and Burgenland-Croatian have an official status in the curriculum, along with English as a foreign language (see Table 2.1). The school puts emphasis on its multilingual identity and posters and signs and has at least two languages present (German, Burgenland-Croatian and at times English). In interviews, teachers describe the changes from a time when everybody was able to speak Burgenland-Croatian, some 50 years ago:

Teacher A1 (translated from German): When I was attending first grade, everybody knew Croatian. All children. Everybody could speak Croatian, because the parents and grandparents knew it. But now, more people are moving to the town and they simply learn it [at school, but don't use it any more].

A shared observation in many minority language schools in Austria is the decline of language skills of students (and parents). While Burgenland-Croatian, as well as Hungarian and Slovene in other regions, were still commonly used until the 1960s, many families reacted to political pressure with language shift and opted for German as the language of perceived social success. Many teachers voice their opinion of having to revitalize and teach a vernacular language that students have little or no exposure to prior to school. Teaching methods that target first language speakers, as the curriculum suggests, are thus deemed unfit for these students.

In School B, structured multilingualism includes German as the main language of the school and its surroundings, and English in the bilingual classes as well as Spanish in the Spanish classes. For the teachers, German and English are the main languages of communication, as most of the teachers have been trained in Austria and many of the English language native speakers use English in the school context as their German competence varies. Both English and Spanish are visible in the linguistic landscapes of the school as important languages that often have international ties and a wide communicative range, and students are required to have some prior knowledge of these languages. Parents have to apply to the school in order for their children to join these forms of ME. Other languages that the students speak are present in the posters at the school entrance and in small posters with information on several languages; however, the function of multilingualism is primarily symbolic in these instances.

As part of the work agreement with the school, I prepared a workshop for all teachers of the school, which they attended as a form of internal training. After an introduction to ME and lived language experiences, I collected individual and group opinions from the teachers, focusing on their ideas of the ideal language situation in School B. After brainstorming on the ideal school situation for them, they produced phrases on small sheets of paper that were then pinned to a display wall. The prompt suggested they start with the word 'Ideally, ...', but this was not always used. This form of anonymous collection was meant to allow for a more open expression and to show the frequency and range of ideas and opinions. Among the most common phrases were the following three, with slightly different wordings but expressing the same ideas (the phrases were in both

English and German, and have been translated into English for the purpose of this chapter):

- Note 1: Ideally, I can speak all languages
- Note 2: Ideally, the students are given more than two years to learn a second language
- Note 3: Ideally, all the languages receive adequate support

The 27 collected phrases firstly point to the wishes of the teachers to be competent speakers in more (or all) languages. Secondly, they point to the organizational challenges that multilingual students encounter: students in need of acquiring German as the language of instruction could ideally be granted a two-year grace period (or 'extraordinary status') where their achievements would not be given a mark. The period of two years is considered too short by many, among them the teachers of this school. Thirdly, the teachers point to more abstract support that could be given to the working languages used in the school as well as the home languages spoken by the students. In other activities in the same workshop, it was quite obvious that many teachers had concrete suggestions as to how to support individual students but felt the resources that were needed, both in time and in garnering the right people, were difficult or impossible to attain.

To summarize, the leadership and teachers in School A refer to its form of ME as historically important, which is justified by the presence of a minority language in the area for the last 400 years. School B not only constructs its openness and international understanding through ME in English and Spanish, but also by considering other languages that could be part of the school. Both schools do not comment on the use of German, which is indicative of a very secure standing of this language in the largely German speaking school system.

In both schools, native speakers are valued as a resource for the teaching of English (and Spanish), and in School B they are even labelled as 'native speaker teachers' in contrast to other teachers. As they are not required to have pedagogical training (but do get some training on the job), this reflects on their main qualification which is linked to their home language. While the students in the bilingual classes come from different backgrounds (India, Sri Lanka, Ghana, etc.), the native speaker teachers are from Great Britain, Ireland and the United States. In contrast to English native speakers, the mother tongue teachers (who are also native speakers of their own languages) and teachers of Burgenland-Croatian are never labelled as such. This can be likened to 'native-speakerism' (Holliday, 2015), thereby ascribing authority to native speakers of English.

Language policy and language organization

In the two schools I present here, a number of languages are integrated into the ME. Structural inclusion of certain languages assigns them importance: specific teachers may be assigned to a language or specific hours during the week can be reserved, as can specific classrooms. In School A, Burgenland-Croatian as a regional minority language is promoted in addition to German. All classes are expected to be taught in German and Burgenland-Croatian to the same extent, but almost all children have a higher competence in German when they enter school. The teachers mainly use German as they have all had their education in German and their Burgenland-Croatian competence varies, thereby solely relying on the knowledge of the language acquired through their upbringing in a bilingual family in the region. English is mainly taught by the German speaking teachers. Having the same teachers assigned for ME in both German and Burgenland-Croatian presents some challenges. In contrast to schools that follow a relatively structured approach with regular changes of the language of instruction every day or every week (e.g. Purkarthofer, 2017), School A leaves it to the teachers to structure their bilingual classes.

Two teachers express their preference for having specific teachers for Burgenland-Croatian, and their reasoning is affirmed by others (in the same and in different schools):

Teacher A2 (translated from German): Don't you think it would be better if we had one or two teachers for Croatian in the school, who would only teach Croatian? That would have a more successful outcome.

Teacher A3 (translated from German): To be honest, German and Mathematics are the priority, followed by Croatian, maybe there's still half an hour [for that].

In a language ecology that prioritizes German, Burgenland-Croatian is perceived as an albeit important part of heritage, but less relevant for educational success than other topics (i.e. German or mathematics). Having specific teachers responsible for using and teaching the language, and also reserving certain times for its teaching, are believed to foster its status in the school. During the period of my presence, there were no explicit times or spaces connected to one or the other language. In other interviews, teachers talked about being hesitant to use Burgenland-Croatian in class as it was seen as challenging for the teachers as well as the students.

Very few families continue to use Burgenland-Croatian in their everyday life. This declining trend has been prevalent in the region for the last 50 years and can be explained by social changes from rural to more industrialized work and a more mobile workforce. Still, some parents express their discontent with the perceived lack of abilities of the students in the official second language and they would like the students to become more proficient through learning in school:

> **Parent A1** (translated from German): I don't mind Turkish or Slovak, it does not matter, but if it is a bilingual school where the second language is Croatian, then I find it somewhat important that the children acquire competence in Croatian.

The teachers' hesitations to use Croatian, along with the absence of Burgenland-Croatian outside the school context, gives the students the experience of an imbalance between the two 'official' school languages: students express a certain curiosity towards the Croatian language but they do not talk about it as a fully functional language of schooling.

In School B, languages are distributed in a slightly more structured way. In the bilingual classes, rooms are available for English language activities, and the classes are split into two groups for a certain number of hours per week. The presence of several English speakers has an influence on the communication practices in school. Most of the native speaker teachers in School B are relatively young and have recently relocated to Austria, either for work or for personal reasons such as relationships. While some are very functional in German, this is, however, not required. Their main role is to use and promote the English language and they are even discouraged from speaking German with the students. The other home languages that teachers and students speak are not frequently used. Mother tongue teachers and other teachers are expected to speak German, but during our discussions several teachers talked about their first languages or languages that they have been trying to learn over the years (e.g. Spanish and French but also Turkish and Bosnian-Croatian-Serbian).

Zooming in on the classes: Peripheral Englishes and Croatian languages

At the micro level of classroom interactions, I would like to continue by taking a closer look at the diversity within languages, in the case of English and Croatian. School A, along with the other bilingual schools in the region, teaches Burgenland-Croatian according to the shared standard but recognizes different varieties of the language: starting from the first grades, students are supported in acquiring the variety spoken in their own family, village or town. In the case of students who enter school without prior language competence in Burgenland-Croatian, the local variety of the town or that of the teacher is taught. In the final years of schooling, the students also learn the Croatian-Croatian variety of Croatia. While there has been strong regional pressure to privilege the regional variety, teachers also see the economic use of teaching a more international variety. Incoming children of refugees from the Balkan wars in the 1990s, who spoke the Croatian variety of Croatia, were seen as a potential stronghold to foster the already declining language use of (any variety of) Croatian in the regional bilingual schools. In this example, different language ideologies either come into dialogue or else oppose each other: the close resemblance of the regional minority language and the family language of the newly arrived refugees helped with the successful inclusion in German-Croatian ME, and teachers and students were able to work together more easily than in the monolingual German schools. At the same time, not only the Croatian-Croatian variety but also other related Slavic languages of the region, most notably Slovak, have been seen as a threat to regional varieties of Burgenland-Croatian. Teachers are required to develop strategies to deal with different varieties, and also divergent levels of language competence. Many express their wish for stronger support through out-of-school use of Croatian by families and community members. In light of this, the presence of speakers of (Croatian-)Croatian was often seen favourably and as a welcome source of everyday Croatian interaction.

In School B, the bilingual classes can be seen as a form of rather elite multilingualism, but again, looking at language use in the classes, a high number of students are found to possess a peripheral variety of English as the family language. Students of Sri Lankan or Indian origin or from East and West African countries who have previously been educated in English meet in these bilingual classes and contribute to what Canagarajah calls 'Global Englishes' (Canagarajah, 2013). These classes carry the potential for multilingual encounters, as students with English as their home language learn together with students who have had some exposure to English in kindergarten but come from families with either German or other languages as their home languages. Regardless of this, the students' multilingualism in most cases goes beyond English and German and this is not specifically taken into account in the set-up of the bilingual programme. In the language portraits produced in one of the classes, most students mentioned the many languages they used or that were of relevance to their extended family in different places in the world. A number of languages were relevant for the students but were not addressed in school. These languages will be discussed in the last section.

Multilingual students in ME: What about the others?

From well-included languages and their speakers, I shall now turn now to the languages that are not present in the curriculum. Teachers in both schools described moments of doubt and frustration with their current means of language organization and practice as they felt it was not doing justice to their student population and educational goals. Initiatives to symbolically include different languages had already been adopted but were not producing the desired results. Two examples of how each school reacted to a challenging situation and how these reactions either produced lines of inclusion or opened ways to renegotiate the use and status of the languages in the schools are analysed in this subsection.

In School A, the main struggle that was brought up in interviews was the declining use of Burgenland-Croatian by the students and their families. In the second half of the 20th century, speakers of Burgenland-Croatian had experienced marginalization as German was seen as the language of social success and upward mobility in the area. Parents were told that they should switch to German to give their children better chances in life, and adults commuted weekly from the farms and villages to work in the larger cities among speakers of German and with German as the lingua franca. Burgenland-Croatian has regained its reputation and is evaluated more positively nowadays, but it is still often linked to traditional music, old costumes and the rural farms of the grandparents. To foster the use of Burgenland-Croatian in School A, special classes were formed and taught by teachers with strong skills in Burgenland-Croatian with the intention of providing specific support to students with a family background in Burgenland-Croatian. Teachers argued, as shown in the quote below, that students of Turkish origin, as well as those with other home languages, should be advised against taking these classes, as the focus on German was seen as a priority.

Teacher A1 (translated from German): That was the idea, if we have three classes per grade: one Croatian class, where Croatian is intensively used. While we welcome students to learn Croatian, students of Turkish or other languages can go to the other classes if they should focus on learning German.

In meetings with parents, they expressed their perception of a social hierarchy between the Croatian classes and the other classes formed, as German speaking parents regarded those classes as preferable due to having fewer 'foreign' students in them. At the time of the fieldwork, students from families who spoke Turkish or Kurdish made up almost one-third of the students in certain classes in School A. They had, depending on their length of stay in Austria and other factors, acquired German, the language of instruction, to varying degrees. Students who already spoke Turkish could sign up for two hours of voluntary mother tongue education in the afternoons. Some students were able to learn Burgenland-Croatian rather easily, but in the interviews we conducted with teachers, these students were seen as exceptionally gifted. In these interviews, Burgenland-Croatian was generally considered as a burden to some, while yet remaining a heritage and thus a duty to others. The arrangement of special classes to foster Burgenland-Croatian risks turning into an unintentional exclusionary practice in this respect, making the minority language an educational resource that is only offered to some.

In School B, a relatively similar situation could initially be found. The bilingual German/English classes and Spanish classes were rather sought after, whereas the classes without a specific language focus felt left behind. Given the social composition of the school, these classes without a specific language focus were equally highly multilingual but their multilingual potential was not capitalized on, as the home languages of the students were not systematically used for literacy and learning. While the bilingual programme constructed the use of the target languages as a desirable goal, the different language skills of the students in the classes without a language focus were more often seen as a threat to their German learning. A team of motivated teachers and the school leadership found this imbalance worth addressing and the school has recently started to offer trilingual literacy in German, Turkish and Bosnian-Croatian-Serbian. At the same time, the formerly unnamed German-only classes were renamed as *multilingual classes* (see Table 2.1). Two teachers with expertise in literacy in Turkish and Bosnian-Croatian-Serbian currently come into the classroom for up to 12 hours each week to work alongside the German speaking class teacher. The effects of the changed policy were reported by teachers, and they spoke not only about a changed attitude but also about successful learning experiences and language transfer for better learning. In this way, additional teachers and changes in classroom practice could help to pave way for more inclusive practices.

'Schools [...] ought to be about people reflecting on and critiquing the "Discourse maps" of society', claims Gee (2012: 215), in his work on literacy and social linguistics. In the two examples presented here, we see how ME is intrinsically connected to learning about language use and the position of speakers: while some languages and educational resources are constructed as desirable and valuable, e.g. by offering them to a selected group of students, other resources are perceived as a burden, e.g. when they are linked to staying in school for some extra hours in the afternoon for mother tongue education. Changing the spaces for languages in schools, from the afternoon to integrated teaching in mainstream classes, can also change the status of teachers and students, and can help them to see themselves as part of the specific school.

Normalizing Multilingualism: Ideology, Policy and Organization

Working with students to become 'full and indispensable actors in society – locally, nationally, and globally' (Hornberger, 2009: 198) is the goal of most educational institutions, and the two schools presented here are no exception. In the concluding discussion, I will highlight two aspects of ME that permeate several of the discussed topics – the access to languages and speakers and how hierarchies are produced in ME – and, finally, two options to shape ME to meet the needs of speakers and learners.

Language hierarchies and social ladders: Localized and universalized access

Both schools presented in this chapter are very outspoken about supporting multilingualism and celebrate it through festive activities and multilingual welcome signs. But only some languages are constructed as functional languages in the everyday life of the school and are equipped with forms of social capital such as teaching staff, time and status.

Looking at examples from both School A and School B, we see how access to language and teaching resources is regulated and how language ideologies play out as certain languages and their speakers are given preferential treatment and their position is constructed as more socially desirable. The bilingual students with Croatian and German as well as the primarily German speaking students are normalized in School A, particularly in the Burgenland-Croatian classes, while speakers of Turkish, Kurdish, Hungarian or Slovak are constructed as the 'Other'. Despite this orientation towards monolingualism or maybe rather 'limited bilingualism' at the local level, the school's status as a minority language school in a national context gives it access to more resources, including more teachers and smaller classes, thus benefiting all students.

In a different place, the classes without a language focus in School B have become a multilingual programme in its own right. For these students, this opens a space where dialogue across different lived experiences can take place (Hornberger, 2009: 198) and where more languages than just German are valued and, most importantly, used and developed. Changes are visible within the school and they have also reached a broader level through a network of classes all over Vienna, opting for trilingual literacy practices. Mother tongue teachers have seen their role change from sometimes being mistaken for aides for students who do not speak German to experts for literacy and teaching. Their longer teaching hours in one class (in contrast to earlier fragmented hours in several classes) have strengthened their standing and relationship with the other teachers in the school. Teachers are now able to exchange strategies and materials and form a network of practice across the city. Mother tongue teachers are thus leaving their highly compartmentalized hours of teaching and gaining more universal access to teaching in School B.

What is visible in both examples is the evaluation of languages in a very specific, localized setting, yet these are influenced by a broader context. Language ideologies translate into policy and organization (e.g. the installation of bilingual classes with German and English), but ME programmes also affect individual students. Participation in trilingual literacy programmes is unlikely to change the status of either Turkish or Bosnian-Croatian-Serbian in Austria as a whole, but it renders these linguistic resources highly relevant for the students in their classes. ME is not necessarily or in itself a means of equity and inclusion and it can, just as any social institution, (re)produce social hierarchies to benefit those that are already in possession of a valued capital. On the other hand, it has the potential to open spaces where hierarchies can be questioned and speakers' experiences can be brought into use for teaching and learning.

Including differences: Shape the group or shape the practice?

ME that wants to be relevant has to constantly respond to expectations and changing circumstances. Programmes can: (1) be targeted at a very specific group of students, e.g. with a specific set of language skills; or (2) propose a specific goal to be achieved by the learners in a certain area or school, e.g. to contribute to better learning outcomes of multilingual students or to achieve school leaving exams in several languages. In interviews with teachers in this study, they often express a preference for Option 1, assuming that this leads to homogeneous groups of learners. At the same time, this kind of targeting risks losing relevance in a specific location. A traditional minority language school like School A no longer finds its imagined audience of balanced bilinguals in (only) German and Burgenland-Croatian. In much the same way, the predominantly German programme in School B failed to take the realities of multilingual Viennese students into account. Shaping groups to fit the intended programmes, thereby excluding speakers of other languages, can thus only be seen as one alternative. Multilingual schools are generally composed of young students and adults with diverging skills, different biographical experiences and a myriad of perspectives for their future. Programmes that centre around a specific goal and offer to include change and adaptability might turn out to be more relevant for a larger proportion of the public.

In thinking about inclusion and multilingual students, the construction of target groups is problematic in itself: learners who *'speak a language other than the language of education at home'* or who otherwise are *'learners of the language of education'* may still be dominant in the school language. Studies on language transmission (e.g. Hinton, 2013) show that the languages of schooling enter into the family home with great assertiveness and that parents often struggle to counter the majority ideologies about language use that would be necessary to uphold home languages. Thus, students enter into ME with their full repertoires and their individual learning experiences shaped by ideologies and they are met in school with policy and organization. Shaping ME and its practices so that they are meaningful to those students is a process, encompassing inclusionary strategies and supported by what we know about very specific places and universal ideas at the same time.

Acknowledgements

I am grateful to the teachers and colleagues who invited me into their schools to learn and who discussed observations and findings with me. This work was supported by the Research Council of Norway through its Centres of Excellence funding scheme (Project no. 223265).

Notes

(1) I have omitted some details in the descriptions of the schools for the sake of greater anonymity.
(2) Burgenland-Croatian, a variety of Croatian on the Austrian-Hungarian border, has been recognized as a regional minority language in Austria and since 1955 its speakers have been given the right to bilingual schools and pre-schools.

References

Banks, J.A. (2001) Multicultural education: Characteristics and goals. In J.A. Banks and C. McGee Banks (eds) *Multicultural Education: Issues and Perspectives* (pp. 3–31). New York: Wiley.
BMB, Austrian Ministry of Education (2018) *Schule mehrsprachig*. See http://www.schule-mehrsprachig.at/index.php?id=61 (accessed June 2018).
Busch, B. (2010) School language profiles: Valorizing linguistic resources in heteroglossic situations in South Africa. *Language and Education* 24 (4), 283–294.
Busch, B. (2017) Biographical approaches to research in multilingual settings: Exploring linguistic repertoires. In M. Martin-Jones and D. Martin (eds) *Researching Multilingualism: Critical and Ethnographic Approaches* (pp. 46–60). New York and London: Routledge.
Canagarajah, S. (2013) *Translingual Practice: Global Englishes and Cosmopolitan Relations*. London and New York: Routledge.
Cenoz, J. (2009) *Towards Multilingual Education: Basque Educational Research from an International Perspective*. Bristol: Multilingual Matters.
Creese, A. (2011) Making local practices globally relevant in researching multilingual education. In F.M. Hult and K.A. King (eds) *Educational Linguistics in Practice: Applying the Local Globally and the Global Locally* (pp. 41–55). Bristol: Multilingual Matters.
De Korne, H. and Hornberger, N. (2017) Countering unequal multilingualism through ethnographic monitoring. In M. Martin-Jones and D. Martin (eds) *Researching Multilingualism: Critical and Ethnographic Approaches* (pp. 247–258). New York and London: Routledge.
Dewey, J. (1990 [1915]) *The School and Society and the Child and the Curriculum*. Chicago, IL: University of Chicago Press.
European Commission (2002) *Presidency Conclusions of the Barcelona European Council*. See http://ec.europa.eu/invest-in-research/pdf/download_en/barcelona_european_council.pdf and https://ec.europa.eu/education/policies/multilingualism/learning-languages_en (accessed June 2018).
Gee, J.P. (2012) *Social Linguistics and Literacies: Ideology in Discourse*. London and New York: Routledge.
Gibson, S. (2009) Inclusion vs. neo-liberalism: Empowering the 'other'. In S. Gibson and J. Haynes (eds) *Perspectives on Participation and Inclusion: Engaging Education* (pp. 11–26). London and New York: Continuum.
Giroux, H. (1992) *Border Crossings: Cultural Workers and the Politics of Education*. Abingdon: Routledge.

Hillmert, S. (2009) Soziale Inklusion und Exklusion: die Rolle von Bildung. In R. Stichweh (ed.) *Inklusion und Exklusion: Analysen zur Sozialstruktur und sozialen Ungleichheit* (pp. 85–100). Wiesbaden: Verl. für Sozialwissenschaften.
Hinton, L. (2013) *Bringing our Languages Home: Language Revitalization for Families*. Berkeley, CA: Heyday.
Holliday, A. (2015) Native-speakerism: Taking the concept forward and achieving cultural belief. In A. Swan, P. Aboshiha and A. Holliday (eds) *(En)countering Native-speakerism: Global Perspectives* (pp. 11–25) London: Palgrave Macmillan.
hooks, b. (1994) *Teaching to Transgress: Education as the Practice of Freedom*. Abingdon: Routledge.
Hornberger, N. (2009) Multilingual education policy and practice: Ten certainties (grounded in Indigenous experience). *Language Teaching* 42, 197–211.
Kroskrity, P.V. (2010) Language ideologies – evolving perspectives. In J. Jaspers (ed.) *Society and Language Use* (pp. 192–210). Amsterdam: John Benjamins.
Luhmann, N. (1995) Inklusion und Exklusion. In N. Luhmann (ed.) *Soziologische Aufklärung 6* (pp. 226–251). Opladen: Westdeutscher Verlag.
Mascareño, A. and Carvajal, F. (2015) The different faces of inclusion and exclusion. *CEPAL Review* 116, 127–141.
Musk, N. (2010) Bilingualisms-in-practice at the meso level: An example from a bilingual school in Wales. *International Journal of the Sociology of Language* 202, 41–62.
Norton, B. (2013) *Identity and Language Learning: Extending the Conversation* (2nd edn). Bristol: Multilingual Matters.
Pavlenko, A. and Blackledge, A. (2004) Introduction: New theoretical approaches to the study of negotiation of identities in multilingual contexts. In A. Pavlenko and A. Blackledge (eds) *Negotiation of Identities in Multilingual Contexts* (pp. 1–33). Clevedon: Multilingual Matters.
Purkarthofer, J. (2017) Children's drawings as part of school language profiles: Heteroglossic realities in families and schools. *Applied Linguistics Review* 9 (2–3), 201–223.
Rawls, J. (1972) *A Theory of Justice*. Oxford: Clarendon Press.
UNESCO (2017) *A Guide for Ensuring Inclusion and Equity in Education*. Paris: UNESCO. See http://unesdoc.unesco.org/images/0024/002482/248254e.pdf (accessed 5 November 2018).

The Value of Languages in a Multilingual Classroom

Renata Emilsson Peskova

Board Member of Móðurmál – the Association on Bilingualism, and Co-Founder and Teacher in the Czech Heritage Language School in Iceland

In Iceland, approximately 100 immigrant languages are spoken today (Tungumálatorg, 2014). Languages are much discussed, as an asset or as a barrier in education. Research has shown that the collaborative efforts of authorities, teachers, communities and parents create the best opportunities to include the rich linguistic resources of students in their education (Nieto, 2010; Ragnarsdóttir, 2015). A practical example of such successful collaboration is the long-term support of community heritage language (HL) schools by the City of Reykjavík by providing free classrooms on Saturdays, and schools acknowledging the educational value of the HL classes. Thus, the importance of students' rich linguistic resources is recognized.

However, teachers still feel inadequately equipped for teaching in inclusive classrooms and parents have called for better language support for their children. Plurilingual students are often looked at from a deficit perspective, as shown by this testimony of the mother of a plurilingual boy born and raised in Iceland:

> I am happy about the new parents' meeting at my son's new school. The principal said that our boy does not have Icelandic as a second language but that it is one of his mother tongues and that he will be assessed in it as such. This is the first time I have heard this from any of his schools. Our boy is in the 5th grade now. In the past years he has been called 'a student with Icelandic as second language', 'a non-Icelander', 'a student of foreign origin' etc., even though he has always scored within age-appropriate limits of all screening tests in Icelandic.

The prerequisite for an open dialogue about equitable multilingual education is the understanding that the plurilingualism of children, and each language, are valuable. By removing labels such as 'immigrant', 'heritage' or 'second' and thinking simply about 'student' and 'language' we can open new dimensions in quality multilingual education in inclusive classrooms.

References

Nieto, S. (2010) *The Light in Their Eyes: Creating Multicultural Learning Communities* (10th anniversary edn). New York: Teachers College Press.

Ragnarsdóttir, H. (2015) *Learning Spaces for Inclusion and Social Justice: Success Stories from Immigrant Students and School Communities in Four Nordic Countries. Report on Main Findings from Finland, Iceland, Norway and Sweden.* See http://lsp2015.hi.is/sites/lsp2015.hi.is/files/sh/lsp_final_report_0.pdf.

Tungumálatorg (2014) *Language Square.* See www.tungumalatorg.is.

3 Multilingual Teachers Meet Recently Arrived Students: Language Ideologies and Practices in Preparatory Classes in Germany

Julie A. Panagiotopoulou, Lisa Rosen and Jenna Strzykala

Introduction

The decade-old demand for the increase in the hiring of minority teachers in German educational policy has recently found itself reactivated (on the significance of migrant teachers in the framework of inclusive school development, see Panagiotopoulou & Rosen, 2015a). For instance, on a European level, Friedrich Heckmann's (2008: 83) empirically backed recommendation to enthuse more migrant students about the teaching profession and to urge schools to increase the recruitment of migrant teachers is complemented by a recent European study (Donlevy *et al.*, 2016) conducted on behalf of the European Commission that found that an increasing cultural and linguistic diversity of teachers can contribute to improving the academic success of children and youth from migrant families (Donlevy *et al.*, 2016: 11). Even though the current state of empirical research is described as limited because the majority of studies so far were conducted in the United States and focus on 'long-established migrant groups' and less on 'more recent migrant groups' (Donlevy *et al.*, 2016: 11), the report recommends that the European Commission encourage and support its Member States in developing and implementing measures and strategies on a national level to recruit migrant teachers (Donlevy *et al.*, 2016: 13).

Within the current context of (forced) migration in particular, this demand in educational policy is being updated. For instance, with regard to the reorientation of refugee policy in Germany, the Robert Bosch Foundation recommends that:

> in the future, German language classes taught simultaneously in the dominant family language and in German should become the norm in the acquisition of the German language for refugee children. In order to do so, increasing the hiring of teachers with competences in the home languages of the refugees (…) becomes necessary. (Robert Bosch Stiftung *et al.*, 2016: 18)

As welcome as this recommendation to design the acquisition of German with and through the students' home languages may be from the viewpoint of sociolinguistic migration research, one assumption remains to be questioned: whether teachers do indeed make use of their multilingual resources and skills in day-to-day school life and especially in their lessons. Assuming that they do so can be seen as optimistic for the German speaking context, as we will outline below firstly by means of selected studies on the perspectives of multilingual teachers from migrant families on their own (prospective) language practices in school (in the section, 'Language Ideologies of (Pre-service) Multilingual Minority Teachers'). Secondly, we will then dwell on this question by presenting initial research findings on the educational situation of refugee children in Germany (in the section on 'The Tradition of Exclusion of Refugee Children'). By examining the language pedagogy in a so-called preparatory class for newly arrived children we focus on the analysis of ethnographical data in order to illustrate how the multilingual minority teacher in charge of this class enforces a ban on Arabic (in the section, 'Exclusion of Multilingualism'). The Conclusion to this chapter poses critical questions regarding German language policy and education under the conditions of (forced) migration in light of this case study.

Language Ideologies of (Pre-service) Multilingual Minority Teachers in the German School Context

One of the first studies in German speaking regions that surveyed minority teachers on their teaching practices, their self-conceptions and also on their handling of multilingualism highlights that only a quarter of the approximately 200 respondents deliberately use their multilingualism in their lessons (Georgi, 2013: 228). Furthermore, the study provides evidence pointing towards the official school policy being that multilingualism is not favoured as a teaching resource: at least 40% of the respondents indicate that using minority languages is 'prohibited or frowned upon', in their perception (Georgi, 2013: 228). The ones that do use their multilingual resources report that they do so only on the margins of their teaching and particularly to discipline multilingual students (Georgi, 2013: 230).

In the qualitative section of this same study, one teacher emphasizes that she has 'never at all spoken Turkish somehow' and that the classroom does not provide an 'atmosphere in which she would feel the need to "ally" with the students through the use of Turkish' (Georgi, 2013: 231). A similar argument, but resulting in a categorical rejection of the use of home languages in class, is made by another interviewee: here, it is less about the 'alliance' than about the remaining students' 'non-comprehension', implicating that 'in principle, German is to be spoken' (Georgi, 2013: 231).

Panagiotopoulou and Rosen (2015b, 2016) have reconstructed the monolingual ideologies of multilingual student-teachers at the University of Cologne. A first analysis of 16 peer interviews showed that these student-teachers do not consider their multilingual repertoires as a resource for (future) teaching, but instead view the continuous separation of languages as a special achievement. While doing so, they describe the alienation of their own home languages in school contexts as 'illegitimate or discriminatory only to a limited degree' (Panagiotopoulou & Rosen, 2016: 187). The language ideology of '(neo)linguicism' (Dirim, 2010) they experienced during their own schooling extends into their present teacher education as they barely dissociate themselves from the 'German only' language policy in place (Panagiotopoulou & Rosen, 2015b: 229).

In a representative study (Boos-Nünning & Karakaşoğlu, 2005: 361) young migrant women and girls reported that they had also faced this monolingual policy during their own schooling. Karakaşoğlu (2009: 182) highlights that this is not to be understood as an isolated phenomenon, but as a quantitatively significant issue as well. The prohibition of their heritage language in school is an experience many students with non-German native languages share: among the girls of Turkish heritage, the ratio was 50%. One-third of them experienced this as strongly or very strongly burdening.

Analyses of ten portfolios produced by multilingual student-teachers from migrant families in the context of a university course entitled *Vielfalt im Lehrer*innenzimmer* [Diversity in the teachers' lounge] (Lengyel & Rosen, 2015: 165) have drawn a similar picture. In these written reflections on the use of the participants' multilingual resources in school contexts, the students name advantages and potentials for their teaching and for contact with multilingual pupils and their parents, while expressing the ambivalences and uncertainties they feel: one student, for instance, describes how she intends not to sanction the use of non-German family languages by the pupils and to pick up on multilingualism, following a language awareness approach. However, she also qualifies this prospection on grounds of the institution's 'mistrust' of the use of minority languages: 'If I am addressed in Polish, I would like to reply to the child in Polish. But the German school is still far from this ideal' (Lengyel & Rosen, 2015: 176).

This experience of the German monolingual policy raises questions in regard to the pre-service teachers' future line of work. For instance, one student speaks about a 'negative influence' (Panagiotopoulou & Rosen, 2016: 184) and puts it in a nutshell. Referring to her multilingual resources, she reports: 'as teaching staff I find it to be a bit problematic, how am I supposed to utilise this' (Panagiotopoulou & Rosen, 2016: 185). The students' institutionally critical appraisal showcases the research results depicted in this section: if (and how) migration-related multilingual resources can be made use of in school and especially in preparatory classes for newly arrived migrant students remains an open question from the perspective of (pre-service) multilingual teachers or at least a question that cannot be affirmed per se. In particular, this question cannot be detached from school as a societal institution, from the hierarchies established between school language(s) and home language(s) even before formal education commences and from language ideologies and constructs of difference (Panagiotopoulou, 2017).

The Tradition of Exclusion of Refugee Children in German Schools and Current Research Results regarding Preparatory Classes

More than 20 years ago, Isabell Diehm and Frank-Olaf Radtke criticized the fact that, in the context of educational policy, refugee children were considered as a group primarily in need of a 'German course' in order to gain membership in the monolingually organized German school (Diehm & Radtke, 1999: 119). Further, they criticized the separation of refugee children in schools. That this criticism is as spot on today as ever becomes obvious considering the unaltered reprinting of Diehm and Radtke's chapter with the equally unchanged title, 'Organisational problems in the handling of strangeness' ['*Organisatorische Probleme im Umgang mit dem Fremden*'] in the recently released edited volume, *New Migration and Education: An Interdisciplinary Perspective on Transitions into the German Education System*' (Dewitz *et al*., 2018). At the time, Diehm and Radtke construed in-school separation such as the establishment of preparatory classes as an organizational rather than a pedagogic measure. According to them, what matters here is the production of a supposed homogeneity, which turns out to be an illusion as 'there have always been newcomers as a result of migration processes' (Diehm & Radtke, 1999: 116; see also Radtke, 1996). This separation conflicts with the continuous recommendations of intercultural and inclusive school development according to which it is 'necessary to avoid measures of segregation such as preparatory and reception classes and to privilege internal differentiation of learner groups instead of external differentiation' (Karakaşoğlu *et al*., 2011: 23).

Even in today's Germany, the right to education in the form of compulsory schooling does not apply to undocumented children and those who have not submitted an asylum application (yet). In some federal states, waiting times before compulsory schooling sets in can last between three and six months (Robert Bosch Expert Commission on Considering a Realignment of Refugee Policy, 2015: 9). In addition, in some of Germany's federal states such as Schleswig-Holstein, refugee children with uncertain residency status are taught in refugee accommodation instead of schools (Frieters-Reermann *et al.*, 2013: 76). Depending on the federal state, in cities with a high number of newly arrived children, special 'preparatory classes', 'reception classes' and 'international support classes' are set up for them (Frenzel *et al.*, 2015: 172). Beside these special separated classes, newcomers who are subject to compulsory schooling can be taught in the context of individual integration measures within regular classes (Massumi *et al.*, 2015: 29). This model of schooling is chosen primarily by towns and districts with a lower number of newly arrived pupils and places them 'in regular classes with additional German lessons in small groups' (Frenzen *et al.*, 2015: 172). This form of non-separate or semi-integrative schooling seems, however, to be the exception. In an overview of educational policy and models of schooling, Massumi *et al.* (2015: 29) show with regard to the federal state of North Rhine-Westphalia that in the larger Cologne area during the school year 2014/2015, over 90% of the newly arrived children were being taught in preparatory classes. Children with a legally uncertain status are also at risk of being excluded even from these classes and thus of not having any access to school at all. Those affected are especially refugees with a status of 'permitted' or 'tolerated' residency (the corresponding German terms are *Gestattung* or *Duldung*), those who are no longer subject to general compulsory schooling, those without a status or considered illegal and, finally, unaccompanied children (Frieters-Reermann *et al.*, 2013: 21).

Because of insufficient data and a general lack of research, the extent to which the right to education is being exercised cannot be assessed. On the one hand, statistical data on education participation are 'non-existent' for young refugees in Germany as a group (Korntheuer, 2016: 51). In particular, at the federal and state level, school statistics are still a long way from providing information on the education situation of refugees and asylum applicants (Kemper, 2016: 201). On the other hand, to this day there have been no studies on the effectiveness of various models of schooling for all groups of refugee pupils (Maak, 2014: 321). In addition, research data and findings on the previous education trajectories of children with refugee experiences are 'completely' lacking (Behrensen & Westphal, 2009: 46).

Beside these desiderata, several qualitative research studies do exist that investigate the different models of schooling from the perspective of the students and teachers in a particular federal state (Karakayalı *et al.*, 2016, for Berlin; Maak, 2014 and Ahrenholz & Maak, 2013, for Thuringia; Montanari, 2017, for Lower Saxony).

In addition, a number of research works have been carried out as ethnographic field studies by master's students and doctoral candidates in selected educational institutions in North Rhine-Westphalia and Lower Saxony since 2015 (Gudat, 2017; Panagiotopoulou *et al.*, 2018; tom Dieck, 2017). For instance, Gudat (2017) reveals how translingual metalinguistic conversations of the children were tolerated by the teacher but not recognized as translingual learning strategies with regard to the German language. Furthermore, it can be assumed that refugee pupils are schooled in a way that focuses on (linguistic) deficits. For instance, although the pupils already possess competencies and skills that are relevant for school, these skills are not recognized as such (this applies to their multilingual resources in written language as well). Instead, the students are systematically reduced to their lack of German proficiency and their status as 'GaSL' (German as a second language) students (Panagiotopoulou *et al.*, 2018). Complementing this, tom Dieck (2017) has shown that recently arrived students themselves also perceive the acquisition of the German language as the central prerequisite for social integration and educational success. Following Heller (2008), these 'ethnographies of multilingualism' (Blackledge & Creese, 2010: 58) such as the ones presented above enable a broader view of the language practices of all actors involved, students as well as pedagogues. In our studies, we follow this approach of ethnography by not treating linguistic abilities in isolation, out of context, or even normatively as the expected performance of the learners. In the process, the observed practices of language pedagogy are understood and analysed as inseparably connected to educational conditions and language policies as well as to language ideologies and prevailing social discourses, such as the different prestige of languages (for details, see Panagiotopoulou & Rosen, 2018).

Exclusion of Multilingualism in a Preparatory Class for Recently Arrived Students in North Rhine-Westphalia (Germany): The Ban on Arabic as a Promise of Learning Success?[1]

The ethnographic data presented in the following were collected by Jenna Strzykala within the framework of the educational research project 'Research Workshop Inclusion' (under the direction of Petra Herzmann, Julie A. Panagiotopoulou and Lisa Rosen). The analysis is guided by the language policy framework (Spolsky, 2004) that views linguistic practices, language ideologies and policies as interconnected and interrelated. This means that we 'do not see ideologies and practices as separate entities' (Blackledge & Creese, 2010: 59) but instead we regard language policies in educational institutions as directly linked to the 'social ideologies about bilingualism, multilingualism and monolingualism' (Blackledge & Creese, 2010: 59) as well as to the comprehensive sociopolitical context of migration societies. The following two questions are directive in the analysis of the participant observations conducted in a preparatory class for recently arrived students in North Rhine-Westphalia (Germany):

- What kind of language policies and practices can be observed in a preparatory class with (emergent) multilingual students?
- How do students and teachers negotiate the monoglossic policies and practices in a German school?

Below, we present the school in its immediate context before introducing the class and its teacher.

The field: A secondary school in Cologne, a preparatory class and the monolingual perspective of the multilingual teacher

During the academic year 2014/2015, 1578 recently arrived children were schooled in parallel classes in the Cologne metropolitan area (Massumi *et al.*, 2015: 29). As is characteristic for cities in North Rhine-Westphalia with a comparatively high number of newly migrated children and youths, so-called 'preparatory classes' [*Vorbereitungsklassen*], 'reception classes' [*Auffangklassen*] and 'international remedial classes' [*internationale Förderklassen*] are created specifically for them (Frenzel *et al.*, 2015: 172). One major difference between these types of classes is that 'preparatory classes' are formed ahead of the academic year whereas 'reception classes' are created during the school year; 'international remedial classes' are a type of parallel schooling in vocational schools. The preparatory class we will expand on below is a class in a secondary school in a marginalized suburban neighbourhood of Cologne. The class is one of the preparatory secondary school classes operated in parallel that 777 students attended during the 2014/2015 academic year in Cologne. By comparison, 497 students were assigned to this type of class for recently arrived migrants at primary school level and 304 students to vocational school (Massumi *et al.*, 2015: 29).

The preparatory class in this case is attended by a total of 14 students between the ages of ten and 14. These refugee children do not have much in common with other students at this school. Although both groups of students are accommodated in the same school building, they only meet during recess. They are not grouped in the same classes nor do they have any joint lessons. As newly arrived children, the students of the preparatory class have been homogenized into a group of non-German speakers from seven countries (Bulgaria, Egypt, Iraq, Lebanon, Romania, Serbia and Syria). Their 'German as a second language' teacher, who we will call Ms Keskin, is multilingual herself (in addition to German, she uses Turkish and English in her everyday life) and has obtained an additional certificate in teaching 'German as a second language'. Most of the class lessons are taught by Ms Keskin.

On the first day of observation on 4 September 2015, the ethnographer Jenna Strzykala conducts a conversation with Ms Keskin on her class before lessons start for the day. In Ms Keskin's spontaneous report, she presents the students as a heterogeneous group (of learners) despite their shared experience of forced migration (with one exception). About half of the children are 'newly' migrated, while their parents (with one exception) are non-EU citizens. Along school-relevant competences, Ms Keskin highlights the diversity of her class: the degree and time of alphabetization as well as proficiency in English are mentioned as noteworthy specifics. However, she focuses solely on the (in)existence of linguistic resources that are – from her point of view – meaningful for the German school: their proficiency in the foreign language English is put forward for two students, while neither proficiency in other previous school languages of the rest of the group nor any other further school-relevant competences (e.g. mathematics) are valued.

Reconstructing a purposeful handling of the group's heterogeneity with regard to previous school experiences and language resources was scarcely possible after five weeks of classroom observations as the students were usually expected to work on standardized assignments and worksheets for German language education. However, how and to what extend the home languages used by the children within their peer groups in the context of classroom situations were given an illegitimate status could indeed be documented.

Although Ms Keskin could be observed using her multilingual skills in situations outside lesson teaching – for instance, she spoke English in a phone conversation with one student's father (4 September 2015) – the use of Turkish, however, could only be observed once, in communication with a student we will call Dana (11 September 2015). When asked about it, Ms Keskin explains that it was *'ein türkischer Dialekt, den Dana gebrochen spreche'* [a Turkish dialect Dana speaks brokenly]. She reports using the dialect with Dana *'wenn's persönlich wird oder auch mal für ein starkes Kommando'* [when it comes to personal matters or sometimes for a strong order], *'damit das die Anderen nicht verstehen'* [so that the others don't understand]. Because Dana is *'die Große'* [the big one], it may be uncomfortable for her to be *'vor den Kleinen peinlich berührt'* [seen embarrassed by the little ones] or even scolded in front of them.

Similar to the research findings on the use of multilingualism in lesson teaching by multilingual (student-)teachers presented above, Ms Keskin tends to use her family language, Turkish, only on the fringes of lesson hours to achieve an educational aim (or rather to discipline or counsel a student). In doing so, she excludes her own multilingual practice and presents herself if anything as a German speaking teacher who meets (emergent) multilingual recently arrived students.

In the following subsection, we focus on the practised *ban on Arabic*, its *enforcement almost without any resistance* and its *explicit legitimization*. Based on two excerpts from observation protocols, we will subsequently exemplify how speaking Arabic in the classroom was permitted or purposefully used only to discipline those students who were speaking Arabic and to banish from the classroom the languages they brought in (see subsection 'The ban on Arabic and resistance through whispering'). Later, we will pursue the question as to how the command of German enforced in all situations of day-to-day school life, in informal as well as formal situations, was legitimized by the promise of learning success (see subsection on 'The command of German and the promise of learning success'). All in all, the point is to highlight the pedagogic practice in place within the context of preparatory classes as institutions with regard to power relations, pointing at the issue that recently migrated students are being addressed as *non-(German)speakers* and recruited as second language learners as soon as they are perceived as being in the process of preparation for the German school. In the example we are now going to discuss, this happens in a preparatory class taught by a multilingual teacher of German as a second language with a familial history of migration.

The ban on Arabic and resistance through whispering

> During silent individual work, some students are busy with their workbooks while others are lining up around the class teacher's desk to collect their corrected workbooks. Ms Keskin hands Milan his workbook while saying 'Milan, sag mal den beiden, wenn sie sich noch weiter unterhalten, müssen wir sie trennen' [Milan, tell those two that if they keep chatting with one another we'll have to separate them]. Milan seems to know who this refers to, turns around, walks towards his desk and while passing them addresses Rana and Haya, the two students referred to, in Arabic. They abruptly interrupt their whispered discussion in Arabic and turn to their notebooks. Ms Keskin, who has been observing Milan's mission from her desk, gives a satisfied nod of the head and grabs the next workbook. (J.S., 4 September 2015)

In order to efficiently enforce the command of German and the language ban that comes with it, overseers were used in the day-to-day classroom life of this preparatory class. This role is fulfilled not only by the teacher personally, but additionally by the student Milan, who is a speaker of the forbidden language himself. In the excerpt presented above, the Arabic speaking student is being addressed as an assistant and overseer by Ms Keskin and purposefully instructed to reprimand his Arabic speaking – or in this particular situation, Arabic-whispering – classmates. Milan's role as a deputy language overseer had already been established earlier that day when, during silent individual work, he had noticed Rana and Haya talking to each other and reported them to the teacher by saying '*Frau Keskin, die Zwei sprechen eine Sprache*' [Ms Keskin, those two are speaking one language], followed by Ms Keskin addressing the issue with a friendly but somewhat rhetorical question for Haya: '*Haya, wie war das mit Sprache und Klasse? Welche Sprache sprechen wir, wenn wir hier sind?*' [Haya, remind me what the thing is regarding language and classroom? What language do we speak when we're here?]. Caught red-handed, the girls chorus a monotonous, elongated reply '*Deuuuutsch*' [Geeeermaan]. Considering the obvious routine with which the students seem to admit their wrongdoing and how they subsequently cut off their conversation in Arabic, the unambiguous language ban we have coded as *the ban on Arabic* had already been publicly performed earlier that day.

Addressing Milan as assistant in this particular situation is based on a (situational and only temporarily effective) construction of 'we' versus 'them': '… if they keep chatting with one another we'll have to separate them'. With this ultimatum, the teacher formulates the collective concern of preserving or rather recovering the class's (language) order and, at least implicitly, the concrete task for Milan as well. Consequently, Milan conveys the teacher's reprimand to 'those two' and provokes their sudden silence. The self-evidence with which Milan admonishes his classmates in Arabic leaves room for the assumption that this is a matter of routine (as earlier observations have shown). The new status of the languages that the students bring into the classroom – from medium of communication to means of disciplinary (self) action and linguistic assimilation – puts a distance between the children's current linguistic reality and their past linguistic biographies as well as their supposed language use outside school, and submits the students to the (new) language order. Building on this, we hypothesize that the minority languages lose their previous status as family languages and/or languages of instruction and that within the German preparatory class, they are being pushed into the background of day-to-day lessons at best. From this perspective, breaching the rules by (quietly) using the banished and forbidden language on the proscenium of the class can be construed as an act of resistance (Butler, 1997: 226). However, how does the sanctioning of resistance, or rather of whispering, legitimize itself in front of the students concerned? And, what conceptions of the necessity of this rule are immanent to the teacher's practices? To pursue these questions, we will proceed by going into the teacher's insisting on the command of German – in fact even outside lessons and while the students are not in the middle of class, but during recess, where conversations (albeit whispered) within the peer group are actually (supposedly) permitted.

The command of German and the promise of learning success

> During morning recess in the classroom, the students are allowed to unwrap their breakfast snacks and have whispered conversations with one another. 'Wer auf Toilette muss, kann mitkommen, ich schließ' euch

auf' [Whoever needs to use the toilet can follow me, I'll unlock it for you], Ms Keskin declares. Except for four students (Haya, Karim, Saida and Rana) who stay at their desks having breakfast, all others leave the classroom with the teacher while the door stays open. For a few seconds, all I can hear are chewing sounds, until Saida chatters loudly in Arabic. The remaining three children join in and an animated discussion ensues. About a minute later, Ms Keskin enters the classroom. The discussion ends abruptly, but the teacher seems to have heard it and storms into the middle of the U-shaped desk formation. Unusually loud and determined, she blusters: 'Es reicht, sonst seid ihr beide fällig!' [This is enough, or you're both due!]. While saying this, she looks at Rana and Saida, who are seated next to each other. 'Alle halten sich dran, nur Saida und Rana und Haya und Karim nicht! So lernt die Saida nie was! Deutsch, ja?' [Everyone sticks to it, except for Saida and Rana and Haya and Karim! Like this, Saida will never learn anything! German, ok?]. Everyone stays silent, some nod their heads. Again, all I can hear are chewing sounds while the other students return to the classroom one by one. (J.S., 4 September 2015)

This situation is particularly characteristic of the teacher's double role as both a custodian and a representative of an institution that uses monitoring and punishment (in a Foucauldian sense) or more specifically disciplinary action and sanction. When the custodian leaves the room and after only a few minutes during which only chewing sounds can be heard, the students start to converse in Arabic – an animated discussion ensues despite the shared knowledge that this is actually prohibited, which is why the students silence themselves abruptly as soon as the teacher re-enters the room. Without explicitly naming the rule violation, she admonishes the students to speak only German, otherwise Saida, who just recently migrated, would 'never learn anything'. The collective abstinence from their shared language is justified by a supposed collective responsibility pertaining not only to the new classmate's acquisition of German, but to her ability to learn anything at all. By doing so, the teacher also legitimizes the school's request to its multilingual student body to assimilate linguistically as fast as possible, immediately following their assignment to the preparatory class, thus acting hegemonically and reproducing linguistic power relations – possibly against her own intentions. The students concerned thus become resistant members of a minority that is just in the process of being informed about the illegitimacy of their supposed right to use their (minority) languages – in fact even outside official learning and lesson situations.

Accordingly, the rhetorical question, 'German, ok?', does not leave any room for negotiation. All it does is terminate the teacher's resolute intervention. Hence, hardly any alternatives of action can result from this for the peer group as well as with regard to the inclusion of the student Saida. Thus, the students hush again. This phenomenon has already been reconstructed in other empirical studies in the context of early childhood day-care as well as in connection with the (implicit) intention of preparing multilingual children for monolingual schools (Panagiotopoulou, 2016: 22).

Ms Keskin's unusually loud and assertive insistence on the command of German and the minacious announcement ('This is enough, or you're both due!') leaves room for the assumption that the teacher of German as a second language perceives the parallel use of family languages as a direct threat to her students' learning success or rather the success of the German language training she is accountable for. This is a conviction that can and has been found in other institutions as well, such as day-care facilities, from which allophone potential students are (to be) recruited: 'Indeed, the belief that the use of the home language will delay the learning of the language of the school is one of a number of common fears which Grosjean (2014) calls "myths about multilingualism"' (Young, 2014: 39). In order to fast-track the learning success themselves, to enable a potential academic success in the first place the students are left with the choice of speaking German or not speaking at all.

According to Paul Mecheril and Thomas Quehl (2015: 159), the prevailing 'implicit' and at the same time illusory promise of the German school is: 'Speak (academic) German, and everything is going to be ok'. In the context of the practised German language training within the preparatory class that participated in the ethnographic study, this formula could be further expatiated upon and specified: 'Speak only German in order to learn German, and everything will be ok' – a promise that proves itself illusory and hardly justifiable from the standpoint of (migration) pedagogy under the conditions of forced migration. For while German speaking migration societies such as Germany and Austria increase 'the pressure on allophones to speak German', as Hans-Jürgen Krumm (2015: 3) has criticized, their family language 'oftentimes [remains] the only thing that refugees were able to take and keep on their escape and a necessary island of safety in a foreign world. This means for one that supporting the learning of German should avoid any type of pressure, and that the use of their own language should be permitted, even encouraged'.

Conclusions

The structural actuality that preparatory classes coexist in parallel with inclusive regular classes within the same school provokes the research question of everyday practices of exclusion in the context of German (inclusive) schools. Our first observations allowed for us to reconstruct how students of different ages and with diverse school experiences and academic trajectories are generated as *a learner group not (yet) ready to be integrated* into the German (inclusive) school, using the preparatory class as a measure of homogenization. The main criterion of this homogenization pertains solely to the allegedly inexistent or low German language skills of the potential regular students: 'The denomination *newly migrated children and youths without or with little German-language skills in school* encompasses children and youths who migrate to Germany at a compulsory school age (six years or older) and who do not dispose of any or of enough German-language skills at that point' (Massumi *et al.*, 2015: 13, italics in original). Supposedly, this definition happens 'dynamically', as the text further reads: 'When a student from this group reaches a level of proficiency that allows for a successful participation in regular lessons, he or she is no longer counted as a member of the separately recorded group according to the aforementioned definition' (Massumi *et al.*, 2015: 13).

This definition illustrates firstly that what matters is primarily what the children and youths are not able to do or rather what they should be able to achieve in order to be allowed to participate in regular lessons to begin with. That being said, what still needs to be clarified is what exactly is to be understood by 'successful participation' (Massumi *et al.*, 2015: 13). Moreover, the deficit orientation of this type of categorization is to be discussed critically from the viewpoint of 'educating emerging bilinguals', as it focuses 'on the students' limitations rather than their potential' (García & Kleifgen, 2010: 2).

The definition by Massumi *et al.* also presumes another assessment of the language proficiency of the children from the preparatory class that would be able to determine to what extent they are 'no longer counted as a member of the separately recorded group' (Massumi *et al.*, 2015: 13). The latent promise not to belong to the category of students 'without any or enough German-language skills' (Massumi *et al.*, 2015: 13) any more leaves room for the assumption that they do not automatically count as regular students, but rather as learners of German as a second language at best. Here as well, the denomination draws upon a powerful or rather hierarchically organized differentiation of first language versus second language, native-speakerism versus non-native-speakerism, and which establishes not only a temporal order but a qualitative one, too (Knappik & Dirim, 2013: 22). The ascription that is thereby being made stays relevant for the academic trajectory in Germany and cannot be cancelled out by further performance assessments.

Preparatory classes are thus meant to prepare children and youths linguistically for school. For this reason, they have something in common with pre-school facilities that label their multilingual clientele as 'non-German speaking', referring to 'school' or rather 'school language' (or '*Bildungssprache*' [academic language] according to Mecheril & Quehl, 2015) and classifying them (often implicitly) as not (yet) ready for school.

Multilingualism is thus indirectly or latently linked with a supposedly expectable endangerment of German language training. This view is held by multilingual educators in charge of this so-called 'German language training' as well (Panagiotopoulou & Kassis, 2016). In this respect, it comes as no surprise with regard to the perspectives of (pre-service) teachers reported on in the section on pre-service teachers' language ideologies that the use of family languages in the preparation of newcomers for regular classes in the (inclusive) German school, as is the case in our example, is explicitly presented as a factor of risk to the learning (of German) by a multilingual teacher of German as a second language. Although we cannot establish how widespread this deficit-oriented view of multilingualism is, our exploratory findings may encourage reflection on inclusive school development and inclusive teacher training in a migration society (see also Panagiotopoulou *et al.*, 2020).

Note

(1) The following remarks and analyses trace back to a reworked version of the previously published German contribution by Panagiotopoulou *et al.* (2018) (see reference list).

References

Ahrenholz, B. and Maak, D. (2013) *Zur Situation von SchülerInnen nicht-deutscher Herkunftssprache in Thüringen unter besonderer Berücksichtigung von Seiteneinsteigern. Abschlussbericht zum Projekt 'Mehrsprachigkeit an Thüringer Schulen (MaTS)'* [*On the Situation of Pupils of Non-German Origin in Thuringia with Special Consideration of Newcomers. Final Report on the Project 'Multilingualism in Schools in Thuringia (MaTS)'*]. Research report. See http://www.daz-portal.de/images/Berichte/bm_band_01_mats_bericht_20130618_final.pdf (accessed June 2018).

Behrensen, B. and Westphal, M. (2009) Junge Flüchtlinge – ein blinder Fleck in der Migrations- und Bildungsforschung. Bildung junger Flüchtlinge als Randthema in der migrationspolitischen Diskussion [Young refugees – a blind spot in migration and educational research. The education of young refugees as a side issue in discussions on migration policy]. In L. Krappmann, A. Lob-Hüdepohl, A. Bohmeyer and S. Kurzke-Maasmeier (eds) *Bildung für junge Flüchtlinge – ein Menschenrecht. Erfahrungen, Grundlagen und Perspektiven* (pp. 45–58). Bielefeld: Bertelsmann.

Blackledge, A. and Creese, A. (2010) *Multilingualism: A Critical Perspective*. London: Continuum.

Boos-Nünning, U. and Karakaşoğlu, Y. (2005) *Viele Welten leben: zur Lebenssituation von Mädchen und jungen Frauen mit Migrationshintergrund* [*Living Many Worlds: On the Living Situation of Girls and Young Women with a Migration Background*]. Münster: Waxmann.

Butler, J. (1997) *Hass spricht: Zur Politik des Performativen* [*Hate Speaks: On the Politics of the Performative*]. Berlin: Suhrkamp.

Dewitz, N.v., Terhart, H. and Massumi, M. (eds) (2018) *Neuzuwanderung und Bildung: Eine interdisziplinäre Perspektive auf Übergänge in das deutsche Bildungssystem* [*New Migration and Education: An Interdisciplinary Perspective on Transitions into the German Education System*]. Weinheim: Beltz.

Diehm, I. and Radtke, F.-O. (1999) *Erziehung und Migration: Eine Einführung* [*Education and Migration: An Introduction*]. Stuttgart: Kohlhammer.

Dirim, İ. (2010) 'Wenn man mit Akzent spricht, denken die Leute, dass man auch mit Akzent denkt oder so'. Zur Frage des (Neo)Linguizismus in den Diskursen über die Sprache(n) der Migrationsgesellschaft ['When you speak with an accent people think that you think with an accent as well or something'. On the issue of (neo)linguicism in the discourses on the language(s) of the migration society]. In P. Mecheril, İ. Dirim, M. Gomolla, S.

Hornberg and K. Stojanov (eds) *Spannungsverhältnisse: Assimilationsdiskurse und interkulturell-pädagogische Forschung* (pp. 91–112). Münster: Waxmann.

Donlevy, V., Meierkord, A. and Rajania, A. (2016) *Study on the Diversity within the Teaching Profession with Particular Focus on Migrant and/or Minority Background. Final Report to DG Education and Culture of the European Commission.* Luxembourg: Publications Office of the European Union. See https://op.europa.eu/en/publication-detail/-/publication/e478082d-0a81-11e7-8a35-01aa75ed71a1.

Frenzel, B., Niederhaus, C., Peschel, C. and Rüther, A.K. (2015) 'In unserer Schule sind alle im Grunde ins kalte Wasser gesprungen und alle sind nach ner Weile belohnt worden durch große Erfolge'. Interviews mit Lehrerinnen und Lehrern zu den Besonderheiten des Unterrichtens neu zugewanderter Schülerinnen und Schüler ['In our school basically everyone jumped in at the deep end and all were rewarded with big success after a while'. Interviews with teachers on the specifics of teaching newly migrated students]. In C. Benholz, M. Frank and C. Niederhaus (eds) *Neu zugewanderte Schülerinnen und Schüler – eine Gruppe mit besonderen Potenzialen. Beiträge aus Forschung und Schulpraxis* (pp. 171–196). Münster: Waxmann.

Frieters-Reermann, N., Jere, T., Kafunda, M., Moerschbacher, M., Morad, H., Neuß, B., Offner, M. and Westermann, A. (2013) *Für unser Leben von morgen: Eine kritische Analyse von Bildungsbeschränkungen und -perspektiven minderjähriger Flüchtlinge [For Our Lives of Tomorrow: A Critical Analysis on Educational Restrictions and Perspectives of Underage Refugees].* See https://www.sternsinger.de/fileadmin/bildung/Dokumente/themen/flucht/2014_dks_malawi_studie_fuer_unser_leben_von_morgen_kmw_missio.pdf (accessed May 2018).

García, O. and Kleifgen, J.A. (2010) *Educating Emergent Bilinguals: Policies, Programs, and Practices for English Language Learners.* New York: Teachers College Press.

Georgi, V.B. (2013) Selbstwirksamkeitsüberzeugungen von Lehrkräften mit Migrationshintergrund: Empirische Schlaglichter auf den Umgang mit Mehrsprachigkeit und kultureller Heterogenität [Convictions of self-efficacy of minority teachers: Highlights of the handling of multilingualism and cultural heterogeneity]. In K. Bräu, V.B. Georgi, Y. Karakaşoğlu and C. Rotter (eds) *Lehrerinnen und Lehrer mit Migrationshintergrund: Zur Relevanz eines Merkmals in Theorie, Empirie und Praxis* (pp. 223–241). Münster: Waxmann.

Grosjean, F. (2014) Myths about bilingualism. See http://www.francoisgrosjean.ch/myths_en.html (accessed February 2021).

Gudat, M. (2017) 'Und was heißt das auf Deutsch?': Ethnographische Beobachtungen zur Mehrsprachigkeit in einer NRW-Vorbereitungsklasse ['And what does that mean in German?': Ethnographic observations on multilingualism in a NRW preparation class]. Unpublished MA thesis, University of Cologne.

Heckmann, F. (2008) *Education and Migration. Strategies for Integrating Migrant Children in European Schools and Societies: A Synthesis of Research Findings for Policy-makers.* Brussels: European Commission. See http://www.nesse.fr/nesse/activities/reports/activities/reports/education-and-migration-pdf (accessed May 2018).

Heller, M. (2008) Doing ethnography. In Li Wei and M.G. Moyer (eds) *The Blackwell Guide to Research Methods in Bilingualism and Multilingualism* (pp. 249–262). Malden, MA: Blackwell.

Karakaşoğlu, Y. (2009) Beschwörung und Vernachlässigung der Interkulturellen Bildung im 'Integrationsland' Deutschland – Ein Essay [Invocation and neglect of intercultural education in the 'integration country' of Germany – an essay]. In R. Tippelt and W. Melzer (eds) *Kulturen der Bildung. Beiträge zum 21. Kongress der Deutschen Gesellschaft für Erziehungswissenschaft* (pp. 177–195). Opladen and Farmington Hills, MI: Barbara Budrich.

Karakaşoğlu, Y., Gruhn, M. and Wojciechowicz, A. (2011) *Interkulturelle Schulentwicklung unter der Lupe: (Inter-)Nationale Impulse und Herausforderungen für Steuerungsstrategien am Beispiel Bremen [Intercultural School Development under the Microscope: (Inter-)national Impulses and Challenges for Control Strategies on the Example of Bremen]*. Münster: Waxmann.

Karakayalı, J., zur Nieden, B., Kahveci, Ç., Groß, S., Heller, M. and Güleryüz, T. (2016) *'Willkommensklassen' in Berlin: Mit Segregation zur Inklusion? Eine Expertise für den Mediendienst Integration* ['*Welcome Classes' in Berlin: To Inclusion Through Segregation? An Expertise for the Media Service Integration*]. See https://mediendienst-integration.de/fileadmin/Dateien/Expertise_Willkommensklassen.pdf (accessed June 2018).

Kemper, T. (2016) Zur schulstatistischen Erfassung der Bildungsbeteiligung von Flüchtlingen und Asylbewerbern [Collection of school statistics on the educational participation of refugees and asylum seekers]. *Sonderpädagogische Förderung* 2, 192–202.

Knappik, M. and Dirim, İ. (2013) Native-speakerism in der LehrerInnenbildung [Native-speakerism in teacher education]. *Journal für LehrerInnenbildung* 3, 20–23.

Korntheuer, A. (2016) *Die Bildungsteilhabe junger Flüchtlinge: Faktoren von Inklusion und Exklusion in München und Toronto* [*The Educational Participation of Young Refugees: Factors of Inclusion and Exclusion in Munich and Toronto*]. Münster: Waxmann.

Krumm, H.-J. (2015) Was Freiwillige bei der Sprachunterstützung von Flüchtlingen brauchen – und was nicht [What volunteers need in the language support of refugees – and what they don't]. Universität Wien. See http://www.idvnetz.org/Dateien/HJKrumm%20Kleiner%20Leitfaden%20fuer%20SprachhelferInnen.pdf (accessed May 2018).

Lengyel, D. and Rosen, L. (2015) Diversity in the staff room – ethnic minority student teachers' perspectives on the recruitment of minority teachers. In D. Lengyel and L. Rosen (eds) Minority teachers in different educational contexts: Recent studies from three German-speaking countries. *Tertium Comparationis – Journal für International und Interkulturell Vergleichende Erziehungswissenschaft* 21 (2), 161–184.

Maak, D. (2014) 'es WÄre SCHÖN, wenn es nich (.) OFT so diese RÜCKschläge gäbe': Eingliederung von SeiteneinsteigerInnen mit Deutsch als Zweitsprache in Thüringen ['It would be nice if there weren't always these setbacks': Integration of newcomers with German as a second language in Thuringia]. In B. Ahrenholz and P. Grommes (eds) *Zweitspracherwerb im Jugendalter* (pp. 319–341). Berlin and Boston, MA: De Gruyter.

Massumi, M., von Dewitz, N., Grießbach, J., Terhart, H., Wagner, K., Hippmann, K. and Altinay, L. (2015) *Neu zugewanderte Kinder und Jugendliche im deutschen Schulsystem: Bestandsaufnahme und Empfehlungen* [*Newly Arrived Children and Teenagers in the German School System: Survey and Recommendations*]. Cologne: Mercator-Institut für Sprachförderung und Deutsch als Zweitsprache and Zentrum für LehrerInnenbildung der Universität zu Köln. See http://www.mercator-institut-sprachfoerderung.de/fileadmin/Redaktion/PDF/Publikationen/MI_ZfL_Studie_Zugewanderte_im_deutschen_Schulsystem_final_screen.pdf (accessed May 2018).

Mecheril, P. and Quehl, T. (2015) Die Sprache der Schule: Eine migrationspädagogische Kritik der Bildungssprache [The language of the school: A criticism of the academic language from the perspective of migration pedagogy]. In M. Knappik and N. Thoma (eds) *Sprache und Bildung In Migrationsgesellschaften* (pp. 151–177). Bielefeld: Transcript.

Montanari, E. (2017) Beschulung von neu in das niedersächsische Bildungssystem zugewanderten Schülerinnen und Schülern in der Sekundarstufe I [Schooling of newly arrived pupils in the Lower Saxony education system in the lower secondary level]. Stiftung Universität Hildesheim. See https://hildok.bsz-bw.de/frontdoor/index/index/docId/699 (accessed June 2018).

Panagiotopoulou, A. (2016) Mehrsprachigkeit in der Kindheit: Perspektiven für die frühpädagogische Praxis [Multilingualism in Childhood: Perspectives for Early Childhood Pedagogy]. *Weiterbildungsinitiative Frühpädagogische Fachkräfte, WiFF Expertisen* 46. Munich: Deutsches Jugendinstitut e.V.

Panagiotopoulou, A. (2017) Mehrsprachigkeit und Differenzherstellung in Einrichtungen frühkindlicher Erziehung und Bildung [Multilingualism and doing difference in institutions of early childhood education]. In I. Diehm, M. Kuhn and C. Machold (eds) *Differenz–Ungleichheit–Erziehungswissenschaft* [Difference - Inequality - Educational Science] (pp. 257–274). Wiesbaden: Springer VS.

Panagiotopoulou, A. and Kassis, M. (2016) Frühkindliche Sprachförderung oder Forderung nach Sprachentrennung? Ergebnisse einer ethnographischen Feldstudie in der deutschsprachigen Schweiz [Early childhood language support or demand for language separation? Results from an ethnographic study in German-speaking Switzerland]. In T. Geier and K.U. Zaborowski (eds) *Migration: Auflösungen und Grenzziehungen – Perspektiven einer erziehungswissenschaftlichen Migrationsforschung* (pp. 153–166). Wiesbaden: Springer VS.

Panagiotopoulou, A. and Rosen, L. (2015a) Migration und Inklusion [Migration and inclusion]. In K. Reich, D. Asselhoven and S. Kargl (eds) *Eine inklusive Schule für alle: Das Modell der Inklusiven Universitätsschule Köln* (pp. 158–167). Weinheim: Beltz.

Panagiotopoulou, A. and Rosen, L. (2015b) Professionalism and multilingualism in Greece and Canada: An international comparison of (minority) teachers' views on linguistic diversity and language practices in monolingual vs. multilingual educational systems. In D. Lengyel and L. Rosen (eds) Minority teachers in different educational contexts: Recent studies from three German-speaking countries. *Tertium Comparationis – Journal für International und Interkulturell Vergleichende Erziehungswissenschaft* 21 (2), 225–250.

Panagiotopoulou, A. and Rosen, L. (2016) 'Sprachen werden benutzt, (...) um sich auch gewissermaßen abzugrenzen von anderen Menschen' – Lehramtsstudierende mit Migrationshintergrund plädieren für einsprachiges Handeln im schulischen Kontext ['Languages are being used (...) to delimit oneself from other people' – minority preservice teachers make a case for monolingual actions in school contexts]. In T. Geier and K.U. Zaborowski (eds) *Migration: Auflösungen und Grenzziehungen – Perspektiven einer erziehungswissen-schaftlichen Migrationsforschung* (pp. 171–192). Wiesbaden: Springer VS.

Panagiotopoulou, A. and Rosen, L. (2018) Denied inclusion of migration-related multilingualism: An ethnographic approach to a preparatory class for newly arrived children in Germany. *Language and Education* 32 (5), 394–409.

Panagiotopoulou, A., Rosen, L. and Strzykala, J. (2018) Inklusion von neuzugewanderten Schüler innen durch mehrsprachige Lehrkräfte aus zugewanderten Familien? Deutschförderung unter den Bedingungen von (Flucht-)Migration [Inclusion of newcomers with multilingual minority teachers? Promotion of German under the conditions of (forced) migration]. In A. Wegner and İ. Dirim (eds) *Normative Grundlagen und reflexive Verortungen im Feld DaF und DaZ* (pp. 210–227). Leverkusen: Verlag Barbara Budrich.

Panagiotopoulou, A., Rosen, L. and Strzykala, J. (eds) (2020) *Inclusion, Education and Translanguaging. How to Promote Social Justice in (Teacher) Education?* Wiesbaden: Springer VS. See https://www.springer.com/de/book/9783658281274 (accessed March 2020).

Radtke, F.-O. (1996) Seiteneinsteiger – Über eine fragwürdige Ikone der Schulpolitik [Newcomers – on a questionable icon of school policy]. In G. Auernheimer and P. Gstettner (eds) *Pädagogik in multikulturellen Gesellschaften: Jahrbuch für Pädagogik* (pp. 49–63). Frankfurt am Main: Peter Lang.

Robert Bosch Stiftung, Sachverständigenrat deutscher Stiftungen für Integration und Migration (SVR) and Johansson, S. (2016) Was wir über Flüchtlinge (nicht) wissen. Expertise [What we (don't) know about refugees. Expertise]. See http://www.svr-migration.de/publikationen/was-wir-ueber-fluechtlinge-nicht-wissen/ (accessed May 2018).

Robert Bosch Expertenkommission zur Neuausrichtung der Flüchtlingspolitik (2015) Dossier. Access to Educational Facilities for Refugees: Early Childhood Daycare, Schools and Universities. See http://www.bosch-stiftung.de/content/language1/downloads/Kommissionsbericht_Fluechtlingspolitik_Bildung.pdf (accessed January 2017).

Spolsky, B. (2004) *Language Policy*. Cambridge: Cambridge University Press.

tom Dieck, F. (2017) Inklusions- und Exklusionsprozesse im Sozialraum Schule aus der Perspektive neu zugewanderter Schüler*innen [Processes of inclusion and exclusion in the social space of schools from the perspective of newly immigrated students]. Unpublished MA thesis, University of Osnabrück.

Young, A.S. (2014) Working with super-diversity in Strasbourg pre-schools: Strengthening the role of teaching support staff. *European Journal of Applied Linguistics* 2 (1), 27–52.

Supporting Plurilingual Students by Building Professional Educational Networks

Maryse Adam-Maillet

Inspector for the local authority (LA) of Besançon (France) and Executive Manager of the Roma and newly arrived plurilingual pupils support service

My work is rooted in Franche-Comté, a region in northeastern France bordering Switzerland, in which migrants have settled to work since the Industrial Revolution. Nowadays, Franche-Comté is home to many asylum seekers and unaccompanied minors. I have been involved with the schooling of Roma and newly arrived plurilingual pupils (from pre-school through high school completion) for the past ten years. Relying on a team of teachers trained in French as a second language (FSL) and inspired by the work of researchers such as Cummins (2014) and Hélot (2007), we have started implementing bottom-up educational language policies fostering plurilingualism at the regional level. Confronted with deeply ingrained, monolingual attitudes among stakeholders, we have deployed a policy to train professionals (i.e. managers, head teachers, social workers and FSL teachers as well as teachers of other disciplines).

Our team has been a pioneer in the field of educational inclusion. As preparatory classes (separate classes in which newly arrived children are taught) had failed, we put an end to them 10 years ago. Migrant students are now registered in regular classes and progressively included in regular curricula. Today most classes of FSL use students' plurilingual resources, with the help of online tools to support their empowerment. We try to recruit FSL plurilingual teachers, but, above all, we mostly look for highly motivated individuals.

Designing and implementing an inclusive plurilingual policy has taught us that FSL teachers also need to develop skills to act as conscious mediators with other educational actors (families, teachers of other disciplines, counsellors, social workers). In fact, multilingual teachers (non FSL teachers) barely use their family languages in the classroom. Indeed, many teachers from minority backgrounds do not feel authorised to use a language other than French in the school setting. Teachers cannot be left to stumble along alone; they need planned academic training, including knowledge of how to use plurilingual learning tools and language autobiographies, as well as daily support from the educational authorities and from their fellow teachers.

We have thus, in partnership with researchers (see Krüger & Thamin, this volume), developed a policy of staff training to help stakeholders reflect on their language ideologies and practices through discussion, writing and developing professional networks to support them. Today in our region, learning French as a second language at school is anchored in teachers' and students' inclusive plurilingual practices a great deal of the time.

Note

(1) 'The term "Roma" used at the Council of Europe refers to Roma, Sinti, Kale and related groups in Europe, including Travellers and the Eastern groups (Dom and Lom), and covers the wide diversity of the groups concerned, including persons who identify themselves as Gypsies.' See http://a.cs.coe.int/team20/cahrom/documents/Glossary%20Roma%20EN%20version%2018%20May%202012.pdf.

References

Cummins, J. (2014) L'éducation bilingue: qu'avons-nous appris de cinquante ans de recherche? In I. Nocus, J. Vernaudon and M. Paia (eds) *L'école plurilingue en Outre-mer: Apprendre plusieurs langues, plusieurs langues pour apprendre* (pp. 41–63). Rennes: Presses universitaires de Rennes.

Hélot, C. (2007) *Du bilinguisme en famille au plurilinguisme à l'école*. Paris: L'Harmattan.

4 Parents Speaking *Other* Languages in Early Childhood Settings: A 'Language Barrier' for Building an Inclusive Partnership of Education Between Practitioners and Parents?

Nathalie Thomauske

Introduction

The question of how best to serve or educate a plurilingual and diversified people is at the heart of current scientific and political discourse in Germany and in Europe. As an example, the French President Emmanuel Macron made it one of his election goals. Concerning the European level, one can differentiate between, on the one hand, a certain plurilingualism of the elite which is valued as an asset for Europe and for the globalized market and, on the other hand, the so-called 'integration' of refugees and people with a migration background which is strongly linked to mastery of the national language and perceived as the key to achievement in school. These debates on a European level can also be found in Germany in the results of OECD studies such as the PISA study, which confirmed a huge discrepancy between the results of pupils with and without a migration background, and has resulted in an increasing focus on early childhood education (Baumert *et al.*, 2001).

Concerning the development of language policies in the domain of early childhood education in Germany, one can observe several key discourses. Firstly, there is the idea that learning the 'national language' is the best way to 'integrate' migrants or newcomers such as refugees, which has even been anchored in a 'national plan of integration' on a federal level since 2007 (Beauftragte der Bundesregierung für Migration, Flüchtlinge und Integration, 2007). Hence, the learning of German has been delegated to the early childhood education sector, as it is assumed that the earlier the children acquire the national language the better.

As there is still a research gap when it comes to the de facto language policy in early childhood institutions in Germany (Kitas), in this chapter I would like to elaborate on the following questions:

- How are parents speaking another or an Othered language involved in daily practices in the Kita and how are their plurilingual competencies taken into consideration?
- How do the discourses about the so-called 'integration' or inclusion of languages or linguistic diversity translate into the pedagogical practices of early childhood education?
- What do plurilingual parents wish for their children concerning the acquisition of languages?

To address these questions, I will present some of the results of an international research project where focus group discussions with practitioners and parents were conducted using a polyphonic video-ethnographic approach in France and Germany, among other countries (Thomauske, 2017a; Tobin, 2016). Within a power-sensitive perspective, I will focus on the justifications of de facto language policies of parents speaking Other languages in comparison to those of practitioners working in Kitas. I understand language practices or refer to these practices, as does Shohamy (2006), as talk about de facto language policies (see, for example, Shohamy, 2006: 50f.).

I will elaborate first on the political and theoretical background before describing the methods used in the research project and shed some light on some of the theoretical lenses that I utilized in the analysis of the data. Secondly, I will present some insights into de facto language policies in the domain of early childhood education and the private domain, before I present my conclusions.

Theoretical and Political Background

Since 2002 the German federal government has taken into consideration agreements from the World Summit for Children (2002 in New York) and developed a national Plan of Action in order to improve the education and care of children from an early age (BFSFJ, 2006: 15–18). This led, among other things, to the creation of a federal program called *Frühe Chancen. Schwerpunkt-Kitas: Sprache und Integration* (Early Chances: Language and Integration) between 2011 and 2015. In this program the focus was on children with a migration background who do not yet speak German sufficiently. The goal was better 'integration' of children who are considered as having 'deficits' in the German language. In reality this meant that these children were taken out of the group structure and put into small groups to give them special support in German. Here the concept of 'integration' becomes clear. There is a construction of two groups: the 'normal' group of German speaking adults and children and the 'deficient Other' group of children speaking an Othered language. The latter group has to change or be changed in order to be able to be 'integrated' into the first group. In this understanding, speaking an Other language in a public space such as the Kita is understood as a symbol of a 'parallel society' and therefore as a barrier for 'integration'. However, the evaluation of this approach to language acquisition showed it to be ineffective (Thomauske, 2017a: 135). Language learning depended much more on the quality of the interaction between the educators and the children (such as scaffolding on a daily basis) as well as between the children themselves (Roßbach *et al.*, 2016). That is why the following program *Sprach-Kitas* (Language Day-care Centers) (between 2016 and 2022) focused on the qualification of all the staff members through the help of additional educators (for further information, see https://sprach-kitas.fruehe-chancen.de/).

Another change in focus was the use of the term 'inclusion' which has replaced the notion of 'integration'. Concerning the concept of inclusion, there are several definitions I would like to quote, starting with the UNESCO Commission's definition:

> Inclusion is thus seen as a process of addressing and responding to the diversity of needs of all children, youth and adults through increasing participation in learning, cultures and communities, and reducing and eliminating exclusion within and from education. (UNESCO, 2005: 13)

In order to reduce exclusionary practices in the domain of early childhood education, I argue that educators should avoid Othering and stigmatizing children by taking them out of the group context, which could impede the inherent motivation for learning a new language such as German. An inclusive approach to (language) education based in the everyday life of the Kita is aimed at all children. It is therefore important to arrange the activities or the educational practices so that the child is interested in and motivated and/or inspired to participate in learning a new language.

The third focus in the new program was collaboration with families. For the education of children, parents – as the primary instance of socialization (Zimmermann, 2003) – are seen as 'the first and most important significant others' in the life of their children (Berliner Bildungsprogramm, 2014: 49). That is why it is assumed that a strong bond established through a good collaboration or partnership between the children and their parents, including during the time spent in the Kita, is an important condition for any educational or learning process,. In Germany, the Kita has the duty to inform parents of their educational plans and parents have the right to be informed of these, and this is anchored in German law at a federal level (SGB VIII, Kindertagesförderungsgesetz – KitaFöG) as well as at the level of the Länder (Federal Land in Germany) (see, for example, Berliner Bildungsprogramm, 2014).

However, if the educators and the parents enter into the partnership as equal partners, as this idea of collaboration is based on a normative idea and not yet based on empirical findings (Betz *et al.*, 2017), one could question what this means for each partner (for a detailed description and discussion of the notion of partnership, see Knappmann, 2013; Thomauske, 2017a: 237–255). Practitioners might expect parents to collaborate in Kita matters, meaning that parents should ask them what their children have learned in the Kita or how they could help with the next summer party. On the other hand, parents could expect practitioners to inform them regularly about 'relevant matters of the Kita' (Berliner Bildungsprogramm, 2014: 51) without having to ask. I will come back to that example later on in the analysis of the data. But first I will present the research methods.

Research Methods

The empirical data used in this chapter were collected in an international comparative study called 'Children Crossing Borders' (CCB; Tobin, 2016). CCB represents a collaborative research effort with five partners: the United States, the United Kingdom, Italy, France and Germany. The first aim of CCB was to understand how different early childhood educational systems cared for and educated the children of families with a migration background and what those parents, as well as practitioners working in those systems, desired with respect to the education of the children. In order to access these views and opinions, we conducted ten focus group interviews with parents and five with practitioners in each of the countries. In Germany, the focus groups were conducted in Berlin and Stuttgart (southern Germany) and in Jena (eastern Germany). Based on video-ethnography, a video cue of 20 minutes showing a typical day in an early childhood setting in an urban area (e.g. Berlin, Paris) was used to stimulate focus group discussions of four to ten practitioners watching and discussing the tapes together. Separated from the practitioners, homogeneous parent groups speaking the same language and coming from similar cultural backgrounds and heterogeneous focus groups with parents from a variety of cultural and linguistic backgrounds were organized.

The collected data allowed me to analyze attributions of meaning or legitimizations of parents and practitioners in relation to stated language practices for my PhD study (Thomauske, 2017a). For the purpose of this chapter, I focus more on the notion of collaboration between the Kitas and families in relation to the discourse of 'integration' and 'inclusion'. Concerning the use of focus groups, one can assume that focus group discussions give insights into reflections of larger discourses and shared norms and values (Macnaghten & Myers, 2004: 67). In this sense, discourses are understood as products of discursive practices as well as generating discursive practices, which are 'socially constitutive as well as socially conditioned' (Blackledge, 2005: 4).

The analysis of the data was based on the constructionist version of grounded theory methodology (GTM) (Charmaz, 2014). Selected focus groups (approximately four per country) were analyzed in greater depth with sequences to generate codes and categories through initial and focused coding. Through the in-depth analysis, the patterns of interpretation with respect to the language policy or language practice were identified.

Theoretical and Sensitizing Concepts

In line with GTM using sensitizing concepts (Charmaz, 2014: 160f.), I draw on post-decolonial and critical whiteness studies in order to get a better understanding of the structural position of parents of color and practitioners in relation to language policies (for a detailed discussion, see Thomauske, 2017a: 39–48). From a critical whiteness perspective, I use analytical terms in order to mark the marginalized or dominant position in society, such as People of Color and white. These terms do not designate the physiognomy of a person but their structural position in a hierarchized and racialized society. I also use the term 'speaking a Norm language' instead of speaking German or French as well as the term 'speaking an Other language' instead of speaking the mother tongue in order to designate the difference between devalued and Othered ways of speaking. Following these perspectives, one can assume that we live in (post)colonial nation-states where the people are positioned in racialized hierarchies. This is due to persisting relations of power and a continuity of colonialism since the nation-building processes in relation to colonialism in the 18th and 19th centuries. Following Mignolo (2000), colonial continuities lie hidden in the 'underground' of the national self-image. Through this decolonial lens, 'coloniality' represents the 'darker side' of modernity and eurocentrism (Mignolo, 2000: 22). In this sense colonialism has affected colonized and colonizing societies in a reciprocal way, which means that:

> To the same degree as White forces (White power) subordinated and exploited others, European societies also became colonial societies generating a colonial culture and a way of thinking. (Ha, 2010)

So, this can be one reason why People of Color in Germany still get assigned to a history of migration, even when they themselves were born in Germany. Thus, they are Othered as belonging to a different time, the past (such as third or second-generation migrants), and to a different territory (originating from a different country), never belonging to the dominant society and thereby excluded from the privileges of the White majoritarian society as a consequence (Arndt, 2005: 28).

To identify how relationships of power are constructed and legitimized, I was interested in the construction of hegemony in institutions of education. Hegemony is understood as a combination of exerting pressure and building consensus and it is presumed that institutions of education are key locations where actors (re-)produce, deconstruct and modify hegemony (Gramsci: Gefängnisheft 6, H 10.1, §12, cited in Candeias, 2007: 20).

In my understanding of a hegemonic societal construction based on language or linguistic features, I follow proponents of critical applied linguistics (Pennycook, 2001). In this interdisciplinary perspective of applied linguistics and sociology or social studies, the addressed phenomenon is language in society and its analysis of reconstructing speakers' relations of power through language ideologies (Woolard, 1998). It is presumed that current de facto language policies and understandings of languages or norms of speaking are influenced by a long-established monolingual ideology or an ideology of monolingualism, which has its origins in European nation-building (Blommaert & Verschueren, 1998). One language ideology concerns the idea of separating language spaces and enforcing monolingual ones, which as has been shown above was established in the 16th century as part of the ideology of purification during colonialism and imperialism (see Thomauske, 2017a: 57–95) and became what Holliday (2015) called 'native-speakerism'. The idea that people with a migration background do not master their 'native language' legitimizes the only 'correct' way of speaking the national language, whereas the non-native way of speaking gets racialized as the deficient Other speech (Mecheril & Dirim, 2016). (Socio-)linguists and academics working in the domain of language education argue that it is instead a high competence to be able to switch and to adapt to linguistic necessities in various plurilingual or monolingual situations or, as García and Li Wei (2014) state, they translanguage (see Sánchez & Espinet, Chapter 10, this volume, for a detailed account of translanguaging). These language ideologies contribute to maintaining a certain language order based on a hierarchization of their 'native speakers'. As Blackledge (2005: 31) states: 'Political and popular discourse often comes to regard official languages and standard varieties as essentially superior to unofficial languages and non-standard languages' (see also Shohamy, 2006). This also has a consequence for which languages are valued in the context of early childhood education and which languages are excluded or banned to the private domain.

But from a hegemonic critical perspective, we all co-construct hegemonic relations and contribute to resisting the linguistic nationalism in our daily activities or statements. So, the study of language ideologies and its concept itself enables us also to resist power imbalances (Ek *et al.*, 2013: 199).

De Facto Language Policies in the Domain of Early Childhood Education

In the following section, I will illustrate the theoretical ideas above with some of the results of the data analysis.

Acquiring the 'Norm' language: A means of 'integration' or self-empowerment?

When focus group participants talk about their language policies, they reflect on reasons why a certain language should be spoken or taught in certain contexts. One line of argument concerns the discourse on integration.

The hegemonic position of practitioners and parents is that the Norm language favors the so-called integration of children with a migration background and speaking another language. Focus group participants say that speaking a common language, like German, would impede the creation of 'language groups' or the isolation of children speaking an Other language. One mother talks about the fighting that occurred between 'language groups':

Monja: I don't want my child to always say, I'm an Arab and such – I don't like that. I'm a human first of all and Arabic, that's his business, he does that at home, but not within groups like that. I don't like that at all ((shakes head)). And that was totally extreme in the kindergarten here, with [Monja's son], that they really acted like hooligans. The quarrel was always just between Arabs and Turks, for example, the children. [...] there's always that [fight] between the groups, [between] the different language/mother-tongue groups.[1] (Berlin, Pinocchio, parents)

In Monja's understanding, the children form groups through the common feature of speaking the same language and/or sharing the same natio-ethno-cultural belonging or ascription (Mecheril, 2018). In this position it seems that conflicts between groups are read through a natio-ethno-cultural lens. The fact that there could also be different reasons for forming a friendship group or having conflicts has been discussed in detail elsewhere (Thomauske, 2017a). In addition, the choice of language plays an important role. One way of preventing or working against this kind of group-building is through requiring the children to only speak the national standard language among themselves (Thomauske, 2017a), but not all parents know if this is the best way:

Anna: In our group, for example, there are five Russian speaking children. [...] They have the tendency to group together and play together – the Russian children, you understand? [...] And from the first day and also at the parent-teacher meetings it was said, our children are Russian, they are together. Like subgroups of sorts – the Russians extra, the Germans extra. (.) Well, I don't know if one should forbid it. (Berlin, Löwenzahn, parents)

Anna talks about the fact that these children did not know the Norm language sufficiently at the beginning and therefore tended to group together with other children speaking the same language. It was helpful for the purpose of socializing and accommodating themselves in the new environment. But what is not quite clear is why it becomes a problem. Is it because of the group-building? Is there a wish that everyone should be 'integrated', which could mean in this case that German and Russian ascribed children mix together and play together? As the Russian speaking parents are addressed with this issue and not the German parents, it seems that the task of 'integration' is rather a task of 'assimilation' of the Russians into the Norm speaking group of children.

From an inclusive perspective, one could rather argue that it is a task for everyone to consider: Why is this group-building important for these girls and are they somehow excluded from other groups? If there is a desire to mix the children more, then educators could develop ideas together, perhaps in collaboration with the parents, about what common activities could favor inclusion, such as building on the plurilingual resources of the children (see below). These negative attitudes towards children's group-building reflect the hegemonic discourse mentioned above, in which the national language is the condition of social 'integration'.

But from the perspective of the marginalized, acquiring the Norm language is an important means of gaining access to resources (economic, educational, etc.), as can be seen in the following extract:

Banu: Our expectations ... We are quite happy with our position, with our kids' position, but it could be better, and we trust they can give us that. Discriminating the German, or non-German, or nothing like that happens, it's just that in terms of language Turks start school losing 0–1, we don't want our kids to be in that position. We send our kids to German Kindergarten so they can be educated as them, so they can talk as them. We don't want them to start school losing 0–1. (Berlin, mother)

In this perspective, I would understand acquiring the Norm language as an act of self-empowerment in order to avoid being discriminated against for not speaking German well enough. It becomes obvious that to be able to speak the Norm language is a form of symbolic capital needed in a 'language market' (Bourdieu, 1992: 49) and is intrinsically linked with other forms of capital, such as cultural and economic (Thomauske, 2017a).

Shared responsibilities of language education?

The question we might ask is: Who should acquire the Norm language and how should it be acquired? One way is by separating languages into spaces, such as German-only in the Kita and the 'mother tongue' in the private domain of the families. One could assume that the responsibilities for the transmission of these languages or the child's language education are shared, as is suggested with the idea of partnership. But it seems that there is no real dialogue about who is responsible and how language education should be implemented. It is more about expecting the other group to do their duty. Parents, for example, expect practitioners to 'teach' German and this is the main reason for them bringing their children to the Kita, as the following mother states:

> Nalan: I too think German is important, also from the perspective of pre-school education. Otherwise I can take care of my child at home. (Berlin, Lutzenstraße, parents)

Practitioners, on the other hand, see parents as responsible for teaching the first language to the child. To elaborate on this idea further and how it is connected to the idea of partnership, I would like to discuss the following sequence in a little more detail:

> Britta: Whereas we always preach, at home the native language.
> Kirstin: But, if that [the language] then isn't even really there, you know, then/
> Dana: it's also important that the parents then mostly only speak in the first language and not additionally try to teach broken German. And that then becomes twice half a language. (Berlin, Pinocchio, practitioners)

There are a few underlying assumptions in this sequence:

(1) children need to acquire their 'native language' perfectly;
(2) parents are responsible for the transmission of their 'native language';
(3) parents with a 'migration background' do not 'master' their 'native language' any more, but do not speak German sufficiently well either ('broken German');
(4) language separation or monolingual spaces (speaking only one language) prevent language confusion;
(5) children are in danger of becoming semilingual.

This all leads to the conclusion that parents should speak to their children in their home language, but in a 'correct' way in order to avoid a so-called semilingualism. So here one notices a deficit stance in relation to the linguistic competencies of parents intrinsically linked with language ideologies such as 'native-speakerism'. These parents are constructed as the deficient Other who do not fulfil their duty of transmitting their 'native language' to their children. That is why, in the practitioners' view, children cannot acquire the Norm language, as they are lacking a foundation in their first language in order to be able to build on the second one. In addition to that, it allows the practitioners to put themselves in a higher position of power by paternalizing the parents with regard to their knowing about and how to do language education. Here it is interesting that

Britta uses the term 'preach', which gives a religious connotation to her advice. Taking this image further, the practitioner is a kind of preacher; she knows what to do and is in the position to give advice to the parents, the believers, who should listen to what she says (Thomauske, 2013).

One reason behind this paternalizing stance could be that there is a societal discourse about the risks of the familial living conditions that tend to have a negative impact on the education of these children (Anders & Roßbach, 2014). In this 'deficit' perspective, the negative preconditions of the families have to be compensated for by the school or pre-school system but also by parental education programs (for an overview of these programs, see Tschöpe-Scheffler, 2005). Kitas are seen as a good way to get access to those families that are seen as being in need (Pietsch et al., 2010). This is further reinforced when it comes to children or families with a migration background, speaking an Other language instead of German, which is seen as a disadvantage in the educational system (see, for example, the results of the 2000 and 2015 PISA studies, and the 2016 IGLU study: Baumert et al., 2001; Hußmann et al., 2017; OECD, 2018). The PISA results were or are interpreted in such a way that not only does the pre-school or school system have to be more inclusive, but parents also have to be educated, which can be illustrated with the following example:

Britta: Not a day goes by almost where we don't [tell] the parents, don't just really quickly in the cloak room quickly a conversation in passing, when they have any questions, too, and such: 'at home native language, please, here you speak German now', yes, yes. (Berlin, Pinocchio, practitioner)

As plurilingual people are commanded to assimilate to the Norm language, whereas their Other languages are excluded from the public space of the institution, they are silenced in a way, as they are not in the position to decide for themselves which language they would like to speak, and they are disciplined or admonished to adapt to the German-only policy. As the traditional hegemonic monolingual language order is broken by the use of Other languages in the Kita, the de facto language policies of silencing and banning Other languages in the private domain contribute to maintaining and legitimizing this language order.

The power imbalance between the practitioners and the parents is also noticed by the latter:

Monja: quite a few teachers really don't accept what the parents say, and they speak with us like, a little, as if we don't understand at all what the children have to learn. Yeah, they only know the pedagogical side//
Sumaya: They always know that better, even though it's my child. (Berlin, Pinocchio, parents)

From their perspective, practitioners tend to give advice and do not really listen to parents, which is in opposition to how educational partnerships should be implemented. One reason that appears in the quote above by the parents is the hierarchy of knowledge. Who knows better how to educate the child – the parents or, as it seems in this case, the practitioners who have acquired pedagogical knowledge?

'Visibilizing' the Other languages in the Kita

This leads us to a different political approach to language which could also be found in the data. There are different reasons to include Other languages in the Kita (for a detailed analysis, see Thomauske, 2017b). The first reason is that parents speak about the fear of losing their home languages, because as children learn German, their ability to speak to and understand their relatives seems to disappear (Thomauske *et al.*, 2016). As parents feel mainly responsible for preserving the home languages but fear that this will not be enough, the inclusion of their home languages in the Kita could contribute to the valuing of these languages and thereby motivate children and parents to practice these languages (see in detail Thomauske, 2017b). From a practitioner's point of view, the argument is to demonstrate appreciation towards the home languages of the families. However, when it comes to the question of how it could be possible to take these languages into consideration, most of the practitioners argue that for several reasons, such as the general conditions, insufficient personnel or the linguistic heterogeneity of the children, they cannot imagine how to include them. Other practitioners, however, have shown initiatives of how they manage to include home languages in daily activities or projects in the Kita. In one Kita, parents speaking Other languages participated in diverse pedagogical activities, such as the development of a plurilingual dictionary, creating a plurilingual CD with the voices of the parents or being asked to read or narrate a story in their home language.

By doing these kinds of activities, the different languages of the children and the parents are 'made visible', as one practitioner terms it. This contributes to the valuing of these languages but also to the valuing of their speakers, and it encourages and supports the acquisition of diverse languages. It also reinforces the self-esteem of the children and their parents who receive the message that they can feel proud of their language background.

Beate: So, children want to then bring the parents along for the ride, they think that's great that we have such an interest in that [their languages] [...]

Fiona: Yeah, we've actually recently demanded a lot of the parents with the translations, because we needed the translations from them, too, for various, for all the different things we've got going now, and I also just noticed that really made her proud ... (Stuttgart, practitioners)

In addition, this contributes to establishing or maintaining an inclusive partnership of education between the parents and the practitioners, as the following quote illustrates:

> Claudia: Yeah, and above all, of course, one also addresses the parents about it, who actually sometimes don't have the confidence. There are parents [...] who hold back, for whatever reason one doesn't know, but then one gradually gets to the parents, too, that's also a good method of involving the parents with, yeah in cooperation with the Kita, you know. (Stuttgart, practitioner)

Here it seems that parents start to open up to the institution when they notice that their family backgrounds and languages matter and that they are seen as resources instead of a 'barrier' for the language education of their children. It appears that an important factor in this case is that parents feel listened to and valued. It is not only an acknowledgement but also the inclusion of their (plurilingual) resources in pedagogical projects in the Kita.

Conclusions

To conclude, one could question whether the concept of educational partnership has led to an acknowledgement of the expertise of parents and a de-hierarchization of the relationship between practitioners and parents. The data analysis reveals that different knowledge and skills, such as a higher level of theoretical knowledge with regard to education and care, may lead practitioners rather to give advice to parents about the education of their children instead of entering into a real dialogue with them and listening to their views, wishes or expectations concerning (language) education. The analysis has also shown that other categories of difference contribute to asymmetrical positioning. For example, being part of a white middle-class majority, the practitioner might expect parents and families to assimilate to the mainstream 'German culture and language' in order for them to be able to fulfill their duty of informing the parents in the Kita. By regulating not only the children but also the parents on how to speak at home or in the Kita, the practitioners normalize certain language norms, silence certain ways of speaking and paternalize the children and the parents. I would like to add here that this is only one example and there are other examples of what practitioners do to support a real dialogue (see, for example, Thomauske, 2017a: 336–341). The use of arguments about the so-called 'integration' through the Norm language supports and legitimizes the practitioners' position. The monolingual language order is reproduced as the Norm language is valued whereas the Othered languages are invisibilized and excluded (see also, for example, Gkaintartzi *et al.*, 2015). In answer to the first question, given this position, parents speaking an Other language are not involved in the Kita.

Their plurilingual competencies are rather constructed as a 'barrier' to helping their children to acquire 'proper' German. But the data also show that some practitioners are in favor of the idea of inclusion by enabling plurilingual spaces in the Kita. Thereby the wishes of the parents concerning the support of the bi- or plurilingualism of their children can also be consolidated.

Concerning the establishment of a possible inclusive partnership of education, the analysis made it clear that if their family culture as well as their plurilingual resources are valued and included in pedagogical activities, this can enable the participation of parents. However, what happens in cases where parents do not have the time or energy to do so? Would it be a condition that parents need to participate in order to be able to establish such a partnership? Would practitioners interpret the non-participation of parents as a sign of not collaborating? These questions still have to be answered by further research. In any case, following an inclusive approach, practitioners need to take a step back from the privileged position of the 'knowing' pedagogic professionals and give space to the parents and the children.

Note

(1) The original languages of the quotations were German, Russian, Turkish and Kurdish and were translated into English by a professional translator.

References

Anders, Y. and Roßbach, H.-G. (2014) Empirische Bildungsforschung zu den Auswirkungen frühkindlicher, institutioneller Bildung: Internationale und nationale Ergebnisse. In R. Braches, H. Sünker and C. Röhner (eds) *Handbuch Frühe Kindheit* (pp. 225–350). Leverkusen: Verlag Barbara Budrich.

Arndt, S. (2005) Weißsein: Die verkannte Strukturkategorie Europas und Deutschlands. In M. Eggers, G. Kilomba, P. Piesche and S. Arndt (eds) *Mythen, Masken und Subjekte: Kritische Weißseinsforschung in Deutschland* (pp. 24–28). Münster: Unrast Verlag.

Baumert, J., Klieme, E., Neubrand, M. *et al.* (eds) (2001) *PISA 2000: Basiskompetenzen von Schülerinnen und Schülern im internationalen Vergleich.* Opladen: Waxmann Verlag.

Beauftragte der Bundesregierung für Migration, Flüchtlinge und Integration (BBMFI) (2007) *Nationaler Integrationsplan. Neue Wege – Neue Chancen.* Berlin: Presse und Informationsamt der Bundesregierung.

Berliner Bildungsprogramm (2014) *Das Berliner Bildungsprogramm für die Bildung, Erziehung und Betreuung von Kindern in Tageseinrichtungen bis zu ihrem Schuleintritt.* Berlin: Verlag Das Netz.

Betz, T., Bischoff, S., Eunicke, N., Kayser, L.B. and Zink, K. (2017) *Partner auf Augenhöhe? Forschungsbefunde zur Zusammenarbeit von Familien, Kitas und Schulen mit Blick auf Bildungschancen.* Gütersloh: Bertelsmann Stiftung.

BFSFJ (2006) *Nationaler Aktionsplan: Für ein kindergerechtes Deutschland 2005–2010.* Berlin: Bundesministerium für Familie, Senioren, Frauen und Jugend.

Blackledge, A. (2005) *Discourse and Power in a Multilingual World.* Amsterdam and Philadelphia, PA: John Benjamins.

Blommaert, J. and Verschueren, J. (1998) The role of language in European nationalist ideologies. In P. Kroskrity, B. Schieffelin and K. Woolard (eds) *Language Ideologies: Practice and Theory* (pp. 189–210). New York: Oxford University Press.

Bourdieu, P. (1992) *Was heisst sprechen? Die Ökonomie des sprachlichen Tausches*. Vienna: Braumüller.

Candeias, M. (2007) Gramscianische Konstellationen. Hegemonie und die Durchsetzung neuer Produktions- und Lebensweisen. In A. Merkens and V. Rego Diaz (eds) *Mit Gramsci arbeiten: Texte zur politisch-praktischen Aneignung Antonio Gramscis* (pp. 15–32). Sonderband Neue Folge AS 305. Hamburg: Argument.

Charmaz, K. (2014) *Constructing Grounded Theory* (2nd edn). Los Angeles, CA: Sage.

Ek, L.D., Sánchez, P. and Quijada Cerecer, P.D. (2013) Linguistic violence, insecurity, and work: Language ideologies of Latina/o bilingual teacher candidates in Texas. *International Multilingual Research Journal* 7 (3), 197–219.

García, O. and Li Wei (2014) *Translanguaging: Language, Bilingualism and Education*. Houndmills: Palgrave Macmillan.

Gkaintartzi, A., Kiliari, A. and Tsokalidou, R. (2015) 'Invisible' bilingualism – 'invisible' language ideologies: Greek teachers' attitudes towards immigrant pupils' heritage languages. *International Journal of Bilingual Education and Bilingualism* 18 (1), 60–72.

Ha, K.N. (2010) Postkoloniale Kritik als politisches Projekt. In J. Reuter and P.-I. Villa (eds) *Postkoloniale Soziologie: Empirische Befunde, theoretische Anschlüsse, politische Intervention* (pp. 259–280). Bielefeld: Transcript Verlag.

Holliday, A. (2015) Native-speakerism: Taking the concept forward and achieving cultural belief. In A. Swan, P. Aboshiha and A. Holliday (eds) *(En)Countering Native-speakerism* (pp. 11–25). London: Palgrave Macmillan.

Hußmann, A., Wendt, H., Bos, W. et al. (2017) *IGLU 2016: Lesekompetenzen von Grundschulkindern in Deutschland im internationalen Vergleich*. Münster: Waxmann.

Knappmann, S. (2013) *Der Weg von der 'Anleitung zur Erziehung' zu Eltern als Erziehungspartner in Kindertagesstätten*. Das Online-Familienhandbuch des Staatsinstituts für Frühpädagogik (IFP). Munich: Staatsinstitut für Frühpädagogik (IFP). See http://www.kindergartenpaedagogik.de/la.html (accessed 18 September 2014).

Macnaghten, P. and Myers, G. (2004) Focus groups. In C. Seale, F. Gobojaber, G. Gubrium and D. Silverman (eds) *Qualitative Research Practice* (pp. 65–79). London: Sage.

Mecheril, P. (2018) Orders of belonging and education: Migration pedagogy as criticism. In D. Bachmann-Medick and J. Kugele (eds) *Migration: Changing Concepts, Critical Approaches* (pp. 121–138). Berlin: De Gruyter.

Mecheril, P. and Dirim, I. (2016) Die Sprache(n) der Migrationsgesellschaft. In P. Mecheril (ed.) *Handbuch Migrationspädagogik* (pp. 99–120). Weinheim: Beltz UTB.

Mignolo, W.D. (2000) *Coloniality, Subaltern Knowledges, and Border Thinking*. Princeton, NJ: Princeton University Press.

OECD (2018) *PISA 2015: PISA Results in Focus*. See https://www.oecd.org/pisa/pisa-2015-results-in-focus.pdf.

Pennycook, A. (2001) *Critical Applied Linguistics: A Critical Introduction*. Mahwah, NJ and London: Lawrence Erlbaum.

Pietsch, S., Ziesemer, S. and Fröhlich-Gildhoff, K. (2010) *Zusammenarbeit mit Eltern in Kindertageseinrichtungen – Internationale Perspektiven. Ein Überblick: Studien und Forschungsergebnisse*. Munich: Weiterbildungsinitiative Frühpädagogische Fachkräfte (WiFF), Deutsches Jugendinstitut e.V.

Roßbach, H.-G., Anders, Y. and Tietze, W. (2016) *Wissenschaftliche Evaluation des Bundesprogramms 'Schwerpunkt-Kitas Sprache & Integration'*. Bamberg and Berlin: Bundesministerium für Familie, Senioren, Frauen und Jugend.

Shohamy, E. (2006) *Language Policy: Hidden Agendas and New Approaches*. London and New York: Routledge.
Thomauske, N. (2013) Le débat sur les pratiques langagières dans l'éducation de la petite enfance: L'exemple de Berlin. In M.-N. Rubio and C. Hélot (eds) *Développement du langage et plurilinguisme chez le jeune enfant* (pp. 69–97). Toulouse: Érès.
Thomauske, N. (2017a) *Sprachlos gemacht in Kita und Familie: Ein deutsch-französischer Vergleich von Sprachpolitiken und -praktiken*. Wiesbaden: Springer VS Research.
Thomauske, N. (2017b) Möglichkeitsräume der Umsetzung von de facto Sprachenpolitiken in Einrichtungen der frühkindlichen Bildung: Ein deutsch-französischer Vergleich. In U. Stenger, D. Edelmann, D. Nolte and M. Schulz (eds) *Diversität in der Pädagogik der frühen Kindheit: Im Spannungsfeld zwischen Konstruktion und Normativität* (pp. 234–252). Weinheim and Basel: Beltz Juventa.
Thomauske, N., Gil, D., Fuster, T., Zaninelli, F. and Preissing, C. (2016) Language. In J. Tobin (ed.) *Preschool and Im/migrants in Five Countries: England, France, Germany, Italy and United States of America* (pp. 115–127). Brussels: Peter Lang.
Tobin, J. (ed.) (2016) *Preschool and Im/migrants in Five Countries: England, France, Germany, Italy and United States of America*. Brussels: Peter Lang.
Tschöpe-Scheffler, S. (2005) Unterstützungsangebote zur Stärkung der elterlichen Erziehungsverantwortung oder: starke Eltern haben starke Kinder. *ZSE: Zeitschrift für Soziologie der Erziehung und Sozialisation* 25 (3), 248–262.
UNESCO (2005) *Guidelines for Inclusion: Ensuring Access to Education for All*. Paris: United Nations Educational, Scientific and Cultural Organization. See https://unesdoc.unesco.org/ark:/48223/pf0000140224 (accessed 15 November 2019).
Woolard, K.A. (1998) Introduction: Language ideology as a field of inquiry. In B. Schieffelin, K. Woolard and P. Kroskrity (eds) *Language Ideologies: Practice and Theory* (pp. 3–27). New York: Oxford University Press.
Zimmermann, P. (2003) *Grundwissen Sozialisation: Einführung zur Sozialisation im Kindes- und Jugendalter* (2nd edn). Wiesbaden: VS Verlag für Sozialwissenschaft.

Establishing a Relationship of Trust between Parents and School

Marie-Claire Simonin

Pre-school teacher, France

Relations with parents are often a matter of fear for teachers who prefer to keep their distance. I shared this fear for a long time until I worked with Travellers. In order for them to accept schooling, I had to establish a relationship of great trust and therefore of close proximity. This type of relationship, which was quite exceptional for a teacher in France, taught me a lot. When I arrived at a kindergarten with high linguistic diversity, I realized that I could not work effectively with pupils without knowing their families well. Following this realization, I decided to have an interview with each family and my colleagues did the same. The experience was so conclusive that we decided to implement this practice every year.

These interviews are essentially conversations about the family's history and its linguistic practices and attitudes.[1] We take the time to get to know each other, to talk about the family and the child and about the school. This creates a relationship of mutual trust from the start of the school year. Parents do not perceive our questions as indiscreet; on the contrary, they are touched by the fact that the teacher has taken an interest in them and is listening to them. These interviews bring teachers concrete knowledge about families who are very diverse in terms of their geographical origins, reasons for migration and educational levels (some are illiterate, others are highly qualified). It then becomes impossible for teachers to consider all parents as 'deficient Other[s]' (Thomauske, this volume).

This change in attitudes and relationships allows teachers to build real collaboration between families and the school without placing themselves in a position of superiority. Parents enter the school and take part in activities: they translate the stories read or told by teachers into their languages; they record words in 'digital multilingual picture books' that we use in class and that are also posted on the school's blog[2]; they teach us nursery rhymes in Arabic, Romani, Turkish, Shimaore, Pashto and other languages. Thanks to parents, home languages have a place inside the school. As these interviews can lead to a profound transformation of teachers' attitudes, they also constitute a highly interesting tool for teacher education.

Notes

(1) For details, see 'parents' interviews' at https://www.decolang.net/exemples-de-pratiques-clive.
(2) See the school's blog at http://mat-cologne-besancon.ac-besancon.fr/2020/04/10/nos-comptines-et-imagiers-plurilingues/.

5 'Dutch If Possible, and Also When It's Not': The Inclusion of Multilingualism in Declared, Perceived and Practiced Language Policies in a Brussels Secondary School

Kirsten Rosiers

Introduction

In this chapter, teachers' responsiveness to multilingualism and the inclusion of other languages in a linguistically diverse Brussels (Belgium) secondary classroom with a monolingual policy will be analyzed. Belgium is a multilingual country in which Dutch, French and German are the three officially recognized languages in specific parts of the country: Dutch is the official language in the northern part of the country, French in the southern part and German in a small eastern part. Brussels, Belgium's capital, is officially bilingual Dutch-French, and notwithstanding the presence of many other languages as the result of globalization and migration flows, the lingua franca of the city is French (Blommaert & Rampton, 2011; Janssens, 2013). French is mastered by 88.5% of the inhabitants, whereas it is estimated that 23.1% of the population is fluent in Dutch (Janssens, 2013). Self-reported data based on the home language of the family indicate that 33.6% of the families in Brussels are monolingual French speaking, 5.4% are monolingual Dutch speaking and 14.1% are bilingual Dutch-French speaking (Janssens, 2013).

The bilingual status of the city is not translated into the educational system. Education is a community responsibility: schools belong either to the Dutch speaking Flemish Community or to the French speaking French Community; as a result, bilingual education has not been organized. In this chapter, a Dutch-medium school will be described and analyzed. Many Dutch-medium schools in Brussels have recently been welcoming an increase of pupils speaking other languages than Dutch at home; 71.9% of pupils in secondary education do not speak Dutch at home (Flanders National Administration Agency, 2019). As such schools were once meant to assure the survival of Dutch in a predominantly Francophone city, this has led to attempts to control and accommodate the increasingly multilingual pupil population enrolled in these schools. Policymakers consider the knowledge of Dutch to be the key factor for including all pupils in schools; therefore, a monolingual Dutch policy is prescribed as the main accommodation strategy in education.

The research presented in this chapter is part of a broader research project, 'Between the devil and the deep blue sea' (PI Jürgen Jaspers[1]), which investigates teachers' reconciliation of monolingual school policies with a multilingual reality in Brussels' secondary schools. Within the philosophy of the project, it has been demonstrated that research on language policy tends to divide teachers in two oppositional camps (Jaspers, 2018, 2019). On the one hand, they 'serve as "soldiers" of the system' (Shohamy, 2006: 78) who have internalized the monolingual habitus of policymakers into their own habitus, pursuing an ideology of linguistic homogeneity (Gogolin, 1997; Hélot, 2010). On the other hand, teachers' agency, their different attitudes and practiced policies within schools are emphasized (Bonacina-Pugh, 2012, 2020; Hélot, 2010; Mary & Young, 2017, this volume; Young, 2014). Teachers can interpret, appropriate and/or ignore policies in an interactive frame with their own interpretation of policy, their own ideas about language use and the linguistic needs of their pupils (Hornberger & Johnson, 2011; Leung & Creese, 2008; Puskás & Björk-Willén, 2017; Ricento & Hornberger, 1996). Based on their own experiences, values and perceptions, teachers interpret and negotiate the meaning of top-down policies at a local level, reconciling often contradictory interests (Leung & Creese, 2008). As a result, it can be expected that teachers will be ambiguous in practices and discourses around policy (Creese, 2010). To scrutinize these ambivalences, linguistic-ethnographic research was carried out in one Brussels school within the project's framework. For the purpose of this chapter, language policy in education will be analyzed to unravel how school and teachers reflect on and deal with the inclusion of multilingualism. Language policy research will be explained in the following section. I will describe the methodology of the research before turning to the results, in which policy at a governmental and school level will precede a description of teachers' attitudes and practices. Ambivalences within and between policy levels will be discussed in the concluding remarks.

Table 5.1 Overview of the different levels of language policy

Language policy (< Spolsky, 2004)	In this chapter
Language management	Declared language policy < Shohamy, 2006
Language ideologies and beliefs	Perceived language policy < Bonacina-Pugh, 2012
Language practices	Practiced language policy < Bonacina-Pugh, 2012

Language Policy Research and the Ethnography of Language Policy

Spolsky (2004) identifies language policy as a multifaceted phenomenon that requires an investigation of language management (how language use is organized in texts – declared language policy; Shohamy, 2006), language ideologies (see Mary & Young, this volume, for further definitions of language ideologies) and beliefs (attitudes and conceptualizations of actual use and intended practices – perceived language policy; Bonacina-Pugh, 2012) and language practices (what people do – practiced language policy; Bonacina-Pugh, 2012; cf. Table 5.1 for an overview of the concepts). Language policy as a text is never unilaterally translated in language practices and beliefs due to covert and overt ideological processes playing a part (Shohamy, 2006). A local understanding of policy is necessary, as 'policies pose problems to their subjects, problems that must be solved in context' (Ball, 1997: 270). Therefore, and to understand the *language policy onion* (Ricento & Hornberger, 1996: 402) – a metaphor to refer to the multiple layers of policy, including different agents, levels and processes involved – different layers should be connected (McCarty, 2011). Macro-level language policies at governmental level and micro-level educational practices can be related by means of an ethnography of language policy (Johnson, 2009). By its ethnographic understanding of local context (Hornberger & Johnson, 2011), this method can resolve the lack of 'educational policy interpretation and appropriation that illuminates connections between macro and micro policy' (Johnson, 2009: 139).

Methodology

To explain teachers' attitudes towards multilingualism and language practices, their responses to policies posing problems 'that must be solved in context' (Ball, 1997: 270) and to account for teachers' discourses on these topics that engender multiplicity and layering (Pachler *et al.*, 2008), linguistic-ethnographic research was carried out. This method makes it possible to analyze local actions from the participants' point of view and to relate interactions to the broader social context in which they are produced (Copland & Creese, 2015; Rampton *et al.*, 2015).

Linguistic-ethnographic fieldwork was carried out in one classroom in a Brussels secondary Dutch-medium school during the school year of 2016–2017.

Pupils were in the second year of the general track of secondary education (age +/− 14) and displayed a variety of languages spoken at home (Arabic, Aramaic, Dutch, English, French, Persian, Somali, Spanish, Turkish).

Fieldwork included collecting policy documents, participant observation for four months, 24 hours of audio recordings of classroom interaction, more than 26 hours of audio recordings of individual pupils and more than three hours of focus group interviews with pupils. In a second stage (autumn–winter 2017–2018), these data were complemented with individual interviews with classroom teachers and the head of school (+/− 7 hours). These different data collection tools are used to achieve triangulation, i.e. to check data integrity and to be able to extend inferences from the data (Ritchie, 2003).

The main focus of this chapter is on the in-depth, semi-structured interviews with the teachers. Table 5.2 gives an overview of relevant teacher information. All seven observed teachers of the selected classroom as well as the head of school were interviewed. Interviews were conducted a few months after the in-classroom fieldwork, which enabled the development of a topic list that was tuned to the specificities of teachers and school policy. All interviews were transcribed entirely. For the purpose of this chapter, interviews were analyzed by means of a thematic analysis focusing on emerging topics of inclusion of other languages and multilingualism. This resulted in the emergence of five themes: knowledge of governmental and school language policy; reaction to other languages; perception of pupils' language use; attention to multilingualism; and openness to multilingual education. A qualitative, constant comparative method was used to analyze these themes throughout the interviews (Corbin & Strauss, 1990; Ryan & Bernard, 2000).

Thanks to the multifaceted linguistic-ethnographic dataset, teacher interview data could be complemented with policy documents and classroom interaction data, which made it possible to investigate multilingualism and inclusion at different policy levels. Policy documents were analyzed paying specific attention to the themes of language, inclusion and multilingualism. Classroom interaction data were analyzed and transcribed, taking notice of teachers' engagement with multilingualism and their attention to language policy.

Results: Declared, Perceived and Practiced Language Policy

Declared educational language policy at governmental level

In this chapter, the focus is on a Dutch-medium school in Brussels. As Dutch-medium education in Brussels falls within the area of responsibility of the Flemish government, I will analyze the Flemish educational language policy. Policy texts by consecutive ministers of education highlight the importance of knowledge of Dutch as a key condition to guarantee

Table 5.2 Overview of teachers' interviews and information on teachers' background

Name[a]	General information	Professional information	Subject taught in the selected classroom	Interview data (date and duration)
Janne	• Lives in Brussels' periphery	• Has been a teacher for more than 10 years, in this school	Mathematics and sciences	12 September 2017, 00:35:19
Els	• Lives in Flanders • Monolingual[b]	• Has been a teacher for more than 20 years, in this school	Dutch 2,[c] additional hour	18 September 2017, 00:41:38
Celine	• Lives in Brussels • Raised in Flanders, has lived in Brussels for 20 years	• Has taught in this school for more than 10 years • Worked 10 years in the media before	Head of school[d]	22 September 2017, 01:28:38
Audrey	• Lives in Brussels • Bilingual English-Dutch	• Has taught in this school for 5–10 years	English and history	28 September 2017, 00:48:19
Christine	• Lives in Flanders • Bilingual French-Dutch	• Has taught in the school for more than 20 years	French	16 October 2017, 00:51:42
Mark	• Lives in Flanders • Monolingual	• Has been teaching for 5–10 years, has taught in this school for 2 years	Natural sciences	24 October 2017, 00:47:10
Fabian	• Lives in Flanders • Monolingual	• Has been teaching for more than 20 years, has taught in this school for 2 years	Technology	05 December 2017, 00:28:58
Emily	• Lives in Flanders • Monolingual	• Has been teaching for +/− 15 years, has taught in this school for 5 years	Dutch	22 February 2018, 00:41:48

Notes: [a]All teachers' and pupils' names have been anonymized. [b]I use monolingual for teachers who only speak Dutch at home, bilingual for teachers who are raised bilingual. [c]Pupils have two hours of Dutch during which the class is deduplicated (cf. 'Declared language policy at school' below). During these hours, Emily, the regular teacher of Dutch, is assisted by Els, called 'Dutch 2' for reasons of clarity in this chapter. [d]It should be noted that the fieldwork during the school year of 2016–2017 was the head of school's first year in that position; at the moment of the interview, she was no longer head of school, but had become a regular teacher of Dutch again.

equal opportunities for all pupils, and specify that pupils with other home languages should be mainstreamed in Dutch-medium education (Delarue & De Caluwe, 2015). Following the language education law of 1963, the language of instruction (henceforth, LOI) in schools of the Flemish Community is Dutch. Due to a long struggle for an equal position and recognition of Dutch in Belgium (for an in-depth description, see De Caluwe, 2012), Flemish people and policymakers want to protect Dutch against variation. As a result, integration and education debates in Flanders are guided by a monolingual ideology based on three assumptions (Pulinx *et al.*, 2017; for more information on the language ideological debate, see Blommaert, 2011). Firstly, it is assumed that proficiency in Dutch is necessary for participation in education. Secondly, a home language other than Dutch is considered to be a problem and an obstacle for both educational success (Van den Branden & Verhelst, 2009) and Dutch proficiency (Pulinx *et al.*, 2017). Thirdly, to guarantee educational success, lack of proficiency in Dutch should be addressed (Pulinx *et al.*, 2017). Languages other than Dutch are considered to be a threat to the dominant position of Dutch and to undermine community cohesion (Van den Branden & Verhelst, 2009).

Policy towards multilingualism in Flanders is vague and implicitly restrictive, showing paradoxes in dealing with different languages (Delarue & De Caluwe, 2015). On the one hand, Flemish educational policy acknowledges prestigious languages such as English and French, although these languages are only allowed in foreign language classes and, more recently, in content and language integrated learning. On the other hand, policy regulations are restrictive for immigrant languages: they are forbidden, and non-native speakers should acquire Dutch as soon as possible (Delarue & De Caluwe, 2015; Sierens & Ramaut, 2018). On this matter, Jaspers (2009) distinguishes prestige multilingualism and plebeian multilingualism. Prestige multilingualism – multilingualism of the elite (Blommaert, 2011) – covers knowledge of prestigious languages such as French and English, whereas plebeian multilingualism – multilingualism of the poor (Blommaert, 2011) – involves languages of multi-ethnic, urban groups such as Turkish and Arabic.

In the latest *language* report by one Minister of Education (Smet, 2011, tenure 2009–2014), a recognition of the multilingual reality goes hand in hand with a vague policy towards multilingualism: while Smet asked for more openness to multilingualism and the home languages of pupils,[2] no initiatives to include multilingualism in daily classroom practices were mentioned (Sierens & Ramaut, 2018). Projects that experimented with pupils' home languages in education (e.g. OETC, Van den Branden & Verhelst, 2009) were cancelled by the minister (Smet, 2011).

During the fieldwork on which this chapter reports, the Minister of Education at the time of data collection (Crevits, tenure 2014–2019) continued the language policy of her predecessor. Knowledge of Dutch is seen as a top priority. Other languages are important, although only prestigious ones are mentioned in her policy text (Crevits, 2014). However, for a complete picture it should be mentioned that she displayed a more favorable attitude towards multilingualism in media interviews. Following the publication of a study which she commissioned and which was carried out (Flemish Ministry of Education and Training, 2016), she demonstrated willingness to put multilingualism on the agenda of the Flemish education council. During a loaded media debate in November 2017, she commented positively on a new guideline of one of the three educational groups offering official education in Flanders[3] (GO!). GO! decided to authorize the home languages of pupils on the school's playground, as well as for specific purposes in the classroom, e.g. to translate or to prepare group work. In a reaction to the debate, the head of the subsidized free and Catholic educational group, under which the school I will discuss resides, supported the use of home languages to improve Dutch (Katholiek onderwijs, 2017). In the debate in parliament that week, the Minister of Education was asked to comment on the new guideline. She emphasized its positive aspects and praised the attempt to remove the stigma of multilingualism by using the home language as a scaffold to learn Dutch, specifying, however, that Dutch should still remain the language of education and instruction (Crevits, 2017). It should be mentioned that the minister's more positive stance was not translated into a policy statement.

To conclude, Flemish education policy towards multilingualism is restricted to some statements on home languages and a broad interpretation of multilingualism. Definite policy measures have not been enacted (Pulinx *et al.*, 2017). Multilingualism, and specifically multilingual proficiency in immigrant languages, does not fit the monolingual standard ideology (Vogl, 2012), and is erased from policy texts (Gal & Irvine, 1995).

As schools can organize their own language policy within the broader policy framework of their educational group, I will now turn to a description of one school.

Declared language policy at school level

I will zoom in on one Brussels school which developed a 'severe' stance towards the use of Dutch. This stance is translated in the school's regulations: 'Our school is a Dutch-medium school. Your choice for Dutch-medium education implies that you will encourage your children to learn Dutch, also outside of school'. The statement, taken from the part on 'positive engagement towards the language of instruction' of the school's policy booklet, addresses parents. When a parent enrolls his/her child at the school, both parents and child have to sign a language agreement to demonstrate their understanding of specific language rules. A correct understanding of Dutch being necessary to succeed in all courses is emphasized. Especially for pupils from mixed-language families or families with another home language, school regulations indicate that speaking Dutch at school is often not enough. Therefore, a commitment to read Dutch books or magazines, to watch Dutch television and, eventually, to practice Dutch in the youth movement, sports or leisure clubs is recommended. Interaction at school between parents, teachers and school heads should be carried out in Dutch. It is strongly recommended that one of the parents should master Dutch in a sufficient way.

According to school policy, pupils are expected to speak Dutch at all times: in the classroom, in the hallways, on the playground and during excursions. If they repeatedly fail to speak Dutch, they will be given a language assignment that they have to present to school management. After several linguistic assignments, penalties are imposed. In the implicit language policy of the school, known by all teachers and pupils but not written down in the school's policy booklet, penalties equal language tickets: teachers should in principle write a language ticket when they hear another language (cf. below).

The school language rules follow the governmental policy texts with an emphasis on Dutch proficiency as the primary criterion for success and inclusion. A clear focus on Dutch proficiency contradicts, however, other policy aspects, such as the acknowledgement of a multilingual and multicultural society and the explicit mentioning of tolerance and respect for each other's individuality: 'We want to prepare pupils for harmonious coexistence in a multilingual and multicultural society. In an effort to grow together via communication, we are *"tolerant and respectful towards each person's individuality"*' (my emphasis).

By taking into account 'each person's individuality', this policy aspect is related to UNESCO's definition of inclusion: '[a] process of strengthening the capacity of the education system to reach out to all learners' (UNESCO, 2017: 7). Moreover, the school's curriculum displays a recognition of the bilingual reality of the city, as well as efforts to include students. In the first grade, French speakers have an extra hour of Dutch, Dutch speakers have an extra hour of French. In the second grade, classes are split into two groups during two hours of Dutch class, aimed at helping students to improve in Dutch. Note that only French is considered and that the main focus remains Dutch proficiency. Moreover, it is not explained how exactly the school intends to implement a tolerant and respectful attitude towards each person's individuality.

Perceived and practiced language policy of teachers at the classroom level

I will analyze how the seven classroom teachers and the head of school consider multilingualism and inclusion, by describing the five themes that emerged from the interview analysis: (1) knowledge of governmental and school language policy; (2) reaction to other languages; (3) perception of pupils' language use; (4) attention to multilingualism; and (5) openness to multilingual education. To contextualize teachers' attitudes and practices, it should be noted that all teachers in this school had not been trained to teach in multilingual schools.

Knowledge of governmental and school language policy

Fabian, the teacher of technology, is the only teacher who knows the governmental policy on language and multilingualism. His comments are related to the media debate on the changing policy in GO!-schools (see

Subsection on 'Declared educational language policy at governmental level', above) which took place in the week before his interview. He specifically did not approve of the new GO!-guideline and articulated that the inclusion of multilingualism would be 'a heavy door in their face'. He had been a teacher in a GO!-school for more than 20 years and, during that time, teachers were 'fighting against it':

> we couldn't win, also, because racism and so on, is also at the basis of it, if you do not tolerate someone speaking Arabic, you get finger-pointed, you are a racist (…) and now they are opening an umbrella and they say, it is all possible, then we don't have to sanction any more, so it is a little bit, I think, opening the withdrawing umbrella. (Interview, Fabian, 5 December 2017)

In this quote, Fabian displays a monolingual attitude and a less nuanced vision (cf. 'they say, it is *all* possible').

When asked about their opinions on the school language policy, teachers were aware of the language ticketing policy, but they did not know all the details and they did not like the ticketing sanctions. Teachers gave various reasons for not issuing tickets, for example, stating that they do not like to punish pupils and that they prefer using other strategies to prevent pupils speaking other languages. In the next section, I will describe how teachers reacted when they heard other languages.

Reaction to other languages

According to the declared language policy of the school, teachers have to sanction pupils when they speak other languages. Interview data revealed that teachers are expected to give language tickets. Although it does not mean that teachers never issue a language ticket, it is nevertheless worth mentioning that I never witnessed a teacher issuing or even mentioning a language ticket during the fieldwork period. In the interviews, teachers indicated that they rarely issue language tickets during the year. However, teachers did react to pupils' speaking other languages: in interviews, teachers mentioned drawing pupils' attention to the rule of not speaking other languages, encouraging them in a friendly or jocular way to speak Dutch or switch to Dutch (Janne, Fabian, Emily, Christine, Els, Audrey). Only if pupils repeatedly failed to speak Dutch or if they did not accept the teacher's request did teachers mention that they sanctioned pupils, by writing a note in the school diary (Janne, Mark) or by giving them a Dutch task (Fabian).

Although pupils were aware of the restricted language policy and rarely used other languages when teachers could hear them, the following extracts demonstrate teachers' rare reactions to other languages in classroom practice.

As mentioned previously, teachers rarely impose language policy; however, in the first extract from a mathematics class, the teacher, Janne, imposes the language policy by asking a pupil to sit on his chair in the right way.

Example 1 Teacher imposing language policy
Mylas is the name of a pupil

		Original	English translation
1	Mylas	Ik zat **gecoinceerd**	I got **stuck**
2	Teacher Janne	'**gecoinceerd**', ik zat ingesloten.	**stuck**, I got stuck
3		Gebruik wat meer Nederlandse	Use more Dutch words
4		woorden	

Fieldwork note, 23 March 2017, 3rd hour, mathematics, Janne.

Mylas is using a hybrid word: he uses a French lexical item 'coincé' with Dutch conjugation rules ('ge' and -d, Line 1). The teacher repeats the hybrid word 'gecoinceerd' and gives the Dutch equivalent 'ingesloten' (Line 2). She then asks him to use more Dutch words (Lines 3–4). In doing so, she evidences that French is not authorized in the classroom. This is comparable to the non-legitimateness of Spanish in an induction classroom in France, as mentioned by Bonacina-Pugh (2020). Els (teacher of Dutch 2) also imposes Dutch: during a small group activity, she walks into the classroom while pupils are working in groups. She appears to have heard French and she reacts by saying out loud, 'Dutch if possible, and also when it's not' (audio recording, 4 May 2017).

During other interactional moments, teachers are sensitive to other languages and accept them in the classroom. This was especially the case during English class with Audrey. In the following extract, she introduced the grammatical construction of the degrees of comparison.

Example 2 Teacher associating different languages
Bold: French
Italics: English

1	TA	Dus als je vergelijkt, dan zit je bij de	So if you compare, than you are at the
2		*comparative*	*comparative*
3	Pupil	Ah **comparatif**	Ah **comparative**
4	TA	int Frans **comparatif**	In French **comparative**
5	Pupil	**comparatif**	**Comparative**
(…)			
6	TA	Als je de hoogst overtreffende trap	If you have the most outstanding
7		hebt,	position,
8		dan heb je *a superlative*	then you have *a superlative*
9	Pupil	**Superlatif**	**Superlative**
10	TA	**Superlatif**	**Superlative**
11	TA	Als je da ni goe kan onthouden, dan	If you cannot remember it, then you can
12		onthou je da met superman,	remember it with superman, superman is
13		superman is	
14		altijd de sterkte, de knapste, de snelste,	always the strongest, the most handsome,
15		*whatever*, ja, **superlatif**, *superlative*	the quickest, *whatever*, yes, **superlative**, *superlative*

Audio recording, 27 April 2017, 4th hour, English, Audrey.

After one pupil's association of the term in English 'comparative' to the French term 'comparatif' (Line 3), the teacher Audrey accepts this usage and even repeats the French equivalent in her practiced language policy (Line 4). The acceptance of other languages was also observed by Bonacina-Pugh (2020). Audrey explicitly links French and English in the subsequent explanation, to scaffold pupils' learning by associating the lingua franca, French, to the LOI (Line 11–15, cf. also Mary & Young, 2017). In the interview, Audrey comments on the association of different languages:

> Erm, if it is to understand something or if they associate different aspects, then it is not a problem for me, but, if it is really swearing at each other in another language, so that I cannot understand, then it is.
> (…)
> Yes, a lot of words in English have also a French equivalent or something that resembles it, and if they draw links, then I find it quite positive in fact, because they make associations between the different languages and then I don't have a problem with that at all. (Interview, Audrey, 29 September 2017)

Pupils can also draw on other languages for school-related work: Audrey recognizes linguistic diversity as a benefit and as a tool for pupils' learning process, which mirrors UNESCO's (2017) guidelines for equity and inclusion. Her instrumental view of using other languages for pedagogical purposes resonates with the views of one of the teachers in Leung and Creese (2008), who appeared to accept another language if it could help pupils to get 'the job done'. Audrey's tolerance of other languages for pedagogical purposes is shared by the head of school. She indicates in the interview that she accepts the use of other languages for pedagogical purposes: pupils can use other languages in her classroom to help each other. However, it is also her opinion that pupils should 'put the switch on Dutch' when they enter school.

Teachers also ignore other languages because 'you cannot react every time' (Interview, Emily, 22 February 2018). In the third extract from technology class, Nahid is swearing in French (Line 2). The teacher does not comment on her use of French, nor on the insult, but on her behavior (Lines 4–13).

Example 3 Teacher ignores other languages
Bold: French

1	TF	We wachten weer tot het stil wordt	We wait again until it is quiet
2	Nahid	**Ta gueule**, Musafe:h	**Shut up**, Musafe:h
3	Nahid	**Ta g**	Sh

4	TF	Nu heb ik daarstraks xxx kunde u ni	I just have xxx can you imagine, tried to
5		inbeelden proberen aan te tonen da	demonstrate that negative behavior
6		negatief gedrag nooit ni, xxx en dan blijft	never, no xxx and then you keep on doing it.
7		ge nog verder doen. Praten en storen das	talking and disturbing is also negative behavior
8		ook negatief gedrag eh mensen, das een	eh guys, it is a business card
9		visitekaartje da ge aflevert eh. (pauze)	you deliver isn't it (pause).
10		Zoals ek gisteren al heb gezegd, de keuze	As I already said yesterday,
11		da je hebt gemaakt, de studiekeuze voor	the choice you made, the study option
12		volgend jaar, das een goeie keuze die je	for the next year is a good choice you made
13		hebt gemaakt	

Audio recording, 3 May 2017, 3rd and 4th hours, technology, Fabian.

Sometimes teachers also react in a jocular way to other languages. Els and Christine both have standard phrases:

Example 4 Jocular reactions to the use of other languages

Dutch is a beautiful language in a Dutch college, next door is the French college.
 (Interview, Els, 18 September 2017)
This seems to be beautiful Dutch.
 (Interview, Christine, 16 October 2017)

Janne's language use is related to these jocular comments. She uses other languages herself, for fun.

Example 5 Teacher using other languages for fun
Bold: French

		Original	English translation
1	Teacher Janne	zo snel als je kan, da's zo **à l'aise**	As quickly as you can, this is **at ease**

Fieldwork note, 6 March 2017, 7th hour, mathematics, Janne.

Janne asked one of the pupils to distribute some documents as quickly as he could, because now he is doing it '*à l'aise*', 'at ease'. During other moments, she also rhymed with this specific utterance '*à l'aise in den Delhaize*' ('at ease in Delhaize'; Delhaize is a supermarket brand).

Perception of pupils' language use

Teachers' opinions on pupils' language use differ gradually, from a negative deficit-vision (Cummins, 2000) 'can you call it Dutch for some of them? No, isn't it, seriously' (Interview, Els, 18 September 2017) to positive 'there is trouble and affliction when talking about French (…), but for me, it is normal, they do their best to say it in proper Dutch' (Interview, Mark, 24 October 2017).

Teachers are concerned with the (lack of) exposure to and practice of Dutch: using other languages is related to a lack of exposure to Dutch at home, which is the responsibility of parents (according to Janne). Pupils should speak Dutch with one another, as it is assumed that it offers an extra opportunity to practice (in the opinion of Janne and Emily).

The two bilingual teachers (Christine and Audrey) mention their personal bilingual background as a reason for understanding pupils better than other teachers: it causes no problems if pupils mix different languages: 'I am bilingual myself, you know, I did the same before' (Interview, Audrey, 28 September 2017).

Attention to multilingualism

Teachers differ in their opinions on the attention that should be paid to multilingualism and how multilingualism should be included at school. For a first group of teachers (Janne, Fabian and Els), the school policy is good as it stands. For Janne, awareness of pupils speaking other languages at home does not come with an openness to other languages; on the contrary, she is concerned about students' mastery of Dutch.

> I think most of our colleagues keep that in mind, yes, this is simply the reality, so we do understand, but showing responsiveness to multilingualism on the playground, I would have serious problems with it, that they would talk in a mixed way, because I think 'where will you practice your Dutch', so. (Interview, Janne, 12 September 2017)

Els is even afraid that more openness to other languages would lead to more French and to no Dutch any more. For Fabian, a Dutch-medium school equals speaking Dutch, and for the parents as well. His opinion is a literal prolongation of the school policy – 'Your choice for Dutch-medium education implies that you will encourage your children to learn Dutch, also outside of school':

> I think that we understand that they are multilingual and that they are raised in French, but on the other hand, they clearly made the choice to come to a Dutch-medium school, otherwise they should have been on the other side, the French side, so I think that if you choose as a parent to educate your child in a Dutch-medium school, then you should agree on it for hundred percent and support it as well (…) But if we communicate with parents in Dutch, they don't understand us (2.0). Then they expect sometimes, although not always, but some parents expect that we would go along with French. (…) because we are in Brussels, and that is the wrong attitude (…) You choose Dutch, then you should use the Dutch language as well. (Interview, Fabian, 5 December 2017)

Fabian displays no openness to or interest in multilingualism and the languages spoken at home. Moreover, a restricted notion of multilingualism is apparent in his discourse. Firstly, he only mentions French, which is not the multilingual reality of many pupils. Although the interviewer tried to introduce some other home languages during the interview, as demonstrated in the bold parts in the passage below, he only mentioned prestigious languages (see also Subsection on 'Declared educational language policy at governmental level'; Jaspers, 2009):

Interviewer:	Does the school pay enough attention to multilingualism?
Fabian:	Yes, yes, I do think so, here, this school for sure
Interviewer:	How then, how?
Fabian:	I, and even from the pupils themselves, because, I am in the school board, our pupils, even from the third grade, they want to learn more languages
Interviewer:	**Yes to I, but they, no Arabic or Turkish then?**
Fabian:	No, they even ask to follow Spanish (…)
Interviewer:	**But and their own languages, is there enough attention**
Fabian (firmly):	yes
Interviewer:	**The languages that they bring from home**
Fabian:	yes yes
Interviewer:	**And in which way?**
Fabian:	I think that anyway, but then I am talking of the third grade, that there the the, the Dutch language, on the level of teaching Dutch, quite, ample is to follow if they want to go to university or higher education, that they have enough basis, even so for French and English as well and for German as well so I think that that is completely, that it is good, and if you notice that these pupils request to have Spanish as well, then I think that our language policy is super
	(Interview, Fabian, 5 December 2017)

In line with Fabian, most teachers mainly commented on the pupils' use of French. Although many pupils in the selected classroom also speak other languages at home, French is Brussels' lingua franca (Janssens, 2013), shared by almost all pupils. Research on pupils' language use in a Brussels Dutch-medium primary classroom demonstrated that when pupils spoke another language, they almost exclusively used French (Rosiers *et al.*, 2018).

A first group of teachers are aware of the pupils' multilingualism, but feel that multilingualism should not be promoted; on the contrary, they feel that pupils should be supported by giving them more opportunities to speak Dutch.

Teachers' fear of pupils lagging behind in Dutch does not mean that they are not interested in the pupils' multilingual background. During her first years as a teacher, Els asked the pupils to prepare a specific dish from their country, and nowadays she is still interested in pupils' roots. Note, however, that these interests in pupils' multilingualism occur rarely and mostly at the margins of the central learning activities. A similar trend on allowing other languages during less important moments was observed by Jaspers (2015) and Rosiers *et al.* (2018).

A second group of teachers (Mark and Emily) are in favor of a more open policy on multilingualism. Both teachers agree on the importance of paying more attention to pupils' multilingualism. Emily already tries to do so and mentions other languages as a scaffold for learning Dutch, which is reminiscent of the GO!-policy (see Subsection on 'Declared educational language policy at governmental level'):

> these pupils already have difficulties with Dutch, because it is not their mother tongue, and they speak actually, if you think of it, almost never Dutch isn't it, outside of school, not at least with their parents, erm, between themselves, maybe, but, yes, I think that it is true to pay more attention to it, and it can also help to their, to involve their, language, French, erm, yes. (Interview, Emily, 22 February 2018)

However, later on in the interview, her opinion changes: she agrees with the school's focus on Dutch, as pupils already engage enough with their own language outside of school. Ambiguity (Creese, 2010, see introduction) and 'multiplicity and layering' (Pachler *et al.*, 2008: 440, see introduction) are clearly observable in the fluctuating discourse of this teacher.

A third group of teachers – the bilingual teachers, who are also the teachers of foreign languages (French and English) and the head of school – differ from the above groups. Although Christine mentions taking care of other languages by giving pupils as much Dutch as possible, she is also in favor of more languages at school, as is Audrey. Both teachers would prefer more attention to the languages they teach at school: Audrey would like a content course in a language other than Dutch and Christine promotes French and English playtime. According to the head of school, there is a need for investment in multilingualism. However, she feels that if they provide too much support for multilingual pupils, this can change the school into a specialized multilingual school, to the detriment of Dutch speaking pupils from Brussels' periphery, which is not what she wants either.

Openness to multilingual education

When teachers were asked to comment on multilingual education, they all had one specific type of multilingual education in mind, viz. content and language integrated learning (CLIL). All teachers were in favor of CLIL, except the teachers of Dutch. In the opinion of the latter, CLIL would make education more complex. For Els, it is important that pupils first learn the language of the school in a proper way, because they are enrolled in a Dutch-medium school. The teacher of technology is not against CLIL but calls for caution as well: CLIL may be beneficial for pupils who are good at languages, whereas it may hinder other pupils' success.

Teachers' attitudes to the use of pupils' home languages during group work was also discussed. Again, teachers of Dutch were not in favor.

According to Els, this would be too complex, and Emily mentioned a widespread fear of not being able to control or help pupils when not speaking their language(s) (Strobbe, 2016; Van den Branden & Verhelst, 2009). The foreign language teachers displayed a more positive attitude, although Audrey is also worried:

> I can agree, but I would find it difficult as a teacher to give feedback or guidance to help them (…) because I don't understand (…) what they do at home to succeed in a task, I don't care, but if I am there, I want to help as well. (Interview, Audrey, 28 September 2017)

Christine thinks that teachers should move to an evolution in which they accept other languages during group work, but mentions that mixing can be chaotic, and everyone should still understand each other. The head of school is in favor of multilingual education, but feels it should be implemented with adaptations for the Brussels education system, by merging Dutch- and French-medium education. She is more reticent towards other languages during group work, as she believes it may lead to an increased use of French instead of the use of other home languages.

These secondary school teachers share the same fears of losing control as the Flemish pre-primary and primary teachers cited in the study of Sierens and Ramaut (2018) on the implementation of a multilingual pedagogy. The authors point to a language ideological and a pedagogical challenge for teachers, the former being the challenge of a monolingual vision, the latter a challenge of teacher control for efficient classroom and learning management.

It is striking that the teachers of non-language courses interpret the use of other languages for group work as less problematic. Janne, the teacher of mathematics, expressed wanting to try it out. Mark, the teacher of natural sciences, has already implemented this type of multilingual education in practice: pupils were asked to write a report in Dutch after watching online videos; the latter was allowed in any language. He is more pragmatic than the other teachers: if there was a comprehension problem, he would ask for Dutch information or a translation from another pupil. Fabian, the teacher of technology, is also in favor of using home languages during group work. The fear of lack of control, mentioned by the Dutch teacher, is countered by his statement:

> You perceive it from pupils' behavior, if they are working, or playing, or doing silly, therefore you don't have to understand the language, no, yes. Arabic is a language that today is watched seriously, isn't it (…), so I do think that there are, major problems, if it would be French or English, languages we do understand a little bit, or German, then would, I think, multiple colleagues would have less problems, compared to really a language we do not understand at all, such as Greek or, I don't know what. (Interview, Fabian, 5 December 2017)

Conclusion: Ambivalences Within and Between Levels

In this chapter, teachers' responsiveness to multilingualism and the inclusion of other languages in a linguistically diverse Brussels school with a monolingual policy was analyzed. Based on linguistic-ethnographic fieldwork, language policy was described at governmental and school policy level and at the level of teachers' opinions and practices in one classroom. In this section, ambivalences on different policy levels will be described and connected to each other.

The analysis of declared language policy (Shohamy, 2006) at **Flemish governmental level** revealed ambivalences in the engagement with multilingualism and the inclusion of other languages. Policymakers emphasize the knowledge of Dutch as the prime criterion to guarantee equal opportunities for all pupils. They acknowledge the multilingual reality, nonetheless without issuing coherent policy guidelines for schools to engage with multilingualism (see also Sierens & Ramaut, 2018; Leung & Creese, 2008, for similar findings in the UK). Moreover, policymakers only value a specific kind of *elite* multilingualism (Jaspers, 2009). The Minister of Education's emphasis on the knowledge of Dutch as the prime and unique criterion for inclusion in policy texts contradicts her opinions in media debates, in which she acknowledges the use of home languages as a scaffold to learn Dutch.

At first sight, the governmental policy is translated rigidly in the selected **school**'s regulations: a Dutch-only policy is emphasized and inclusion in the school means learning and speaking Dutch. The explicit language policy, written down in the school regulations, mentions that pupils should be punished when they speak other languages. The implicit, unwritten policy prescribes teachers to issue a language ticket when they hear other languages. However, in practice, I never saw one during the fieldwork period and teachers mentioned issuing them rarely. Moreover, the strict stance contradicts other aspects of school regulations: the school also strives to include every pupil and wants to prepare pupils to live together respectfully in a multilingual city. How exactly the school wants to implement an attitude towards tolerance and respect is not mentioned in the regulations. The vagueness of the school regulations is reminiscent of the declared policy at governmental level.

The ambivalences between declared policy at governmental and school level are translated into **teachers'** practiced and perceived language policy. Teachers respond to both top-down and bottom-up discourses (Leung & Creese, 2008). In their perceived language policy, teachers agree on the top-down governmental language policy: they applaud the strict focus on Dutch as the only legitimate language and want to make sure that pupils develop competences in the LOI. Teachers adhere to some of the widespread myths about education and multilingualism: they are afraid of losing control when pupils speak other languages; the presence of prestigious languages would be tolerated; and they believe that time spent in other languages is to the detriment of Dutch (see also Rosiers, 2016; Sierens & Ramaut, 2018; Strobbe, 2016; Van den Branden & Verhelst, 2009). In their practiced language policies, teachers endorse this stance by encouraging pupils to use Dutch exclusively (compare with Bonacina-Pugh, 2020). Teachers seem to pursue an ideology of linguistic homogeneity, perpetuating the monolingual habitus of top-down policy-makers' discourses at the governmental level (Gogolin, 1997; Hélot, 2010).

Nonetheless, practiced and perceived language policy data reveal teachers' responsiveness to bottom-up discourses as well. In interviews, teachers show openness to multilingual education and especially to the use of other languages during group work. In classroom practice, teachers legitimize other languages (Bonacina-Pugh, 2020) and accept the instrumental use of French for learning (Leung & Creese, 2008). Ambivalences that occur in perceived and practiced policies at a teacher level respond to ambiguities of declared policy at governmental and school level, resulting in ambivalences within as well as between different policy levels (see Figure 5.1). Teachers are often either depicted as '"soldiers" of the system' (Shohamy, 2006: 78) or as agents of change, without attending to the ambivalences that occur in their practices and discourses. By means of linguistic-ethnographic research, this study demonstrated that teachers may not transform the monolingual habitus entirely, but they do adapt the governmental and school language policy to their own interpretation (e.g. by not issuing language tickets, but by appealing to different solutions to engage with other languages), showing responsiveness to multilingualism and the inclusion of other languages (cf. Creese & Leung, 2003; Hornberger & Johnson, 2011; Puskás & Björk-Willén, 2017; Ricento & Hornberger, 1996).

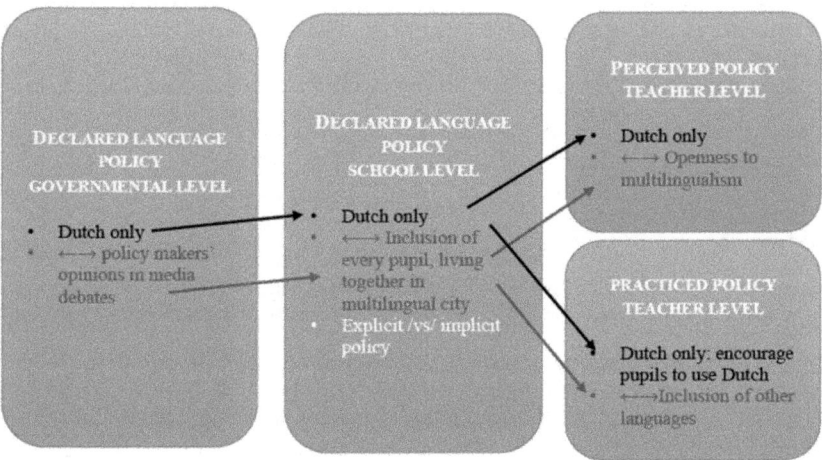

Figure 5.1 Ambivalences within and between different policy levels

When relating the three policy levels to each other, the same ambivalences – in favor of Dutch-only versus in favor of inclusion of multilingualism – occur within and between levels. Nevertheless, a prevailing monolingual ideology dominates at each level. Although openings towards an educational policy of including multilingualism are present at all policy levels, they are vague and even erased. To date, policymakers only acknowledge the use of other languages in education during media debates, whereas they only vaguely touch upon it in their policy documents. It would have a bigger impact on school-level policy and perceived and practiced policy if statements in the media were the topic of specific and well-considered policy texts. If we want to evolve towards a policy that not only mentions inclusion and multilingualism, but also exploits the use of other languages in the most beneficial way, openings at the three levels should be integrated. By means of a policy-practice dialogue and bottom-up initiatives, teachers' views and concerns should be acknowledged, deconstructed and included (Leung & Creese, 2008; Mary & Young, 2017; Young, 2014). Only when top-down and bottom-up discourses tune to each other to include multilingualism, can equal chances for learning be guaranteed for all pupils, whatever linguistic background they have.

Notes

(1) Project funded by the FNRS (PDR T.0091.16, 2016–2020) and the ULB/Brussels-Wallonia Federation (Action de recherche concertée, 2016–2019).
(2) In his concept text on language policy, Smet comments on his vision and writes, 'language organizes our thoughts and our environment. In an environment that is increasingly multilingual, multilingualism is an asset' (Smet, 2011: 3, my translation). Further in the document, he comments on language policy documents and he mentions 'the primacy of standard Dutch as the prioritizing and linking language, the acknowledgement and valuing of the home language if it is not Dutch, the ambition to render each child trilingual, the implementation of an inclusive language policy' (Smet, 2011: 37).
(3) Three educational groups organize official education in Flanders: (1) GO!, i.e. schools owned by the community; (2) subsidized public schools; and (3) and subsidized free, mainly Catholic schools. These three groups reside under the community responsibility for language matters.

References

Ball, S. (1997) Policy sociology and critical social research: A personal review of recent education policy and policy research. *British Educational Research Journal* 23 (3), 257–274.
Blommaert, J. (2011) The long language-ideological debate in Belgium. *Journal of Multicultural Discourses* 6 (3), 241–256.
Blommaert, J. and Rampton, B. (2011) Language and superdiversity. *Diversities* 13 (2), 1–21.
Bonacina-Pugh, F. (2012) Researching 'practiced language policies': Insights from conversation analysis. *Language Policy* 11, 213–234.

Bonacina-Pugh, F. (2020) Legitimizing multilingual practices in the classroom: The role of the 'practiced language policy'. *International Journal of Bilingual Education and Bilingualism* 23 (4), 434–448. doi:10.1080/13670050.2017.1372359

Copland, F. and Creese, A. (2015) *Linguistic Ethnography*. London: Sage.

Corbin, J. and Strauss, A. (1990) Grounded theory research: Procedures, canons and evaluative criteria. *Qualitative Sociology* 13 (1), 3–21.

Creese, A. (2010) Two-teacher classrooms, personalized learning and the inclusion paradigm in the United Kingdom. What's in it for learners of EAL? In K. Menken and O. García (eds) *Negotiating Language Policies in Schools* (pp. 32–51). London and New York: Routledge.

Creese, A. and Leung, C. (2003) Teachers' discursive constructions of ethno-linguistic difference: Professional issues in working with inclusive policy. *Prospect* 18 (2), 3–19.

Crevits, H. (2014) *Beleidsnota 2014–2019*. Brussels: Onderwijs.

Crevits, H. (2017) Leerkrachten mogen maar één taal spreken: Het Nederlands. *De Standaard*, 29 November.

Cummins, J. (2000) *Language, Power and Pedagogy: Bilingual Children in the Crossfire*. Clevedon: Multilingual Matters.

De Caluwe, J. (2012) Dutch in Belgium: Facing multilingualism in a context of regional monolingualism and standard language ideology. In M. Hüning, U. Vogl and O. Moliner (eds) *Standard Languages and Multilingualism in European History* (pp. 259–282). Amsterdam: John Benjamins.

Delarue, S. and De Caluwe, J. (2015) Eliminating social inequality by reinforcing standard language ideology? Language policy for Dutch in Flemish schools. *Current Issues in Language Planning* 16 (1–2), 8–25.

Flanders National Administration Agency (2019) *Local Acculturation and Integration Monitor* [*Lokale inburgerings- en integratiemonitor*]. See https://integratiebeleid.vlaanderen.be/lokale-inburgerings-en-integratiemonitor-editie-2019-0.

Flemish Ministry of Education and Training (2016) *Multilingualism as a Reality in Schools*. See https://onderwijs.vlaanderen.be/nl/meertaligheid-als-realiteit-op-school-mars.

Gal, S. and Irvine, J. (1995) The boundaries of languages and disciplines: How ideologies construct difference. *Social Research* 62 (4), 967–1002.

Gogolin, I. (1997) The 'monolingual habitus' as the common feature in teaching in the language of majority in different countries. *Per Linguam* 13 (2), 38–49.

Hélot, C. (2010) 'Tu sais bien parler Maîtresse!' Negotiating languages other than French in the primary classroom in France. In K. Menken and O. García (eds) *Negotiating Language Education Policies: Educators as Policymakers* (pp. 52–71). New York: Lawrence Erlbaum/Routledge.

Hornberger, N. and Johnson, D. (2011) The ethnography of language policy. In T. McCarty (ed.) *Ethnography and Language Policy* (pp. 273–289). New York: Routledge.

Janssens, R. (2013) *Brio-taalbarometer 3: diversiteit als norm*. Brussels: Brio. See https://www.briobrussel.be/node/14488.

Jaspers, J. (2009) *De klank van de stad*. Leuven: Acco.

Jaspers, J. (2015) Modelling linguistic diversity: The excluding impact of inclusive multilingualism. *Language Policy* 14 (2), 109–129.

Jaspers, J. (2018) Language education policy and sociolinguistics: Toward a new critical engagement. In M. Pérez-Milans and J. Tollefson (eds) *Oxford Handbook of Language Policy and Planning*. Oxford: Oxford University Press.

Jaspers, J. (2019) The deliberative teacher: Wavering between linguistic uniformity and diversity. In J. Jaspers and L. Madsen (eds) *Critical Perspectives on Linguistic Fixity and Fluidity: Languagised Lives* (pp. 217–240). London and New York: Routledge.

Johnson, D. (2009) Ethnography of language policy. *Language Policy* 8, 139–159.

Katholiek onderwijs (2017) Thuistaal kan als uitgangspunt om Nederlands te leren. *Knack*, 22 December.

Leung, C. and Creese, A. (2008) Professional issues in working with ethnolinguistic difference: Inclusive policy in practice. In D. Murray (ed.) *Planning Change, Changing Plans: Innovations in Second Language Teaching* (pp. 155–173). Ann Arbor, MI: University of Michigan Press.

Mary, L. and Young, A. (2017) Engaging with emergent bilinguals and their families in the pre-primary classroom to foster well-being, learning and inclusion. *Language & Intercultural Communication* 17 (4), 455–473.

McCarty, T. (2011) *Ethnography and Language Policy*. London: Routledge.

Pachler, N., Makoe, P., Burns, M. and Blommaert, J. (2008) The things (we think) we (ought to) do. *Teaching and Teacher Education* 24, 437–450.

Pulinx, R., Van Avermaet, P. and Agirdag, O. (2017) Silencing linguistic diversity: The extent, the determinants and consequences of the monolingual beliefs of Flemish teachers. *International Journal of Bilingual Education and Bilingualism* 20 (5), 542–556.

Puskás, T. and Björk-Willén, P. (2017) Dilemmatic aspects of language policies in a trilingual preschool group. *Multilingua* 36 (4), 425–449.

Rampton, B., Maybin, J. and Roberts, C. (2015) Theory and method in linguistic ethnography. In J. Snell, S. Shaw and F. Copland (eds) *Linguistic Ethnography: Interdisciplinary Explorations* (pp. 14–50). Basingstoke: Palgrave Macmillan.

Ricento, T. and Hornberger, N. (1996) Unpeeling the onion: Language planning and policy and the ELT professional. *TESOL Quarterly* 30 (3), 401–428.

Ritchie, J. (2003) The applications of qualitative methods to social research. In J. Ritchie and J. Lewis (eds) *Qualitative Research Practice: A Guide for Social Science Students and Researchers* (pp. 24–46). London: Sage.

Rosiers, K. (2016) Nederlands om te rekenen, Turks om te roddelen? De mythe ontkracht. Een interactie-analyse naar translanguaging in een Gentse superdiverse klas. *Tijdschrift voor Nederlandse Taal- en Letterkunde* 3, 155–179.

Rosiers, K., Van Lancker, I. and Delarue, S. (2018) Beyond the traditional scope of translanguaging. *Language & Communication* 61, 15–28.

Ryan, G.W. and Bernard, H.R. (2000) Data management and analysis methods. In N.K. Denzin and Y.S. Lincoln (eds) *Handbook of Qualitative Research* (2nd edn) (pp. 769–802). London: Sage.

Shohamy, E. (2006) *Language Policy: Hidden Agendas and New Approaches*. London: Routledge.

Sierens, S. and Ramaut, G. (2018) Breaking out of L2-exclusive pedagogies: Teachers valorising immigrant pupils' plurilingual repertoire in urban Dutch-medium classrooms. In P. Van Avermaet, S. Slembrouck, K. Van Gorp, S. Sierens and K. Maryns (eds) *The Multilingual Edge of Education* (pp. 285–311). London: Palgrave.

Smet, P. (2011) *Samen taalgrenzen verleggen: Conceptnota*. See http://www.ond.vlaanderen.be/nieuws/2011/doc/talennota_2011.pdf.

Spolsky, B. (2004) *Language Policy*. Cambridge: Cambridge University Press.

Strobbe, L. (2016) Taalbeleid of talenbeleid? De plaats van meertaligheid op school. In L. Van Praag, S. Sierens, O. Agirdag and L. Peter (eds) *Haal meer uit meertaligheid: Omgaan met talige diversiteit in het basisonderwijs* (pp. 117–130). Leuven/Den Haag: Acco.

UNESCO (2017) *A Guide for Ensuring Inclusion and Equity in Education*. Paris: United Nations Educational, Scientific and Cultural Organization. See http://unesdoc.unesco.org/images/0024/002482/248254e.pdf.

Van den Branden, K. and Verhelst, M. (2009) Naar een volwaardig talenbeleid: Omgaan met meertaligheid in het Vlaams onderwijs. In J. Jaspers (ed.) *De klank van de stad* (pp. 105–137). Leuven: Acco.

Vogl, U. (2012) Multilingualism in a standard language culture. In M. Hüning, U. Vogl and O. Moliner (eds) *Standard Languages and Multilingualism in European History* (pp. 1–42). Amsterdam: John Benjamins.
Young, A. (2014) Unpacking teachers' language ideologies: Attitudes, beliefs, and practiced language policies in schools in Alsace, France. *Language Awareness* 23 (1–2), 157–171.

The Importance of Supporting Students' First Languages: Avoiding Unintended Consequences

Jordan Foster

ESL and international languages teacher, Edmonton Public Schools (Canada)

As an English as second language (ESL) teacher, I am fortunate to work in a school authority and province that understands the value of encouraging the use of students' home languages. In Alberta, *The ESL Guide to Implementation* (Alberta Education, 2007), intended for teachers and administrators, explicitly addresses the many benefits of students maintaining and actively using their first language in academic settings.

In my own class, I have seen the benefits of encouraging and supporting the use of students' first language in academic tasks. When encouraged to take notes, conference with classmates, and plan their writing in their first language, students often produced longer texts in English, took more risks with unfamiliar structures, and expressed more complex thoughts and ideas. When students were encouraged to share their languages, cultures, and experiences, I noticed them to be more open and curious about learning and taking risks with expressing themselves in English.

Many language educators incorporate strategies that support literacy development in both the language of instruction and students' first language while also finding ways to celebrate students' linguistic and cultural heritage. These pedagogical practices foster overall bilingualism, from which students benefit cognitively, academically, socially, and emotionally (University of Calgary, 2017).

However, for some, the misconception persists that first language use, either at school or home, is a hindrance to students' English language development. Aside from the lost language learning opportunities this presents, the potentially negative impacts on students' identities need to be considered. In the short term, students may sense that their language and culture are not valued or welcome at school or in the community. Over time, loss of opportunities to use and develop the first language may contribute to language attrition, or loss, and feelings of disconnection from culture and community.

I strongly believe that as educators we must be mindful of the positive personal and academic benefits of students being able to access their full linguistic repertoires to support their learning, as well as the potentially negative consequences of not doing so. It is important that we advocate for use of first language and promote multilingualism in our schools and communities.

References

Alberta Education (2007) *English as a Second Language (ESL): Guide to Implementation – Kindergarten to Grade 9*. Edmonton: Alberta Education Learning and Teaching Resources Branch, accessed 10 April 2021. https://education.alberta.ca/media/563809/esl-guide-to-implementation-k-9.pdf

University of Calgary, Language Research Centre (2017) Literature review on the impact of second language learning. Edmonton, AB: Canadian Association of Second Language Teachers and Second Languages and Intercultural Council of the Alberta Teachers' Association, accessed 10 April 2021. https://www.caslt.org/files/pd/resources/research/Lit-review-Impact-L2-Learning.pdf

6 A Longitudinal Study of Emergent Bilinguals among Chinese Pupils at a Japanese Public School: A Focus on Language Policies and Inclusion

Junko Majima and Chiho Sakurai

Introduction

Demographic change in Japan

In the era of globalization, the number of 'immigrants' with various purposes and reasons for emigrating to Japan has increased over the past several decades. The number of registered foreigners in Japan was 2,731,093 in 2018, the highest in recorded history according to the Ministry of Justice (2019). The number constitutes 1.88% of the total population and continues to grow. Even though the number of foreigners in Japan decreased at the time of the financial crisis of 2007–2008, often called the 'Lehman shock', and following the Great East Japan Earthquake and subsequent nuclear power plant disaster in 2011, overall the number of foreigners has more than doubled over the 25 years between 1991 and 2016.

Who are these people from abroad, then? They are categorized as 'newcomers' and although from a practical standpoint they are 'immigrants', the Japanese government repeatedly states that it 'has no immigration policy' and therefore the word 'immigrants' is not officially used[1] (MIC, 2006). The 'newcomers' are contrasted with the 'old-timers' who came to Japan before and during WWII, mostly from China (5%) and Korea (90%), which were then colonized by Japan (1910–1945). After WWII, 1.4 million Koreans returned to their liberated homeland, while

600,000 remained in Japan for various reasons (Tomozawa & Majima, 2015: 496).

The so-called 'newcomers' consist of several groups of people:

- returnees from China who were orphaned at the end of WWII and began returning to Japan after the normalization of Sino-Japan diplomatic relations in 1972 (20,000 people and their families);
- refugees from countries in Indochina – Vietnam, Laos and Cambodia – since 1975 (113,000 people accepted up to now);
- descendants of Japanese emigrants to South American countries, such as Brazil, Peru, Bolivia, etc., after the Immigration Control and Refugee Recognition Act was changed in 1990 to allow 'Long-Term Residents' and welcomed Japanese-related people as workers to make up for the labor shortage;
- non-Japanese spouses, especially Japanese farmers' wives who came mostly from China, Korea and the Philippines; and
- nurses and caretakers from the Philippines and Indonesia who emigrated through the Economic Partnership Agreement (EPA) in the late 2000s.

In addition, the Japanese government initiated a so-called 'technical intern' system in 1993 with the dual purpose of training young foreigners to become skilled workers and helping to solve the labor shortage in Japanese industries. Up to now, these technical interns have come mostly from China and the Association of Southeast Asian Nations, i.e. so-called ASEAN countries. The number of such technical interns exceeded 270,000 in 2017, but some people, including a UN migrant rights expert, have criticized the system for its working conditions and violation of human rights.[2] New legislation was passed in December 2018 to reform the system and the government plans to accept more workers, but it will take some time to assess the consequences.

Linguistic diversity and monolingual ideologies in Japan

Although the education of 'newcomer' children brought to Japan or born in Japan has been one of the most urgent issues in the field of education for more than two decades, it has not received much nationwide attention until fairly recently. This is mostly attributable to the fact that culturally and linguistically diverse (CLD) children (Cummins & Nakajima, 2011) are relatively small in number (only 0.6% of the school children in Japan as of 2016) and are geographically scattered; thus they are almost invisible to the general public except in some foreigner-dense areas. Japanese bilingual education is heavily informed by prevailing assimilationist and monolingual ideologies and CLD pupils are commonly put into the mainstream classroom of only Japanese pupils.

Although Japan and the Japanese language are actually diverse and complex (Tomozawa & Yoshimura, 2010), Japan has been recognized as a monoglossic society in which the Japanese language is viewed as an 'assimilation' tool to be applied to non-Japanese speaking people. The Japanese school system basically operates on a 'submersion' model (Baker, 2006), in which pupils are faced with the dual task of acquiring a new language and accessing the curriculum through a developing language.

There was no official language education policy issued by the Ministry of Education, Culture, Sports, Science and Technology (MEXT) in Japan concerning teaching Japanese as a second language (JSL) until fairly recently, nor has there been an official discussion of policies concerning children's mother tongue or heritage language, or concerning bilingual education for minority children/people (Majima, 2009).

Immigrant children, however, have been regarded and treated at schools as a 'problem' due to their lack of Japanese knowledge and low achievement rather than as 'proficient native speakers of Chinese (L1)' or 'emergent bilinguals' (García & Kleifgen, 2018). Facing difficulties in keeping up in classes alongside their Japanese peers, many children are unable to develop their mother tongue while learning Japanese.

Official Policies of Japanese Language Education for CLD Pupils

Below we detail the policies implemented primarily by MEXT throughout the past three decades.

Assimilationist ideology concerning CLD environments: 'Benign neglect'

It may not be easy for readers to imagine that even a developed country like Japan, although often characterized as insular, had never had a chance to seriously consider the consequences of an influx of foreign people. The small number of foreigners in Japan's public schools for most of its modern history has made it seem unnecessary to take into serious consideration foreign children's education. Teachers have not been prepared or trained to cope with pupils who do not speak Japanese. School principals and local boards of education are generally reluctant to address issues that are 'invisible' until they are forced to face such pupils in their schools or school districts, at which time administrators' first and only concern is teaching the Japanese language. Children of immigrants usually speak their mother tongue or home language, but their proficiency in this language has largely been neglected. Apart from government policies, there has been research in the field of teaching JSL to young learners conducted in the last couple of decades, but the focus is mostly on the development and acquisition of the Japanese language (Hifumi, 1996; Nishikawa *et al.*, 2015).

Although efforts to support the mother tongue of minority children have not been attacked directly, the ideology that 'when you are in Japan, all you need is the Japanese language' is commonly accepted and consequently children's home languages are neglected. In addition, MEXT maintains a position assuming responsibility for the education of 'Japanese nationals' only, whereas foreign children can be granted public education if they ask for it.

It was only in 1991 that MEXT started the official 'Survey on foreign pupils who need Japanese language instruction at public schools in Japan'. The first nationwide survey showed that 5463 foreign pupils needed Japanese language instruction. The most recent survey from 2016 shows that in addition to the 34,335 foreign pupils, 9612 Japanese nationals also need Japanese language education. This number – 43,947 pupils, the highest on record – is 6.3 times that of the first year the survey was conducted.

The number of foreign pupils accounts for only 0.6% of all school-age children in Japan, and the percentage of those who need language instruction is only about 0.3%. MEXT has long been seemingly reluctant to forthrightly address the issue of education of foreign pupils, partially because the number was deemed negligible but also because the Fundamental Law of Education concerns only Japanese nationals. The law does not mention foreign nationals in Japan, thus allowing the ministry and the general public to continue neglecting this issue, which Kurita (2004) calls 'benign neglect'. The situation can be compared to what Cummins (2014: 4) describes in the Canadian context: 'Mid-1980s–mid-2000s: This period was characterized by benign neglect of students' languages. Maintenance of home languages was seen as an issue for the parents rather than the school, and implicit "English-only zone" policies continued to operate in schools'.

A brief history of the evolution of educational policies and support for CLD pupils in Japan

In the first half of the 1990s, the foreign pupils sitting in Japanese classrooms were instructed and urged to learn the Japanese language and school culture, which Ohta (2000) calls 'education in the framework of national education'. As such, the pupils were culturally deprived of their heritage language and culture and expected to assimilate to the mainstream Japanese school system (Sakurai, 2018). During the second half of the 1990s, CLD pupils faced tremendous difficulties and challenges in understanding subject curricula even after acquiring Japanese proficiency at the survival level. The challenge was to help foreign pupils to develop their cognitive ability and understanding and do well in class.

Teachers and researchers have since developed new ways of teaching, and the focus has shifted from 'teaching language only' to 'teaching content', i.e. school subjects such as math, science, etc., using the Japanese language, influenced by the content-based approach. In the 2000s, MEXT supported the project to publish the 'JSL Curriculum' for elementary and junior high school pupils, integrating the various subject and language curricula.

MEXT has been offering annual seminars for JSL teachers, school principals and local education board members on issues related to JSL methodologies and pedagogies. It has also financially supported 'projects for special education for returnees and foreign pupils', and compiled the *Guidebook for Attendance at Japanese Public Schools* (2005, revised 2015). The guidebook was published in the seven most commonly spoken languages: English, Korean, Vietnamese, Filipino, Chinese, Portuguese and Spanish.

MEXT also compiled the *Manual for Conducting Seminars for Foreign Pupils' Education* (2014a). The year 2014 was important, as MEXT developed and published the first official assessment tool, the *Dialogic Language Assessment for JSL pupils (DLA)* (MEXT, 2014b). The Dialogic Language Assessment (DLA) was modified over the years (Sakurai, 2018) and the former version of the DLA is the assessment tool used in our research between 2012 and 2016, as we explain later. Another reason why 2014 is monumental is that Japanese language education for non-native pupils became legally recognized as part of Japan's formal education policy, where it is treated as a 'special curriculum'. This marks the first time in history that MEXT made JSL education for CLD pupils official and legitimate education policy.

Supporting the Home Language of CLD Children

The next challenge concerns the home language of CLD pupils.[3] Most of society are generally not concerned about CLD pupils or their education; the majority default to a position of benign neglect at best, as they tend not to actively familiarize themselves with CLD pupils and have little knowledge of bilingual or multilingual education for minorities in society. As Mary and Young (2017) report on schools in France, pre-school teachers often instruct parents to speak the language of schooling instead of their home language or heritage language, under the assumption that it is for the sake of the children and will facilitate their acquisition of the school language. Unfortunately, the same thing has often occurred in Japan. Prohibiting children from using their home language leads to a series of negative psychological consequences, beginning with shame and disdain for their home language and culture, eventually extending to their parents, which may end up with children suffering from low self-esteem and identity crises (Nakajima, 2016).

The significance of one's mother tongue and its development for bilingual education was slowly beginning to be understood around the year

2000, when bilingual education theories and research primarily from North America – such as Cummins (1984), Nakajima (1998, 2001, 2016) and Baker (2006), among others – was introduced and gradually accepted among researchers and teachers in Japan.

MEXT, however, has failed to acknowledge these developments regarding the importance of one's home language, by continuing its stance in admitting the use of L1 solely as an aid to help children improve Japanese proficiency. MEXT has never made explicit the goal of helping CLD children become bilingual or multilingual, proficient in both Japanese and their home language; they are exclusively concerned with Japanese language proficiency. The Ministry has made no comment so far about acquiring one's mother tongue as a linguistic human right (Skutnabb-Kangas, 1981).

Research site background: One public school's endeavor

As we have described above, it was only about 30 years ago that Japanese public schools began to face newcomer CLD pupils in critical numbers, and therefore there are few specialists and/or researchers as well as scarce empirical research in this field. Some of the literature documented mainly focuses on the difficulties CLD pupils face. We thought it important to grasp CLD pupils' development not only of Japanese but of both their home language and Japanese to better understand the development of each child as a whole. We have developed a close and trusting relationship with one public school in Osaka, where our research was approved for as long as a decade. Although it took almost a decade for the school staff and school principals as well as the local board of education and the community to understand the importance of the pupils' L1, the principal of the elementary school of our research site and his staff teachers have successfully created and worked on different approaches and practices with inclusion in mind.

We conducted a longitudinal study by following a total of 110 pupils to assess their bilingual proficiency in L1 Chinese and L2 Japanese, using a former version of the DLA (MEXT, 2014). We discuss the results below in light of inclusive education.

Kiyota (2007) proposed a model to teach foreign pupils school subjects with the help of their L1 so that their knowledge of academic subjects, mother tongue and Japanese language could improve simultaneously, hand in hand. A number of researchers (Kiyota, 2016; Namekawa, 2019; Sakurai, 2008) have reported on the successful results of such a model. For example, Sakurai (2008) showed that a low-achieving Peruvian pupil demonstrated improvement in his L1 Spanish competence, cognitive development and Japanese proficiency with the help of his L1.

The public elementary school where we conducted our research was having difficulties with CLD Chinese pupils a decade ago, and many

Chinese pupils did not get adequate support for their home language, Chinese. This school is unique in the sense that administrators, faculty and staff have worked hard to help the school implement inclusive education, trying out a variety of practices. The following are some examples of those practices; they are from the field notes of the authors, taken while observing JSL classes and in personal conversations with the principal and the school staff:

- Employment of a Chinese full-time teacher in 2012.
- 'Pull-out classes' for Chinese pupils, where the native Chinese teacher sometimes uses Chinese for instruction and cognitive awareness of the two languages.
- Better communication with Chinese pupils' parents: in order to promote mutual understanding, the Chinese teacher improved ways of translating aspects of school culture.
- Multilingual signs and posters in the school building.
- Schoolwide cross-cultural understanding classes offered by the school.
- Teachers' praise of and expression of respect for Chinese pupils speaking Chinese.
- School-wide composition project organized by the school principal: the topics of the compositions were 'Pride', 'Dream' and 'Connections'. Some Chinese pupils wrote in Chinese and translated into Japanese. Excellent compositions were selected and have been published in the school's newsletters since 2014.
- Bilingual presentations at the graduation ceremony were encouraged, where every sixth grader gets a chance to declare what they feel, such as gratitude to their parents and hopes for junior high school.

At the research site, we observed a number of effective practices for inclusive education without MEXT instructions. From casual conversations to formal addresses at the graduation ceremony, the school principal acted to promote inclusive education to help CLD pupils become more independent, achieve higher self-esteem and adopt positive attitudes towards learning something new.

A competent, native Chinese teacher with specialized training played an invaluable role. She was able to provide what García and Li Wei (2014) call 'translanguaging' instruction in pull-out Japanese classes for Chinese pupils (see also Sánchez & Espinet, this volume). She communicated with the parents in such a way that parents' attendance at parent-teacher association meetings increased to 100%. As she was an excellent role model, some CLD children expressed their wish to become a school teacher like her, which is remarkable considering no Chinese pupil had wanted to become a school teacher before. All of these suggest the tremendous and positive impact this individual bilingual teacher had on CLD pupils and their families.

Our longitudinal research focused on 110 pupils, from whom we collected language assessment data comprising 176 samples in Japanese and 137 samples in Chinese, among which 91 sets are of the same pupils in both languages. As we did not want to interfere with regular school plans, our research was conducted at the school's convenience.

The data presented here constitute part of a long and large-scale study (Majima & Sakurai, 2017; Majima et al., 2019). For more details on the bilingual assessment tool used in this research, see Sakurai (2018).

Empirical Research of Bilingual Proficiency of Chinese Pupils

Research

The study presented here is based on data collected between 2011 and 2016, but the entire study was conducted over a period of eight years, from 2008 to 2016, with more than 110 participating pupils at a school located in an area where Japanese returnees from China after WWII and their Chinese families are concentrated.[4]

Purpose

Our research group aims at understanding the children's language proficiency and development in two languages – not only in Japanese, as preceding Japanese researchers have studied, but also in L1 Chinese – and understanding the pupils holistically. This study aims to show the linguistic and personal development of Chinese 'newcomer' pupils at a Japanese public elementary school in Osaka Prefecture.

Research site

The research was conducted at a relatively small Japanese public elementary school in what is regarded as a relatively low-income area located near a housing complex with Chinese residents. The school has received an increasing number of Chinese pupils since around 1990, and at the time of the research more than 70 members (23%) of the school population of approximately 300 (in 2014, which fell to 200 in 2018) are of Chinese heritage; most of them were born in Japan or arrived in Japan at a very young age.

We focused on 17 Chinese pupils among the 60 students total who entered Grade 1 (G1) in 2011, when the ratio of Chinese students in the school was at a record high. We assessed their Japanese and Chinese proficiency when they were G1 (first graders who were six years old), G3 (third graders who were eight years old) and G5 (fifth graders who were 10 years old). The 17 G1 pupils decreased to 14 G3 and, later, to 12 G5 pupils, due mostly to the parents' job situations which resulted in them moving away from the city.

Research questions

Our concern lies in the plurilingual proficiency among Chinese pupils studying in Japan, and we wanted to track the development of their mother tongue (Chinese) and the local language (Japanese). In order to assess the language proficiency of the young learners, ordinary paper-pencil tests like the ones used for the majority of students at school is considered inappropriate. We decided to assess students through a one-on-one language assessment tool, a former version of the DLA, which takes 30–40 minutes per pupil. (For a more detailed explanation of the validity and merits of this tool, see Nakajima & Sakurai, 2012; Sakurai, 2018). The research questions for this study were:

- **RQ1**: How well is the pupils' L2 Japanese proficiency developed in speaking and reading?
  Did the pupils develop their Japanese proficiency incrementally over the years? What is their achievement in Japanese in terms of the JSL stages assessed by the DLA?
- **RQ2**: How well is the pupils' L1 Chinese maintained over the school years?
- Is there a relationship between their Chinese (L1) proficiency and Japanese reading skills? Chinese pupils are assumed to have a home language, but how proficient are they?
- **RQ3**: How do the pupils negotiate their identities? What is their attitude towards their languages, their parents and their future?

Methods

In order to respond to the three research questions, we adopted a mixed-methods approach. The DLA was used for RQ1 and RQ2, whereas we conducted interviews with the sixth graders (G6) to respond to RQ3. The procedure of the assessment is as follows:

- Warm-up conversation.
- Basic daily vocabulary checked with 55 picture cards.
- Basic task with situation cards to explain the procedure of one day's actions (for example, we asked the students questions such as: 'explain what you see in the picture of a room' and 'tell one of the well-known children's stories you see on the card').
- Cognitive task with picture cards to explain things such as an earthquake, the process of digestion, environmental pollution and global warming.
- Listening to a story and then retelling the story.
- Reading task: students had to choose and read a whole book, then recount the story and answer comprehension questions.
- Questions about reading habits and activities.

Table 6.1 JSL assessment framework 'Overall proficiency' (DLA, MEXT, 2014)

Stage	In relation to the regular classroom	Stage in terms of support
6	Understand topics related to the subject matter and actively participate in classroom activities	Autonomous learning with support
5	Understand topics related to the subject matter with help and participate in classroom activities with some support	Autonomous learning with support
4	Understand topics in daily life and participate in classwork	Individual learning support
3	Understand topics in daily life with help and partially participate in classwork	Individual learning support
2	Make progress with help in Japanese learning for school life	Initial support
1	Just started Japanese learning necessary for school life	Initial support

One-on-one interviewing is certainly time-consuming, but each pupil's unique situation can be observed in detail, which can never be fully rendered through paper-pencil classroom tests. As the testers were well-trained and always recognized the child's efforts and responses with positive feedback, the children were usually satisfied with their achievement at the end of the assessment. The dialogic assessment was audio recorded and then transcribed into Japanese. In the case of interviews in Chinese, the recorded audio was transcribed into Chinese and then translated to Japanese, which was carried out by Chinese graduate students majoring in Japanese language studies.

Collected and transcribed data were assessed according to the analysis and diagnosis procedures of the DLA and located within the six calibrated stages shown in Table 6.1. The assessment was conducted by two native speakers of the language to secure its validity. (See MEXT, 2014, and Sakurai, 2018, for more detailed theories and procedures of the DLA.)

Pupils at Stages 1–4 need individual support; in Stage 5 and above, they are able to follow the regular class with some specific and supplementary support. The DLA consists of four language skills, but for this specific study we have collected data on speaking and reading skills only. The authors and the teachers in charge of the non-native Japanese students at the elementary school worked together to evaluate the results, and the Chinese data were analyzed and evaluated by Chinese graduate student researchers as mentioned previously.

In order to respond to RQ3, we conducted individual follow-up interviews asking about students' language proficiencies, identity and their future. We interviewed 12 pupils individually for 15–20 minutes each.

As for research ethics, we had permission to conduct research from the school principal and the teachers, and we strictly follow the guidelines of Osaka University Research Ethics. In publishing the results, we respect children's and teachers' privacy and ensure that individual identities are not revealed.

Results

L2 Japanese speaking and reading proficiency

RQ1: How well is pupils' L2 Japanese proficiency developed in speaking and reading over the school years?

The stages of CLD pupils' speaking skills are shown in Figure 6.1. As a general tendency, as pupils progress through the school grades, they simultaneously progress through the six stages. In G1, many of them are still in Stage 2 or 3, for which 'pull-out' individual instruction is strongly recommended. As they get older, more pupils reach Stages 5 and 6, at which time they are able to participate in the regular classroom.

We then analyzed the results of the reading skills (Table 6.2). Figure 6.2 shows that a majority of children are in Stage 3 in G1, and more pupils reach Stage 5 or 6 as they get older. When we compare the results of speaking and reading skills, however, fewer pupils achieved Stages 5 and 6 in reading than in speaking skills. This suggests that speaking skills develop

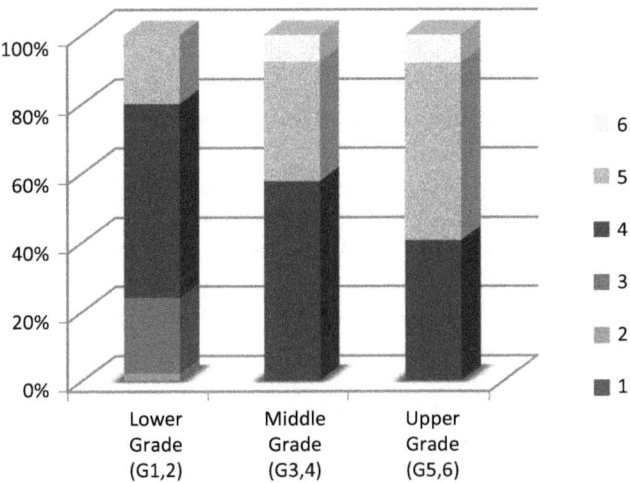

Figure 6.1 Japanese speaking proficiency in DLA stages (*n* = 113)

Table 6.2 Japanese reading proficiency in DLA stages (*n* = 96)

Reading stages	Lower grade (G1,2)	Middle grade (G3,4)	Upper grade (G5,6)	Total
1	0	0	0	0
2	0	0	0	0
3	16	4	3	23
4	9	13	17	39
5	7	7	14	28
6	2	1	3	6
計	34	25	37	96

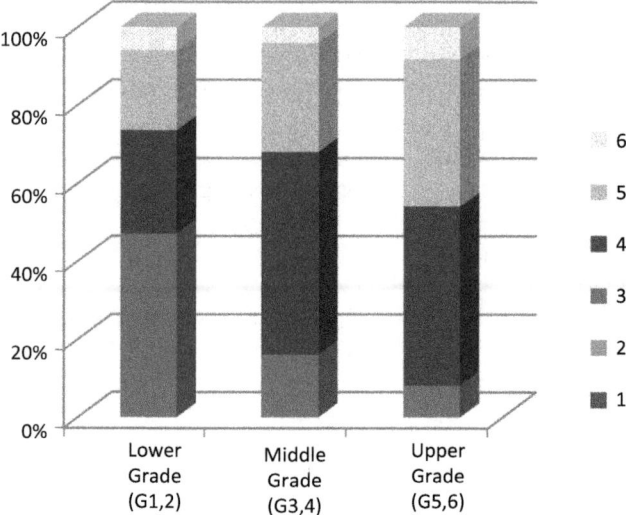

Figure 6.2 Japanese reading proficiency in DLA stages (*n* = 96)

faster than reading skills, which supports preceding studies such as Cummins (1984).

When we consider these results, it becomes clear that a considerable percentage of pupils who were either born in Japan or brought to Japan at a very young age are still in Stage 3 or 4 and require individual support in order to fully participate in regular class. Therefore, it is important to understand that even though these pupils do not appear to have problems in daily conversation, many of them have difficulty in following the content of classes, which suggests that they need careful and considerate support over the long term of their education.

L1 Chinese proficiency

RQ2: What is the relationship between Chinese pupils' Chinese (L1) proficiency and Japanese reading skills?

Chinese pupils were divided into three groups according to their L1 proficiency:

- listening comprehension only bilingual group: pupils are able to listen to and comprehend their L1, but cannot speak it;
- conversational bilingual group: pupils are able to listen to and speak their L1, but are not literate in this language;
- biliterate in both languages (bi-literal) group: pupils can read in their L1 in addition to demonstrating conversational fluency.

We then analyzed the relationship between these three types of L1 proficiency and the Japanese reading assessment.

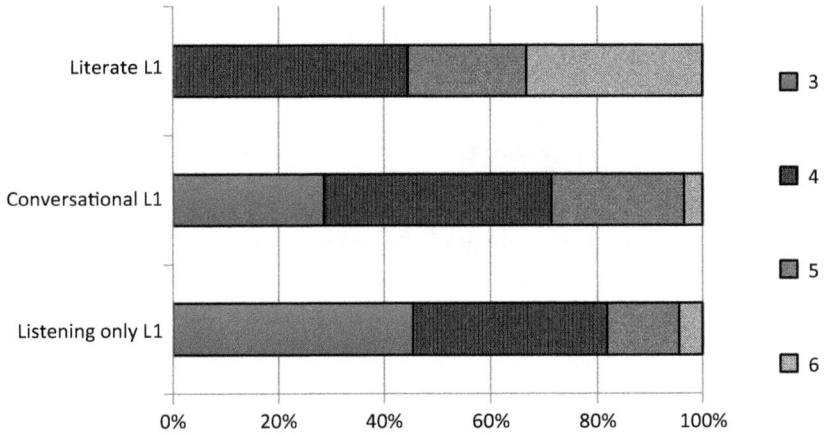

Figure 6.3 L1 Chinese proficiency and Japanese reading proficiency

Figure 6.3 shows the three types of L1 Chinese proficiency and the ratio of pupils in each group belonging to each stage from 1 to 6 within the JSL for reading proficiency. The lower bar indicates (a) 'L1 listening comprehension only', the middle bar is (b) 'Conversational L1' and the top bar shows (c) 'Literate L1'.

The results show a remarkable tendency for those who have high L1 proficiency to achieve higher proficiency in L2 Japanese reading. The bottom bar in Figure 6.3 indicates that the 'Listening only L1' pupils consist of 40% at Stage 3, 35% at Stage 4 and only about 12% at Stages 5 and 6 in Japanese reading proficiency. The middle bar shows that the largest percentage of 'Conversational L1' pupils fall into Stage 4. The top bar indicates that 'Literate L1' pupils achieve the highest level overall, where one-third of the pupils were assessed to be at Stage 6 in their L2 Japanese reading proficiency.

This presents a profound and important implication: L1 proficiency is likely to be interrelated with L2 literacy, as shown by Cummins (1984) and others. Those children who are losing their L1 may experience greater difficulty in developing their reading skills in L2 Japanese compared to those who have maintained and developed their L1 in speaking. Group (a) – the listening only comprehension group – appears to have greater difficulty in acquiring L2 reading compared to Group (b), and Group (c) – the bi-literal group – achieved the highest L2 literacy of all three groups.

Before moving on to RQ3, let us briefly mention that, according to an interview conducted at the time, the 12 G5 pupils' bilingual literacy graduated to G6. A closer look at the development of the two languages of these 12 (previously 14) pupils in Majima *et al.* (2019) reveals that five of them had become literate during their years in K–G2 in Chinese texts and four had started reading Chinese. This points to an emergent biliteracy and suggests that in the long run we may be able to observe more pupils becoming literate in their L1 as well.

Identity

RQ3 sought to investigate the following questions: How do pupils negotiate their identity? What is their attitude towards their languages, parents and their future? As mentioned above, we conducted one-on-one interviews with 12 G6 pupils. The questions were about their self-recognition in the two languages, their relationship with their parents, and their identity and future. When they were asked in which language they feel more confident and comfortable, all of them answered 'Japanese'. Thus, we may conclude that the local language is stronger in this sense than their L1 home language. One of the pupils in this group said that she does not know Chinese at all, but the rest said that they speak Chinese every day.

When they were asked about their parents, one respondent said that he is very proud of his father because his father is fluent in both languages and helps facilitate communication in the family, with his mother not knowing much Japanese and the respondent not being fluent in Chinese. This child used the word 'respect' towards his father in regard to his father's language proficiency, which shows the importance of language in his family life. Another boy complained that his mother often talks so fast in Chinese that he cannot follow. He said that he roughly grasps the meaning of his mother's speech, in which she urges him to study more. Asked what to do when he does not understand his mother, he said, 'I just ignore her'. He tried to understand his mother, but when he could not, he said that he just gave up entirely on the conversation with her. This shows a discrepancy of L1/heritage Chinese language proficiency among family members, which may lead to misunderstanding and further family problems in the future.

The next question in the interview was targeted at understanding the respondents' identity. 'How would you respond if someone asks you, "You speak Japanese so well. Are you Japanese?"?' Only one respondent said s/he would respond with 'Yes, I am Japanese'; two other pupils said they would respond, 'I am both Chinese and Japanese' and 'I am half Chinese and half Japanese', respectively. The rest of the nine pupils said they would answer, 'No, I am Chinese' or 'I am Chinese but I can speak Japanese'. Only one child among 12 G6 students seemed to have shifted her identity completely to identify as Japanese. We learned later that it was the educational/living strategy that her parents had chosen as they had decided to naturalize and gain Japanese citizenship. Other children, however, were developing their Chinese with mixed Japanese identity. It was encouraging to observe that nobody seemed to have negative feelings towards or felt ashamed of their Chinese background. This may well be related to the inclusive environment of the school discussed earlier.

The results of the follow-up interviews showed that most of the pupils have become orally bilingual but not biliterate, and have developed identity as Chinese or 'Chinese who can speak Japanese'. The results can be explained within the 'educational framework of literacy attainment'

(Cummins & Nakajima, 2011). Even though the pupils are not as literate in their home language as they are in Japanese, they seem confident and comfortable at school, gradually acquiring high self-esteem identifying as Chinese or simply being themselves. Crucially, this took place in an overall educationally supportive and encouraging environment, to the extent that five of them gained emergent literacy in Chinese without formal Chinese education.

Conclusion

MEXT has not only been slow in implementing language policies to support CLD pupils, but it has neglected developing these pupils' L1. Our research takes the example of a struggling Japanese public school with many Chinese pupils who have not only overcome difficulties and developed Japanese proficiency, but many of whom have demonstrated development in L1 Chinese through spoken interaction at home, and some of whom have even slowly developed emergent L1 literacy. Our study suggests that those who acquired L1 Chinese tend to have higher Japanese literacy in school. Most of them have also developed a grounded identity, and the researchers were given the impression that they will stand tall and proud in Japanese society as encouraged by the school principal and staff. The competent bilingual teacher clearly played an important role at school, giving the children not only cultural and linguistic knowledge but empowerment in the development of their identities.

In the era of globalization, it is no easy task to promote additive bilingualism among CLD pupils in Japan when Japanese government policy and the majority of society are supportive of monolingual and assimilationist ideologies. Nevertheless, most of the Chinese CLD pupils in our longitudinal study showed development in both Chinese and Japanese proficiency with a positive attitude towards their heritage language and culture.

A number of activities and phenomena were observed at the school that fostered a school climate that is supportive and encouraging of Chinese CLD pupils as well as the majority of pupils; these include hiring a Chinese native teacher, multilingual posters in the school building, bilingual presentations at the graduation ceremony and high attendance of Chinese parents at school bilingual activities, to name a few. These children offer hope when they are regarded as 'seeds' of potential for the future development of Japan and not merely as a source of problems to be dealt with.

Our research results supported those of preceding studies conducted outside of Japan, such as in North America and in Europe. Importantly, our conclusions based on the longitudinal empirical and bilingual data we collected constitute the first of their kind for a Japanese public school, which supports a more careful consideration and integration of the home language of CLD pupils in their education. This follows from the observation that high proficiency in pupils' home language is correlated with higher achievement in their local/school language (Japanese in this case).

The implications from this research encourage teachers and researchers to conduct assessments not only in pupils' school language but in both their school and home languages, even in a monoglossic society such as that of Japan, so that CLD children can be understood and supported better in a more holistic manner. In June 2019, the Japanese National Diet passed the Japanese Language Promotion Law, in which Article 7 mentions the importance of the home language in the process of teaching Japanese to foreign pupils.[5] It is hoped that the national and local governments and boards of education will be granted more substantial budgets and resources to better equip communities and schools to help CLD pupils become bilingual, or possibly bi-literal, according to their wishes and needs and with the understanding and help of their majority Japanese peers.

Notes

(1) We will use the word 'immigrant' for practical reasons in this chapter as there is no more precise alternative.
(2) The press conference is reported on the website of the United Nations Information Centre. See https://www.unic.or.jp/news_press/features_backgrounders/2805/?lang=en.
(3) The term 'home language' is used in this chapter, by which we refer to the pupil's mother tongue, but we understand that other terms can be used such as 'heritage language' as well as 'ancestral', 'ethnic', 'immigrant', 'international', 'minority', 'non-official', 'third' (after English and French) in different contexts (Cummins, 2014: 2).
(4) Our study was realized with the financial support of 'KAKEN-HI', i.e. Grants-in-Aid for Scientific Research by the Japanese Government, for eight years. The research we report in this chapter is a part of that study.
(5) The law to promote Japanese-Language Education can be read in Japanese at the website of the Agency of Cultural Affairs, MEXT. See http://www.bunka.go.jp/seisaku/bunka_gyosei/shokan_horei/other/suishin_houritsu/pdf/r1418257_02.pdf.

References

Baker, C. (2006) *Foundations of Bilingual Education and Bilingualism* (4th edn). Clevedon: Multilingual Matters.
Cummins, J. (1984) *Bilingualism and Special Education: Issues in Assessment and Pedagogy*. Clevedon: Multilingual Matters.
Cummins, J. (2014) Mainstreaming plurilingualism: Restructuring heritage language provision in schools. In P.P. Trifonas and T. Aravossitas (eds) *Rethinking Heritage Language Education* (pp. 1–19). Cambridge: Cambridge University Press.
Cummins, J. and Nakajima, K. (2011) *Gengo Mainoritii wo sasaeru kyoiku* [*Education Supporting Linguistic Minorities*]. Tokyo: Keio University Press.
García, O. and Kleifgen, J.A. (2018) *Educating Emergent Bilinguals: Policies, Programs, and Practices for English Learners* (2nd edn). New York: Teachers College Press.
García, O. and Li Wei (2014) *Translanguaging and Education*. London: Palgrave Macmillan.

Hifumi, T. (1996) Nenshousha no goi shuutoku katei to gengo shiyou joukyou ni kansuru kousatsu [Vocabulary acquisition process and language use among younger learners: A case of Vietnamese children in Japan]. *Nihongo Kyoiku [Journal of Teaching Japanese as a Foreign Language]* 90, 13–24.

Kiyota, J. (2007) *Bogo wo katsuyou shita naiyou juushi no kyouka-gakushuu-shien-houhou no kouchiku ni mukete [Towards Constructing Content-Based Learning Supporting Method Using Mother Tongue]*. Tokyo: Hitsuji Shobo.

Kiyota, J. (2016) *Gaikoku kara kita kodomo no manabi wo sasaeru [Supporting Language Minority Children's Learning]*. Tokyo: Bunrikaku Publishing.

Kurita, Y. (2004) Gengoken no kenpougaku teki kousatsu (1): Kanada Kenpou hanrei wo sozai ni [Constitutional considerations on linguistic human rights (1): A study based on the court rules on Canadian constitution]. *Kyudai-Hogaku [Legal Studies at Kyushu University]* 87, 1–68.

Majima, J. (2009) Gaikokujin jidou seito eno bogo kyouiku shien no juuyousei ni tsuite [Importance of supporting mother tongues of foreign pupils.] *Report on the Educational Project for Supporting Mother Tongue* (pp. 38–43). Kobe: Hyogo Prefectural Board of Education.

Majima, J. and Sakurai, C. (2017) CLDji no fukusuu-gengo-nouryoku no kankei ni tsuite: Osaka-fuka no kouritsu-shougakkou deno chousakenkyuu yori. [Bilingual development among culturally linguistically diverse children: A study at a public elementary school in Osaka Prefecture]. *Matani Ronshu* 11, 41–57.

Majima, J. (ed.), Sakurai, C., Nakajima, K. *et al.* (2019) *Bogo wo nakusanai nihongo kyouiku wa kanouka? Teijuu ni-seiji no ni-gengo nouryoku [Is Teaching Japanese Without Losing their Mother Tongue Possible? Bilingual Proficiencies among Second Generation Immigrants]*. Osaka: Osaka University Press.

Mary, L. and Young, A. (2017) Engaging with emergent bilinguals and their families in the pre-primary classroom to foster well-being, learning and inclusion. *Language & Intercultural Communication* 17 (4), 455–473. doi:10.1080/14708477.2017.1368147

MEXT (Ministry of Education, Culture, Sports, Science and Technology-Japan) (2005, revised 2015) *Monbu kagaku sho 'Gaikokujinjidouseito no tame no syugakushien gaidobukku' [Guidebook for Foreign Pupils' Attendance at Japanese Public Schools]*.

MEXT (Ministry of Education, Culture, Sports, Science and Technology-Japan) (2014a) *Monbu kagaku sho 'Gaikokujinjidouseito kyouiku kensyu manyuaru' [Manual for Conducting Seminars for Foreign Pupils' Education]*.

MEXT (Ministry of Education, Culture, Sports, Science and Technology-Japan) (2014b) *Monbu kagaku sho 'Gaikokujin jidou seito no tameno JSL taiwagata assessment DLA' [JSL Dialogic Language Assessment for Foreign Children and Students]*. See http://www.mext.go.jp/a_menu/shotou/clarinet/003/1345413.htm (accessed 20 May 2018).

MIC (Ministry of Internal Affairs and Communication of Japan) (2006) *Report on Study of Promoting Multicultural Symbiotic Societies*. See http://www.soumu.go.jp/kokusai/pdf/sonota_b5.pdf.

Ministry of Justice, Japan (2019) Heisei 30 nendomatsu genzai ni okeru Zairyuu gaikokujin suu ni tsuite [Press release on the number of Foreign Residents at the end of 2018 in Japan]. See http://www.moj.go.jp/nyuukokukanri/kouhou/nyuukoku-kanri04_00081.html.

Nakajima, K. (1998/2001/2016) *Bilingual kyoiku no houhou [Ways for Bilingual Education]*. Tokyo: ALC.

Nakajima, K. and Sakurai, C. (2012) *Dialogic Reading Assessment*. JSPS Grants-in-Aid for Scientific Research Report (B) 21320096.

Namekawa, E. (2019) *Gengo-shousuu-ha no kodomo no gainen-hattatsu wo unagasu kyouka gakushuu shien [Encouraging Concept Development in an Academic Learning Support Class for Language Minority Students]*. Tokyo: Koko Publishing.

Nishikawa, T., Aoki, Y., Hosono, N. and Higuchi, M. (2015) Nihon umare/sodachi no JSL no kodomo no nihongo-ryoku [Japanese proficiency of JSL children born/raised in Japan]. *Nihongo Kyoiku [Journal of Teaching of Japanese as a Foreign Language]* 160, 64–78.

Ohta, Y. (2000) *Nyu-kama-no kodomo to nihon no gakkou* [*Newcomer Children and Japanese Schools*]. Tokyo: Kokusai-shoin.
Sakurai, C. (2008) Gaikokujin jidou no manabi wo unagasu zaiseki-gakkyuu no arikata: Bogo-ryoku to nihongo-ryoku no shinchou wo mezashite [Designing a mainstream class to facilitate the development of minority-language children in both Japanese and their other tongue]. *Mother Tongue, Heritage Language, and Bilingual Education (MHB) Research* 4, 1–26.
Sakurai, C. (2018) *Gaikoku ni roots wo motsu kodomo no Bilingual dokusho-ryoku* [*Bilingual Reading Proficiency of Children Who Have Roots in Foreign Countries*]. Osaka: Osaka University Press.
Skutnabb-Kangas, T. (1981) *Bilingualism or Not: The Education of Minorities*. Clevedon: Multilingual Matters.
Tomozawa, A. and Majima, J. (2015) Bilingual education in Japan: Slow but steady progress. In W.E. Wright, S. Boun and O. García (eds) *The Handbook of Bilingual and Multilingual Education* (1st edn) (pp. 493–503). Oxford: John Wiley.
Tomozawa, A. and Yoshimura, M. (2010) Japan. In J.A. Fishman and O. García (eds) *The Handbook of Language and Ethnic Identity* (2nd edn) (pp. 486–500). New York: Oxford University Press.

Inclusive Practices in Multilingual Schools

Andy Hancock

Head of Graduate School of Education & Sport, University of Edinburgh

In Scotland, the context in which I work, multilingual classrooms are becoming the norm as a result of globalization and forced migration. Despite this increasing diversity, monolingual ideologies and monocultural practices still prevail and the teaching profession is not representative of the diverse communities it serves. However, my experience of working with a Chinese bilingual teacher illustrates how it is possible to intervene and disrupt dominant school practices. Many educationalists have a deficit view of minority learners based purely on their performance in the language of instruction. This can be reversed by providing spaces for pupils to draw on all the languages at their disposal to reinforce concepts, support understanding and access the curriculum. These pedagogies draw heavily on Cummins's concept of common underlying proficiency, social justice principles and inclusive practices (Hancock, 2020). In this way, the learning environment both promotes and reaffirms the linguistic identities of bilingual learners through translanguaging and secure constructions of self while also sending a powerful message to monolingual peers, namely, that all languages are valued within mainstream classrooms.

I have argued that engagement with families is an integral aspect of the bilingual teacher's role. In one school the timings of teacher-parent consultations were changed to take into account Chinese parents' unsocial working hours, and attendance increased significantly. Home visits have been used to gain a deeper understanding about family lives and this knowledge is used as a bridge to pupils' learning. I am currently exploring pupils learning heritage languages and literacies in the home and in the community. I have highlighted ways in which complementary schools and mainstream schooling can collaborate further and connect with pupils' lived experiences. All the above demonstrate a range of ways in which bilingual teachers can act as mediators of languages and identity formation. However, this needs the support of school leadership and transformative educators to create spaces for counter-narratives from those in the minority.

Reference

Hancock, A. (2020) Inclusive practices for pupils with English as an additional language. In R. Arshad, T. Wrigley and L. Pratt (eds) *Social Justice Re-Examined: Dilemmas and Solutions for the Classroom Teacher* (2nd edn) (pp. 122–134). London: UCL Institute of Education Press.

7 'To Make Headway You Have to Go Against the Flow': Resisting Dominant Discourses and Supporting Emergent Bilinguals in a Multilingual Pre-School in France

Latisha Mary and Andrea S. Young

Introduction

With rises in migration in recent years contributing to increasingly linguistically diverse classrooms in Europe and around the world, the need to support children who speak a language other than the language of schooling has become urgent. Despite changes in both French (MEN, 2015) and European (European Commission, 2015) policy documents promoting language diversity and inclusive language policies, many teachers in France continue to hold monolingual ideologies and implement 'French-only' policies, depriving young bilingual and emergent bilingual pupils of their most important linguistic resources for learning – their home languages. Despite working within this monolingual habitus, some teachers manage to resist and challenge prevailing deficit discourses and develop inclusive classroom practices that support young emergent bilingual children. This chapter focuses on one such pre-school teacher working with three- and four-year-old emergent bilingual children in France whose inclusive language practices broke with the monolingual norm. Drawing on video recordings of classroom activities over the course of an entire school year, in-depth interviews with the teacher and extracts from her written reflections, we investigate the beliefs, experiences and knowledge that contributed to the development of her language ideology with the aim of understanding how this developed over time and in turn motivated her actions in the classroom. Through our analysis we detail the origins of her teacher language ideologies, in particular her strong beliefs with regard to social justice, her positive image of the children, her critical awareness of language and language acquisition and her willingness to question the prevailing monolingual discourses and practices. In our discussion, we draw on these data in a bid to understand how teacher educators might contribute to the development and evolution of pre-service and practising teachers' language ideologies and which elements in curriculum development they might harness to create more equitable classrooms for their multilingual pupils.

Language Ideologies and Classroom Practices: Key Findings from Research

Language ideologies have been defined as individuals' 'beliefs, or feelings about languages as used in their social worlds' (Kroskrity, 2004: 98), expressed similarly by Spolsky (2004: 14) as 'what people think should be done' with language. Silverstein (1979: 193) defines language ideologies as 'sets of beliefs about language articulated by users as a rationalization or justification of perceived language structure and use'. Thus, language ideologies not only concern the beliefs and attitudes that individuals hold about language, but also the practices through which these beliefs are performed (Gal, 1998, cited in Razfar, 2012) and 'what people do' with language (Spolsky, 2004: 14). These sets of beliefs which inform action, conscious or unconscious, are developed through the sociocultural experiences of individuals and contribute to their perception and evaluation of language use, including their understanding of language acquisition and the value and place they attribute to different languages (Kroskrity, 2004; Spolsky, 2004).

Research in the area of teacher cognition (Borg, 2003) and teacher language ideologies (Kroskrity, 2004; Pettit, 2011; Razfar, 2012) has drawn attention to the link between teachers' beliefs and their practices in the classroom (see Mary & Young, 2020, for a detailed literature review). Teachers' beliefs about languages, about the children or parents who speak languages other than the language of schooling and about how second languages are acquired, will have an impact on the place attributed to children's home languages in the classroom and whether these will be silenced or used as a resource for learning (Hélot, 2010; Pulinx *et al.*, 2017; Young, 2014a). These ideologies will also play a role in the ways in which teachers interpret and implement or challenge and negotiate top-down language policies, contributing to the nature and degree of agency they exercise in the classroom with regard to supporting their bilingual and emergent bilingual learners (Mattheoudakis *et al.*, 2017; Pulinx *et al.*, 2017). Given that teachers' beliefs and practices may have long-term positive or negative consequences on pupils' language development and learning and that issues of power are at play (Cummins, 2000; Saxena & Martin-Jones, 2013; Woollard, 1998), it is vital to understand where such ideologies come from, how they are formed and how they may evolve over time (Crookes, 2015).

Critical Teacher Language Awareness, Critical Engagement and Agency: Initial Steps Towards Creating Equitable Classrooms

Cummins (2009) and Palmer and Martinez (2013) stress that educators always have a degree of freedom within their institutions to challenge inequitable language policies and practices. Cummins (2009: 262) specifies, however, that the first step in doing so involves a re-examination of the sets of beliefs or 'normalized assumptions' practitioners hold with regard to their linguistically and culturally diverse students and their language practices. This requires teachers to *critically* engage with their beliefs about what providing effective education in linguistically diverse contexts means. Likewise, in his investigation into teacher philosophies, Crookes (2015: 491) focuses on what he calls teachers' 'critical cognitions' and 'critical philosophies of teaching' which he defines as 'a form of critical, self-reflective teacher cognition which draws on the insights of critical theory' and emphasises the role that cognitive assumptions and relations of power often have in challenging and changing inequitable situations in classrooms. He argues that in order for these to be uncovered and changed, teachers first need to be able to question the practices and the contexts in which they are working. García (2017: 270) also stresses the need for teachers to question their assumptions about language practices, and in particular about the ways in which their 'multilingual students use their languages and make sense of their multilingual worlds'. She advocates the need to develop *critically aware language teachers* who are willing to take on the role of 'language activists' in the classroom. Being a language activist implies the ability to question normative assumptions about what constitutes equitable language practices in the classroom, as well as the ability to then challenge practices that do not support (emergent) bilingual children's personal and academic development. This chapter seeks to investigate this area by focusing on the ways in which one critically aware pre-school teacher, Sylvie, dared to question and disrupt the status quo despite the prevalent dominant monolingual deficit discourses in her environment and the factors that led to her exercising agency in the classroom.

Context and Aim of Study

At the start of our longitudinal study investigating Sylvie's inclusive practices in her multilingual pre-school classroom with emergent bilingual three- and four-year-old children, Sylvie had been teaching for 35 years, 31 of which had been in multilingual classrooms. During her 18 years of teaching children in their first year of pre-primary she had developed a number of culturally and linguistically inclusive practices that broke from the monolingual norm. In addition to documenting these practices and their impact on the children and their families (see Mary & Young, 2017a, and 2017b for a detailed account), we also questioned what might have motivated this one particular teacher to disrupt the status quo and challenge the dominant monolingual ideologies so prevalent in her environment. With the goal of better understanding how her language ideology had developed over time and how this in turn had impacted on her 'practiced language policies' (Bonacina-Pugh, 2012), we endeavoured to analyse her beliefs, knowledge and experience with regard to language practices in the classroom, first and second language acquisition and relationships established with children and parents who spoke a language other than the language of schooling at home.

In the following section we describe the general educational context in France within which Sylvie was working as well as her local school and classroom context, providing a backdrop to a better understanding of the role her own language ideology played in the disruption of dominant discourses.

Macro Institutional Context

We have previously discussed the monolingual habitus of French education contexts (Mary & Young, 2018a; Young, 2017), the historical and ideological roots that embed it in French society and that persist in spite of attempts by various agencies such as the MEN (Ministère de l'Éducation nationale), the DGLFLF (Délégation Générale à la Langue Française et aux Langues de France) and the Council of Europe to promote a more inclusive, plurilingual approach to education. The engrained idea that, as the language of the République (Article 2 of the Constitution, modified by constitutional law no. 95-880 on 4 August 1995), French is the only language that should be permitted within the precincts of schools is still upheld in many schools in France (Young, 2014a, 2014b, 2017). This is of course both paradoxical, within an educational policy context where plurilingualism is encouraged through the studying in and through multiple languages at school, and simultaneously nonsensical in a de facto multilingual context where children are exposed daily to a wide variety of languages spoken by family and peers and in society at large. Yet many schools in France, as in many other contexts, are still attempting to establish monolingual islands in multilingual oceans (Jordens *et al.*, 2018), refusing to engage with civil society through innovative practices that help children to make sense of their multilingual worlds. Multilingual environments in France are still frequently viewed as a threat to the supremacy and development of the national language, French, and as such, schools sometimes consider it their duty to eradicate all other languages, just as was the case in the 19th century with respect to the indigenous, regional languages of France, in order to promote French and nurture competences exclusively in this language (Kremnitz, 2013).

The foundation of the nation-state and the creation and development of a national identity through the promotion of French as the unique official language are not solely to blame for the prevailing monolingual habitus present in many French schools. Teacher education has for far too long ignored the need to equip future and practising teachers to work effectively in multilingual contexts, leaving them to 'fumble along' (Murakami, 2008) on their own. Consequently, with scant information and training about multilingualism and limited experience of how to support bi/plurilingual learners, many teachers feel insecure in their role when it comes to engaging with children and their families who speak a language other than the language of schooling.

Micro Local Context

The class in which this research was conducted was a first year of formal education class (*petite section de maternelle*). Pre-primary education in France is free and has recently become mandatory from the age of three (MEN, 2019a). In theory, newly arrived pupils are provided with additional support from the age of six in the form of pull-out French as a second language classes (UPE2A, *Unité pédagogique pour élèves allophones arrivants*) taught by a specialist teacher. In practice, this is subject to the availability of resources and many children are not able to benefit from such arrangements. Furthermore, due to a common belief that young children acquire a language quickly by being immersed in it (Mary & Young, 2018a), no additional support is provided by a specialist teacher for children under the age of six (MEN, 2012). This leaves the responsibility for supporting the language development of young, emergent bilingual children solely in the hands of the mainstream classroom teachers, many of whom have little or no knowledge of bilingualism and/or second language acquisition (Mary & Young, 2018b).

It is within this context that Sylvie, the teacher in our study and head teacher of the school, perseveres in her struggle to help the three- to four-year-old emergent bilingual pupils in her class access education on an equal footing with their French speaking peers. Our ethnographic, longitudinal study of Sylvie's classroom, which took place between September 2014 and July 2015, focused on the innovative and inclusive practices implemented in the classroom and the ways in which she supported the language and personal development of her emergent bilingual pupils. The school was located in an area identified by the education authorities as 'high priority' (low socioeconomic status), and a high proportion of the children (15) spoke a language other than French, the language of schooling, at home. The classroom observed comprised 23 children, of whom eight spoke French at home, five Turkish, two Albanian, two Serbian, five Arabic and one spoke both Creole from Réunion Island and French.

Methodology and Data Collection

Data were collected at regular intervals throughout the school year during bi-monthly visits to the school, during which classroom practices and interactions between children, parents, classroom teacher and teaching assistants were filmed over the course of an entire morning on 17 separate occasions. In addition, semi-structured interviews were conducted with the class teacher, classroom assistants, intercultural mediator, parents and French as a foreign language teacher (with whom some of the mothers were learning French). For the purposes of this chapter, which investigates the origins and evolution of Sylvie's ideologies and the link between these and her inclusive classroom practices, we draw mainly on the video footage, classroom observations and semi-structured interviews with Sylvie (consisting of four in-depth interviews conducted in September, January and February and lasting from 23' to 55' each), as well as her personal written reflections on her classroom practices. As mentioned in the previous sections, this study aimed to explore which beliefs, knowledge and experiences might have motivated this teacher to disrupt the status quo and challenge the dominant monolingual discourses so prevalent in her environment. In particular, our analysis of this data aimed to explore the following research questions:

- RQ1: What concrete examples (practiced language policies) of inclusive educational practices that challenged and broke with existing monolingual ideologies and deficit discourses did we observe?
- RQ2: In what ways did Sylvie's language ideology motivate her actions and enable her to resist dominant deficit discourses?
- RQ3: What beliefs, experiences and knowledge contributed to the development and evolution of this language ideology?

In order to answer the above research questions, we drew on a reflective narrative framework (Derry *et al.*, 2010) to analyse the video footage. This involved viewing and transcribing the recorded data in a bid to identify key segments for investigation which were then reviewed with Sylvie, during which time we asked her to comment on and explain what she was doing and why. In addition, the interview transcripts and Sylvie's written reflections were examined and coded using the constant comparative method (Ryan *et al.*, 2000; Wellington, 2004). Emerging themes and concepts were first coded, using the key notions detailed in Biesta *et al.*'s (2015) ecological model as a framework. These were then refined, compared and contrasted in a bid to uncover her past experiences, identify her future aspirations and describe her present circumstances – the three key influences on agency outlined by Biesta *et al.* (2015) – and to form a coherent picture in relation to the aforementioned research questions. Below, we first detail Sylvie's educational practices which broke with the monolingual norm, before exploring the origins of her language ideologies, namely her strong beliefs with regard to social justice, her positive vision/image of the children, her critical awareness of language and language acquisition and her willingness to question the prevailing monolingual discourses and practices.

Breaking With the Monolingual Norm: Inclusive Educational Practices Observed in Sylvie's Classroom

In this section we provide examples of the prevailing monolingual deficit discourses that Sylvie regularly encountered throughout her career and describe the inclusive educational practices we observed in her classroom that broke with this norm. We specifically detail the ways in which she welcomed parents into the classroom and used children's languages as resources. During one exchange with Sylvie, she shared with us an example of the difficulties she systematically encountered in maintaining her alternative practices in the face of the assimilationist attitudes expressed by her colleagues:

> But every time I said something, even remotely, during CPD about these language questions they would systematically throw it back in my face, colleagues that is eh, 'but parents should speak French, it's shameful, I myself am from a Spanish immigrant background', Italian whatever, etc., … I got pulled up systematically 'and it's not right these parents who give up, who only speak Turkish at home'. (Interview, Sylvie, 26 January 2016, our translation)

This statement reveals the monolingual habitus present in the institutional context in which Sylvie worked. Even the teachers who themselves came from a migrant background expressed the belief that the best approach to educating emergent bilingual children was the exclusive use of French at the expense of the home languages.

Despite being surrounded by assimilationist attitudes towards the children and parents who spoke other languages at home, Sylvie continued to remain open to these languages and to welcome their presence in the classroom. She did this through establishing an open classroom policy where the presence of parents and their home languages were not only welcomed, but also considered as an important resource for the children's learning and well-being.

Open-door policy: Welcoming parents into the classroom

We regularly observed Sylvie welcoming parents into the classroom and inviting them to engage in various activities with the children in the languages of their choice. This open-door classroom policy is uncommon in France as traditionally parents tend to be excluded from the classroom. In spite of the most recent curriculum guidelines (MEN, 2015) for pre-primary, reiterated in the back to school Ministerial note (MEN, 2019b) which emphasise the importance of including parents in the education process and developing practices that foster co-educational partnerships between schools and families, relationships between teachers and parents tend to remain rather formal and distant, sometimes marked by a lack of trust and occasionally of respect (see Krüger & Thamin, this volume, for a detailed account). True, home-school, educational partnership initiatives are thus relatively rare in France, with each party tending to stay within the confines of their own sphere of action, the professional at school and the parental at home.

Although Sylvie managed to swim against this current, she was aware that her practice of opening up the classroom to parents was seen as problematic by some of her colleagues and superiors:

> For 15 years there was an inspector, who still works for the Ministry of Education, who said, referring to me, 'I don't work with that school because the head teacher is crazy'. That's how it started. Because two school teachers had said that it was chaos in my classroom, parents in the playground, parents in the corridors, in the classrooms, headscarves in the school, well, everything you can imagine. (Interview, Sylvie, 26 January 2016, our translation)

These negative comments, related by Sylvie, equate the presence of parents with chaos and reflect the ideals of 19th century France when teachers strove to ensure that both religious and family influences would not enter the realm of school, believing that in so doing they were affording all young citizens of the République equal opportunities, free from outside interference. In direct opposition to these firmly held beliefs, Sylvie demonstrated the value of the parents' presence in a variety of ways, such as inviting them to participate in joint readings of children's books in their home languages, alongside French, or encouraging them to lead an activity with a small group of children. The extract below illustrates how she viewed parents as an important resource for the teacher too, enabling her to learn more about the children, their cultures, their languages and their practices at home, and how this knowledge allowed her to ease the children's transition between home and school.

> The parents' presence in the classroom inevitably changes the appearance and atmosphere of the classroom. It allows me to overcome ethnocentric behaviour and to know more about how the children actually live, what they regularly do, their values, their customs and to understand them better

and therefore to respect them more and communicate better with them. Entering into French culture can then be experienced as an additional asset which doesn't require the painful amputation of their home culture. (Sylvie's written reflections on practice, 21 April 2016, our translation)

Sylvie's desire to better understand the children's home lives and cultures demonstrates her ability to decentre as well as her sense of empathy for the challenges that parents and children were facing. She viewed the knowledge she gained through the parents' presence as fundamental to building communication and contributing to the children's well-being.

Using children's languages as resources

Extract 7.1 First day of pre-school, 2 September 2014

N.B. For the purpose of this chapter the transcripts have been translated from French into English, leaving the **original Turkish words** and adding (*their translation into English*).

		English translation
01	Teacher	What have you been doing? What is it? **Ne var**? *(What is it?)* What is it? [Child holds out something he's made out of playdough]
02	Child 1	[Unclear] **tatlı** ? (sweetie ?)
03	Teacher	What?
04	Child 1	[Unclear] **tatlı** ? (sweetie ?)
05	Teacher	A sweetie! Ah, OK! Is it for me? Can you eat it? [Teacher takes playdough and pretends to taste it]
06	Teacher	Do you like sweeties, you? You, do you like sweeties?
07	Child 1	[Nods head yes and smiles]
08	Teacher	[Smiles and gives the child the playdough]
09	Teacher	[Turning to child 2 who shows her her doll] Ah, G.! [name of child]
10	Teacher	[Turning back to child 1] Another one again? Two sweeties. **Iki** *(two)*. Two sweeties. Two sweeties. More? Shall we make a lot of them? **Çok çok**? *(a lot a lot)* A lot, a lot? Ok, let's make some sweeties.
11	Teacher	[Turning to child 2] Is that your baby? What's his name? [Points to doll] **Ad ne**? *(what's his name?)*
12	Child 2	**Bebek**. (baby)
13	Teacher	He's called **bebek**. He's called baby then. Ok. Look. Is he hungry? **Aciktum**? (I open?) [demonstrates giving the baby a bottle].
14	Child 2	[Unclear]
15	Teacher	Here. [Gives child bottle] Feed him. Sit down. Sit down.
16	Teacher	[Turns to child 1] Now then, how many sweeties have you made? One, two, three [counts as she points to each sweet]. **Bir, iki, üç** *(one, two, three)* [counts as she points to each sweet]. One, two, three. Shall we make some more? Ok, I'm going to make three too. One [counts as she points to the sweet]
17	Child 1	Oh, a lot!

In this extract, we observe Sylvie's use of translanguaging (Baker, 2011; García, 2009) – her spontaneous, purposeful and flexible use of the children's home languages as a pedagogical tool to scaffold their learning and foster their understanding (for a detailed account of her use of translanguaging in the classroom see Mary & Young, 2017b; see also Sanchez & Espinet, this volume, for a more in-depth look at translanguaging pedagogy). Although she herself was not fluent in any of the children's languages, she had managed to learn a certain number of words in the children's home languages which she then used to mediate their learning and understanding. These practices permeated her daily classroom activities as she spontaneously made use of translanguaging whenever the opportunity arose and provided support for learning and recognition of children's and parents' *funds of knowledge* (González *et al.*, 2005).

Our previous studies with pre-service (Mary & Young, 2018a) and practising (Young, 2014a, 2014b) teachers have highlighted teachers' concerns about using children's home languages in the classroom and their fear that these might somehow dampen a child's desire to learn the language of schooling. Although Sylvie had learned over time that merely immersing children in a '*bain de langage*' (language bath) did not provide sufficient means for these children to 'learn French well enough to catch up with their peers', she had already been open to including children's home languages in the classroom from the very start of her teaching in multilingual classrooms.

> I've always wanted to learn more about their home languages, even when I was at the primary level, I tried to learn about their cultures, at that time it was Arabic culture. You knew some words, some expressions, but that was it, and I did the same thing straight away with Turkish, [learned] some words. But what changed was that the more Turkish speaking children I had in the class, in fact I couldn't help it, the more I worked alone with them, the more Turkish they provided me with. In fact, in the beginning I learned things without realising it. But then again ... I was actually open to it. (Interview, Sylvie, 26 January 2016, our translation)

Resisting Dominant Discourses: Beliefs, Experiences and Knowledge that Contributed to Sylvie's Language Ideology

How is it that Sylvie was able to break the mould and resist such deficit discourses which viewed children's and parents' home languages as an obstacle to their learning and mastery of the language of schooling?

Below, we analyse and detail the origins of her language ideologies, in particular: her strong beliefs with regard to social justice; her positive vision/image of the children; her critical awareness of language and language acquisition; and her willingness to question the prevailing monolingual discourses and practices.

Critical consciousness and beliefs with regard to social justice

Crookes (2015) points to critical theory and critical consciousness (Freire, 1973) as the foundations on which teachers' critical teacher cognition and critical philosophy of language teaching can be built. The data collected during the semi-structured interviews and informal exchanges with Sylvie highlight the influence that authors working within a critical theory framework had on her own thinking and her interest in issues related to questions of social justice prior to her teacher training programme. She mentions reading one influential text in particular, *Lettre ouverte à une maîtresse d'école par les enfants de l'école de Barbiana* (Enfants de Barbiana, 1968), in her last year of secondary school. This text questioned the lack of equity in schools at the time and eventually inspired her to pursue a career in teaching.

> I remember that there was a definition I had kept for a long time that said 'school is like a hospital that takes care of healthy people and sends the sick ones away'. I started out [in teacher education] with those kinds of ideas. (Interview, Sylvie, 26 January 2016, our translation)

Sylvie's interest in critical views of education continued throughout her undergraduate studies in philosophy, where she engaged with the work of Pierre Bourdieu and Célestin Freinet, among other critical pedagogues, through works such as *Les Héritiers* (Bourdieu & Passeron, 1964), *L'école capitaliste en France* (Baudelot & Establet, 1971) and *Pour l'école du peuple* (Freinet, 1974), which proposed critical analyses of the education system and emphasised its role in reproducing social inequalities. Her critical consciousness and awareness of the lack of social justice in schools which developed during this time moved her to question inequitable practices and imparted a sense of mission early on in her career.

> I entered school [the teaching profession] in order to change school, and to provide children with the arms of emancipation such as reading, writing and mastering oral communication, etcetera, I thought that everyone was supposed be ready at their stations, in order to change society, but at that time we thought we could make a difference, could change society, achieve greater equality, more fraternity, well, we still haven't given up. (Interview, Sylvie, 26 January 2016, our translation)

The strong military-like expressions (**arms** of emancipation, everyone ready at their **stations**) used by Sylvie to describe her role as a teacher in society evoke an image of a soldier preparing for battle. Her philosophy of teaching had already started to develop prior to entering the teaching profession and imparted in her a sense of responsibility to change the school system and disrupt the status quo with the goal of changing society as a whole. This critical view of school as an unjust system fuelled her desire for change and served as a catalyst for her to challenge the system and to take risks despite being immersed in an environment which discouraged her from doing so.

Intercultural competences and positive image of the children and their families

During our exchanges with Sylvie we became aware that she had displayed various components of intercultural competence early on in her career. In line with Spitzberg and Changnon's (2009) definition of intercultural competence, she regularly displayed an openness to others, knowledge of children's and families' cultural identities and different perspectives and an ability to empathise and to understand the children and families in her classroom. She not only demonstrated openness but also strove to 'establish positive and constructive relationships' (Huber & Reynolds, 2014: 16) with children and families whose cultural background was different from her own. One factor she often spoke about was the importance of respecting the children's languages and cultures.

> It has always been my view that, long before the talk about bilingualism, about plurilingualism, I have always thought that it was good that they keep their language(s) … and to respect their language(s) and I always had books in the classroom that spoke about other countries, I always [had these] … even in primary school. (Interview, Sylvie, 26 January 2016, our translation)

This openness was part of her humanistic culture and was intrinsically linked to her understanding of learning and the belief that valuing children's home languages and cultures was a necessary step towards helping the children feel accepted and engaging them in learning. In the following extract, she explains why she chose to use the word *lahmacun* (Turkish pizzas popular with Turkish families) when interacting with a Turkish speaking child during a classroom activity. Her explanation focuses on her desire to communicate to children that she is aware that their home environment and the school environment are two separate worlds and on her goal of helping children make the transition between these two worlds in order to facilitate learning.

> [...] I think he's very familiar with the word 'lahmacun' [...] showing him that his world is not unknown to me, that there is not a separation between school and home, and that I know a little bit about what they are experiencing … for children, school is a completely sealed environment and closed off from the home … if the school doesn't have this approach … it's difficult for the child. They are two very very separate worlds. … I try to build bridges between the two. So, the fact of saying little words like that …, which refer to their daily lives, it's a way for me to try to show them that I know a bit about their, their daily lives too. (Interview, Sylvie, 30 September 2015, our translation)

This extract highlights her ability to see things from the children's perspective and to display empathy towards them. In addition to her efforts to understand what the children/families might be feeling, she also purposefully employs strategies in order to communicate this understanding to them.

Critical awareness of language and language acquisition: Beliefs about emergent bilingual children

Sylvie also saw the emergent bilingual and bilingual children in her class as being full of potential and capable of attaining the same targets as their French speaking peers.

> I was immediately struck by the difficulties of a number of children from immigrant backgrounds. Why did these children, although of perfectly normal intelligence, encounter so many difficulties in school subjects? This has been the leitmotiv throughout my career and I wanted to understand better in order to find solutions. After 17 years in primary education I wanted to go and see what was happening beforehand, in the first year of pre-school in the same neighbourhood. (Sylvie's written reflections on practice, 21 April 2016, our translation)

> When I worked exclusively with them I really discovered that they knew a lot of things in fact. (Interview, Sylvie, 12 January 2016, our translation)

We notice here that, in addition to her high expectations for these children, she also holds a view of them as developing bilinguals already possessing an important amount of knowledge. Instead of blaming the children or their families for the difficulties they encountered, she sought answers elsewhere. She questioned the system and exercised agency within her institutional context in order to better understand the different factors involved.

> ... I also saw their potential. Because they are children who have great potential, and have the opportunity to become bilingual. For now, it is not exactly the case, because it's not taken into account enough. (Interview, Sylvie, 30 September 2014, our translation)

Viewing these children as emergent bilinguals full of potential is in direct contrast to some of the deficit discourses prevalent among teachers and educators in many schools (Gkaintartzi & Tsokalidou, 2011; Moons, 2010; Pulinx *et al.*, 2017; Thomauske, 2011; Young, 2014b). She views the children as intelligent and capable and recognises the school's role in contributing to the underachievement these children were experiencing. She thus sets high, albeit attainable, goals for the children, in particular in the area of literacy and literacy engagement. Although she was concerned with the children's acquisition and mastery of French, the language of schooling, she did not focus solely on this but rather expressed an awareness of the importance of developing their home languages and of the positive impact the transfer of knowledge from one language to another would have on their language and literacy development, particularly through the use of bilingual picture books, as seen in the extract below:

> I have made choices, and my choice is to say that before entering primary school they have to be speaking, their speech has to be fluid and they have

to be engaging with books in French ... I tried to find, [...] means through which we can concretely ... and even now I think I'm only at the beginning stages with the strategies and tools. For example, there are translated books, I'm starting to have a lot of them but a lot more are needed. We need a lot more, a whole lot more ... I really think it's a good starting point that, lots of books, the same in their home languages and in French, and going back and forth between them. (Interview, Sylvie, 26 January 2016, our translation)

Willingness to take risks and reflect critically on her practices

As mentioned previously, Sylvie's ability to reflect critically and call into question the normative practices of her institution contributed to the development and evolution of her language ideology. This reflects Cummins' (2009: 262) claim that the exercise of agency or 'articulation of choices' implies 'a re-examination of the normalized assumptions about curriculum, assessment, and instruction that constrict both identity options for culturally diverse students and their cognitive and academic engagement'. We see in the following extract that calling into question the normative practices in her environment, 'going against the flow', was part of her broader philosophy of teaching and was seen as a means to make progress:

No, I'm not afraid. That's the difference, but that's tied to my political culture in its broader sense not in the narrow sense, I wasn't afraid of going against the tide. Sometimes teachers are afraid. And inevitably, I think that to make headway, you have to, at some point you have to go against the flow. (Interview, Sylvie, 26 January 2016, our translation)

Discussion

We have highlighted the inclusive language practices Sylvie managed to implement, despite being faced with monolingual deficit discourses in her environment and have described and analysed her experiences and beliefs in order to better understand the origins and evolution of her language ideologies. We now draw on our analysis of Sylvie's language ideologies in a bid to understand (1) how teacher educators might contribute to the development and evolution of pre-service and practising teachers' language ideologies and (2) which elements in curriculum development might move them to create more equitable classrooms for their multilingual pupils.

Our analysis of Sylvie's language ideology demonstrated that from the start of her career she was already capable of reflecting critically on the various situations and contexts within which she found herself. Whereas this reflection was initiated by her strong commitment to social justice, her knowledge and awareness of social inequity and the practices that contributed to it also played a key role in the development of her beliefs about language practices. How then might we as teacher educators draw on these findings in order to raise student-teachers' awareness of inequitable relations of power in the classroom and to foster their critical reflection and ability to question deficit monolingual discourses?

One starting point is to ensure that modules in teacher education programmes provide robust, research-based knowledge of issues concerning second language acquisition, bilingualism and identity investment (Palmer & Martinez, 2013), while also exploring the complexity of language and its relationship to social identities, discrimination and oppression (García, 2017) with the aim of critically engaging (student-) teachers with these issues.

However, as research has already shown (Horan & Hersi, 2011; Mary & Young, 2010, 2018a), simply providing student-teachers with this knowledge alone is insufficient to have a lasting impact on their beliefs, attitudes and practices as these (future) practitioners often come to courses with already established attitudes and ideologies about language which limit their ability to take on new information (Commerford, 2005; Garmon, 2004). When confronted with this newly acquired knowledge, students also need to be provided with opportunities to exchange, engage in debate and confront their views and experiences with others in order to gain a deeper understanding of the issues.

A second step towards critical engagement with questions of equity and social justice concerns efforts to raise student-teachers' sense of empathy and openness to other cultures and languages. Given that many students in initial teacher education lack first-hand experiences with linguistic and cultural diversity, teacher education programmes need then to provide them with experiences that promote intercultural competence and foster their understanding of the challenges their bilingual and emergent bilingual pupils and their families face. Designing tasks in which students are required to actively engage with minority groups (Dolby, 2012), experience language immersion/submersion (Suarez, 2003) or take on the perspective of victims of language discrimination (Rios *et al.*, 2003) have been suggested as effective means of raising student-teachers' awareness and sense of empathy.

To conclude, we suggest that a further and important way forward is to foster future/practising teachers' awareness of their own agency by presenting them with examples of culturally and linguistically inclusive pedagogies in action through the use of filmed extracts of classroom practices (Mary & Young, 2018a). One of the ambitions of this longitudinal research was that by presenting examples of inclusive classroom language policies, such as Sylvie's, we might foster a greater desire and belief in the capacity to act among (future) teachers within their institutional contexts. Our belief is that by providing access to actual examples of research-informed practice, supported by robust knowledge of second language acquisition and bilingualism, we might stimulate critical reflection in our student-teachers, kindle awareness of their own agency and thus foster their willingness to 'go against the flow', to disrupt monolingual deficit discourses and to develop and implement culturally and linguistically inclusive practices in their classrooms.

References

Baker, C. (2011) *Foundations of Bilingual Education and Bilingualism* (5th edn). Bristol: Multilingual Matters.
Baudelet, C. and Establet, R. (1971) *L'école capitaliste en France*. Paris: François Maspero.
Biesta, G., Priestly, M. and Robinson, S. (2015) The role of beliefs in teacher agency. *Teachers and Teaching* 21 (6), 624–640.
Bonacina Pugh, F. (2012) Researching 'practiced language policies': Insights from conversation analysis. *Language Policy* 11 (3), 213–234.
Borg, S. (2003) Teacher cognition in language teaching: A review of research on what language teachers think, know, believe and do. *Language Teaching* 36, 81–109.
Bourdieu, P. and Passeron, J.-P. (1964) *Les Héritiers*. Paris: Éditions de Minuit.
Commerford, S.A. (2005) Engaging through learning – learning through engaging: An alternative approach to professional learning about human diversity. *Social Work Education* 24 (1), 113–135.
Crookes, G.V. (2015) Redrawing the boundaries on theory, research, and practice concerning language teachers' philosophies and language teacher cognition: Toward a critical perspective. *The Modern Language Journal* 99 (3), 485–499.
Cummins, J. (2000) *Language, Power and Pedagogy: Bilingual Children in the Crossfire*. Clevedon: Multilingual Matters.
Cummins, J. (2009) Pedagogies of choice: Challenging coercive relations of power in classrooms and communities. *International Journal of Bilingual Education and Bilingualism* 12 (3), 261–271.
Derry, S.J., Pea, R.D., Barron, B. *et al.* (2010) Conducting video research in the learning sciences: Guidance on selection, analysis, technology, and ethics. *Journal of the Learning Sciences* 19, 3–53.
Dolby, N. (2012) *Rethinking Multicultural Education for the Next Generation*. New York: Routledge.
Enfants de Barbiana (1968) *Lettre ouverte à une maîtresse d'école par les enfants de l'école de Barbiana*. Paris: Mercure de France.
European Commission (2015) *Europe 2020: From Indicators and Targets to Performance and Delivery*. Brussels: European Political Strategy Centre. See https://ec.europa.eu/epsc/sites/epsc/files/strategic_note_issue_6.pdf (accessed 20 October 2018).
Freinet, C. (1974) *Pour l'école du peuple*. Paris: Maspero.
Freire, P. (1973) *Education for Critical Consciousness*. New York: Seabury Press.
Gal, S. (1998) Multiplicity and contention among language ideologies. In B. Schieffelin, K. Woollard and P. Kroskrity (eds) *Language Ideologies: Practice and Theory* (pp. 317–331). New York: Oxford University Press.
García, O. (2009) Education, multilingualism and translanguaging in the 21st century. In T. Skutnabb-Kangas, R. Phillipson, A.K. Mohanty and M. Panda (eds) *Social Justice Through Multilingual Education* (pp. 140–158). Bristol: Multilingual Matters.
García, O. (2017) Critical multilingual language awareness and teacher education. In J. Cenoz, D. Gorter and S. May (eds) *Language Awareness and Multilingualism: Encyclopedia of Language and Education* (pp. 263–280). Heidelberg: Springer.
Garmon, M.A. (2004) Changing preservice teachers' attitudes/beliefs about diversity: What are the critical factors? *Journal of Teacher Education* 55, 201–213.

Gkaintartzi, A. and Tsokalidou, R. (2011) 'She is a very good child but she doesn't speak': The invisibility of children's bilingualism and teacher ideology. *Journal of Pragmatics* 43, 588–601.

González, N., Moll, L.C. and Amanti, C. (2005) *Funds of Knowledge: Theorising Practices in Households, Communities and Classrooms*. Mahwah, NJ: Lawrence Erlbaum.

Hélot, C. (2010) 'Tu sais bien parler Maîtresse!': Negotiating language other than French in the primary classroom in France. In K. Menken and O. García (eds) *Negotiating Language Education Policies: Educators as Policy Makers* (pp. 52–71). New York: Erlbaum/Routledge.

Horan, D.A. and Hersi, A.A. (2011) Preparing for diversity: The alternatives to 'linguistic coursework' for student teachers in the USA. In S. Ellis and E. McCartney (eds) *Applied Linguistics and Primary School Teaching* (pp. 44–52). Cambridge: Cambridge University Press.

Huber, J. and Reynolds, C. (eds) (2014) *Developing Intercultural Competence Through Education*. Pestalozzi Series 3. Strasbourg: Council of Europe Publishing.

Jordens, K., Van Den Branden, K. and Van Gorp, K. (2018) Multilingual islands in a monolingual sea: Language choice patterns during group work. *International Journal of Bilingual Education and Bilingualism* 21 (8), 943–955.

Kremnitz, G. (ed.) (2013) *Histoire sociale des langues de France*. Rennes: Presse universitaire de Rennes.

Kroskrity, P.V. (2004) Language ideologies. In A. Duranti (ed.) *A Companion to Linguistic Anthropology* (pp. 496–517). Oxford: Blackwell.

Mary, L. and Young, A. (2010) Preparing teachers for the multilingual classroom: Nurturing reflective, critical awareness. In S.H. Ehrhart, C. Hélot and A. Le Nevez (eds) *Plurilinguisme et formation des enseignants: Une approche critique/ Plurilingualism and Teacher Education: A Critical Approach* (pp. 195–219). Frankfurt am Main: Peter Lang.

Mary, L. and Young, A.S. (2017a) Engaging with emergent bilinguals and their families in the pre-primary classroom to foster well-being, learning and inclusion. *Language & Intercultural Communication* 17 (4), 455–473.

Mary, L. and Young, A.S. (2017b) From silencing to translanguaging: Turning the tide to support emergent bilinguals in transition from home to pre-school. In B. Paulsrud, J. Rosén, B. Straszer and Å. Wedin (eds) *New Perspectives on Translanguaging and Education* (pp. 108–128). Bristol: Multilingual Matters.

Mary, L. and Young, A.S. (2018a) 'Black, blanc, beur': The challenges and opportunities for developing teacher language awareness in the French educational context. In C. Hélot, C. Frijns, K. Van Gorp and S. Sierens (eds) *Language Awareness in Multilingual Classrooms in Europe: From Theory to Practice* (pp. 275–299). Berlin: De Gruyter Mouton.

Mary, L. and Young, A.S. (2018b) Parents in the playground, headscarves in the school and an inspector taken hostage: Exercising agency and challenging dominant deficit discourses in a multilingual pre-school in France. *Language, Culture and Curriculum* 31 (3), 318–332. doi:10.1080/07908318.2018.1504403

Mary, L. and Young, A. (2020) Teachers' beliefs and attitudes towards home language maintenance and their effects. In A. Schalley and S. Eisenchlas (eds) *Handbook of Home Language Maintenance and Development*. Berlin: De Gruyter Mouton.

Mattheoudakis, M., Chatzidaki, A. and Maligkoudi, C. (2017) Greek teachers' views on linguistic and cultural diversity. *Selected Papers on Theoretical and Applied Linguistics* 22, 358–371.

MEN (2012) *Circulaire no. 2012-141 du 2 octobre 2012 relative à l'organisation de la scolarité des élèves allophones nouvellement arrivés*. Paris: Ministère de l'Éducation Nationale.

MEN (2015) *Programmes maternelle. Programme d'enseignement de l'école maternelle. Bulletin officiel spécial no.2 du 26 mars 2015*. Paris: Ministère de l'Éducation Nationale.

MEN (2019a) *La loi pour une École de la confiance a été promulguée au Journal Officiel le 28 juillet 2019*. Paris: Ministère de l'Éducation Nationale.
MEN (2019b) *Circulaire de rentrée 2019: Les priorités pour l'école primaire. Note de service no. 2019-087 du 28-5-2019*. Paris: Ministère de l'Éducation Nationale.
Moons, C. (2010) Kindergarten teachers speak: Working with language diversity in the classroom. Unpublished Masters thesis, McGill University.
Murakami, C. (2008) 'Everybody is just fumbling along': An investigation of views regarding EAL training and support provisions in a rural area. *Language and Education* 22 (4), 265–282.
Palmer, D. and Martinez, R.A. (2013) Teacher agency in bilingual spaces: A fresh look at preparing teachers to educate Latina/o bilingual children. *Review of Research in Education* 37, 269–297.
Pettit, S.K. (2011) Teachers' beliefs about English language learners in the mainstream classroom: A review of the literature. *International Multilingual Research Journal* 5, 123–147.
Pulinx, R., Van Avermaet, P. and Agirdag, O. (2017) Silencing linguistic diversity: The extent, the determinants and consequences of the monolingual beliefs of Flemish teachers. *International Journal of Bilingual Education and Bilingualism* 20 (5), 542–556.
Razfar, A. (2012) Narrating beliefs: A language ideologies approach to teacher beliefs. *Anthropology & Education Quarterly* 43 (1), 61–81.
Rios, F., Trent, A. and Vega-Castañeda, L. (2003) Social perspective taking: Advancing empathy and advocating justice. *Equity & Excellence in Education* 36 (1), 5–14.
Ryan, G.W., Bernard, H.R. and Beck, C.T. (2000) Data management and analysis methods. In N.K. Denzin and Y.S. Lincoln (eds) *Handbook of Qualitative Research* (2nd edn). Thousand Oaks, CA: Sage.
Saxena, M. and Martin-Jones, M. (2013) Multilingual resources in classroom interaction: Ethnographic and discourse analytic perspectives. *Language and Education* 27, 285–297.
Silverstein, M. (1979) Language structure and linguistic ideology. In P. Clyne, W.F. Hanks and C.L. Hofbauer (eds) *The Elements: A Parasession on Linguistic Units and Levels* (pp. 193–247). Chicago, IL: Chicago Linguistic Society.
Spitzberg, B.H. and Chagnon, G. (2009) Conceptualizing intercultural competence. In D.K. Deardorff (ed.) *The Sage Handbook of Intercultural Competence* (pp. 2–52). Thousand Oaks, CA: Sage.
Spolsky, B. (2004) *Language Policy*. Cambridge: Cambridge University Press.
Suarez, D. (2003) The development of empathetic dispositions through global experiences. *Educational Horizons* 81 (4), 180–182.
Thomauske, N. (2011) The relevance of multilingualism for teachers and immigrant parents in early childhood education and care in Germany and in France. *Intercultural Education* 22 (4), 327–336.
Wellington, J. (2004) *Educational Research: Contemporary Issues and Practical Approaches*. London: Continuum.
Woollard, K.A. (1998) Language ideology as a field of inquiry. In B. Schieffelin, K. Woollard and P. Kroskrity (eds) *Language Ideologies: Practice and Theory* (pp. 3–47). New York: Oxford University Press.
Young, A.S. (2014a) Unpacking teachers' language ideologies: Attitudes, beliefs and practiced language policies in schools in Alsace, France. *Language Awareness* 23 (1–2), 157–171.
Young, A. (2014b) Looking through the language lens: Monolingual taint or plurilingual tint? In J. Conteh and G. Meier (eds) *The Multilingual Turn in Languages Education: Opportunities and Challenges* (pp. 89–109). Bristol: Multilingual Matters.
Young A.S. (2017) 'Non, moi je lui dis pas en turc, ou en portugais, ou en, j'sais pas moi en arabe': Exploring teacher ideologies in multilingual/cultural preschool contexts in France. *Bellaterra* 10 (2), 11–24.

From a Monolingual to a Multilingual Approach in Primary Schools in the Netherlands

Frederike Groothoff

Peripatetic language support advisor in primary education in Amstelveen (NL) and Founder of LangWhich

When I started my first job as a primary school teacher in a school for newly arrived migrant pupils I heard myself and my colleagues say 'At this school we only speak Dutch' (the majority language in the Netherlands, and the language of instruction at Dutch schools). The multilingual identities and multilingual resources of the pupils were ignored because we as teachers were not aware of the assets of well-maintained home languages.

Later, during my time as a part-time PhD student at Utrecht University, I learned about culturally and linguistically inclusive pedagogies, which I immediately applied in my class. I, for example, encouraged pupils to compare a certain grammatical phenomenon in Dutch with rules in their home language, I asked my pupils to read in their home language once a week during circle time, and we collected beautiful words in many different languages on our word wall (we found out that 'dragonfly' is pronounced like 'helicopter' in Arabic).

When I started sharing my knowledge and practices with my colleagues, my principal allowed me to dig deeper into the subject. It resulted in me writing a language policy document for the school. Within a few years we changed our monolingual language policy to a more open one which supported positive attitudes towards home languages. By the time I left this school, there was a welcome sign in multiple languages, a book collection with books in many different languages, hallways with pupils' work in different languages, colleagues with multilingual practices in their classes, and a school song that included different languages and melodies from the backgrounds of the pupils.

It is quite easy to spread these ideas in your own (digital) network, although you might encounter a little resistance in the beginning. I started by sharing insights from research-informed practices with my direct colleagues and on Facebook. Then I explained how easy it is to adopt inclusive classroom language policies. Teachers can start immediately with, for example, a multilingual sign from the internet. The beginning might seem small, but it will result in something big: confident and happy pupils because their teachers are curious, respectful, and open towards their languages and cultures.

8 Rethinking Inclusion: A Case Study of an Innovative University Diploma Programme for Refugee Students in Grenoble (France)

Stéphanie Galligani and Diana-Lee Simon

Introduction

Grenoble Alpes University (UGA hereafter), situated in the heart of the French Alps, has long been a destination for migrants. Within the broader European context of unprecedented migration, numbers of migrants, refugees and asylum seekers on the university campus have increased considerably, raising important questions as to their place in the host country/university, the role and policy of the university regarding their language education, and indeed their integration and inclusion in society. Initially, informal initiatives of intensive French classes were launched in an attempt to meet the most urgent needs of refugee students. These, however, soon proved inadequate to deal with the influx of refugees. Since UGA's official policy is resolutely humanitarian – offering hospitality to refugee students and providing support and solidarity for their education, particularly their French language education – an innovative programme was initiated in 2015 leading to a new, specially conceived Diploma, at the heart of the present study.

Against a backdrop of European policy for the linguistic inclusion of adult refugees, this chapter explores the issues of integration and inclusion with reference to a case study involving French language education for migrant students at UGA in France. It focuses on teacher perceptions of their roles and functions in inclusive language education on the one hand, and on the importance of interpersonal relations between the teachers and refugee students on the other, revealed through the analysis of a series of personal interviews conducted by the authors. Furthermore, it raises the broader social issues of cohesion and surmounting social determinism.

Theoretical Framework on Inclusion: From Policies to Ideologies

The notion of inclusion will be addressed here on a macro level with regard to formal European language policies concerning education for migrants, where we trace a conceptual shift from 'integration' to 'inclusion' in official texts. This backdrop will allow us to re-examine the notion as it emerges in the field on a more micro level through the discourse of actors involved in the project, reflecting teacher ideologies in which inclusion emerges as a driving force and is inextricably linked to social cohesion.

From integration to inclusion, and beyond inclusion to inscription

Integration, a complex process: Towards a sociological perspective

It is worthwhile to distinguish between integration policy and integration. As Schnapper (2009) points out, the term integration is somewhat ambiguous. It refers both to policy and to sociology. In terms of policy, for example, France in the 1990s appointed a Minister of Integration (Kofi Yamgnane); today it sports a Ministry of Immigration, Integration, National Identity and Co-development. On the other hand, integration refers to a sociological concept derived initially from Emile Durkheim's work *Suicide* in 1897, but in common use by sociologists today. In the context of migration, integration has taken on pejorative overtones, since integration policy aimed at migrants and their descendants tends paradoxically to generate tensions and sometimes feelings of exclusion and stigmatization. These negative sentiments allude to the confusion between integration policy and the process of integration in society and, as Schnapper (2009: 21) rightly suggests, both forms of integration concern not only migrants and their descendants, but society as a whole. Consequently, a distinction between integration policies – in the sense of the measures taken to define and apply political will – and the sociological process of integration is necessary. The former are adopted by all European governments, while the latter – a social process – is more complex and subject to critical reflection and research-based knowledge.

Casting a retrospective glance over a century of research conducted by sociologists in the Durkheim tradition on interethnic issues related to the migratory phenomenon in the United States of America, Schnapper (2009) synthesizes what she considers to be the milestones. Her overview provides us with two important concepts. Firstly, she notes that processes of integration vary according to different domains of life in the community, or its dimensions. The cultural integration (Schnapper, 2009: 22) of migrants and their descendants – adoption of the cultural models of the host society – seems more readily achieved than what she calls their structural integration (Schnapper, 2009: 22), participation in different social spheres and in particular the labour market. These differences may generate social tensions and frustrations. Secondly, as a process, she underscores the fact that integration is not a simple, straightforward process. It implies social interactions involving complex affiliations in linguistic, cultural and religious terms as well as values, to mention but a few of the many facets of social plurality that come into play, and in some cases produce tensions and may even lead to marginalization or exclusion. In this perspective, a person is never entirely 'integrated'; integration cannot be considered as an absolute, but is dependent on circumstances and context. We now turn our attention to integration in European education policies where a strong opposition to the social phenomenon of exclusion has made the notion of inclusion central.

Inclusion at the heart of formalized European education policies

The question of 'inclusive education' was the subject of the 2005 UNESCO Report, *Guidelines for Inclusion: Ensuring Access to Education for All*, in a collective effort to identify groups of people who, for reasons of physical, mental or social impairment, were excluded from society. The report advocates 'education for all' as a means to afford equal chances to all individuals to participate in the development of their nations (UNESCO, 2005: 4).

It underlines the importance of teacher attitudes towards inclusion and advocates an 'inclusive approach' (UNESCO, 2005: 23) on a policy level. Attitudes of teachers are said to direct actions in classrooms and society. Inclusion is put forward as a guiding principle with important benefits for all refugee students in terms of a more enriching learning environment in which diversity is seen as a positive force. Education is seen as a powerful vehicle for empowering socially marginalized adults to change their life chances so as to be able to participate more fully in their communities. In this report, empowerment refers to 'acquiring the awareness and skills necessary to take charge of one's own life chances' (UNESCO, 2005: 28).

The question of inclusive education in EU policy documents thus originates from the importance given to the integration of 'special needs' pupils in mainstream schools, raising questions of cost and organization to facilitate such inclusion. This resulted in a reconceptualization of the process of inclusion, emphasizing the need to reorganize and innovate in schools in order to adopt pedagogical methods suited to the diverse needs of pupils. UNESCO views inclusion as 'a dynamic approach of responding positively to pupil diversity and of seeing individual differences not as problems, but as opportunities for enriching learning' (UNESCO, 2005: 12). At the core of inclusive education is the Declaration of Human Rights 1948, which states that:

> Everyone has the right to education ... Education shall be free, at least in the elementary and fundamental stages. Elementary education shall be compulsory. Education shall be directed to the full development of human personality and to the strengthening of respect for human rights and fundamental freedoms. It shall promote understanding, tolerance and friendship among all nations, racial or religious groups, and shall further the activities of the United Nations for the maintenance of peace. (Art. 26, *Universal Declaration of Human Rights*. See https://www.un.org/en/universal-declaration-human-rights/ (accessed 11 July 2019))

The vision of inclusion in education here is that of a complex, dynamic process: it applies to all learners without distinction:

- It is one that welcomes diversity and aims to respond to it.
- It is about removing barriers and providing equal access to education.

At a national level, these same principles find their echo in the education policy of the French Ministry of Education (MEN), published on 8 July 2013. In a complement to Article 2 of this policy, the Code of Education ensures inclusion in schools for all children without distinction. It ensures social mixing of the school population within educational institutions (MEN, 2013). Within this national framework, inclusive pedagogy aims at full participation of all pupils in all aspects of life in school and the community, without distinction regarding their impairments or the diversity of their profiles. Policy documents support the notion of inclusion in schools and thus support endeavours and practices that favour inclusion at all levels of education. Furthermore, at a European level, the UNESCO *Guide for Ensuring Inclusion and Equity in Education* (UNESCO, 2017: 24) stipulates that:

> Policy is made at all levels of an education system, not least at the level of the classroom. As such, the transition to inclusion and equity is not simply a technical or an organizational change. Rather, it is a move in a clearly philosophical direction. (Fulcher, 1989, as cited in UNESCO, 2017: 24)

In the context of migration, 'inclusion' is often associated with the adjective 'social' in order to designate a dynamic process implying responsibilities and concerted efforts made by refugees themselves, by Member States and the administrations of local or regional communities welcoming migrants, and by those of supporting social partners, the civil service and volunteers (European Parliament Resolution, 5 July 2016). The term in policy documents thus refers to a dynamic and interactive process for the individual and society.

Furthermore, the question of inclusion as a collective social responsibility is raised at an institutional level by the Council of Europe in a recent Report on *The Linguistic Integration of Adult Migrants* (Beacco *et al.*,

2017) where an inclusive approach is advocated. In this report, language learning is not isolated from other dimensions of inclusion. This implies that civil society, employers, associations of all kinds and language teachers ought to share responsibility for the linguistic integration of adult migrants.

These official texts confirm that inclusion as a value is a central principle within European education policies (Beacco & Coste, 2017). As a top-down model, the texts are destined to inspire and support educational initiatives for all.

Inscription: The preferred term within a socio-anthropological perspective

The terminology, particularly the term integration, is called into question from an ethnographic and anthropological perspective by Moro, an ethnopsychiatrist and psychoanalyst who has worked extensively with migrant children and their families. In order to adopt a viewpoint less tainted by the idea of domination of one group over another or of a group over an individual, she prefers the less ethnocentric term 'inscription' in society (Moro, 2012: 167). The latter refers to a dynamic social process involving the mixing and mingling of cultures and, from a psychological point of view, (identity) reconstruction. It signifies, for example, that the person adopts a number of French values, desires and symbols, yet without relinquishing or losing his/her identity. Furthermore, the process of inscription includes a time factor. It implies, according to Moro, a societal movement of change over several generations, and involves the building of new social relationships within the pluralistic context of contemporary France. She suggests that the word inscription be declined in the plural in accordance with the multiple affiliations – in anthropological terms – of social actors, tributary to mobility characteristic of contemporary, plural societies (Coste & Simon, 2009; Lahire, 2001). This term, and more particularly the societal process it alludes to, will be of particular interest to us when we reflect on the wider social relevance of relationships generated between the actors.

Against the above backdrop, we propose to adopt a micro perspective in order to examine the perceptions of the key actors in our study, including teachers, their representations and ideologies and the point of view expressed by the refugee students interviewed, with particular reference to the notion of inclusion, the term we have retained for the purposes of this study.

Education for inclusion: Teacher ideologies, roles and functions

In a recent article on language education for inclusion of adult migrants, García (2017) advocates a broad, translanguaging perspective and insists on the fact that teaching adult migrants effectively requires of teachers not only a departure from an authoritative stance, but also changes in their roles and functions. Before defining these, the concept of translanguaging needs to be contextualized. The term has come to be used to refer to 'the complex and fluid language practices of bilinguals and the pedagogical approaches that leverage those practices' (García, 2017: 16). In examining declared practices rather than discourse, we insist on the idea of students' holistic repertoires in both linguistic and cultural terms, and retain the following forceful principles behind translanguaging: building on existing strengths of learners, giving a voice to learners and enabling learners to 'do' language and to make meaning as an act of identity. We consider these specific features of translanguaging as highly pertinent within our analytical framework.

The new roles identified by García (2017: 22) include: *the detective, the co-learner, the builder* and *the transformer*. A teacher needs to be a *detective* in the sense of taking into account the adult learner as a person with his/her previous knowledge and particular ways of making meaning. The idea of the *co-learner* demands that the teacher be in a position to learn from the adult learner and provide opportunities for active participation, for doing. With regard to less distant relations, the teacher is challenged to be a *builder*, which implies stepping down from a high position and creating favourable conditions for interaction and learning. This implies bridging differences in age, gender, class, educational level, etc., accommodating differences and differentials, and providing stimulating learning opportunities that engage learners. Finally, as a *transformer* of the social reality of adult migrants, teachers 'must be ready to build on the human ability to re-mix and recontextualize; that is, to inscribe language performances and identities into new contexts' (García, 2017: 22).

In relation to the above theoretical framework, the two research questions retained are as follows: 'How can the process of social and academic inclusion be observed through the roles and functions of the different actors involved in the language training of refugee students and of what broader social significance are the underlying human dynamics?'

Origin, Features and Implementation of the Innovative Diploma Project: DU PASS B2

In 2015, the Director of the CUEF (Centre Universitaire d'Études Françaises) – a component of UGA specializing in French language teaching at all levels – designed a tailor-made language programme to meet the special needs of refugee students. This was largely a result of personal initiative at the outset. Having gained approval and financial support from the governing bodies of UGA, the programme is now certified by a University Diploma, the DU PASS B2 (*Diplôme d'Université Passerelle solidarité – objectif B2*; solidarity bridging diploma, aimed at achieving a B2 level in French). Designed to train refugee students whose studies have been interrupted by severe war and/or economic conditions in their home countries, it aims at bridging the gap between their pre-migration studies and pursuit of their courses post-migration. It thus enables them to reconnect with the university milieu while developing adequate language proficiency in French as well as gaining experience in academic methodology

(French for academic purposes). As the Programme Manager said in an interview, it is important 'that they become fully aware of what it means, in concrete terms, to be a student at UGA' [A6]. While the first semester offers intensive language instruction in French, the second invites refugee students to attend specialized courses in fields of their choice so that 'they really have a foot in the door' [A6] in preparation for building their professional careers. Her central concern is including the students in order to ensure their social and academic inclusion.

Admission to the DU PASS B2 is granted in accordance with strict criteria. Firstly, students have to be war or economic refugees, aged 18–26, and have to have been students in their home country prior to their arrival in France. In 2015–2016, students enrolled in the programme were war refugees from Syria, Iraq and other Arab speaking countries, whereas in 2016–2017 the spectrum was enlarged to Albania, Armenia, Sudan and Kosovo. Secondly, these students have to show a strong desire to resume their studies; they have to have been in France for a short period of time and to have previously acquired at least an A2 level in French with a B1 level underway. Some have studied French in their home countries while others have been given French tuition by volunteer organizations in France.

Of the 17 refugee students enrolled in the DU PASS B2 in 2015–2016, 15 gained entry into bachelor's or master's degree programmes at UGA in musicology, English, Russian and French as a foreign language, at the Grenoble School of Management or the Grenoble Polytechnic School. The Director at the time noted that 'almost all gained entry into their chosen fields and many of them validated their B2 level in French with extraordinary motivation, and it was not necessarily the most advanced students in French who had the strongest drive and achieved the B2 goal. Some did not manage to reach B2 level, but were still accepted by some Departments' [L17]. The programme capacity has been increased steadily, with 19 refugee students enrolled in the course in the second year (2016–2017) and 22 in the third year (2017–2018).

At the time of its conception, this Diploma was a unique example in the French university context. Since then, other French universities have followed suit; for example, Strasbourg and Toulouse Jean Jaurès universities both offer diploma programmes for migrant students to facilitate their integration within the French university system, as do Vincennes – Saint Denis (Paris 8) and Bourgogne universities, to mention but a few. At a national level, a network of 40 universities was founded in 2017, the MEnS (Migrants dans l'enseignement supérieur), to support inclusive educational initiatives in higher education.

Research Design and Methodology

This highly innovative Diploma programme at UGA aims to meet the needs of a sensitive sector of the student population with a view to their inclusion in mainstream courses and, as such, was naturally of interest to us as researchers within the same university. By conducting exploratory research, our aim was to offer insights into the personal implication of the key actors involved and provide initial feedback on the course, while enhancing the programme through deeper reflection on its academic and social relevance.

In order to acquire a deeper understanding of the ideologies and declared practices of engaged actors and their implications in terms of inclusion and broader social cohesion, the following research questions were formulated. (1) To what extent may inclusive ideologies and practices be seen as a driving force for transformation, both at an individual and at a social level? We intend to reflect on this vast question from a micro perspective involving a case study with wider relevance. (2) How do teachers perceive their own practices in response to the special needs of adult refugee learners in the university context? (3) In what ways are teacher roles and functions challenged? (4) What characterizes teacher stances likely to contribute to inclusion? Furthermore, we wish to pay particular attention to the broader social implications of the teaching-learning process in terms of the human relationships generated. We will examine the latter in systemic terms within the wider framework of collective action. To this end we draw on social theory as inspired by Mauss (2010 [1923–1924]) so as to highlight the subtler impact of the giving-receiving-reciprocating principle (Mauss, 2010 [1923–1924]: 161) at work, which we see as seeds sown to cultivate social cohesion.

In terms of methodology, a qualitative research design was adopted in the form of comprehensive interviews (Kaufmann, 1996) conducted with university staff and migrant students. Three key actors agreed to be interviewed, namely the CUEF Director and initiator of the course, the Programme Manager for the DU PASS B2 and a teacher of French as a foreign language within the programme. The choice of semi-structured face-to-face interviews seemed the most appropriate way to provide the interviewees with the opportunity to express their thoughts, beliefs, perceptions and personal implication. Conducted in French within the institutional context of UGA in March 2017, the interviews lasted approximatively half an hour each, were recorded with prior consent and then were transcribed for the purpose of our research. The participants were highly cooperative and generous with their time and spoke willingly of their commitment in personal terms. Our interpretation aims to reveal underlying values at the heart of an inclusive educational process.

A second series of comprehensive interviews was conducted with three voluntary migrant students enrolled in the programme: two male refugees – an Albanian student from Kosovo (V) and a Syrian student from Aleppo (M) – and one female refugee student also from Aleppo (H). Interviewing the students raised a number of deontological questions, not the least being their consent, their ability to express themselves in French and the sensitive nature of their itineraries. Consequently, the questions retained as a guide for the semi-structured interviews were limited essentially to their perceptions of the language class and their experiences of living in Grenoble. Volunteers were given the questions in advance of the interviews to enable them to familiarize themselves with the contents, reflect on their experiences and boost their confidence for the interviews which were to be conducted in French, the foreign language they were acquiring. Using the latter as a medium for the interviews might have been questionable, but the students appeared willing, courageous and proud to respond in French. Regarding their language proficiency, all had an attested B1 level in French (a requirement for enrolment in the DU PASS B2) and were working towards a B2 level as mentioned previously. Prior to the interviews, the students had met the researchers briefly. The class was thus informed that a research project was underway and invited to participate, helping instil a favourable relationship of mutual confidence necessary for the success of the interviews. Conducted in a vacant staff room at UGA, the interviews lasted a quarter of an hour each and were filmed, with the students' prior consent and with the researchers' commitment to use the contents solely for research purposes. The camera had been set up in advance and remained in a fixed position focusing on the interviewee. The transcription[1] of these interviews provides personal information from the subjects themselves on their impressions of the course and life experiences on the campus. Analysis of extracts (translated into English) on the theme of inclusion as it transpires in the discourse of the migrant students sheds light on social cohesion as a process.

Innovative Teacher Roles for Inclusion: Towards Transformation of Social Reality

Selected extracts from the interview conducted with the teacher are analysed below using the categories proposed by García (2017) to highlight the roles and functions that we believe potentially contribute to academic and social inclusion. Our interpretation involves a double process of mediation: interpreting the informant's message and translating extracts from French into English.

The teacher interviewed works with adult refugee students for eight hours a week (five devoted to French for academic purposes and three to French as a foreign language), and is a skilled detective as she chooses to focus on her students, their ability level and what they already know. 'I started off with very basic things, because B1 is also being able to present one's trajectory, one's course of study, so I thought I'd do that for two sessions, but it took two weeks, that's what happens!' [G18]. Furthermore, she skilfully chose practical themes directly related to students' immediate concerns in order to fully engage them: an oral comprehension task on 'how to succeed in my studies in France', for example, followed by written work on university documents, courses and timetables, etc., to familiarize adult learners with academic documentation and help them read and interpret it. These activities proved much more time-consuming than predicted: '[...] at first I thought it would take 15 minutes, but each time it took two hours, but then again it was important, because cooperation amongst students developed within the group and I felt it was important for the cohesion of the group' [G18]. Loss of teaching time is apparently compensated for by a gain in social cohesion, allowing for precious links to develop between the students as a group. She values and sows the seeds of social inclusion and cohesion, which she considers crucial as reflected in her spontaneous 'definition': 'inclusion for me, there is the idea of an existing group, being included in it' [G22]. As a work theme, she also focuses on 'successful studies in economic management' as a motivating factor inviting them to project themselves professionally, revealing her underlying concern for inclusion. This seems to be her unconditional priority: 'French for Academic Purposes, it [the aim] will be firstly to integrate in the university' [G18], translating ambitions of both social and structural integration.

Furthermore, there was evidence in the interview of her relinquishing her role as sole source of knowledge and adopting her stance as co-learner when she solicited their active engagement in an oral expression task in which they were invited to prepare a short talk on their country of origin as preparation for a written task requiring argumentation skills. This opened a space for personal expression reminiscent of identity texts (Cummins & Early, 2011) and for sharing of their personal knowledge with the group. This oral production task resulted in a talk on Armenia, in which the student spoke of the genocide, followed the next day by one on Azerbaijan, sparking off social and political tensions within the group. The teacher too was taken aback to a certain extent when the student discourse, aimed initially at 'developing oral skills', proved to be of a highly intimate and personal nature in terms of expressing real-life experience. As she expressed it: 'they were bearing witness and one realizes that it touches on very delicate personal issues, being their home country they have left ...' [G12]. These tensions were apparently eased, however, thanks to interpersonal exchanges she observed between the students themselves during break time. It is worth noting here that a task aimed at developing oral skills with a group of refugee students is by no means devoid of social meaning, the proof being that these students continued their discussions more informally during the break in order to iron out misunderstandings and ill-feelings inadvertently inflicted on their classmates. In this context, the role of the teacher as a builder is demanding and not devoid of risk as it requires creating and managing a space for expression of strong differing opinions, thus offering new challenges for orchestrating classroom interaction and putting mediation skills into practice, in some cases to maintain cohesion within the group.

With regard to her commitment and voiced didactic and pedagogical choices as well as ethical concerns, she could, on a micro scale, be considered a transformer of social reality in the sense of generating opportunities for social bonding and cohesion; indeed, analysis of her discourse reveals that her practice is fuelled by the concern for inclusion. Reflecting on the course, she surmises: 'this DU Passerelle B2, is the first step they can take in "security". I put it in inverted commas because they are all in a situation of insecurity [...] it is the stepping stone to successful integration' [G22]. Grappling with the notions of 'inclusion' and 'integration', she considers that: 'before integration there is something more local, they'll first be included in something, a programme which enables them to be integrated little by little, well administratively, culturally, etc., so there is social cohesion because they belong to a group which is recognized here in Grenoble, it's the university, its institutions [...]' [G22]. Her vision appears to a certain extent to embrace the complexity of the social processes involved in integration at different levels as described by Schnapper (2009), including both cultural and structural dimensions.

Since the above analysis pertains to one particular teacher, it can by no means be generalized. Nonetheless, we wish to underscore the fact that inclusion and social cohesion within the class as a group emerge here as core values in this teacher's agency and in our view may be seen as a driving force behind her ideology. It is worth noting that the Director, the Programme Manager and the teacher are all fully engaged on a personal level with the refugee students both within the university context and outside it if we take into account their involvement in voluntary work for associations devoted to social causes. Their strong motivation and personal commitment – beyond professional duty – stem no doubt from their involvement with migrants and their life stories, resulting in an acute sense of urgency and social responsibility.

Giving Voice to Adult Refugee Students: Towards Participatory Social Cohesion

Conducting personal interviews with the refugee students was motivated by the belief that their active participation in the research project itself, inviting them to express their personal feelings and thoughts about their experience of the French Diploma course and their lives in Grenoble, would reinforce their sense of belonging, in terms of academic and social inclusion. Giving them a voice, affording them a participatory place in the research discussions centred on the DU PASS B2 course and taking into account their point of view may be seen as a new space for inclusion and empowerment, of the kind that elevates their social positions, enhancing their status and as such creating new opportunities for reversing social determinism (Cummins, 2012).

The three interviewees struck a common chord, expressing their complete and unconditional satisfaction regarding the quality of the French course and teaching (contents, methods, materials and also the language laboratory, mentioned several times): 'Yes, we are very happy with the course. We have oral and written comprehension courses. We are punctual, serious students and we try to do our very best and our teachers are all ... well, just excellent! Excellent in their profession!' [V24].

Furthermore, a profound feeling of gratitude is openly expressed in very personal terms as illustrated here: 'I have deep feelings within me regarding the CUEF. It's not only the work, not simply the work they work with their hearts ... really each person who works here ... I don't have the words to express it, to explain your kindness, your work' [M22]. It is above all the human dimensions of the experience of the teaching/learning at the CUEF that are highlighted by this interviewee. He finds himself 'at a loss for words' to express adequately his deep sense of gratitude for the human kindness pervading the teachers' work. The teacher-learner relationship in its affective and social dimensions emerges as primordial; he is struck by the human values underpinning teacher attitudes and practice.

Well beyond granting access to knowledge, the university is above all a place where social relations are cultivated: 'Yes, in fact the good life in Grenoble for me began thanks to the university because as I told you I meet other students, and every time we go out together, to visit museums, mountains, so it was great for me' [M28]. The discourse brings to light cultural dimensions of their life experience: 'this course was not only linguistic, but also cultural, because it enabled us to discover the culture of French society, for example there were visits to town and trips to discover France' [H12]. Opening opportunities for social interaction and cultural discovery but also for bewilderment in confrontation with Otherness, these events and outings appear to contribute to their sense of social inclusion, while inviting renewed identity construction, activating an ongoing process of inscription.

The qualitative analysis of our interviews with teacher and learners has enabled us to show how teacher roles and functions are challenged, necessitating confidence, empathy and mediation skills. The social and affective relationship between teacher and learners emerges as a crucial factor in an inclusive approach aimed at sowing the seeds of social and academic inclusion, as well as fostering social cohesion.

Conclusion: New Perspectives

A conclusion in two parts will enable us firstly to widen our perspectives with regard to the broader sense of inclusion and cohesion as a dynamic social system. Secondly, a retrospective glance at our exploration of the Diploma project will enable us to highlight the strengths of the analyses, to point out certain limits and to suggest new perspectives for necessary continued research.

Collective action, social cohesion and inclusion as a dynamic system: The reciprocity principle or *'don et contre-don'*

Social cohesion is a central concern, but what evidence do we have, if any, of the process involving the creation of human relationships as a social system? We propose to reconsider the chain of actions engaged, by taking into account the deep ethical values that inspired them and their symbolic force in social terms. To this end, we look at the core values of giving-receiving-reciprocating (*donner-recevoir-rendre*) as played out by the actors in our case study, in light of social theory developed by the French sociologist and anthropologist Mauss (1923–1924). His observations and analyses of how primitive societies function revealed that giving (of goods, materials, etc.) was always followed by reciprocation, carried out in accordance with pre-established, underlying social conventions, giving rise to the triple obligation of giving-receiving-reciprocating. Reciprocity is thus the fundamental mode of interpersonal or inter-group relations. As Villa Correa (2014: 313) points out, giving is seen by Mauss as initiating a dynamic social process which generates and cultivates social relationships. Furthermore, 'all forms of exchange occur within structures in which actors are mutually or reciprocally dependent on one another for valued outcomes' (Molm *et al.*, 2007, cited in Villa Correa, 2014: 313). Giving thus constitutes a social system where the mutual dependence of actors exerts a binding force, and it is in this respect that it may be seen as contributing to social cohesion.

How can the theory of reciprocity be applied to our case study? The personal initiative of the Director in responding with unconditional generosity in order to 'find an emergency solution' by engaging her colleagues and launching the programme may be interpreted as a reciprocal gesture (reciprocating) when we learn from the data that she had herself lived the experience of exile and been welcomed and given a place (receiving) which enabled her to regain control of her life and continue her studies. The symbolic force of the initial gift (she) received, remains active and the refugees are now the potential recipients. The programme director, for her part, is conscious of the necessity for the refugees to become recipients when she recounts how a trainer-teacher (who had also arrived in France as a foreigner and been given a place) urges migrant students to accept all that is given to them by the institution and exhorts that they 'become aware themselves that they're in a different environment with different work modes and that they'd have to work very hard, and that they ought to take all that's given to them, all that's offered to them, to integrate and be able to pursue their studies' [A20]. The phenomenon of giving-receiving-reciprocating appears as an underlying leitmotif in the discourse, even if reciprocation on behalf of the refugee students in turn remains an unknown for the future. An active social process is nonetheless present, one in which inclusion is the central issue and the different actors create possibilities for progressive inscription and social bonding.

Strengths, limits and new perspectives

It may not be hyperbolic to suggest that the university as an institution plays a key role in the education and inclusion of adult migrants in society, equipping them to regain status, autonomy and expertise, to acquire language competency and academic skills so they may effectively reconnect with their desired fields of study in preparation for the future. As we have seen in this forceful example of an initially bottom-up incentive, it is a key arena for generating interpersonal relations with intricate social ramifications which may certainly function as a system with regard to social cohesion.

For such a programme, what, we may ask, are the key issues to be addressed in the future? Initially launched in 2015 as an urgent response to the dire needs of adult refugee students, such a programme's chances of survival in the long term may legitimately be questioned. Indeed, it has served as a model to other universities in the French context where it has inspired similar initiatives as mentioned previously, which is encouraging. It remains, nevertheless, a fragile component dependent on university policy and special funding in order to ensure free access for the students. It is also dependent on political and administrative changes. Dare we mention that the corollary for inclusion of 'the happy few' means exclusion for others, through lack of funds, means and resources?

Secondly, our modest exploration is but the beginning of a research project which needs to be extended and nourished by further research including classroom observation and assessment of learners' language competencies and attitudes, etc., including a diachronic study of students' university trajectories after the course and their inclusion in the workplace.

Finally, despite the limited scope of this case study, the interviews indicate how such a project can contribute effectively to the social, cultural and linguistic inclusion of adult migrant refugees in society, by generating and developing human relations. Moreover, actors become inscribed in a new network of social relations, thus enabling them to reconnect and pursue their studies under the best possible conditions, as fully fledged social actors. The impact in terms of empowering individuals and activating the complex processes of inscription and social cohesion is not, therefore, to be underestimated.

Transcription codes adopted :

L : CUEF Director
A : Programme Manager
G : FFL Teacher

Three migrant students in the programme :

V : an Albanian male student from Kosovo
M : a Syrian male student from Aleppo
H : a female refugee student from Aleppo

Note

(1) We thank Iulii Dolgova warmly for her much appreciated assistance in transcribing the interviews.

References

Beacco, J.C. and Coste, D. (2017) *L'Éducation plurilingue et interculturelle. La perspective du Conseil de l'Europe*. Paris: Didier.
Beacco, J.C., Krumm, H.J., Little, D. and Thalgott, P. (eds) (2017) *The Linguistic Integration of Adult Migrants/L'intégration linguistique des migrants adultes. Some Lessons from Research/Les enseignements de la recherche*. Berlin and Boston, MA: Conseil de l'Europe, De Gruyter Mouton. See https://rm.coe.int/the-linguistic-integration-of-adult-migrants-lessons-from-research-l-i/168070a67f (accessed July 2018).
Coste, D. and Simon, D.L. (2009) The plurilingual social actor: Language, citizenship, education. *International Journal of Multilingualism* 6 (2), 168–185. See http://www.tandfonline.com/doi/pdf/10.1080/14790710902846723 (accessed May 2017).
Cummins, J. (2012) Language awareness and academic achievement among migrant students. In D. Balsiger, D. Betrix-Köhler, J.F. de Pietro and C. Perregaux (eds) *Éveil aux langues et approches plurielles: De la formation des enseignants aux pratiques de classe* (pp. 41–54). Paris: L'Harmattan.
Cummins, J. and Early, M. (2011) *Identity Texts: The Collaborative Creation of Power in Multilingual Schools*. Stoke-on-Trent: Trentham Books.
European Parliament (2016) *Resolution of 5 July 2016 on Refugees: Social Inclusion and Integration into the Labour Market*. See http://www.europarl.europa.eu/sides/getDoc.do?pubRef=-//EP//TEXT+TA+P8-TA-2016-0297+0+DOC+XML+V0//EN (accessed June 2018).
García, O. (2017) Problematizing linguistic integration of migrants: The role of translanguaging and language teachers. In J.C. Beacco, H.J. Krumm, D. Little and P. Thalgott (eds) *The Linguistic Integration of Adult Migrants/L'intégration linguistique des migrants adultes. Some Lessons from Research/Les enseignements de la recherche* (pp. 11–26). Berlin and Boston, MA: Conseil de l'Europe, De Gruyter Mouton.
Kaufmann, J.C. (1996) *L'entretien compréhensif*. Paris: Nathan.
Lahire, B. (2001) *L'homme pluriel: Les ressorts de l'action*. Paris: Armand Colin/Nathan.
Mauss, M. (2010 [1923–1924]) *Essai sur le don: Forme et raison de l'échange dans les sociétés archaïques* (12th edn). Paris: PUF.
MEN (2013) *Loi no. 2013-595 du 8 juillet 2013 d'orientation et de programmation pour la refondation de l'École de la République*. Paris: Ministère de l'Éducation Nationale. See http://www.education.gouv.fr/cid102387/loi-n-2013-595-du-8-juillet-2013-d-orientation-et-de-programmation-pour-la-refondation-de-l-ecole-de-la-republique.html (accessed June 2018).
Moro, M.R. (2012) *Les enfants de l'immigration: Une chance pour demain*. Paris: Bayard.
Schnapper, D. (2009) Penser l'intégration. In J. Archibald and S. Galligani (eds) *Langue(s) et immigration(s): Société, école, travail* (pp. 19–31). Paris: L'Harmattan.
UNESCO (2005) *Guidelines for Inclusion: Ensuring Access to Education for All*. Paris: United Nations Educational, Scientific and Cultural Organization. See https://unesdoc.unesco.org/ark:/48223/pf0000140224 (accessed July 2019).
UNESCO (2017) *A Guide for Ensuring Inclusion and Equity in Education*. Paris: United Nations Educational, Scientific and Cultural Organization. See http://unesdoc.unesco.org/images/0024/002482/248254e.pdf (accessed July 2018).
Villa Correa, B.E. (2014) Les enjeux socio-économiques de l'enseignement plurilingue en milieu rural en Colombie: Le cas de l'Oriente d'Antiquoia. Unpublished PhD thesis, Université de Grenoble.

The Empowering Role of Teachers

Samúel Lefever

University of Iceland, School of Education

In our work with immigrant students in Iceland we have seen the impact that teachers can have on the students' academic, social and personal development. Research conducted with newly arrived young adults in secondary school has shed light on the varying roles of teachers which are along the same lines as those described by García (2017).

Repeatedly students talked about how teachers went to extra lengths to help them in their studies and social integration. They valued teachers who took time to dialogue with them, showed an interest in their lives, believed in them and accepted them for who they were (*co-learner*). As *detectives*, the teachers strove to recognize and build on the students' cultural and linguistic backgrounds, and by activating students' knowledge and skills, helped increase their academic engagement.

The teachers also put emphasis on creating conducive conditions for interaction and inclusion (*builder*). They wanted to break down possible barriers between teachers and students and build open and supportive relationships with the immigrant students. One teacher expressed his role in this way:

> They [students] don't really get to know a teacher very often as a person, they know them as an academic instructor, so once you break down that barrier, ... they might start listening to you when you start teaching them life skills and the knowledge that they need to get to the next level.

The teachers also wanted to help their students feel included, both at school and in their lives outside school (*transformer*). They encouraged them to participate in discussions, share their experiences and believe in themselves.

Our research has shown us how teachers, by giving students a voice and a sense of belonging, can play an integral role in empowering young immigrant adults and help them to become successful participants in society.

Reference

García, O. (2017) Problematizing linguistic integration of migrants: The role of translanguaging and language teachers. In J.C. Beacco, H.J. Krumm, D. Little and P. Thalgott (eds) *The Linguistic Integration of Adult Migrants/L'intégration linguistique des migrants adultes. Some Lessons from Research/Les enseignements de la recherche* (pp. 11–26). Berlin and Boston, MA: Conseil de l'Europe, De Gruyter Mouton.

Part 2

'Actuality Implies Possibility'[1]: New Practices of Inclusion

Note

(1) Cummins, J. (2019) Multilingual literacies: Opposing theoretical claims and pedagogical practices in the Canadian context. *Cahiers Internationaux de Sociolinguistique* 16 (2), 90.

9 Experiences, Challenges and Potential of Implementing a Participatory Approach to Designing Educational Material For and With Refugee Women in Greece

Roula Kitsiou, Sofia Tsioli, George Androulakis and Inaam Alibrahim

Introduction: The Glocal Social Context

In this chapter we have adopted the term *reception crisis* (Spyropoulou & Christopoulos, 2016) instead of refugee crisis, since we do not refer to a *new* phenomenon but to the intensity of the migration flows. Based on a global perspective of migration, the refugee flows have placed many European countries in an *in transit* condition. After the EU-Turkey Refugee Agreement, Greece became an *in limbo* country trapping refugees locally, preventing them from being reunited with their families and hindering European mobility in general. The glocal social context is consequently characterized by both local and global considerations about the phenomenon of migration. The prolonged forced residency of refugees leads to the reproduction of inappropriate reception practices and structures, racist attitudes and increasing xenophobia (Cabot, 2014).

In 2015, approximately 856,723 people arrived in Greece, whereas in 2016, because of the EU-Turkey Agreement, 173,450 people entered the country (UNHCR, 2016, as mentioned in Kourachanis, 2018: 4). Regarding the contexts that are of specific interest for this chapter, approximately 3996 refugees arrived in Lesvos in May 2016, and 5673 people arrived in February 2017. Regarding Athens, 5187 people resided in camps up to May 2016 while in February 2017 there were 5166 people.

A particularly vulnerable group within the refugee population is women. Previous research has shown that this particular group has limited access to public spaces which results in limited access to information as well. This is mainly due to their caring responsibilities which do not leave them time to participate in information-sharing activities and sessions/social events (see Project PRESS research data in Daskalaki *et al.*, 2017). Refugee women face particular challenges related to their gender, their roles and their positions both in their society of origin and in the host society (see, for example, Jabbar, 2010). In many cases they might have already been harmed by traditional practices in their countries of origin, where they may have experienced exclusion from meaningful participation in community structures or they may have been victims of sex- and gender-based violence or destitution (UNHCR, 2011).

Kramsch (2018), taking into consideration the intense social pace, points out the necessity for a critical approach targeted towards the human agent, i.e. one that takes into consideration individuals' feelings and human relations that seem to be threatened by rapid changes and mobility. Drawing from this perspective and applying it to the field of education, we may then perceive educators as cultural workers (Giroux, 2001) with an increased responsibility to act in a way that inspires their students to stand up for their rights. In this sense, education and more specifically language education plays a crucial role in creating women-friendly spaces and in raising awareness about women's rights, options and ways to fight for access to new paths with regard to their professional, family, social and personal lives.

The present chapter adopts an inclusive framework of approaching language education and aims to explore how a group of women with multiple languages, cultures, religious traditions, ages, life and professional experiences, as well as educational and professional backgrounds, have worked and interacted in the digital workplace of Skype and through email (computer-mediated collaboration), in order to create educational material for second language education addressed to women with a refugee background. Taking into account the special conditions of transit and limbo as the context of the whole endeavour, the group opted for empowerment and intercultural awareness-raising through dialogic and reflexive practices, while valuing women's identities through integrating non-Western perspectives in the final product of the educational material. The authors of this chapter have been involved in various stages and sub-teams of the project, as well as in the research that is presented here (see Figures 9.1 and 9.2).

The Project PRESS

The Project PRESS aimed to provide education to newly arrived refugees from various backgrounds in Greece. It was an initiative of the

THE PROJECT 'PRESS'
Interdisciplinary team
Scientific coordinator: G. Androulakis (sociolinguist)
PROJECT structure: **Axis 1**: Fieldwork Research on the Communication, Language, and Educational Needs and Expectations of Refugees (ethnographic interdisciplinary research: anthropological & sociolinguistic research) **Axis 2**: Linguistic, Cultural and Social Integration of Children and Adults **Axis 3**: Awareness Raising, Support Services and Long-term Educational Empowerment
Coordinators/ Main researchers: A. Apostolidou, (anthropologist), I. Daskalaki (anthropologist), S. Tsioli (applied linguist)

Figure 9.1 Project PRESS structure and interdisciplinary coordinating team

Hellenic Open University and was implemented from June 2016 to December 2017. It included a series of educational interventions, most of which concerned language education for children, adolescents and adults with a refugee background, in an emergency situation context (see Hos, 2016). In order to design and implement meaningful and appropriate actions for the target groups involved, the first stage of the project included interdisciplinary ethnographic research tools such as participant observation, semi-structured interviews, language portraits and discussions with refugees along with questionnaires (Daskalaki *et al.*, 2017).

The PRESS research team was composed of sociolinguists and social anthropologists (see Figure 9.1) who observed, recorded and reported the situation in the Greek context, identifying current needs and future aspirations of various refugee groups residing in refugee camps in three geographical sites in Greece (Lesvos, Attica and Thessaloniki) during the first phase of the project. The interdisciplinary ethnographic research carried out from October 2016 to May 2017 resulted in data that were analysed qualitatively following discussions with researchers from different disciplines. This analysis informed the work of other project teams during the second phase, which designed and implemented educational interventions for the linguistic and cultural education and integration of refugees of various age groups.

The focus in this chapter is on the Action: *Informal-Non Formal Education with Women* of Axis 2, which aimed at refugees' linguistic and cultural integration, and education through non-formal and informal learning interventions. It was implemented in two Greek geographical regions (Lesvos and Attica) using a participatory and interdisciplinary approach and included three cycles of development-implementation-feedback-reflection-review stages. Its implementation involved the collaboration of the following work teams: (a) the educational material development team, which constitutes the focus of this chapter; (b) the team of the educational actions implementation; (c) the women-participants in Attica and Lesvos; (d) the scientific consultant of the action, (e) the coordination

> **Axis 2: Linguistic, Cultural and Social Integration of Children and Adults**
> **Action "Informal-Non Formal Education with Women"**
>
> Educational material development team "Languages without borders":
> Profiles of the team members as research participants in the present study
>
> **Inaam Alibrahim** (coded as **IA**) (art educator, MA student-Language Education for Refugees and Migrants): Age group: 30-40 years old, refugee background (Syria), Arabic-first language, Greek-second language, English- foreign language. During the implementation of the project she lived in Athens (Greece). She was also member of the implementation team.
>
> **Mary Margaroni** (coded as **MM**) (anthropologist, Greek and German language educator, theatre studies among others): Age group: 40-50 years old, migrant background (Greece), Greek-first language, French-second language, English, Dutch-foreign languages. During the implementation of the project she lived in Liége (Belgium) and Thessaloniki (Greece).
>
> **Iro-Maria Pantelouka** (coded as **IP**) (teacher, MA student-Modern Learning Environments & Development of Educational Materials): Age group: 20-30 years old. non-migrant background, Greek-first language, English-second language. During the implementation of the project she lived in Volos (Greece).
>
> **Leila Moghaddan** (coded as **LM**) (BA in international relations, interpreter in Farsi): Age group: 30-40 years old, migrant background (Iran), Farsi-first language, Arabic-school language, English, Greek-second languages. During the implementation of the project she lived in Athens (Greece).
>
> **Sofia Tsioli** (applied linguist): Scientific coordinator of Axis 2 and Action 18. She was involved in all the stages and sub-teams of the project.
>
> _Action implementation – facilitators_: I. Alibrahim (art educator), K. Korozis (Greek language teacher), M. Mogli (English language teacher), T.-K. Tsintoni (Greek language teacher)
>
> _External Scientific Consultant_: R. Tsokalidou (sociolinguist)
>
> _Researchers of the present study_: R. Kitsiou (main researcher), S. Tsioli (researcher)

Figure 9.2 Participants in Action 'Informal-Non Formal Education with Women'

team, and (f) the scientific coordinator of the project. These teams consisted of multilingual team members including people with a refugee or migrant background (see Figure 9.2).

'Languages Without Borders' Team and Material

Focusing on the educational material development team, in this section we present and discuss (a) the team's constructed identity, (b) the principles and methodological approaches employed and (c) the educational material rationale and elements. More specifically, we draw on data mainly collected through four distant (via Skype) semi-structured interviews (duration 40–50 minutes each) with the four members of the educational material team. The interviews were conducted by two of this chapter's authors in Greek (see Figure 9.2) and the recorded data were analysed qualitatively. In this chapter we present and discuss several extracts drawn from these interviews, which we translated into English.

The chapter also includes reflective comments from one of the researchers who participated in all stages of the action as her thoughts could shed light on aspects of the interview data that are not visible to out-group researchers and could add an insider view/emic perspective. Table 9.1 presents the subsequent and concurrent phases of the fieldwork, the development of educational material, the educational interventions, the reflection and the review of the material.

The educational material development team

All the members of the *Languages Without Borders* team are women of different ages, educational and professional backgrounds and personal life status. This has resulted in building a multifaceted women's identity team profile integrating aspects of motherhood, (forced) migration, conventional and digital literacy skills and mindset, arts- and language-based shared vision for social change, activism, intercultural curiosity and empathy, love for teamwork, lifelong learning and serving the educational rights of underprivileged groups. All four of them are determined, active and open-minded women pursuing better conditions for living and for raising their children.

Their linguistic repertoires include Arabic, English, Farsi, French, Greek and 'bits of other languages' (Blommaert & Backus, 2013: 22) such as Dutch or German. The working language of their collaboration was Greek (mediation language). Maintaining or continuing to expand these personal linguistic repertoires in refugee and migration contexts or resettlement circles was reported as one of their main concerns for their wellbeing mainly for their personal lives:

> it is a great concern [...] not to lose, right, this contact with language and this possibility of expression, that I consider very very important, not only as expression but also as a fundamental let's say part of my own identity. (MM, Greek migrant woman)

This personal need seems to be further transformed and translated into an empathetic stance towards language learning, maintenance or sustainability as complementary options for relocating between different countries, places, cultures and languages. In addition, previous experience from working with groups with a refugee or migrant background indicates an increased understanding of their needs and culturally appropriate approaches so as to connect with them in language experiences that they have the opportunity to co-shape: 'she [referring to another member of the team with a refugee background] has amazing ideas and she comes in IMMEDIATE *contact with refugee population* and she is *the only one* who *we* trust regarding if something is *culturally sensitive*' (IP, Greek non-migrant woman).

The team's constructed identity can be summarized in the following extract: 'each one offers something that *the other one lacks* within the team' (MM, Greek migrant woman), whereas their team spirit is reflected in the material they have collaboratively developed:

Table 9.1 Subsequent and concurrent processes

Phase	Subsequent and concurrent processes						
Fieldwork research June 2016–May 2017	**RES** June 2016– September 2016	**RES** September 2016– January 2017	**RES** January 2017– April 2017	**RES** May 2017			
Action Cycle A September 2017–May 2017		**DES** September 2016– January 2017	**DEV** January 2017– April 2017	**I** May 2017			
Action Cycle B May 2017–July 2017					**REF → DEV** May 2017	**DEV&I** June 2017– July 2017	
Action Cycle C July 2017–August 2017						**REF → DEV** July 2017	**DEV&I** July 2017– August 2017
Final product August 2017–September 2017							**REF → REV** August 2017– September 2017

Notes: DES, Design; DEV, Development; I, Implementation; REF, Reflection; RES, Research; REV, Review.

It has *a united soul* [...] you will see that it is, as if it is one person that has created it but with many cultures and many cultural elements and languages. (IA, Syrian refugee woman)

Finally, the team's *soul* is multimodally represented in the painting 'Ballet Dancers' by Colin Ju, which depicts – according to MM – African women dancing. It has been included in the educational material and symbolizes, according to one of the team's members, a medium of their in-group communication through art. After the interviews were completed, we asked all of the participants to choose a photo, picture, item, song, lyric, etc., that symbolized their experiences from participating in this action. One of them shared the painting 'Ballet Dancers', explaining that it was one of the team's favourite pictures which they finally unanimously chose to include in the material.

Principles and methodological decisions

In this section we refer to the most important principles that informed our methodological decisions. The educational interventions aimed to develop a *space* of (linguistic) well-being for women (Frimberger, 2016). In other words, the main concern of the educational action was women's empowerment, through the development of their linguistic and social capabilities (focusing on the Greek and English languages) and through approaches that legitimize different linguistic-cultural features of their repertoires. The creation of educational material that *allows* equal access to all women of refugee background and respects their multiple identities was a significant challenge during the attempt we discuss here. The adoption of alternative approaches – other than the existing dominant approaches adopted for the Greek context – was necessary for creating meaningful and bottom-up sets of educational resources that could be useful for the here-and-now communicative and language needs of refugee women.

This actually means that educator-facilitators were strongly encouraged to adapt and transform the material, deciding together with their students what would be useful for them each time. Therefore, this data-driven material is perceived more as a resource to be used creatively and in specific spatiotemporal contexts, rather than in a predetermined way. In order to further tailor the material to the students' needs and preferences, the development team required the educator-facilitators to deliver daily reports including students' feedback about the content and format of the material that guided the various reviewing stages. Therefore, similarly to the initial stage of the ethnographic fieldwork that informed the open syllabus, the final product was again informed by women refugees' perspectives.

Specifically, the design's conceptualization was research driven (see the first two sections), and had the following main orientations:

participatory methodology, translanguaging, critical pedagogy, task-based learning and an arts-based approach.

- *A participatory methodology* was employed so as to take into account current language and educational needs and expectations, previous diversified language and educational experiences (see, for example, Hall, 1981), as well as the gender experience, as negotiated by women with several ethnic backgrounds. The participation of refugee women was active throughout the educational action (development of the educational material, implementation of the educational interventions, feedback, reflexive dialogues and revision of the educational material and interventions). In sum, 91 women and two men participated in the construction and realization of the courses in Attica and Lesvos. More specifically, 11 women assumed the roles of facilitators (3), material developers (4) and scientific consultants (4), whereas two men served as facilitator and consultant, respectively, and 80 women of refugee background with diverse linguistic and cultural *routes*, experiences and desires, who were mainly from Syria, Afghanistan, Iran, Iraq, and Erythruria, participated in and co-constructed the intervention.
- *Translanguaging*, which often appears in linguistically and culturally superdiverse (Vertovec, 2007) environments (see, for example, García, 2009; Li Wei, 2016; Sanchez & Espinet, this volume), was employed as a critical theoretical framework to explore and empower women in the process of using and expanding their linguistic resources across registers, dialects and conventional languages (see the following section), in order to question the repetitive monolingual approach.
- *Critical pedagogy* was a guiding notion in the project, as one of its principles requires challenging the dominant perspectives of one's sociocultural context and personal stereotypes, reviewing one's worldview and enhancing one's repertoires and resources in order to develop ways to struggle for one's rights, for social justice and for societal transformation (see, for example, Freire, 2001).
- A *task-based learning and teaching (TBLT) methodology* was adopted, as the emphasis was on realizing successful communicative events and not on language accuracy or defining levels of language proficiency (see Van den Branden *et al.*, 2007).
- An *arts-based approach* was used as a means of expanding the restricted perception of artistic expression from a supplementary tool for linguistic codes – as the dominant codes of communication – to a means of equal importance in the communicative arena through a social semiotic perspective (see, for example, Frimberger, 2016).

Furthermore, another important parameter of the material's design and philosophy is its interdisciplinarity, which calls for approaching language through the lens of other disciplines. This means that using the material requires the presence of professionals from other disciplines, such as nurses, doctors, lawyers and social workers who, along with the facilitators involved in language teaching, participate in interventions with topics such as women's health, women's political and social rights, violence, etc.

Another crucial aspect of this action's design is the concept of *space*. Educational interventions have been developed and implemented through a multi-level use of *space*. The writers took into account the *space* where the action's interventions were implemented, the *spaces* where women were staying and the *spaces* where they spent their everyday lives and where they accomplish most of their communicative events. This means that the material developed includes activities that may be implemented within a classroom, in non-conventional classroom-alternative spaces transformed into *classrooms*, such as in the case of conducting a class in the forest within a camp in order to talk about women's health issues – or in real everyday communication conditions, such as in a shop or walking around the city.

Finally, a highly innovative element of this material is that it includes 'bi-dimensional objectives' (Tsioli, 2017), i.e. there are educational objectives and learning outcomes with regard to both refugee women and facilitators. On a practical level, this means that facilitators take on a learning position in the educational process while taking part in the same communicative activities, sharing feelings of language uncertainty and exploring new linguistic and cultural routes as well as investing their identities in the process (see also Galligani & Simon, this volume, for similar accounts of co-learning).

The following extract summarizes the most important aspects of the material and its philosophy, as reported by the developers of the material:

> It is not linear [...] male, female facilitators in collaboration with and agreeing with the female participants co-decide, right, what they will use from that [...] various parts of the material relate to how to fight for their rights [...] it is an awakening material. [...] it is cultural awareness, pointing out aspects of a woman's identity [...]. (MM, Greek migrant woman)

Educational material structure and elements

The educational material (see the cover in Figure 9.3) is designed to be used with and for women with a refugee background and local women, as well as teachers and facilitators who are involved in the language education of women with a refugee background experiencing emergency conditions. To this end, an open syllabus was developed, based on themes that emerged from the ethnographic interdisciplinary (sociolinguistic and anthropological) fieldwork research (Daskalaki *et al.*, 2017) as well as from the data that emerged from the participatory approach adopted. The topic areas refer to women's identities, needs and interests.

Figure 9.3 'Languages Without Borders' educational material cover

The educational material includes three main themes (*Communication, Everyday Life* and *Human Rights*), and 14 tasks with sub-tasks. For example, concerning the themes *Communication* and *Human Rights*, they include the following tasks, respectively:

- **Task:** I share elements of culture (cultural repertoires): hairstyle or make-up.
  Sub-task: I buy materials and I create my own natural cosmetics.
- **Task:** I struggle for my rights as a woman.
  Sub-task: I create and publish a video for the protection of women's rights on social media.

Multimodality is employed using authentic resources (photos, videos, letters, forms, etc.). Four basic working languages are used (Arabic, English, Farsi and Greek) in a context of translanguaging – not in a mode of translation, but in a complementary, translingual way (Canagarajah, 2018). For example, linguistic features of *conventional* languages occupy their unique space within the spatial limits of the page and can be understood only in a complementary way with the other ones (see Figures 9.4a and 9.4b). For example, in the following task of social awareness-raising (Figure 9.4a), the digital article about gathering food supplies for refugees is presented using Greek for the activity's wording and the article's title (Figures 9.4a.1 and 9.4a.2), English (Figure 9.4a.3) and Arabic (Figure 9.4a.4) complementarily for the article's content, and Greek (Figure 9.4a.5) and Farsi (Figure 9.4a.6) for citizens' quotes within the article.

Using the metaphor of *complementary* and *substitute goods* from the field of economics, we may refer to the translation of one language to

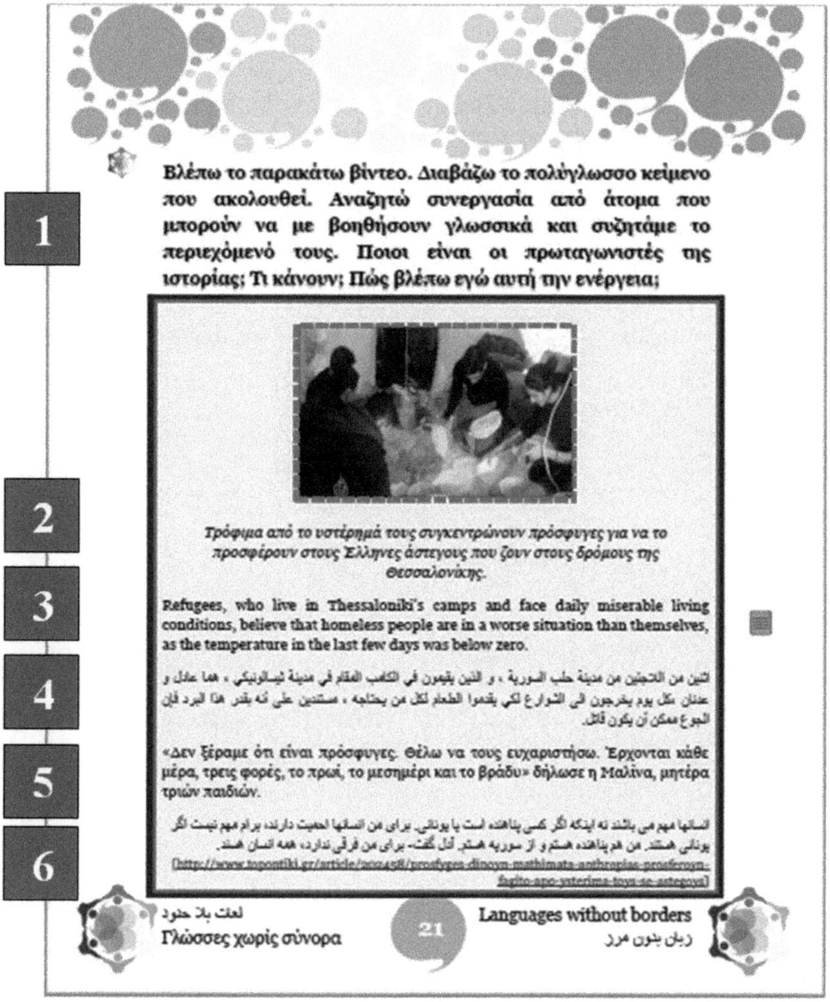

Figure 9.4a Translingual activities

another as substitute *goods*, whereas translanguaging involves languages as complementary *goods*. In this way we support the idea that languages in practice can cooperate in a complementary and inclusive way; they *need* each other in order to shape meaning. This notion is then transferred to students with supplementary repertoires who *need* each other. Students are encouraged to work together towards collaborative meaning-making in order to be able to address the requirements of activities such as the activity shown in Figure 9.4a.

To sum up, the project has attempted to: (a) bring to the surface and value the linguistic-cultural features of women's repertoires; (b) address

Figure 9.4b Translingual activities

the themes of the tasks through a multidimensional framework that reflects the various cultures encountered in the specific educational interventions; and (c) encourage the facilitators to use and engage with other linguistic codes and dialects, breaking down hierarchies in the participant-facilitator interaction. The translanguaging framework seems to promote the subjective and collective well-being of women participants and to create a sense of security that encourages women participants to express themselves within their group after overcoming their fear of a personal inability to carry out a linguistic task.

Working Together: Participatory Approaches in/for (Digital) Translingual Spaces

Working in the field of inclusive teaching and learning as researchers and practitioners requires being open, flexible and always ready to adopt alternative methodological approaches, if it is to benefit the students. Based on our experience from this action, we realize that this can be a very challenging and thought-provoking task, especially when trying to integrate different voices in one common final product in a respectful and critical manner, such as in the case of the *Language Without Borders* educational material. Being culturally different and working together was identified by research participants as the most important asset of the team. In this section we refer to some of the most important challenges faced by the educational material developers, the four women involved, while trying to collaborate through computer-mediated communication for the needs of this project. Specifically, we discuss the challenges and potential of working together with refugee or migrant women in order to apply participatory, interdisciplinary methods and innovative aspects of TBLT in conventional and unconventional spaces of non-formal and informal learning.

Challenges and potential of participatory approaches

Applying translingual practices

One key methodological decision cross-cutting all the actions of project PRESS was the adoption of a translanguaging framework, as mentioned before. This decision resulted from the fieldwork data which reflected the fluid and complex linguistic and communicative needs of refugee target groups (see Daskalaki *et al.*, 2017). Employing this principle, though, as a main guideline in a theoretical mode for the teams who would implement the actions of the project, was not enough. Each group had to negotiate and use its own practices and repertoires so as to decide and (re)arrange languages or linguistic features in a continuum of substitutive or complementary techniques in order to apply translanguaging.

One of the most important challenges the developers of *Languages Without Borders* had to face was how to integrate languages in a translingual and not a translational mode. In many cases they felt they had to write everything in Greek first, and then translate it into other languages. This mainly occurred at the beginning of their cooperation, since Greek was their mediation language. Not every team member was familiar with the concepts of translanguaging and translingual practices and the transition from theory to practice requires negotiation and imagination. In addition, the monolingual mindset that is implicitly preserved through national linguistic policies and is reproduced in everyday lives of citizens clearly affected their choices at the beginning. It was only after systematic cooperation that they managed to question stereotypical beliefs and started re-imagining the content of the page as a palette of many linguistic and spatial possibilities.

It would have been more balanced and creative, as reported by the Arabic speaking developer (see the data extract below), to use Arabic or Farsi as an initial resource of ideas and then translate these ideas into Greek, so as to offer additional ways to think about the worlds of women. It was difficult to avoid imposing the *Greek way of thinking* (if such a thing exists), especially with regard to matters of sociopolitical current affairs (see, for example, the digital article topic in Figure 9.4a). In this case, Greek was functioning as a restraining factor for translanguaging in the sense that in using the Greek language the material developers focused only on what had happened in Greece instead of focusing on what had happened across all the involved countries, such as in Iran and in Syria, in the here(s)-and-now(s).

Using Greek as a mediation language to transfer ideas originating in Arabic or Farsi seemed to function as a filter that reshaped the initial idea and preserved the power relations of that moment while bringing those linguistic and cultural features into contact with one another. On the contrary, using English – which was a second, third or foreign language to all of the women involved – also as a mediation language would have perhaps questioned the dominance of the Greek way of thinking. More specifically, according to the researchers' perspective, the Greek language was related to the specific sociopolitical load that dominated other ideas at the time, whereas English, while functioning as a second language or mediation language for them as well, was used in a *decontextualized mode*, in a sociopolitically indifferent way at the time of their collaboration. This may have possibly facilitated the practice of maintaining some distance from the initial thoughts and ideas that originate from different contexts, which were intended to be represented in the material so as to integrate snapshots of women's lives and practices and thus creatively integrate multiple perspectives. In this regard, one of the research participants stated:

> it is *first written in Greek* and then in other languages. Ideally it should be written from the start in *Arabic* [...] first a reference is made about something using some 'Greek' and then about something else in some 'Arabic' 'Farsi' [...] if there was *communication in English* maybe it would not have been the same thing. (IA, Syrian refugee woman)

Criticality and cultural sensitivity of the material

Developing educational material that is useful and that addresses the current needs of refugee women, who live in conditions of transit and limbo, requires making critical decisions about topics and issues to discuss, which are politically and socially sensitive in nature. From our perspective, education is conceived as a political act and drawing on critical pedagogy principles we need to rethink what may be critical for the lives of the specific target group, in the specific sociohistorical moment and across the sociopolitical contexts that matter to them. The spiral development of the material in three consequent circles was a crucial element of the process that guided the material developers to design context-based tasks including critical language activities in spaces of their locally defined everyday rout(in)es. This spiral development of the material was informed by the refugee women's feedback each time, after their participation in pilot courses (see Principles and Methodological Decisions section).

But how critical should the material be? The following data extract reveals the tension and difficulty of one of the four women of the team in answering this question:

[...] there were *different perspectives* within the team, we weren't sure up to which point we could go on [...] *to what extent* let's say on the one hand we *respect* the specific characteristics of *a culture*, let's say regarding issues like *children's marriage* or to what extent we could at least with a picture to give a hint so as to be *at the facilitators' disposal* and own will, if they will choose according to their team to work on this issue or to leave it out, because as the material works as a bank they have that choice. [...] *not* to create material that presents everything as beautiful and nice [...] *more thought-provoking* material that also addresses some issues that are not so good-looking, [...] *as a voice of support*. (MM, Greek migrant woman)

This question was not easy for the people involved in the action to answer and there were many discussions in order to make common decisions that would allow for all the perspectives to be represented within the material. Finding a balance between criticality, awareness-raising, call for action, resistance, change and struggle on the one hand, and cultural sensitivity on the other, proved to be a very challenging endeavour for the team, according to the ideological positions, ideas, beliefs and representations of the material developers.

For example, the issue of early marriage could be both seen both as a specific characteristic of a culture or an unwanted condition that should be questioned, and as a duty of the educators to raise awareness on this issue through dialogic and reflexive discussions within a critical pedagogy framework. So, the team members had to ask themselves to what extent their decisions were respectful of a culture or critical of unjust social conditions. In addition, feelings of empathy were very important in deciding whether to include topics that would perhaps put women participants in a difficult position by recalling traumatic scenes they or their loved ones had already experienced. For example, in an educational visit to an art gallery, some of the students felt offended because they saw some paintings that involved nude bodies.

So, it was not about which argument was the strongest within the team, because all perspectives were important in different aspects. The solution was to provide many options in the educational material and to render facilitators, in collaboration with students, responsible for deciding what was appropriate in each case, respectfully critical or critically respectful. The following extract is indicative of the issues of concern:

> a simple example now that doesn't concern only refugees, but the more general conditions, for example *it is not possible to speak* I believe about *how we cook this food* and that cake and the other one *and not to have pictures* anyway, stimulus *for reflection about ten hundreds of people who do not have food* or we cannot speak about what we wear at a *wedding*, and if the wedding dress is white or gold or I don't know what else, and not to *talk about children's weddings*. [...] but I can understand that this may bring forward negative connotations and to drag let's say into surface *traumata* from people and possibly the facilitators and educators not to have, not to be let's say qualified to deal with these issues, but for example, *I cannot even imagine that there will be educational material referring to women* that doesn't even include the *issue of female genital mutilation*, that I know they are very *sensitive*, on the other hand if we want it to be thought-provoking *material*, etc., at least I believe that *there must be a seed*. (MM, Greek migrant woman)

In designing educational material that promotes critical thinking and critical pedagogy principles and encourages awareness-raising of women's rights and options, cultural sensitivity may even be seen as a compromise to some of the actors involved. Then, one has to focus on what will be more useful for those women who will attend the courses. How could the material simultaneously work as an awareness-raising medium but also value their cultural baggage/capital? Through a Western-oriented perspective, some practices may be considered as traditional or *exotic*, such as in the case of clothing, working, birth control, interacting with men or interacting with women from Western contexts. On the other hand, team members were all very careful not to include cultural references that could have religious connotations; if the Arabic or Farsi speaking members said, for example, that a given picture implies a religious message, then they would immediately replace the picture with one that was accepted as religiously neutral.

Computer-mediated collaboration: Developing meta-working awareness

Working in a distant mode through computer-mediated collaboration was very time consuming but team members reported having 'gained team-ness' (a term coined for the needs of translating the respective Greek word that means *the quality/property of being, behaving and feeling as a member of a team*, 'ομαδικότητα', and using the morphology of the English word 'togetherness'), i.e. collaborating in a synchronous mode facilitated getting to know each other better and starting to feel a sense of belonging to a team. In general, taking into account the current modes of living and moving, many everyday tasks are realized in a distant mode.

Having the opportunity to work in digital spaces removes the restrictions of physical space and the borders of conventionally embodied working experiences, providing the actors involved with a palette of digital tools that have a great potential to construct and expand the borders of *conventional* translanguaging spaces that involve physical presence and to transmedia meaning-making (Tagg & Jankowicz-Pytel, 2016) in more complex digital or blended environments.

Additionally, team members tried different models of working until they arrived at their final work plan and working practices as a team. Specifically, at first, they worked individually and met in order to share and present, not negotiate, the outcomes of their personal work: this led to multiple voices and styles in the material that were not particularly student-friendly. Consequently, during the second phase, which was characterized as their 'most democratic phase', they met in a synchronous computer-mediated mode and completed every task together: i.e. they looked for resources together, decided upon wordings, pictures, order of activities, etc. As this practice was extremely time consuming and they realized that they would not be able to prepare the material on time, they entered the third phase of their collaboration style and method: they prepared some material individually but then decided upon the final shape and content of the activities all together through Skype or email. Trying out all these processes helped them to develop what they called 'meta-working' skills and knowledge. The most important characteristic of their collaboration is that they shared roles and every member's skills and capabilities were valued. In addition, they all claimed that they learned different things from each other, expanding their linguistic and cultural resources and their intercultural communicative skills.

Becoming Together: Language Education as a Dynamic Space of Mutual Empowerment

Participating in this educational experience, the four women, as educational material developers and members of a multilingual and multicultural team with a common goal and a shared vision, have tried to address the needs of the refugee women as participants in the educational intervention. In this endeavour they took into consideration the participants' views and tried to integrate different perspectives including their entire linguistic, cultural, social and spatial repertoires. This experience has expanded their resources and has resulted in the reconstruction of their identities through integrated perspectives. They have reconsidered Greek, Arabic and Farsi culture through dialogic practices, and have had the chance to get involved in educational processes after a long time working in other contexts. One of the research participants reported:

> I feel like a fish that has returned to its waters. (IA, Syrian refugee woman)

This is an extract that reflects this woman's professional self-fulfilment as a member of the team, and her performance of a professional identity in Greece. Moreover, translanguaging facilitated the women's capabilities to create their own translingual working space as reflected by the educational material as a final product of their practices, beyond the dominance of Greek and English as filters for Farsi or Arabic. In this sense their 'meta-working' awareness, a term they coined themselves, includes translingual practices and maybe – going one step further – transmedia meaning-making practices performed in digital spaces of interaction.

Blurring the boundaries among the roles of the teacher-facilitator and the student-participant was an important aspect towards recognizing language education as a mutual empowerment space. Translanguaging as applied here facilitated this interchange of roles, where both teachers and students participate with the potential to exchange and share resources rather than to transfer linguistic or cultural elements in a one-dimensional mode (see our discussion about using languages as complementary and substitute *goods* in the section on 'Educational material structure and elements'). We conclude that in such participatory approaches it is difficult to differentiate between who learns and who teaches, who designs and who reviews, who applies, who creates, who researches and who reflects. Participants have dynamic roles and alternate between learning, teaching or giving feedback to inform teaching, researching or learning, etc. Mutual educational empowerment occurs in an unforced way and within translingual spaces at various levels, including one or more languages and superficial or deeper levels of translanguaging (see Tsokalidou's typology of translanguaging, 2017).

In this way we may rethink translanguaging as transforming working and learning spaces into spaces of inclusion and mutual empowerment where complementary uses of languages require collaborative meaning-making. Employing translingual practices to design and implement language education may be an act of resistance to dominant ways of doing and experiencing language that helps personal voices emerge in their uniqueness and explore their creative potential. Understanding the relationships between conventionality and innovation in these translingual, transcultural and creative practices is complex. At the same time, it is most crucial given the current sociopolitical context so as to facilitate, in the long term, a form of critical citizenship and the conditions for agency, especially for women.

We have presented the challenges and potential that participatory methodologies can offer in terms of applying translingual practices in a creative and integrated manner that can result in meaningful educational material 'with a common soul'. There is still more to explore, though, if we closely examine how women *working* together also *become* together, reconstructing elements of their identities through focusing on aspects of their personal and educational *herstories* which include a reflection of the operation of agency in their educational lives and the ultimate aim of empowering all the women involved.

References

Blommaert, J. and Backus, A. (2013) Superdiverse repertoires and the individual. In I. de Saint Jacques and J.-J. Weber (eds) *Multimodality and Multilingualism: Current Challenges for Educational Studies* (pp. 11–32). Rotterdam: Sense.

Cabot, H. (2014) *On the Doorstep of Europe: Asylum and Citizenship in Greece*. Philadelphia, PA: University of Pennsylvania Press.

Canagarajah, S. (2018) Translingual practice as spatial repertoires: Expanding the paradigm beyond structuralist orientations. *Applied Linguistics* 39 (1), 31–54.

Daskalaki, I., Tsioli, S. and Androulakis, G. (2017) Project PRESS: Ethnographic approaches of refugees' education in Greece. *Proceedings of the 9th International Conference in Open and Distance Learning* 9 (4A), 19–33.

Freire, P. (2001) *Pedagogy of the Oppressed*. New York: Continuum.

Frimberger, K. (2016) Towards a well-being focussed language pedagogy: Enabling arts-based, multilingual learning spaces for young people with refugee backgrounds. *Pedagogy, Culture & Society* 24 (20), 285–299.

García, O. (2009) Education, multilingualism and translanguaging in the 21st century. In A. Mohanty, M. Panda, R. Phillipson and T. Skutnabb-Kangas (eds) *Multilingual Education for Social Justice: Globalising the Local* (pp. 128–145). New Delhi: Orient Blackswan.

Giroux, H. (2001) *Theory and Resistance in Education: Towards Pedagogy for the Opposition*. London: Bergin & Garvey.

Hall, B. (1981) Participatory research, popular knowledge and power: A personal reflection. *Convergence* 14, 16–19.

Hos, R. (2016) Education in emergencies: Case of a community school for Syrian refugees. *European Journal of Educational Research* 5 (2), 53–60.

Jabbar, S. (2010) *An Investigation into Adult Education for Palestinian Women Refugees*. Saarbrucken: Verlag dr Muller.

Kourachanis, N. (2018) Asylum seekers, hotspot approach and anti-social policy responses in Greece (2015–2017). *Journal of International Migration and Integration* 19 (4), 1153–1167.

Kramsch, C. (2018) Trans-spatial utopias. *Applied Linguistics* 39 (1), 108–115.

Li Wei (2016) New Chinglish and the post-multilingualism challenge: Translanguaging ELF in China. *Journal of English as a Lingua Franca* 5, 1–25.

Spyropoulou, A. and Christopoulos, D. (2016) *Refugees: Will We Make It? A Management Account and Recommendations for a Way Out*. Athens: Papazisi [in Greek].

Tagg, C. and Jankowicz-Pytel, D. (2016) From translanguaging to transmedia meaning-making. *TlangBlog*, 23 June. See https://tlangblog.wordpress.com/2016/06/23/from-translanguaging-to-transmedia-meaning-making/ (accessed September 2019).

Tsioli, S. (2017) PRESS axis 2: Linguistic-cultural and social integration of refugees. Paper presented at the Refugee Education and Support Workshop, 24 June, Athens.

Tsokalidou, R. (2017) *SiðaYes Beyond Bilingualism to Translanguaging*. Athens: Gutenberg.

UNHCR (2011) *Guidelines for Protecting Women and Girls During First Entry and Asylum Procedures in Greece*. Geneva: UN High Commissioner for Refugees. See http://www.isotita.gr/wp-content/uploads/2017/04/Asylum_Guidelines_en_nov2011.pdf (accessed September 2019).

Van den Branden, K., Van Gorp, K. and Verhelst, M. (2007) Tasks in action: Task-based language education from a classroom-based perspective. In K. Van den Branden, K. Van Gorp and M. Verhelst (eds) *Tasks in Action: Task-based Language Education from a Classroom-based Perspective* (pp. 1–7). Newcastle: Cambridge Scholars.

Vertovec, S. (2007) Super-diversity and its implications. *Ethnic and Racial Studies* 30 (6), 1024–1054.

Recognizing Parents as Resources

Sylvie Birot-Freyburger

Former head teacher, Dieppe Pre-school, France (retired)

At the pre-school where I worked for over 20 years, the majority of the children came from families who had immigrated to France and in many of the families one or both of the parents did not speak French. In this multilingual context, I always considered the parents as a wonderful resource, for me and for the children in the class, as they had so many things to teach us. They were often present in the classroom and I often positioned myself as a learner by asking them to explain a number of things to me about their languages, lifestyles and customs and about the different ways in which they interacted with their children at home.

Through our exchanges, we discovered many similarities between Arabic and Turkish, Arabic and French, and Turkish and French. I learned so many interesting things which helped me to better understand the families and their ways of doing things. I regularly sought their help regarding a wide variety of subjects, and also particularly encouraged them to support each other.

When we first organized French as a second language classes at the school, we thought about how to facilitate access to the classes for the mothers. We decided that classes would take place during regular school hours and that babies would be welcome and children would be allowed to move freely between their own classroom and the mothers' classroom. Within this context, the mothers continued to show the same caring and supportive attitudes towards each other, and the French teacher was able to build on the mothers' knowledge. This seemed to have an empowering effect on them. Instead of passively attending the class, they took it upon themselves to set up the room before the teacher arrived, make coffee and took it in turns to make pastries. They enjoyed coming to class; it was a space where they felt a sense of freedom and recognition.

10 Transforming Our Classrooms to Embrace Students' Multilingualism Through Translanguaging Pedagogy

Maite T. Sánchez and Ivana Espinet

In a second grade classroom at a school in Brooklyn, New York, Ms Martin (pseudonym[1]) directs her students to continue to work on a project:

> '*We are going to keep working in our language groups to brainstorm questions for our family members. Students who chose Spanish tables, please go to your table.*' [12 students proceed to two tables where there are laptops and tablets.] '*If you chose the English table, please go to yours.*' [Five students go to one table]. '*If you are in the Chinese table, please go there now.*' [Six students go to their table.] '*Jabir, I see that you are already in your table. Great.*' [He already has his laptop and has started searching for words in Arabic.]

Ms Martin's students are working on interview questions for family members about their own schooling experiences, in English and/or the family members' home languages. This is part of a project that culminates with children writing non-fiction pieces about schools around the world. At the Chinese table, one child is teaching another one how to write Chinese characters. Three boys also hover around a laptop, looking up words and writing them in Chinese characters. At the next table, Camila writes, '*Qué ropa usabas para ir a la escuela?*' ['Which clothes did you wear to school?'] She checks with her partner how to write a question in Spanish and then she continues writing. Jabir – who is learning to read and write Arabic in Saturday school – tells the teacher that in Arabic, you write from right to left.

In an eighth grade English language arts class with Ms Cooper, at another school in Brooklyn, New York:

- 'Quiet on the set! Camera ready? Three, two, one, Action!'
- 'Buenos días. ¡Bienvenidos a la escuela MS 22! En este segmento, vamos a presentar una variedad de historias sobre la gente sin casa. La primera historia la trae Rosa Barrios.' [Good morning. Welcome to MS 22's school! In this segment, we'll present several stories about homeless people. The first story is from Rosa Barrios.]
- Cut!

Ms Cooper's room has been transformed into a television studio. At the front of the class, three eighth graders sit around a table ready to share news stories that they wrote, two of them in Spanish and one in English. At the other side of the room, a group of students take turns fulfilling different crew roles. The camera operator sets up the new shot. The director helps her and tells Rosa, the next reporter, to get ready and look at the camera. At the other side of the classroom, two other groups of students are getting ready to record their news stories in Haitian-Creole, Arabic and English.

In this chapter, we focus on Ms Martin's and Ms Cooper's classrooms, two linguistically diverse classrooms in New York City that are formally identified as having English as the main language of instruction. However, these two teachers implement a translanguaging pedagogy in which students are encouraged to access their full language repertoire for learning (García & Kleyn, 2016). While these teachers have used translanguaging pedagogy to support students' learning of English, we specifically focus on how they have implemented a translanguaging transformative pedagogy that challenges traditional classroom practices that privilege English. These two teachers shaped classroom communities into learning environments in which students were empowered to perform multilingually, contesting the prevalent hierarchy that posits English as more valuable than other languages. Before examining in depth Ms Martin's and Ms Cooper's classroom practices, we will provide the context of the schooling of multilingual students in New York City and introduce the notion of translanguaging and its pedagogical implications.

Multilingual Students and Their Educational Experiences in New York City

New York City (NYC) is the largest urban center in the United States with almost 42% of the public school-age population in the city reporting speaking a language other than English (LOTE) at home during the 2013/2014 school year, the latest year of publicly available information (New York City Independent Budget Office, 2015). The top LOTEs that students report speaking at home are Spanish, Chinese (Mandarin, Cantonese and other), Bengali, Russian and Arabic (New York City Independent Budget Office, 2015).

When a new student is enrolled in a public school in NYC, state guidelines require that parents or guardians fill out a home language identification survey. If they report speaking a LOTE at home, they are given an English language assessment to determine their English language proficiency level. When their level is below a state-determined one, they are identified as a Multilingual Language Learner/English Language Learner (MLL/ELL) as opposed to an English Proficient (EP) student (New York State Education Department, 2015). In this chapter, we are using the label 'MLL/ELLs' to refer to students who have been formally identified through the state assessment as MLL/ELLs, while we use the label 'multilingual students' when we are referring to any student who speaks a LOTE at home, whether or not they have been formally identified. The latest publicly available data (2018/2019 school year) reports that between 13.2 y 13.7% of school-age students in NYC have been identified as MLL/ELL (New York City Department of Education, 2020, 2021), and 27% of students who report LOTE have been identified as EP (New York City Independent Budget Office, 2015).

Per federal, New York State and NYC laws, students formally identified as MLL/ELLs are required to receive specialized instruction that addresses their English language learning needs. New York is one of the few states in the United States that offers bilingual education in public schools (Carrasquillo et al., 2014), but the majority of MLL/ELLs (84%) receive schooling through the English-as-a-New Language (ENL) program where language arts and content-area instruction are taught in English using specific ENL strategies by either one dually certified teacher (in content and ENL) or two teachers, one being an ENL teacher. MLL/ELLs can be in a classroom solely with other MLL/ELLs or mixed with students identified as EPs.

As is the case of most multilingual students in the United States (Gándara & Hopkins, 2010; García, 2009; García & Kleifgen, 2018; Palmer & Martínez, 2016), and despite New York State and NYC efforts to enact policies to increase the number of MLL/ELLs in bilingual education (Carrasquillo et al., 2014), in NYC the great majority of multilingual students are educated primarily through English-only lenses (Menken, 2013). These classrooms can often be spaces in which multilingual students feel invisible or excluded (Suárez-Orozco et al., 2010; Valenzuela, 1999). Therefore, most of these students' bi-multilingual experiences are excluded from schools and are not considered to be assets that can enhance and support their educational experiences.

Bringing Students' Multilingual Practices into Their Educational Experiences: Translanguaging Pedagogy

For many years, educators and researchers have acknowledged the importance of using students' home languages to support learning the formal language of instruction (Celic, 2009; Moll *et al*., 2005; Valenzuela, 1999). The introduction of the concept of translanguaging in educational settings has brought into the field a more critical lens on the role of multilingual students' language practices in education. Baker (2001) first pointed out the term 'translanguaging' (translated from the Welsh *trawsieithu*) to describe a pedagogical strategy used by Cen Williams in which English and Welsh were used for different purposes (i.e. reading in one language, writing in another) in order to obtain deeper understanding of the subject matter, to develop the weaker language and for integration purposes. García (2009) then expanded the term to refer to how multilingual people use their linguistic resources flexibly when in multilingual communities. Otheguy *et al*. (2015, 2019) explain that our traditional notions of language (i.e. 'English' or 'Spanish'), are socially constructed categories, the result of historical and political processes of nation-state building during colonial and post-colonial times. However, when looked at from the internal perspective of bilingual speakers, languages have their own complex system of words and sounds that make up a vibrant repertoire that is constantly shaped by social interaction. Depending on the situation, bilingual speakers might feel more free (with language practices being more fluid) or more constrained (with language practices being perceived as more in line with one named language).

Translanguaging has reframed the understanding of multilingual language practices in education. It has highlighted that educational institutions have traditionally privileged an external named language perspective of language, while the internal perspectives of multilingual speakers have not been considered. Therefore, translanguaging theory and its pedagogical implications have highlighted the need for the internal perspective of language of multilinguals to be part of their educational experiences, not only to support the language of instruction but also because it is an essential component of students' lives and their learning. In this way, the complex and varied experiences of multilingual students are validated in their schools. Since 2011, there has been an increase in the research into pedagogical practices that support translanguaging in education (de los Ríos & Seltzer, 2017; García & Kleyn, 2016; Gort & Sembiante, 2015).

Teachers who understand that multilingual learners translanguage have a positioning – a 'stance' as García *et al*. (2016) called it – that recognizes that all of their language practices, not only in English, are essential for learning (García & Kleifgen, 2018). Teachers with a translanguaging stance understand that in classrooms with multilingual students there is an undercurrent that is always present: the diverse, fluid language and cultural practices that flow through classrooms, even when silent or invisible. García *et al.* (2016: 21) call this translanguaging undercurrent 'the corriente'. These teachers capitalize on the students' multilingual practices in instruction and understand that by disrupting monolingual language education policies, they can better serve the needs of bilingual students (García & Kleyn, 2016; García & Li Wei, 2014; García *et al.*, 2016; Menken & Sánchez, 2019).

Teachers with a translanguaging stance also understand that in order to bring students' home languages into their learning experience, they need to carefully design their instruction (García & Kleyn, 2016; Menken & Sánchez, 2019). García *et al.* (2016) state that designing instruction based on translanguaging theory requires three elements: instruction that capitalizes on collaboration among students; the use of multilingual and multimodal instructional resources; and translanguaging pedagogical practices, specific instructional strategies that allow students to bring their full language repertoire to their learning but also to show their 'linguistic virtuosity' (García & Kleyn, 2016: 23). Sánchez *et al.* (2018) have made a distinction between translanguaging pedagogy that is used for scaffolding purposes – to help children who cannot yet perform the school tasks in the language of instruction by using their home languages as resources – and pedagogy intended for transformation of the hegemony of the national language. The latter means that teachers design instruction to create opportunities for multilingual students to use all their linguistic resources to read, write and think in ways that challenge the language hierarchies in the classrooms, that mirror societal language hierarchies (García & Li Wei, 2014). In this way, translanguaging transformative pedagogy is a culturally sustaining pedagogy (Paris & Alim, 2017) in which the students' identities are affirmed and critically developed to challenge inequities that schools and other institutions perpetuate. While the use of students' home languages as scaffolding has been studied for a long time (Celic, 2009; Moll *et al.*, 2005), the transformative power of this pedagogy has only recently been documented (Ascenzi-Moreno & Espinosa, 2017; Espinet *et al.*, 2018; García & Li Wei, 2014; García-Mateus & Palmer, 2017).

The teachers whom we briefly introduced at the beginning of this chapter, Ms Martin and Ms Cooper, have participated in a professional development (PD) and research project called CUNY-NYSIEB which is framed on a vision of dynamic bilingualism and translanguaging (CUNY-NYSIEB, 2019). Both authors of this chapter have been Project Directors of CUNY-NYSIEB and have also provided direct PD to Ms Martin and Ms Cooper alongside other members of the team. We chose to study these teachers because, despite working in two linguistically diverse classrooms in NYC that are formally identified as having English as the main language of instruction, they quickly understood that classrooms with multilingual learners should not be spaces that posit English as more valuable than other languages. Instead they empowered their students to perform multilingually, expanding their practices both in English and in their other languages (García & Li Wei, 2014; García *et al.*, 2016; Sánchez *et al.*, 2018).

Methodology

In this study, we used a comparative case study approach (Creswell, 2013; Stake, 1995) of Ms Martin and Ms Cooper exploring the following question: *In what ways have these teachers implemented translanguaging pedagogy in their classrooms with multilingual students?* We analyzed field notes of classroom observations and PD sessions done by the chapter authors as well as other members of the CUNY-NYSIEB research team, student work and transcription of interviews (one with Ms Martin and two with Ms Cooper). For Ms Martin's class, we analyzed data collected during a four-month period during her first year of participation in CUNY-NYSIEB, while for Ms Copper, we analyzed data collected through a two-year period, in her third and fourth year of participation in CUNY-NYSIEB. We analyzed the data as per the guidance of Miles *et al.* (2013), involving first- and second-level coding. We then chose examples of classroom moments that showed evidence of translanguaging pedagogy, focusing primarily on transformative spaces (García & Li Wei, 2014; Sánchez *et al.*, 2018), given that there is limited research on this topic. Below, we will provide more details about these teachers.

Ms Martin

Ms Martin is a second grade general education classroom teacher in charge of teaching all subjects. She started her career nine years ago as a transitional bilingual education teacher before becoming a general education teacher five years ago. She also holds an ENL teacher certification. She learned Spanish as an adult and has always had an interest in other cultures and other languages. In 2018/2019, Ms Martin started participating in a 'racial equity' inquiry group in her school organized by the district that explored how to ensure that students see themselves in the work that the teachers do in the classrooms. She also joined CUNY-NYSIEB's 'Translanguaging Study Group' in which teachers of classrooms in which English is the main language of instruction from different schools in NYC, and who were interested in examining their own classroom practices, began to think about ways to design their curricula so students' languages and cultures were at the core. This group met monthly during the 2018/2019 school year and also received classroom support from the CUNY-NYSIEB team to help them implement translanguaging pedagogy in their classrooms.

Ms Cooper

Ms Cooper is an eighth grade English language arts teacher in charge of teaching English language and literature at another public school in Brooklyn. She is a veteran teacher with more than 18 years of experience teaching English language arts. She is the daughter of Jamaican immigrants. Over the years, she has learned some French and has come to understand some Spanish. She has also learned a few words and sentence structures in Haitian-Creole and Arabic. In February 2013, Ms Cooper's school was accepted into the 'Leadership Component' of CUNY-NYSIEB in which 14 schools in New York received PD sessions on translanguaging for a year and a half. Ms Cooper participated in those sessions but also received further individualized support with monthly and/or bi-monthly classroom visits to help her plan and implement translanguaging pedagogy in her classrooms. Once her school finalized its participation in CUNY-NYSIEB in June 2014, Ms Cooper continued to be actively involved with CUNY-NYSIEB by furthering the implementation of translanguaging pedagogy with the support of the team but also by sharing her practices with other educators in New York in face-to-face and virtual meetings.

In the next section, we present evidence of the ways in which these two teachers have implemented translanguaging pedagogy in their classrooms, with an emphasis on practices that challenge the hegemony of English in the classroom.

Findings

We present each teacher's practice separately. We first describe the context of each classroom and the reasons why each teacher was interested in translanguaging pedagogy. Then we provide examples in which teachers have planned instruction to intentionally leverage all of their students' language practices for purposes that go beyond solely their learning of English. Finally, we discuss the changes that these teachers observed in their students.

Ms Martin's implementation of translanguaging pedagogy

Ms Martin's second grade class had 25 students: 56% had been identified as MLL/ELLs and the remaining as EP, but almost 90% spoke LOTEs at home. Spanish was the more prevalent LOTE (14 students), followed by Mandarin (six students), Arabic or Mandinka (one student each). Three students spoke solely English at home.

As a teacher in a classroom in which English is the main language of instruction but with a majority of multilingual students, Ms Martin observed that many of them did not want to use their home languages in the classroom, or share about what was really happening in their lives. Over the past few years she has been growing more uncomfortable with the disconnect between the experiences that students have at school – all through English – and those that they have outside of school. Before joining CUNY-NYSIEB's Translanguaging Study Group, she had been encouraging her students to use their home languages among themselves, had partnered newcomers with language partners and had used Spanish herself to provide support to students who spoke Spanish, particularly newcomers. All these are considered examples of translanguaging pedagogy for scaffolding purposes (García & Li Wei, 2014; Sánchez *et al.*, 2018) in which home language is used to support the learning of the school's language of instruction, in this case English. When Ms Martin joined the Translanguaging Study Group, she shared how she had begun to wonder whether inadvertently, besides privileging English, she was also privileging Spanish speaking students over the other multilingual students in her classroom (Field Notes, PD Session, 8 December 2018). With the support of the CUNY-NYSIEB team, Ms Martin began to strategically plan instruction to intentionally leverage all of her students' home and community language practices and identities, not only to support their learning of English, but also to grow and expand them. In the paragraphs, below, we describe three such activities.

Ms Martin realized that the book *The Ugly Vegetables* (Lin, 2001) could be a great opportunity to bring her Chinese speaking students' culture and language into the classroom and leverage everyone's languages and cultural practices. The text is about a Chinese girl whose mom is planting vegetables that she calls 'ugly Chinese vegetables' because she does not like them. In the book, the mother tells her daughter the name of the vegetables in Chinese. 'This is a "xiao hu gua", Mommy said, handing me a bumpy, curled vegetable' (Lin, 2001: 14). At the end of the book, the character realizes her vegetables are delicious. After reading the book, Ms Martin asked the students who spoke Chinese to teach their classmates how to say the names of the vegetables in the book and to explain what they were. Then she asked all of her students to think about foods that they would like to add if they were to rewrite the book using their home languages. The children wrote names of foods on sticky notes in Spanish, English, Arabic and Chinese and they made a multilingual, multicultural class list. Ms Martin mentioned that this first activity was eye-opening because it revealed how excited and creative the children became when they had a chance to share their knowledge of their languages and cultures (Field Notes, PD Session, 8 December 2018).

Then, Ms Martin designed an activity in which students had the option of trying translanguaging in writing. She knew the students had different levels of literacies in their home language but because their schooling had been done solely in English, they had few opportunities to practice them in school. After going on a field trip, she asked the children to choose someone with whom they would like to share what they learned on the trip; most of them selected a family member. She told the children: 'Think about what language does that person feels most comfortable speaking. If you want, you can use it to write to them. You can include a word, a sentence, or write everything in it.' Ms Martin then organized the classroom in different language tables, according to the languages in which the children chose to write their pieces (English, Spanish, Chinese and Arabic). Since many of the children needed help with translating words, Ms Martin let them use an online translation tool. Those students who had had some literacy instruction in their home language helped others at their tables, becoming the experts. Some multilingual students wrote full sentences in their home languages, while others wrote mostly in English with a few words in other languages. As the class worked, one student whose father is from Mexico commented: 'Now my dad will be able to read it!' The students were also curious to learn about each other's languages. For example, another student who spoke English and Mandinka at home chose to sit at the Spanish table because she wanted to share what she had learned during the field trip with a friend who spoke Spanish. Some students asked classmates from different tables how to say some of the words that they were writing (Field Notes, PD Session, 26 January 2019).

This experience inspired Ms Martin to revise the ways in which she had used a book from the school's curriculum, 'Schools around the World', in order to bring students' multilingualism and their families' experiences into her classroom. We shared a small glimpse of it in the vignette at the beginning of this chapter (Field Notes, Classroom Observation, 6 February 2019). Ms Martin started this redesigned project by reading the book and asking her students what they knew about their parents' schooling experiences. She then proposed that the children interview their parents, in the language that they speak with them, so they could learn more about their schooling experiences or what they did instead of going to school, and to write non-fiction pieces about them. Ms Martin modeled how to write interview questions and gave her students the option to work in language tables to write in their home languages. Students chose to write questions for family members in Mandarin, Spanish, Arabic and English. They collaborated and helped each other in writing and in looking for words through internet translation sites (Field Notes, Classroom Observation, 6 February 2019).

After implementing these three activities in which students' home language, literacies and cultures were included and expanded, Ms Martin reflected that she had seen changes in her multilingual students. Her students were used to performing in English-only at school, but they started to feel that their bilingualism was an asset and something of which to be proud. She commented on the students' participation in their language tables and the changes she had seen in the students' use of their home languages in her classroom:

> Once they're doing this work [in their language tables] they're saying it [in Spanish or Chinese], 'Who knows how to say this?' They're sharing, they're talking [in English and in their home languages.] And even some students were not writing the question [that I asked], they were writing other things [in their home languages with the help of] Google translate. But I'm glad, because that means they're happy, they're having fun, they're using their home languages also in the classroom. (Personal communication, 6 February 2019)

Ms Martin described how one of her students, whose parents speak Spanish but who has never received instruction in Spanish, 'really wants to write in Spanish with his parents. So that's interesting, and he's really trying [to write in Spanish]' (Personal communication, 6 February 2019). She also commented on another student whose family is from Yemen and who had received some instruction at home in Arabic. He is the only Arabic speaker in the class, so he does not have a language partner in his language table, 'but he's so motivated. He just goes off [to work on Arabic]. He's by himself, he's writing, he's really, really engaged. So that's also really, really nice to see' (Personal communication, 6 February 2019).

The three examples of instruction that Ms Martin implemented in her class are examples of translanguaging transformative pedagogy (García & Li Wei, 2014; Sánchez et al., 2018), in which multilingualism is the norm, rather than an English-only space that invisibilizes her students' multilingual language practices and those of their families.

Ms Cooper's implementation of translanguaging pedagogy

Ms Cooper, who taught eighth grade classes for the two years for which we collected data, had a similar student demographic: 19–20 students, approximately a third of them identified as MLL/ELLs, with a handful of them being recent arrivals to the United States, and the remainder as EP. However, most of them spoke languages other than English at home, including Spanish, Haitian-Creole, Arabic, Bengali, French and Fulani.

Ms Cooper collaborated with an ENL teacher who came to her classroom three times a week to provide support to the students who were classified as MLL/ELLs. She realized that solely relying on the ENL teacher was not enough if she wanted to support her multilingual students (Field Notes, PD Session, 10 November 2014). The analysis of field notes from classroom visits from January 2014 through May 2015 shows that with the support of the CUNY-NYSIEB team, Ms Cooper developed a translanguaging pedagogy that leveraged her students' use of their home languages to access content and develop and share their ideas, even when producing a final product in English. For example, she searched for translations of books that she used in her class. At the beginning of each unit, she created a multilingual word wall with the key vocabulary for the unit. For multilingual students in the early stages of English development, she also created and distributed handouts with instructions in English and in other languages. She used internet translation tools but also asked for support from the school community and students to help her with translations. As she started developing these practices, she noticed that her newcomer students were able to participate in class and contribute to the class community in more meaningful ways. She also noted that students labeled as EP started sharing that they also spoke languages other than English in their homes (Field Notes, PD Session, 6 February 2015). But Ms Cooper's translanguaging practices went beyond their use as scaffolding for newcomer students so that they could learn English. She also carefully planned lessons where multilingualism, and not English-only, was the norm. In the paragraphs below, we will describe two such activities aimed at creating spaces to transform her classroom into a multilingual learning environment (García & Li Wei, 2014; Sánchez et al., 2018).

The first project in which Ms Cooper allowed the students' multilingualism, and not English, to be at the center of instruction happened in 2016, when she engaged the students in writing multilingual poems based on their New Year's traditions. Firstly, the students read the poem, '1975: Year of the Cat' from the book *Inside Out and Back Again* (Lai, 2011), about a New Year's Day in Vietnam, where the author translanguages in writing in Vietnamese and English. Rather than finding the English translation of the words in Vietnamese, Ms Cooper asked the students to write, in their language of choice, about why the author chose to include words in Vietnamese and not include the English translation, and then to discuss this with the group. The students had lively discussions about the author's interest in showing her culture, her language and the bilingual practices of her community. Ms Cooper then asked the students to share their families' New Year's traditions and write a poem about them. She encouraged them to include words from their home languages when they made sense in the text. At the end of the project, the students read their poems aloud to the rest of the class. They included New Year's traditions from Haiti, the Dominican Republic, Yemen, El Salvador, Jamaica, Bangladesh, Mexico and others (Ebe & Chapman-Santiago, 2016). Ms Cooper commented that this first project inspired her to continue to create spaces for projects that leverage students' translanguaging in her classroom, rather than having solely English-medium ones (Field Notes, PD Session, 8 February 2016).

The vignette at the beginning of this chapter described the last stages of a project in Ms Cooper's class in which her multilingual students worked on a unit about social issues and whose final product was a multilingual newscast. The project began with the students discussing what constitutes a social issue, and brainstorming personal connections to those issues in the language of their choice (Field Notes, Classroom Observation, 17 May 2016). Each student wrote a first draft of a story using their home language, English or both. One of the students wrote about a friend from school in her home country who had lost a house in a fire, another wrote about domestic violence and a number of them wrote about police harassment. Inspired by a culturally sustaining pedagogy (Paris & Alim, 2017), Ms. Cooper then asked the students to critically investigate and peel back how oppressive institutions and policies that are historically created connect to their issues. After doing research, including using multilingual newspapers, each student revised their original writing to produce a news report that combined the personal stories with the research that they had gathered. The students could write it in English, in their home language or in both (Field Notes, Classroom Observation, 3 June 2016).

Then, students worked in multilingual groups to videotape a newscast featuring their individual stories. In preparation for having students create their newscast, Ms Cooper introduced the students to the various crew roles (director, camera operator, news anchor and reporters). Each group planned a segment that would feature the individual stories using the students' home languages and English. Once the students finalized the videos, Ms Cooper showed them in her other classrooms, and to her colleagues (Field Notes, Classroom Observation, 14 June 2016).

These classroom examples highlight the collaborative work that multilingual students in Ms Cooper's classes engaged with that provided opportunities to translanguage as they make sense of new content and produce written and creative work in multiple languages to construct new knowledge, demonstrate their learning and highlight multilingual and critical-thinking resources that students bring (García *et al.*, 2016). Ms Cooper reflected on her experiences with her students as they translanguaged in the classroom:

> Students are more aware (about all their languages and cultures), and more sympathetic, empathetic, and well-informed (…) Having them have their voice, it's always empowering. So, that's my favorite; I love that. I love when the students feel that they have a voice, and it's not just me (…) And they get to appreciate each others' language. (Personal communication, 30 November 2016)

By allowing the students to draw from their full linguistic repertoire into the classroom, Ms Cooper increased the amount and complexity of the students' participation, allowed them to voice their ideas and opinions and showed that English is not the only language that is valued in her classroom (García & Li Wei, 2014; García *et al.*, 2016; Sánchez *et al.*, 2018).

Bringing Students' Multilingualism into the Classroom to Transform Language Hierarchies

The majority of multilingual students in New York, as in the rest of the United States, attend English-only school environments with the explicit goal of learning solely English (Gándara & Hopkins, 2010; García, 2009; García & Kleifgen, 2018; Palmer & Martínez, 2016). These classrooms can often be spaces in which multilingual learners feel excluded or invisible (Suárez-Orozco et al., 2010; Valenzuela, 1999). While Ms Martin's and Ms Cooper's classrooms are formally identified as English-medium ones, they have made efforts to design and implement instructional spaces in their classrooms that are rooted in translanguaging transformative pedagogy (García & Li Wei, 2014; García et al., 2016; Sánchez et al., 2018). We provided evidence that these teachers have developed a translanguaging stance, the firm belief that by bringing forth their multilingual students' full language repertoires, they can work against the linguistic hierarchy that positions English as more valuable than other languages (García et al., 2016; Menken & Sánchez, 2019).

As Ms Martin learned about translanguaging pedagogy, she began to design instructional activities in which her multilingual students could incorporate their home languages into their learning and to provide a vehicle for family members to extend their own children's learning as well as that of other children in the class (Moll et al., 2005). Because the previous schooling experiences of her students did not validate their multilingual practices, they started to discover the value of their multilingualism in their learning, and to feel excited about accessing their home languages in class. Ms Cooper's students feel comfortable translanguaging in her classroom given that she has been developing her translanguaging and culturally sustaining pedagogy (García & Li Wei, 2014; García et al., 2016; Paris & Alim, 2017; Sánchez et al., 2018) for the past few years. Besides creating materials in multiple languages and allowing students to access their home language to learn English, Ms Cooper has developed transformative spaces (García & Li Wei, 2014; Sánchez et al., 2018) where students can perform multilingually and have also extended her multilingual students' practices to include multimodality (García et al., 2016).

Ms Martin's and Ms Cooper's inclusion of students' home languages in their classroom go beyond the use of scaffolds to aid in their learning of English. They have come to understand that in order to successfully educate multilingual students in a country where the hegemony of English is all-encompassing, they need to contest that hegemony in their classrooms through translanguaging transformative pedagogy (García & Li Wei, 2014; Sánchez et al., 2018). Instead of having English-only classrooms, they are creating learning environments in which students are empowered to perform and share their knowledge and experiences multilingually and, in doing so, they potentially develop critical multilingual identities.

Acknowledgements

We would like to thank Ms Martin and Ms Cooper for opening the doors of their classrooms and to other members of the CUNY-NYSIEB team for working with these teachers and collecting data in their classrooms.

Note

(1) The names of the teachers and their students are pseudonyms.

References

Ascenzi-Moreno, L. and Espinosa, C.M. (2017) Opening up spaces for their whole selves: A case study group's exploration of translanguaging practices in writing. *NYS TESOL Journal* 5 (1), 10–29.
Baker, C. (2001) *Foundations of Bilingual Education and Bilingualism* (3rd edn). Clevedon: Multilingual Matters.
Carrasquillo, A., Rodriguez, D. and Kaplan, L. (2014) New York State Education Department policies, mandates, and initiatives on the education of English language learners. *Journal of Multilingual Education Research* 5 (5), 67–91.
Celic, C.M. (2009) *English Language Learners Day by Day, K-6: A Complete Guide to Literacy, Content-Area, and Language Instruction*. Portsmouth, NH: Heinemann.
Creswell, J.W. (2013) *Qualitative Inquiry and Research Design: Choosing Among Five Approaches*. Thousand Oaks, CA: Sage.
CUNY-NYSIEB (2019) *Our Vision*. See https://www.cuny-nysieb.org/our-vision/ (accessed August 2020).
de los Ríos, C.V. and Seltzer, K. (2017) Translanguaging, coloniality, and English classrooms: An exploration of two bicoastal urban classrooms. *Research in the Teaching of English* 52 (1), 55–75.
Ebe, A.E. and Chapman-Santiago, C. (2016) Student voices shining through: Exploring translanguaging as a literary device. In O. García and T. Kleyn (eds) *Translanguaging with Multilingual Students: Learning from Classroom Moments* (pp. 57–82). New York, NY: Routledge.
Espinet, I., Collins, B. and Ebe, A.E. (2018) 'I'm multilingual': Leveraging students' translanguaging practices to strengthen the school community. In A.M. Lazar and P.R. Schmidt (eds) *Schools of Promise for Multilingual Students: Transforming Literacies, Learning, and Lives* (pp. 118–133). New York, NY: Teachers College Press.
Gándara, P.M. and Hopkins, M. (eds) (2010) *Forbidden Language: English Learners and Restrictive Language Policies*. New York, NY: Teachers College Press.
García, O. (2009) *Bilingual Education in the 21st Century: A Global Perspective*. Malden, MA: Wiley-Blackwell.
García, O. and Kleifgen, J.A. (2018) *Educating Emergent Bilinguals: Policies, Programs, and Practices for English Language Learners* (2nd edn). New York, NY: Teachers College Press.
García, O. and Kleyn, T. (eds) (2016) *Translanguaging with Multilingual Students: Learning from Classroom Moments*. New York, NY: Routledge.
García, O. and Li Wei (2014) *Translanguaging: Language, Bilingualism and Education*. New York, NY: Palgrave Macmillan.
García, O., Johnson, S. and Seltzer, K. (2016) *The Translanguaging Classroom: Leveraging Student Bilingualism for Learning*. Philadelphia, PA: Caslon.

García-Mateus, S. and Palmer, D. (2017) Translanguaging pedagogies for positive identities in two-way dual language bilingual education. *Journal of Language, Identity & Education* 16 (4), 245–255.

Gort, M. and Sembiante, S.F. (2015) Navigating hybridized language learning spaces through translanguaging pedagogy: Dual language preschool teachers' languaging practices in support of emergent bilingual children's performance of academic discourse. *International Multilingual Research Journal* 9 (1), 7–25.

Lai, T. (2011) *Inside Out and Back Again*. New York, NY: HarperCollins.

Lin, G. (2001) *The Ugly Vegetables*. Watertown, MA: Charlesbridge.

Menken, K. (2013) Restrictive language education policies and emergent bilingual youth: A perfect storm with imperfect outcomes. *Theory into Practice* 52 (3), 160–168.

Menken, K. and Sánchez, M.T. (2019) Translanguaging in English-only schools: From pedagogy to stance in the disruption of monolingual policies and practices. *TESOL Quarterly* 53 (3), 741–767.

Miles, B., Huberman, A.M. and Saldaña, J. (2013) *Qualitative Data Analysis: A Methods Sourcebook*. Los Angeles, CA: Sage.

Moll, L., Amanti, C., Neff, D. and González, N. (2005) Funds of knowledge for teaching: Using a qualitative approach to connect homes and classrooms. In N. González, L. Moll and C. Amanti (eds) *Funds of Knowledge: Theorizing Practices in Households, Communities, and Classrooms* (pp. 71–88). Mahwah, NJ: Lawrence Erlbaum.

New York City Department of Education (2020) *2018–2019 English Language Learner Demographic Report*. See https://infohub.nyced.org/docs/default-source/default-document-library/ell-demographic-report.pdf (accessed March 2021).

New York City Department of Education (2021) *DOE Data at a Glance*. See https://www.schools.nyc.gov/about-us/reports/doe-data-at-a-glance (accessed March 2021).

New York City Independent Budget Office (2015) *New York City Public School Indicators: Demographics, Resources, Outcomes*. See https://www.ibo.nyc.ny.us/iboreports/new-york-city-public-school-indicators-demographics-resources-outcomes-october-2015.pdf (accessed September 2019).

New York State Education Department (2015) *English Language Learners (ELLs): Screening, Identification, Placement, Review, and Exit Criteria*. See http://www.nysed.gov/common/nysed/files/bilingual/ellidchartrev.pdf (accessed September 2019).

Otheguy, R., García, O. and Reid, W. (2015) Clarifying translanguaging and deconstructing named languages: A perspective from linguistics. *Applied Linguistics Review* 6 (3), 281–307.

Otheguy, R., García, O. and Reid, W. (2019) A translanguaging view of the linguistic system of bilinguals. *Applied Linguistics Review* 10 (4), 625–651.

Palmer, D. and Martínez, R.A. (2016) Research and policy. Developing biliteracy: What do teachers really need do know about language? *Language Arts* 93 (5), 379–385.

Paris, D. and Alim, H.S. (eds) (2017) *Culturally Sustaining Pedagogies: Teaching and Learning for Justice in a Changing World*. New York, NY: Teachers College Press.

Sánchez, M.T., García, O. and Solorza, C. (2018) Reframing language allocation policy in dual language bilingual education. *Bilingual Research Journal* 41 (1), 37–51.

Stake, R.E. (1995) *The Art of Case Study Research*. Thousand Oaks, CA: Sage.

Suárez-Orozco, C., Suárez-Orozco, M.M. and Todorova, I. (2010) *Learning a New Land: Immigrant Students in American Society*. Cambridge, MA: Belknap Press.

Valenzuela, A. (1999) *Subtractive Schooling: U.S.-Mexican Youth and the Politics of Caring*. New York, NY: State University of New York Press.

Monolingualism as a Cure for Language Disorder?

Joy Pénard

Speech-language pathologist, Basel, Switzerland

When our family lived in Germany, my four-year-old announced we were to speak German now. When I told her this was not possible since our families spoke only French and English, she recanted, deciding being multilingual had its purposes. This demonstrates that the monolingual mindset is so pervasive that young children perceive it. This perspective is also prevalent among professionals. As recently as the year 2000 during my studies, I received the message that monolingualism was the preferred recommendation for a bilingual child with a language disorder. We, as professionals, must put an end to this practice. All children can be bilingual (Thordardottir, 2006).

Eliminating a language does not alleviate a language disorder. It only removes their existing language foundation. As a speech therapist, I take all languages into consideration. Allowing the child to build on an already existing language foundation bolsters the acquisition of the new language by using the child's knowledge as a bridge. Children also need their languages to speak with family. Suggesting people simply learn the majority language, and abandon all others, damages relationships and cuts ties with their history and culture.

I encourage educational professionals to become advocates for translanguaging by learning words in each of the languages they find in their classrooms and call for less judgement of colleagues or parents who may have an accent in whatever languages they speak, and who perhaps even make mistakes in grammar or spelling. Communication, in all languages, and better understanding, should be our primordial consideration.

Reference

Thordardottir, E. (2006) Language intervention from a bilingual mindset. *The ASHA Leader* 11 (10), 6–21.

11 'Spaces of Power, Spaces of Resistance': Identity Negotiation Through Autobiography with Newcomer Immigrant Students

Timea Kádas Pickel

Introduction

The aim of this chapter is to examine how young immigrant adolescents have engaged in a process of identity reconstruction through a pedagogical project involving an autobiographical approach to literacy. In the following, we will show how their participation in this project has changed their vision of the world and of themselves, and allowed them to see themselves and their peers with new insights.

The project was carried out in 2012, in a secondary school induction class attended by pupils who had recently arrived in France. Our research consisted of developing a project around the notion of identity with the objective of improving their French language competence and more particularly their written expression skills. The project was initially influenced by the work of Cummins and Early (2011) on what they call *identity texts*. We encouraged students to write in their first languages before writing in French and included an artistic dimension through a photographic project on self-portraiture. In this chapter, we first summarize the research work around the notion of identity, a complex notion at the borders of several scientific disciplines and central to our reflection on the inclusion of young adolescents in a French secondary school class. In the second part, we introduce newly arrived students and illustrate the richness of their multilingual repertoire as a means of learning the language of instruction. We briefly describe the implementation of the project, as well as the various stages of its development. Finally, we present an analysis of the textual productions of seven students, as well as their discourses.

Theoretical Framework

The theoretical framework adopted in the present chapter is anchored at the nexus of critical and poststructuralist theories of identity (Block, 2007; Bourdieu, 1991; Foucault, 1982; Norton, 2000; Pavlenko & Blackledge, 2004) with a focus on autobiography and narrative identity (Ricoeur, 1985). The notion of identity is a complex one that has been studied by many researchers from different scientific backgrounds. We present below a synthesis of readings that have helped us to better understand its multiple dimensions in order to be able to develop an innovative pedagogical project with young teenagers who at the time of the study had recently arrived in France and were enrolled in an induction class.

Evolving theories of identity: From initial understandings to a poststructuralist view

The first definitions that emerged from Durkheim's sociology (2010 [1895]), for whom the individual was the product of the social conditions in which s/he developed, emphasized the social dimension of the concept of self and identity. Mead (1963 [1934]), one of the precursors of social psychology, was among the first to reflect on the concept of 'self'. By departing from the vision of the individual as an isolated element, he insists on the importance of the Other and of social experience in the production of self-awareness which 'develops in a given individual as a result of the relationships that the latter maintains with the totality of social processes and with the individuals who are committed to them' (Mead, 1963 [1934]: 115). He defines identity, the Self, as the product of an internal conversation between what others reflect back to us, our personal vision of ourselves and our interpretation of others' perceptions of us. It is therefore through the eyes of others that the concept of self is constructed.

Neuroscientific research has also focused on the concept of self. For example, Damasio (1999) reports on the different levels of consciousness that define the concept of self, whose most evolved form is a kind of extended consciousness in which the 'I' evolves through the new contexts it encounters, giving birth to what he defines as the autobiographical Self. He also describes the importance of the role of autobiographical memory in this process, a memory that encompasses our memories of the past but also our expectations and aspirations for the future and that participates in the construction of the autobiographical Self. Thus 'the autobiographical self [...] is the end product not just of our innate biases and actual life experiences, but of the reworking of memories of those experiences under the influence of those factors' (Damasio, 1999: 230).

As a result, the autobiographical Self evolves throughout life and encompasses not only elements of the past but also perspectives for the future. The evolution of the Self, according to Damasio (1999: 230), will be determined by 'the balance between the two influences: the lived past and the anticipated future'.

For Foucault (2001a: 1032), the constitution of the subject and of its identity relies on a set of 'techniques of the self' which 'are offered or prescribed to individuals to fix their identity, to maintain or transform it according to a certain number of goals, and this through relations of self-control or self-knowledge' (my translation). Moreover, the notion of power, analysed as a relationship of multiple forces – of both resistance and creation – is central to Foucault's theory. These power relations traverse the self, forcing it to continually recreate itself and resist the forces that are imposed upon it, the objective being the affirmation of the individual as different, both 'subject to someone else by control and dependence; and tied to his own identity by a conscience or self-knowledge' (Foucault, 1982: 781). Finally, for Bourdieu (1991: 287), the concept of identity refers to 'that perceived-being which exists fundamentally through recognition by other people' (my translation).

The poststructuralist vision of researchers such as Norton (2000) and Pavlenko and Blackledge (2004) over the past two decades has redefined the notion of identity and captured its complexity. The poststructuralists revisited the notion of identity, describing it not as a fixed entity for life, but as fragmented and contested by nature. Furthermore, it is now recognized that the concept of identity is multidimensional (Kanouté, 2002) and there is also a greater emphasis on how identity is constructed in discourse (Block, 2010).

In the case of migrants, identity construction can be particularly complex and dynamic in nature. When individuals move across geographical and psychological borders, immersing themselves in new sociocultural environments, they find that their sense of identity is destabilized and that they enter a period of struggle to reach a balance (Block, 2007: 864). This state in which the individual seeks to reposition his identity between past and present results in a negotiation of the difference in which 'past and present meet and transform each other' (Papastergiadis, 2000: 170, in Block, 2007: 864). Moreover, in a migratory context, the family and school are the two privileged instances for identity reconstruction by young people confronted with situations of exile (Kanouté, 2002).

Different aspects of identity negotiation

Voice

Another important notion in the realization of Self, and therefore in the (re)construction of its identity, is the notion of voice. In research on 'voice and difference policies', Giroux (1992) looks at how students function as agents and how they become 'voiceless' in some contexts or even silenced when they experience real or imagined bullying. This is particularly the case at school, as Giroux (1992: 203) points out, where 'the voices of subordinate groups, those whose first language is not English, and whose capital is either marginalized or denigrated by the dominant school culture' are silenced. Similarly, for Miller (2004: 293), 'students from subordinate groups are silenced because they are unable to represent themselves or to negotiate their identities through their first language at school'.

In her research in the United States, Delpit (1995) introduced the notion of 'silenced dialogue' to explain why black adolescents have difficulty succeeding in school. She raised the issue of teaching strategies that put students in greater difficulty at school. She suggests that teachers should build more on students' cultures when making pedagogical choices, in order to help them decode the 'white' middle-class culture that represents the 'culture of power', that is, the legitimate school culture.

Kinloch (2012) uses Delpit's notion of 'silenced dialogue' to focus more on the voices of young people that are inaudible. She calls on teachers to create learning situations and environments in which young people can engage in a dialogue 'to find out who they are, how they feel, and how they can become "authentic chroniclers" of their own experiences' (Kinloch, 2012: 111). It is in such learning situations that their voices will become audible. The notion of silent dialogue, Kinloch (2012: 112) points out, could prove useful for seeing 'the ways conflict, miscommunication, learning, and power impact classroom literacy engagements and students' perceptions of school and schooling'. Numerous studies have shown that students do better when school activities make sense to them and when they know their voices matter (Cummins & Early, 2011; Kinloch, 2010, 2012; Morrell, 2004).

Narrative identity

Through the stories we write about ourselves, we try to give unity to our existence. *Narrative identity* appears to be an issue both for individuals and for groups who (re)construct their identity through 'great' narratives (*grands récits*): 'the notion of narrative identity still shows its fruitfulness: the individual and the community constitute themselves in their identity by receiving such narratives, which become for both of them their actual history' (Ricoeur, 1985: 356, my translation).

Moreover, in a television interview, Ricoeur (1997) explains the notion of identity by drawing attention to the link between identity (who am I?) and memory (what I know I am), and identity (*mêmeté*) and otherness (what others say I am). Thus, the answer to the initial question (who am I?) is sought in the other's gaze; therefore, as Ricoeur specifies, we can only construct our identity in relation to what is different, what is not 'I'.

Identity and empowerment through identity texts

Through the migratory experience and the change of environment, the capital (linguistic, social, economic and cultural) of newly arrived pupils is rendered invisible in the French school system whose educational language policies insist above all on integration through the most rapid acquisition of French possible (MEN, 2012). In the case of immigrant students, it is important that schools help to recreate a kind of symbolic capital in order to enable them to gain recognition and to build or (re)build legitimacy in the eyes of others.

Leveraging students' multilingual repertoires is one way to achieve this symbolic capital. Numerous studies have highlighted the close link between language and identity. This is why valuing migrant pupils' languages rather than ignoring them, and using them as a resource (Ruiz, 1984) to initiate the process of identity reconstruction, proves indispensable:

> we all succeed best ... when we feel that our private and personal selves are accepted within the larger public spheres that we inhabit and are not separated and dislocated from them. (Conteh, 2003: 23)

We also believe, in the continuity of the work carried out in particular by Hélot and Young (2003), that when 'schools are interested in languages spoken and transmitted in the family environment, they enable students on the one hand to better assume their linguistic and cultural heritage and to better construct their identity, and on the other hand to consider their differences as riches to be shared' (Hélot & Young, 2003: 192).

The innovative works of Cummins (2006) and Cummins and Early (2011) on what they call 'identity texts', are among the means to implement a pedagogy of empowerment and identity reconstruction for migrant students. As Cummins (2006) points out, the term 'identity texts' is introduced to emphasize 'the importance of identity negotiation and societal power relations in understanding the nature of classroom interactions' (Cummins, 2006: 52). The school, as a privileged space for the reconstruction of the identity of students in situations of exile, should enable the creation of interpersonal spaces within the classroom in order to support the development of both second/additional languages and family languages (Cummins, 2006). Moreover, as Cummins and Early (2011) have shown with concrete empirical examples, this notion of identity texts allows literacy instruction to be rethought from both a multilingual and a multimodal perspective through the joint use of students' languages and new technologies. This approach thus contributes to giving students the 'power to act' which in turn gives them access to symbolic capital in Bourdieu's sense. For, as Bourdieu (1997: 200) explains, symbolic capital 'exists only in and through the esteem, recognition, belief, confidence of others' (my translation), all indispensable elements in the reconstruction of the identity of students who find themselves in a migratory context.

Negotiation of Identities in a French Induction Class: An Inclusive Pedagogical Project

Newly arrived students and their multilingual repertoire in the French school system

The newly arrived students are students of foreign nationality who have recently arrived on French territory with little or no command of the French language, their families having migrated for economic or political reasons. Some pupils are unaccompanied minors; that is, they arrive alone without family on French territory. As soon as they arrive, newly arrived students are enrolled in a regular school class and in addition follow (when possible) French second language instruction designed for newly arrived students in an 'induction class' (*Unité Pédagogique pour Elèves Allophones Arrivants/UPE2A*) for a minimum of 12 hours at the secondary level.

Since the 1970s when the first specific structures for migrant students were created in France, a succession of denominations has been used to name these foreign/migrant students. We note, however, that the latter denomination 'allophone students', although it recognizes that these students are proficient in a language other than French, does not remove the ambiguity linked to their denomination. Numerous studies in the field of bilingualism (García, 2009; García & Kleifgen, 2010; Hélot, 2011) have shown that these students are mostly bilingual or even multilingual and that they are committed to acquiring the language of schooling as soon as they arrive. As a result, they evolve in a bilingual learning situation, even if their first language(s) is/are invisible in the school context. One may therefore wonder whether the terms 'bilingual' or 'plurilingual' or at least 'emergent bilingual'/'*bilingues en devenir*' (Hélot, 2007) would not be more appropriate terms in order to focus not on what these students lack in terms of skills, but rather on what they have already acquired as a linguistic resource.

To illustrate our point, we present in tabular form the languages constituting the linguistic repertoire of the five students we selected from a larger study (Kádas Pickel, 2017). For the purpose of this chapter, the student's names have been changed to protect their identities (Table 11.1).

Table 11.1 Participating students

Students	Sex	Age	Country of origin	First language	Other languages
Diego	M	12	Portugal	Cape Verdean	Portuguese, French
Arpad	M	13	Hungary	Hungarian	English, French
Zohra	F	14	Italy	Italian	Moroccan Arabic, French
Mandana	F	15	Afghanistan	Pashto	Dari, Urdu, English, French
Edina	F	15	Hungary	Hungarian	English, French

Methodology and Project Design

Since we worked with students who were beginners in French as the language of instruction, we wanted to give them the opportunity to express themselves through writing supported by other means of expression. We therefore decided to set up a photographic project centred on the notion of self-portrait in order to encourage students to explore the notion of identity.

In line with Cummins and Early's (2011) 'identity texts', our approach was inspired by action-research methodology. Students were encouraged to write multilingually about their experiences of migration. In addition, we decided to include another tool, known as Photovoice (Wang & Burris, 1997), which leads to a process of empowerment among participants and encourages their participation in the proposed project: 'Photovoice is accessible to anyone who can learn to handle an instamatic camera; and, what is more, it does not presume the ability to read and write' (Wang & Burris, 1997: 372). Based on the theories of Freire (1973) and feminist theories, Photovoice was first used in the field of health. We wanted to explore the use of Photovoice in a specific school context, that of newly arrived students in vulnerable situations in their everyday lives. Our project was based around our readings on the production of identity texts (Cummins & Early, 2011) and on Photovoice (Wang & Burris, 1997).

The project took place over four months during the 2011/2012 school year in a lower secondary school in Mulhouse (France) where the 'induction class' comprised 22 students and 15 different languages, in addition to French. For the purpose of this chapter we analysed the speeches and the textual productions of five students, aged 12–15 years old, extracted from a larger study (Kádas Pickel, 2017). These five students also participated in the focus group interview, conducted a year later, which allows us to report both their thoughts and discussions on the project as well as their writings. This project was carried out in three stages, as detailed below.

Objectives and implementation of the autobiographical project

With this project, our general objective was to work on the notion of identity, that is to say, on image – both the image of oneself and the image that others have of us. Thus, we encouraged students to write structured autobiographical texts, either in prose or in verse. Our pedagogical objective was the teaching of written expression skills, one of the most difficult skills to develop in a short period of time. However, the project was also about involving students in creative activities that had meaning for them.

Step 1: Writing

In order to enable the students to produce long, structured texts in French, we encouraged them to express themselves first in their first language(s). After writing their life story, they selected or summarized a part of it and translated it into French to share with others. This first stage served as a springboard for the production of poetic texts, first through the search for rhymes and the writing of pictorial sentences, and then based on a model, Jacques Prévert's (1946) poem 'Je suis comme je suis' (I am as I am). Inspired by this poem, the students wrote their own versions. Through this process, they developed not only their physical psychological portraits but also, in some cases, they put their life stories into verse.

Step 2: Photography

During this second stage, the students worked with a professional photographer for two weeks and learned the different techniques for taking pictures. They then worked in pairs to produce portraits of themselves. The various photoshoots gave rise to discussions about photographic techniques and also to critical analysis of a new mode of expression through image. The students learned how to decode an image, from their own photos, allowing them to construct meaning through photography. In the final step, students reworked some photos using black and white printing to add text, thus gaining access to a new form of expression through multimodal literacy (Cummins, 2009; Martin-Jones, 2011).

Step 3: Correspondence

This third stage of the project focused on the relationship between identity and otherness by learning about the experiences of other students living a similar situation in another country. During this phase, students corresponded with newly arrived students at a high school in the Bronx, New York. These students were mainly from French-speaking African countries, which is why correspondence was possible in French. Students formulated questions on topics they wanted to address and then each student selected two questions. The questions were pasted onto cards made by the students with one of their photos on them. Replies were received a few weeks later. The entire project culminated in the presentation of their textual and photographic productions in an out-of-school exhibition that added value to their work.

Analysis of Students' Texts and Discourses

In the final section of this chapter, we propose a three-point analysis of the notion of identity as it can be interpreted from the students' autobiographical writings and speeches. The texts and speeches presented in this chapter were initially produced in French and then translated by me into English.

Narrative identity, memory, autobiography

As Ricoeur (1990) points out, looking at oneself and defining one's identity cannot be done without reflection on the role of memory. The work on autobiographical memory described by Damasio (1999) participates in the reconstruction of the autobiographical Self. The use of narrative gives rise to what Ricoeur (1985) calls 'narrative identity'. Ricoeur interests us because he insists on the narrative dimension of identity or how, through a narrative, whether autobiographical or not, the individual can build an identity, put into words, that helps him to better understand what he has experienced. This construction of identity is what our students expressed in the focus group interview:

Arpad: You know your story better I find because I never thought when I lived in my country I did not think too much about my past I lived in the present but what I meant to say was that I always thought about tomorrow.

Zohra: I just wanted to say that when I arrived the first day I thought about my life as it was in Italy, how I lived, where I lived, with whom ... while when we were in Italy we were at home in our country we didn't think about what we did yesterday or what we had done the day before yesterday.

The students testify how this writing exercise made them think and allowed them, as Arpad says, to better know their history. Before the experience of exile, students did not question the past because 'we were home' (Zohra) and it was the future that was important. But the fact of being 'elsewhere' makes you think about your past, from 'the first day' (Zohra).

The writing process provides them with the means to reflect on their own history as well as the means to do it safely, because in this act of writing, students commit themselves personally to write both for themselves and for others:

Mandana: For example, someone who doesn't want to tell his past to others like that, if he writes in his language, others they don't understand

Edina: [I] know what I'd like to share with others because I don't want to say what's a little delicate, a little intimate, but not say everything ... yes, so I knew what I wanted to say

Zohra: We take out everything we have

Arpad: [It allows you to] be a little more hidden from others

Mandana: We feel more comfortable

The initial use of the first language allows students to later select the elements that they want to share with the others. This step is an important one because it gives students a sense of freedom in writing their life story; the student can be both 'more hidden from others' through the first language, while also being 'more comfortable'.

Reflecting on one's experience of exile, by putting it into words, can also help an individual to evolve, to accept change (Damasio, 1999) and to envisage a better future. This sentiment is what Arpad tries to express in his prose text and accompanying photo:

Arpad: What is important is not where you come from but where you are now and where you are going.

What he also expresses through his text is that once the work of memory has been carried out, that is to say, once the narrative of life has been allowed an anchoring in time, as the guiding thread of identity, one can detach oneself from it; as Arpad says, 'what is important is not where you come from', in order to turn towards the present and the future ('but where you are now and where you are going'). Identity always has a temporal dimension in the sense that it is built either in continuity or in rupture with life's events.

Identity and otherness

Foucault (2001b: 861), in an interview with the Italian press in 1978, speaks of the experience of the spoken and written: 'I am an experimenter in the sense that I write to change myself and to no longer think the same thing as previously' (my translation). These words resonate with the text and words of one of the students, Zohra, who, by the reflection she initiated through her writing work, understood who she was and became aware of her mistakes, such as the way she perceived the Other.

Born in Italy to Moroccan parents, Zohra arrived in France at the age of 14. The autobiographical writing project was already well advanced when she joined the induction class. With the help of two other Italian students who had arrived at the beginning of the school year, she joined the project without difficulty and wrote her autobiographical text in Italian, then translated it into French. She recounts the change, following her migratory experience, in the way she looked at others, at immigrants:

> Before, I didn't like ... immigrants and I thought they should stay in their country! Now I am here in France and I am like them, an emigrant, in another country where I was not born and where I don't come from, where my parents don't come from. Now I am the one who leaves her homeland to aspire to a better future, to be able to study, find a good job and build my life without problems ... When I was in Italy, I was racist, I made fun of others and now I am in the same situation. I must admit, it's not easy to leave everything behind. We must not forget where our language and traditions come from. (Zohra)

This text is surprising in terms of the level and quality of the language used, given that Zohra had only been in class for three months when she wrote it. Similarly, the content of the remarks testifies, on the one hand, to the importance of the retrospection work and, on the other hand, to the depth of the reflection undertaken. This leads us to make the following observations: (1) she had excellent Italian language skills, which allowed her to transfer quickly to a second language (Cummins, 2000) and (2) the use of the first language for the initial stage of writing allowed Zohra to reflect at her cognitive level. Furthermore, by engaging in reflection through autobiographical writing, Zohra has shown much more involvement than in traditional school work (Cummins & Early, 2011). Through this painful experience as an immigrant, she has embarked on a process of identity reconstruction, the first stage of which is the evolution of her thinking and her outlook on the Other. Here she is in line with Foucault's comments that we mentioned at the beginning of this section. Her experience as an immigrant, in finding herself in the place of those she previously rejected, but also the reflection she initiated through the autobiographical project, led her to evolve and changed her vision of others. She testifies to this in the focus group interview: 'I have learned to respect people whoever they are, as they are, because like others have done with me, I have to do with others.'

At the end of the project, when we asked the students about what they had learned, they insisted above all on the change to their points of view, at the individual and collective level:

> Diego: It gave me a new way to see myself and my friends
> Zohra: And to see the world
> Mandana: The work we did with friends it was an opportunity to talk and to know each other better

They also mention the importance of the emotional dimension to group work:

> Mandana: It allowed us to know ourselves a little better because we were talking to each other
> Zohra: It was fun. There was nobody in the school yard.
> Arpad: We had a moment to talk as we had just arrived [in France]
> Mandana: Yes
> Zohra: And we were afraid to speak French in front of the others

They appreciated the dialogue, getting to know one another better, but also sharing 'intimate' moments, working in pairs, without being exposed to the regard of others and without 'shame'. The project was therefore an opportunity for socialization, made possible by allowing students to work by themselves, in groups and on written expression.

Empowerment

In this pedagogical project, the plurilingual repertoires of students were put forward and considered as resources (Ruiz, 1984) in the production of autobiographical stories. The official French curricula do not define a strict framework within which second language learning must take place, which leaves room for experimentation with other pedagogical practices such as taking students' first languages into account. In doing this, their first languages achieve a certain legitimacy, in the sense of Bourdieu (1977). For newly arrived students, thinking and writing in French is still an extremely difficult exercise. By giving students the opportunity to use their first languages, they were able to think at the level of their cognitive abilities (Cummins, 2000; Cummins & Early, 2011), which gave them a sense of comfort and security:

> Zohra: We had more vocabulary and more words
> Arpad: We were somewhat hidden from others
> Mandana: We felt more comfortable
> Zohra: We gave everything we had

Working in the first language provides access to linguistic and cultural resources, that is, *capital* in Bourdieu's sense, that would otherwise remain inaccessible in the second language. Working with students' languages is a means of giving them this symbolic power and setting up a process of empowerment (Cummins, 2000; Cummins & Early, 2011) with the legitimation of their linguistic repertoires (Bourdieu, 1977). It is a question of making visible and legitimizing both pupils' languages and their previous knowledge acquired in their countries of origin.

The aim of the project, to write identity texts and produce portraits, was not only to work in class, but also to produce a public exhibition showing the pupils' creativity to an out-of-school public as well as to various actors in the educational world. This provided an opportunity for the students to have their artistic productions recognized and valued, as Cummins and Early (2011) explain. During the official opening, which took place in one of the most important art galleries in the students' local town of Mulhouse, the students were able to measure the impact of their texts and photographs on the people who viewed them, as testified by the following excerpts from their remarks during the retrospective interview:

> Arpad: There was a lady who came and told me at least five times that it was really beautiful
> Edina: It was great they just told me that it's great, it's nice, it's well done and everything
> Diego: Especially my brother he said it's well done, it's well done
> Mandana: It was a lady she came to me she talked to me a lot and it was great and it must encourage you and that in a very short time you did some very interesting things

The recognition of their status as 'artists' particularly marked the students and the fact that people they did not know were interested in them. They testify to this in the following remarks:

Arpad:	It was really weird, the lady she came, she asked me are you the artists of this project? Can I have an autograph from you? And it was weird because I didn't know her and there were lots of people who said that to me.
Diego:	Me too
Interviewer:	How did you feel?
Arpad:	Like a STAR
Diego:	I also told myself that only stars give autographs
Interviewer:	And what did it do to you when the lady called you an artist?
Arpad:	I didn't know what to think at the time
Edina:	I didn't have words for it 'ah she's talking about me?'
Diego:	My brother said 'You? An artist?'

A new view of themselves emerged, one they initially had difficulty identifying with, and which required a moment of reflection in order to grasp the effect and the impact on their identity. The role of how others view them in their identity construction is highlighted in the following extract:

Arpad:	What made me most proud was that people liked our photos
Mandana:	There were hundreds, not hundreds but almost hundreds of people coming to look and read my text; journalists who came to discover our texts
Diego:	And our photos
Zohra:	It was like on TV when you see people
Arpad:	Like in the movies

The exhibition was thus an encounter with the way others see them, through which their potential as artists was recognized and which allowed them to experience a sense of empowerment (Cummins, 1996, 2009) and for some of them also a sense of unreality.

Conclusion

In this chapter, I have presented an analysis of the notion of identity as it emerges from the multimodal literary productions and discourses of newly arrived students. I drew on the work of Cummins and Early (2011) on identity texts, which I combined with Wang and Burris' (1997) Photovoice methodology, in order to engage students in meaningful literacy activities. In France, French second language literacy instruction tends to remain very traditional, focusing on linguistic and literary knowledge, which Martin-Jones (2011) defines as solitary literacy, while multimodal literacy is shared literacy (Cummins, 2009). I believe that new forms of literacy instruction are essential in order to meet the needs of newly arrived students. First of all, research has shown how important the use of the first language is in second language learning, hence the importance of understanding plurilingual literacy. Secondly, with students who are in the process of learning the language of instruction, it is important to develop activities that correspond to students' level of cognitive development while still allowing them to express themselves fully. As such, it is important to understand the notion of multimodal literacy that opens up the exploration of semiotic systems other than language, such as image, photo, video. Thirdly, it is important to take into account the emotional dimension, especially for those students who are in vulnerable social situations, who need to rebuild a positive self-image and not feel deprived of all their previously acquired skills.

The project I have described showed us how creative students can be and how they are able to invest in learning when they are given the means. I would like to end with a few words from the students, who spoke to us during the interview about how this project resonated in them and how they will keep it 'in the heart' and 'in the head' (Arpad) because they have worked above all for themselves. They realized that they had had a unique experience thanks to this unforgettable project, about which one of them jokingly quipped to the others: 'you are going to tell this to your grandchildren' (Diego).

References

Block, D. (2007) The rise of identity in SLA research, post Firth and Wagner (1997). *The Modern Language Journal* 91, 863–876.
Block, D. (2010) *Second Language Identities*. London: Continuum.
Bourdieu, P. (1977) L'économie des échanges linguistiques. *Langue française* 34, 17–34.
Bourdieu, P. (1991) *Language and Symbolic Power*. Cambridge, MA: Harvard University Press.
Bourdieu, P. (1997) *Méditations pascaliennes*. Paris: Seuil.
Conteh, J. (2003) *Succeeding in Diversity: Culture, Language and Learning in Primary Classrooms*. Stoke-on-Trent: Trentham Books.
Cummins, J. (1996) *Negotiating Identities: Education for Empowerment in a Diverse Society*. Ontario, CA: California Association for Bilingual Education.
Cummins, J. (2000) *Language, Power and Pedagogy: Bilingual Children in the Crossfire*. Clevedon: Multilingual Matters.
Cummins, J. (2006) Identity texts: The imaginative construction of self through multiliteracies pedagogy. In O. García, T. Skutnabb-Kangas and M.E. Torres-Guzmán (eds) *Imagining Multilingual Schools: Languages in Education and Glocalization* (pp. 51–68). Clevedon: Multilingual Matters.
Cummins, J. (2009) Transformative multiliteracies pedagogy: School-based strategies for closing the achievement gap. *Multiple Voices for Ethnically Diverse Exceptional Learners* 11 (2), 38–56.
Cummins, J. and Early, M. (2011) *Identity Texts: The Collaborative Creation of Power in Multilingual Schools*. Stoke-on-Trent: Trentham Books.
Damasio, A.R. (1999) *The Feeling of What Happens: Body and Emotion in the Making of Consciousness*. New York: Harcourt Brace.
Delpit, L.D. (1995) *Other People's Children: Cultural Conflict in the Classroom*. New York: New Press.
Durkheim, E. (2010 [1895]) *Les règles de la méthode sociologique*. Paris: Editions Flammarion.

Foucault, M. (1982) The subject and power. *Critical Inquiry* 8 (4), 777–795.
Foucault, M. (2001a) Subjectivité et vérité. Annuaire du Collège de France, 81e année. Histoire des systèmes de pensée, 1981. *Dits et écrits II* (pp. 1032–1037). Paris: Gallimard.
Foucault, M. (2001b) Entretien avec Michel Foucault/Conversazione con Michel Foucault (entretien avec D. Trombadori, Paris, fin 1978). In *Il Contributo*, 4e année, no. 1, janvier–mars 1980, pp. 23–84. *Dits et écrits II* (pp. 860–914). Paris: Gallimard.
Freire, P. (1973) *Education for Critical Consciousness*. London: Continuum.
García, O. (2009) *Bilingual Education in the 21st Century: A Global Perspective*. West Sussex: Wiley-Blackwell.
Garcia, O., Kleifgen, J.A. and Cummins, J. (2010) *Educating Emergent Bilinguals: Policies, Programs, and Practices for English Language Learners*. New York: Teachers College Press.
Giroux, H. (1992) Resisting difference: Cultural studies and the discourse of critical pedagogy. *Cultural Studies* 1 (1), 199–212.
Hélot, C. (2007) *Du bilinguisme en famille au plurilinguisme à l'école*. Paris: L'Harmattan.
Hélot, C. (2011) Children's literature in the multilingual classroom: Developing multilingual literacy acquisition. In C. Hélot and M. Ó Laoire (eds) *Language Policy for the Multilingual Classroom: Pedagogy of the Possible* (pp. 42–64). Bristol: Multilingual Matters.
Hélot, C. and Young, A. (2003) Education à la diversité linguistique et culturelle: Le rôle des parents dans un projet d'éveil aux langues en cycle 2. *LIDIL (revue de linguistique et de didactique des langues), (Hors Série, Le plurilinguisme en construction dans le système éducatif. Contextes, Dispositifs, Acteurs* 187–200.
Kádas Pickel, T. (2017) L'intégration des élèves nouvellement arrivés en France dans l'espace scolaire français: Langues, représentations, identités en contexte [The integration of newcomer students into the French education system: Languages, social representations and identities in context]. Unpublished doctoral dissertation, University of Strasbourg.
Kanouté, F. (2002) Profils d'acculturation d'élèves issus de l'immigration récente à Montréal. *Revue des sciences de l'éducation* 28 (1), 171–190.
Kinloch, V. (2010) *Harlem on Our Minds: Place, Race, and the Literacies of Urban Youth*. New York: Teachers College Press.
Kinloch, V. (2012) *Crossing Boundaries: Teaching and Learning with Urban Youth*. New York: Teachers College Press.
Martin-Jones, M. (2011) Languages, texts and literacy practices: An ethnographic lens on bilingual vocational education in Wales. In T.L. McCarty (ed.) *Ethnography and Language Policy*. New York and London: Routledge.
Mead, G.H. (1963 [1934]) *Mind, Self, and Society (L'esprit, le soi et la société)*. Chicago, IL: University of Chicago Press (Paris: Presses Universitaires de France).
MEN (2012) *Organisation de la scolarité des élèves allophones nouvellement arrivés*. Paris: Ministère de l'Education Nationale.
Miller, J. (2004) Identity and language use: The politics of speaking ESL in schools. In A. Pavlenko and A. Blackledge (eds) *Negotiation of Identities in Multilingual Contexts* (pp. 290–315). Clevedon: Multilingual Matters.
Morrell, E. (2004) *Becoming Critical Researchers: Literacy and Empowerment for Urban Youth*. New York: Peter Lang.
Norton, B. (2000) *Identity and Language Learning: Gender, Ethnicity and Educational Change* (1st edn). Harlow: Pearson Education.
Papastergiadis, N. (2000) *The Turbulence of Migration*. Cambridge: Polity Press.
Pavlenko, A. and Blackledge, A. (2004) *Negotiation of Identities in Multilingual Contexts*. Clevedon: Multilingual Matters.

Prévert, J. (1946) 'Je suis comme je suis'. In *Paroles*. Paris: Le Point du Jour.
Ricoeur, P. (1985) *Temps et Récit: Le Temps raconté*. Paris: Seuil.
Ricoeur, P. (1990) *Soi-même comme un autre*. Paris: Seuil.
Ricoeur, P. (1997) Interview. *Pensée de notre temps*. Paris: Ina – Arte France 2005.
Ruiz, R. (1984) Orientations in language planning. *NABE Journal* 8 (2), 15–34.
Wang, C. and Burris, M.A. (1997) Photovoice: Concept, methodology, and use for participatory needs assessment. *Health Education & Behavior* 24 (3), 369–387.

Understanding, Adapting and Being Noticed in a New School Context

Kia Kimhag

University of Gävle, Sweden, Fil.mag., Department of Education

For several years, I have been working with exchange students and migrants both as a lecturer and as a partner in national and international projects. From my experience during different projects, it has been very clear that when a person is newly arrived to a country they also walk into a new context (Kimhag, 2012) where they have a lack of understanding of different systems and belonging in different social constructions. Bronfenbrenner (1979) explains how the child is influenced and socialized through experience on four levels: micro, eso, exo and macro. Before, in their home country, they had other people around. Newly arrived migrants have lost most or all of these people and at the same time have also lost their familiar context. Zohra noticed in the chapter (Kádas Pickel, this volume) that 'we must not forget where our language and traditions come from'. The lack of understanding and belonging in the microsystem and the new context makes it more difficult to find a path and easier to fall outside of the community, school and different social contexts.

What image of school and meaning of teachers does the child bring with them? The mother tongue tutors in the projects ENABLE[1] and Studiehandledare[2] became a bridge between the child and the teachers, the lessons and the social structurers in the new school context.

Newly arrived migrants (*Studiehandledare*) with a teacher background were trained for four months to be able to work in Swedish schools as mother tongue tutors. They learned how to work as tutors, how to support the migrant children and how to integrate them into the school context. They reflected on these together through lectures and discussions with teachers at school. By pinpointing cultural likenesses and/or differences a deeper understanding of the Swedish educational system, curriculum, values and norms was developed. They felt that they could make a difference with migrant children. Their knowledge and experience were noticed and they could feel that someone saw and respected them. They learnt what the expectations were and how to behave in the school context. This provided them with self-confidence and a hope for a brighter future. Similarly, the children described by Kádas Pickel changed their vision of the world and themselves: someone had noticed them as artists; they felt like stars.

Notes

(1) ENABLE Self-learning for Arabic Refugee Children – Building a Concept for Mother-tongue Trainers and Teachers. KA 2 project, 2017–2019. See www.enable-tamkin.com.
(2) *Framtid Studiehandledare* (School Tutors in Mother Tongue). ESF project, 2016–2018. See https://esf.se/sv/Resultat/Projektbanken-2014-2020/Alla-Projekt/Framtid---studiehandledare/.

References

Bronfenbrenner, U. (1979) *The Ecology of Human Development*. Cambridge, MA: Harvard University Press.
Kimhag, K. (2012) Practice abroad: How to adapt a new school system. In J.D. Ganck and W. Baeten (eds) *Mobility Framework and Standard for Teacher Trainees* (pp. 17–37). Antwerp: Garant.

12 Framing Critical Perspectives on Migration, Fairness and Belonging Through the Lens of Young People's Multilingual Digital Stories

Vicky Macleroy

Introduction

This chapter explores critical perspectives of young people (7–14 years old) on issues of migration, fairness and belonging in three schools across Cyprus, England and Palestine. It seeks to address how young people draw on their full linguistic repertoire to investigate complex questions of identity, integration and inclusion. The multilingual digital stories presented in this chapter were inspired by the students' desire to be viewed in a different light. The young filmmakers wanted to present themselves as people with talents and skills, with individual stories and empathy, as well as thoughtful citizens documenting their identities and cultures. This chapter presents vignettes from three schools that were part of a five-year project, Critical Connections: Multilingual Digital Storytelling (2012–2017), which worked across schools, homes and communities, but perceived schools as the hub for transformative pedagogy. Young people engaged with digital technology to compose their alternative stories and worked collaboratively to present strong messages of resistance and hope. They explored themes of fairness and belonging through a project-based approach to language learning that fosters learner agency and multilingualism.

The project, funded by the Paul Hamlyn Foundation, reflects the work of the foundation with its commitment to innovation and its vision for engaging schools and implementing project-based learning based on four interconnecting layers: placed (the activity is located in a world that the student recognizes); purposeful (the activity feels authentic); passion-led (the activity enlists the outside passions of both students and teachers); and pervasive (the activity enables the student to continue learning outside the classroom) (PHF & Innovation Unit, 2012: 8). Imagining, hypothesizing and transforming knowledge lies at the core of our work in multilingual digital storytelling. This chapter will interrogate how young people sought to represent their notions of migration, fairness and belonging and present alternative perspectives on their languages and cultures.

What is Multilingual Digital Storytelling?

Ganley, in her foreword to *Digital Storytelling: Capturing Lives, Creating Community* (Lambert, 2013), writes passionately about the excitement and engagement of her students in digital storytelling and endorses Lambert's notion that 'a healthy community – no matter the setting – is grounded in belonging, in understanding, in plurality' (Ganley, 2013: xi). In discussing digital storytelling, Lambert talks about having agency: 'Being the author of your own life, of the way you move through the world, is a fundamental idea in democracy' (Lambert, 2013: 2). This approach to digital storytelling came out of folk culture, cultural activism and experimental theatre and Lambert (2013) defined digital storytelling as possessing these seven components: self-revelatory; personal or first person voice; a lived experience; photos more than moving images; soundtrack; length and design (under five minutes); and intention (process over product). Our project extended these ideas into the field of language learning and collaborative creativity with a greater focus on audience (online, schools and annual film festivals): 'When stories are created in different languages or combinations of languages, they often carry greater cultural authenticity. They also embody and give positive expression to plurilingual repertoires within individuals and societies providing a deeper literacy experience and a basis for greater intercultural respect and understanding' (Anderson & Macleroy, 2016: 1). We defined multilingual digital storytelling in our project as a short multilingual story (3–5 minutes) made using photographs, moving images, artwork, sculpture, objects, shadow puppetry, stop motion animation, green screen, poetry, dance and drama. Teacher and learner agency were fostered, the stories were told from a personal perspective and interculturality was a vital component.

Critical Connections: Multilingual Digital Storytelling Project (2012–2017)

This was an international project to enhance literacy in schools using digital storytelling as a means to encourage students to engage with language learning and embrace intercultural literacy as well as digital literacy. The project involved over 1500 young people, across primary and secondary age ranges (6–18 years old), in creating and sharing digital stories in a bilingual version. The project included over 15 languages: Arabic, Bengali, Bulgarian, Croatian, English (mother tongue, English as an additional language, English as a foreign language), Estonian, French, German, Greek, Hungarian, Mandarin Chinese, Portuguese, Spanish, Tamil and Turkish. Teacher professional development was an integral part of the project and over 50 lead teachers implemented the digital storytelling work in over 30 supplementary and mainstream schools in England and in six other countries (Algeria, America, Cyprus, Luxembourg, Palestine, Taiwan). The project moved across the following themes: inside out, journeys, fairness and belonging. The multilingual digital stories have been shared within classrooms and schools, across schools, at film festivals and on the project website: https://goldsmithsmdst.com/.

Research questions were developed under the following strands: language learning and use; mechanisms for critical engagement; learner autonomy, student voice, social justice and advocacy; sites of learning; and narrative composition, storytelling and creative pedagogy. The following research questions are addressed in this chapter through three vignettes that draw on video recordings of the digital storytelling process, interviews with students and teachers, and three digital stories.

(1) How do young people use digital storytelling to embody their languages, cultures, identities and interests?
(2) How does multilingual digital storytelling extend notions of literacy and inclusion?

Literature Review

In this section, I explore the theoretical framework for the analysis of the three vignettes and focus on perspectives of inclusion, identity, and literacy in the context of multilingual digital storytelling.

Reimagining perspectives on inclusion in multilingual digital storytelling

Inclusion in classrooms is intimately connected with how a child feels in those spaces and whether their ideas are valued and listened to. In articulating her understanding of engaged pedagogy, hooks argues that everyone influences the classroom dynamic and everyone's presence should be acknowledged: 'As a classroom community, our capacity to generate excitement is deeply affected by our interest in one another, in hearing one another's voices, in recognizing one another's presence' (hooks, 1994: 8). Thus, an inclusive classroom needs to be open to young people's languages, cultures and experiences in order to help them make sense of learning. Sheehy (2013), in thinking about what types of borders are useful and which are not, talks about how 'school borders thicken so that more school space and time are devoted to one literacy practice: test preparation' (Sheehy, 2013: 407), and says that what we should, in fact, be looking at more closely is the migration of ideas, people, and objects across specific school borders. Therefore, developing a transdisciplinary approach to learning in schools can help learners inhabit these borders and connect their separated worlds. In discussing translanguaging, García (2017) conceptualizes the notion of being in the borderlands: 'whether we can let ourselves be open to just being in the borderlands, inclusive borderlands, without being forced to cross borders. Only then will we be able as human beings to experience liberation and creativity, as we bring down the walls that separate us' (García, 2017: 19).

I would also argue that reimagining perspectives on inclusion sees these borderlands and spaces as complex and messy. Phipps and Gonzalez (2004), in thinking about intercultural being, the politics of languages and how people make sense of and shape the world, coin the phrase 'messy cultures' and put forward the notion that 'cultures are messy, heavy, people-ridden' (Phipps & Gonzalez, 2004: 61). Their concept of culture is steeped in tradition and experience and ideas of weight, complexity and density, describing culture as 'humming with life' (Phipps & Gonzalez, 2004: 51). This concept of messiness fits with ideas that recognize the contradictions inherent in inclusion and the vibrancy of life. It also recognizes the importance of learners being open to uncertainty and questioning their own viewpoints by listening to others: 'to enter other cultures is to re-enter one's own' (Phipps & Gonzalez, 2004: 3). Valuing the different languages, cultures, experiences and stories children embody in all their complexity lies counter to ideas of inclusion around a single fixed literacy. Children are often forced to chase after an illusory fixed literacy that seems distant from their own rich and noisy experience of language in its multivoicedness. School literacy is often about exclusion rather than inclusion as much school-based learning builds on answers and 'falls short of preparing pupils to work innovatively and creatively in processes that involve give and take and openness towards the uncertain' (Nyboe & Drotner, 2008: 173).

In fostering inclusion and collaboration, learners need to be supported to take risks and to be given the tools to come up with their own ideas. It is this process of developing ideas and creating collaboratively that students find challenging and demanding. Cremin and Maybin (2013) discuss the importance of students developing 'ideational fluency' and note that there are few studies that explicitly examine young people's 'collaborative construction of new meanings through imagined experience' (Cremin & Maybin, 2013: 281). In the process of making multilingual digital stories, young people are asked their opinions about what makes a good digital story and they have to decide collaboratively on what matters to them and look critically at themselves as well as others. In this approach to language learning, empathy and openness are vital and Mercer believes 'it can be powerful for learners to actively imagine other lives through literature, films, role-plays, photos and art' (Mercer, 2016: 104).

In using multilingual digital storytelling to reimagine perspectives on inclusion and carve out spaces for languages, the willingness of classroom teachers and students to take risks, experiment, work collaboratively and learn new skills was at the core of the project's success. This way of working runs counter to current trends in the education system in England where the school curriculum 'does little to foster cross-disciplinary working' (Sefton-Green & Brown, 2014: 9) and 'all sense of process has disappeared by packing excessive content into each school year' (Wrigley, 2014: 35). The danger of this new curriculum in England is that there is no space to include children's messy and complex ideas and it undermines 'critical preparation for democratic citizenship and lacks any sense of the need to involve young people in active debate or inquiry or challenge' (Wrigley, 2014: 35). Multilingual digital storytelling allows young people to define inclusion on their terms.

Reconceptualizing identity in multilingual digital storytelling spaces

In reconceptualizing identity in multilingual digital storytelling spaces, learner agency was a core principle in the meaning-making process. Darvin and Norton (2014) argue that digital storytelling is a powerful medium for affirming identities for 'migrant learners who traverse transnational spaces and ways of thinking' (Darvin & Norton, 2014: 61). Digital storytelling links with research exploring youth, theatre and the ethical imaginary that looks at how concepts of care and hope can develop young people's broader civic engagement (Kushnir, 2017). With our project's focus on multilingualism and the creation of bilingual digital texts, young people had to imagine how to use language in new contexts and negotiate interfaces between different cultural landscapes: 'A key principle underlying the approach has been to allow students to represent themselves and their bilingual/plurilingual repertoires positively through their work' (Anderson & Macleroy, 2017: 8).

In proposing ways to expand our conceptualization of the goals of language teaching and learning, Leung and Scarino (2016) return to important notions of personal development and aesthetics. They argue that any exchange in communication involves interpreting self and others and examine how the aesthetic 'opens space for exploring the multiplicity of meanings, the openness and uncertainty of the interpretation and creation of meanings, and how historical and cultural references are encoded' (Leung & Scarino, 2016: 89). Thus, in developing as multilingual users, language learners are involved in expressions of imagination, creativity, playfulness, comparison, critical appreciation and meaning-making.

Nyboe and Drotner (2008) use the term 'competences of complexity' in relation to creating digital narratives to describe what they see as an aesthetic practice of sense-making, perception and manipulation in which young people push boundaries of themselves and others. Providing space in the digital storytelling process for students to explore, make meaning and represent their multilingual selves was a crucial part of learner agency, creativity and interculturality in the project. This transformative pedagogical approach builds on the work on identity texts (Cummins & Early, 2011) which capture the intercultural and interlinguistic experiences of students and their multiple and fluid identity positions. However, these multilingual identity spaces have to be promoted and fostered across different sites of learning to give students the confidence and desire to express alternative perspectives in and through their languages.

Phipps and Gonzalez (2004) point out that languages are an integral part of students' identities and how they shape their environment and so making space for students' languages in schools and education becomes a social justice issue. By focusing on encounters, on meaning and on understanding, the concept of 'being intercultural' moves beyond language versus culture and beyond the 'captivities of culture' (Phipps & Gonzalez, 2004: 168). Students need to be given the courage and confidence to interrogate language and cultural practices. Habib (2017) argues that students should be given the chance to contest cultural traditions and practices. She discusses local and global belongings and how students learn about identity itself: 'students need a space to interrogate how identities are influenced and affected by social structures too, and how this impacts upon their everyday lives. We can give students the chance to critique cultural mores, as they reflect upon social constraints and challenges for freedom' (Habib, 2017: 144).

In making multilingual digital stories, students are given the space to think about how their languages and cultures are perceived by others and to interrogate their own identities, experiences and place in the world. Lambert (2013) recognizes the powerful effect of transforming personal stories into film and how this process helps people to imagine other viewpoints and reconceptualize identities: 'the story allows some shifts in perspective about events in our lives, and we believe that those shifts are particularly useful to work in identity' (Lambert, 2013: 12).

Reshaping literacy in multilingual digital storytelling

Views of literacy are continually evolving, but approaches towards teaching literacy 'have a tendency to revert back to a notion of literacy as a set of technical skills that need to be mastered' (Anderson & Macleroy Obied, 2011: 18). In contrast, I argue here that to become literate means to make sense of oral, written, visual and digital forms of expression and communication. In reshaping notions of literacy in multilingual digital storytelling, literacy became entwined with images of movement and physicality. Making the digital stories gave students the freedom to explore outdoor spaces in their representations of migration, fairness and belonging. Connecting literacy with the action of the feet, the freedom to roam, to explore, to get lost and to learn to map real and imagined worlds draws on the work of Mackey in her story of learning to be literate where she was 'surprised at a recurring scrap of a nebulous mental image: it always involved feet' (Mackey, 2010: 325). She develops the notion of 'reading from the feet up' and interpreting the world through the action of the feet as 'many children learn to read just at the same time they are beginning to move through their own world more significantly' (Mackey, 2010: 325). This concept of 'foot knowledge' is intricately linked with the way a child learns to move through stories and imagine in multidimensional ways.

In extending concepts of literacy and thinking about the physicality of learning to be literate, Heath (2013) explores the idea of 'the hand of play in literacy learning' and the need for whole-body movement to expand language learning. She connects this view of literacy to language learning for additional languages where role playing and re-enactment improve fluency and advance empathy. As our digital storytelling work developed, drama became a more integral part of our approach to language learning and storying. This links with the work of Alrutz (2015) on digital storytelling, applied theatre and youth, where she recognizes the power of personal narratives to move people and the power of performance to disrupt systems of power. She explores these connections between digital storytelling and applied theatre and how performing one's personal story matters, as it places value on individuals and their experiences and engaging in applied theatre means 'valuing the ideas and input of the participants, emphasizing collaborative discovery and revision, and creating a space for reciprocity between participants, facilitators and audiences of the work' (Alrutz, 2015: 13). In our project, drama became integral to providing space to develop literacy across students' languages in the making of their digital stories.

In our approach to developing literacy in the making of multilingual digital stories, we were inspired by the work of Pahl and Rowsell (2010) on artifactual literacies and we used objects and cultural artefacts to enable students to explore, uncover and tell stories about migration and belonging. Pahl and Escott (2019) use young people's films as a lens for an expanded view of language and literacy and see understandings of literacy as 'moving along a continuum that includes language, visual, together with material, gesture and non-verbal modes of communication' (Pahl & Escott, 2019: 806). From this perspective, literacy is bound up with the languages and materials it is formed from and this is transforming how literacy is conceptualized. Mills and Comber (2013) recognize the spatial turn in literacy research with its shift towards the materiality of lived, embodied and situated experience and how 'material spaces and places shape the identity and literate practices of youth' (Mills & Comber, 2013: 413).

In making digital stories, young people are learning to work in and across different modes of communication and it is this translation of meaning across multiple modes that expands and extends their literacy. Mills (2016) views this transmediation process as key to understanding how multimodal literacy practices work. Learners have to invent connections across modes and 'choose from multimodal semiotic resources that do not have direct equivalence, thus inviting creativity and transformation' (Mills, 2016: 68). Transmediation is a complex and challenging literacy process as it involves transforming knowledge by degrees, recognizing the limitations and possibilities of the different sign-making systems and learning how to use the tool itself. An added level of complexity for young people in developing their multilingual digital stories is the act of translation. It is in this act of translation that language learning deepens and students grapple with the complexities and ambiguities of their languages and how to make meaning as they move between their languages: 'the creative, human activity of translation is at the heart of languaging and being intercultural' (Phipps & Gonzalez, 2004: 149). As well as translating across their languages, young people had to think about audience and how the voiceover would be heard in the target language and the subtitles read and seen on the screen in another language (usually in English).

Narrative approaches to data analysis within a critical ethnography

Our multilingual digital storytelling project was a cross-disciplinary qualitative study in which we adopted a critical ethnographic perspective incorporating a social justice dimension and making links to ecological, collaborative and multimodal perspectives (Anderson & Macleroy, 2016: 134). Ecological perspectives were important in viewing the educational setting as a hierarchy of nested ecosystems, collaborative perspectives were important in recognizing the importance of incorporating the multiple perspectives of teachers, students, parents and community members, and multimodal perspectives were important in understanding how different sign systems work together to make meaning.

The corpora presented here were analysed using narrative and biographical analysis. This allows the researcher to construct a narrative analysis with illuminating quotations from participants. Narrative analysis together with biographical data enables the researcher to focus on key decision points in the story or narrative, critical events, key places and key experiences. A narrative analysis 'keeps text and context together, retains the integrity of people rather than fragmenting bits of them into common themes and codes and enables evolving situations, causes and consequences to be charted' (Cohen *et al.*, 2018: 665). This approach to analysis views 'narratives as powerful, human and integrated; truly qualitative' (Cohen *et al.*, 2018: 665).

The corpora were collected from video recordings and photographs (observing the making of digital stories in schools; presenting digital stories at film festivals; interviews with students, teachers, parents and community members) and documentary materials (school policies; teaching plans and materials; students' work including notes, storyboards; field notes; digital stories in draft and final versions). The Critical Connections pedagogical framework was developed with a ten-stage model across pre-production, production and post-production for embedding digital storytelling within a thematic unit of work. The ten-stage model evolved through trials in different school contexts and regular meetings with project teachers (Anderson & Macleroy, 2016). It should be noted that all the research participants took part with consent and teachers and schools were named and students acknowledged as filmmakers in the research. This fully funded research project had ethical approval from our university ethics board and signed consent from all research participants that their digital stories, photographs, recorded interviews and film footage could be used for educational purposes.

For most project teachers, allowing students to exercise more control over their learning was a major pedagogical shift, but what stood out for these teachers was how students moved beyond their expectations and demonstrated 'increased engagement and depth of learning' (Anderson, 2016: 233). Teachers and students took part in media training and workshops to develop their filmmaking and editing skills. The following three vignettes were selected for narrative analysis in response to the research questions as they present strong narratives about how young people perceive and interpret inclusion.

Introduction to the Vignettes

These digital stories will be explored as vignettes to illustrate the work of the project and its potential for challenging dominant discourses on migration and displacement. The first Arabic-English digital story, *Young Palestinian Talents*, encourages young people to take pride in their lives, challenging existing stereotyping: 'There is a tendency to show "the other" in specific terms. The Palestinian is often shown to be a victim, or a freedom fighter or a terrorist, but seldom as a normal human being who wants to live and enjoy life to the full' (Teacher, Ealing Arabic School). The second Bulgarian-English digital story, *Question Mark Movie*, challenges the way that adults categorize children as numbers and they argue forcefully to be seen as individual children by their educators. The third Greek-English digital story, *Irene – a refugee's story*, is filmed in Cyprus in a sculpture park and shows how seven-year-old children can empathize and imagine stories of migration and loss.

The bilingual digital stories are full of movement, exploration and vitality as young people investigate and represent their environments and think more deeply about being in a place and belonging. Learner agency was a core principle at all stages of the project and as the project expanded, the role of drama, media and the arts became more prominent in the making of the digital stories. They were given the time and space to reimagine perspectives on inclusion and the platform to present and exhibit their stories to a wider international audience.

Vignette from Hajjah Rashda El Masri School (a mainstream girls' secondary school in Nablus, Palestine)

Young people were given the freedom to explore complex issues of identity and inclusion from their own standpoint. The Arabic-English digital story *Young Palestinian Talents* was created by four teenage girls (14–15 year-olds) at their school in Nablus, Palestine. The school was interested in the multilingual digital storytelling project to develop students' skills in English as a foreign language, improve their ability in storytelling and empower and encourage the girls to become more confident in expressing themselves in English. Reem, a lead Arabic teacher on the project in London, forged the link with the girls' school in Nablus, her childhood city. The girls who were involved in the project wanted to position young Palestinians in a different light, not framed as the victim or trapped. Reem commented that although the girls involved in the project had all been 'subjected to the hardship of life under occupation; they still reflected a part of them that celebrated hope despite the difficulties and hardship' (Teacher, EAS). Reem describes the talent, imagination and resilience of the students in making their film as truly amazing and 'a brilliant document of what was happening on the ground at that time' (Teacher, EAS). In making their digital story, the girls wanted Palestinians to be seen as ordinary people with talents and desires. They captured this emotion and reflected a confident and exuberant side of their nature (Figure 12.1).

Young Palestinian Talents opens with a collage of photos and the voiceover in English: 'Each Palestinian has a dream, a talent that he wishes to be real'. The girls then shift the focus to their lives: 'Each one of us has her own story and her own adventure with her talent so let's start the journey of our young Palestinian talents by telling you about us'. The girls choose to film outside in a park overlooking Nablus where a noisy background adds to the rough, authentic nature of the footage. This digital story is full of movement, colour and life. In their search for young Palestinians with talents they uncover the way people make art in and around the margins of a city. The film shifts to a young unicyclist performing tricks in a deserted yard with a high wall and with background music adding to the upbeat mood. As the story moves through the

Figure 12.1 Screenshot of the Arabic-English digital story, *Young Palestinian Talents*

landscape the girls discover more talents and the film shifts seamlessly into Arabic when they share the poetry, rap and songs of young Palestinians. A young Palestinian performs a rap he has written in Arabic about injustice in Palestine, collective responsibility and standing up for your rights. He moves though the urban landscape with graffiti as his backdrop and the strong rhythm of rap in his footsteps. The digital story ends outside in the park with the strong message that young Palestinian talents need to be nurtured and cared for and their stories heard by a wider audience.

Young Palestinian Talents was exhibited at the film festival in London in 2014 under the theme of journeys. In Skype interviews with the students in 2018, carried out by the lead Arabic teacher in England, they reflected upon making the film: 'The idea came to us when we were walking ... you hear a beautiful voice or you see someone who has some talent and they do not receive their just recognition and cannot show their talent' (Student, HRMS). One of the students talked about how making the digital story changed her personality, her experience and her perception of herself and another student viewed it as an exceptional film that showcased their goal to show young Palestinians in a different way. Another student added: 'This was one of the most beautiful experiences of my life. I was very enthusiastic and motivated and very much enjoyed making the film'. Finally, a student captured the experience in two words: 'confidence and courage'.

The narrative analysis of *Young Palestinian Talents* demonstrates how students have made the key decision to take literacy outside the classroom and present their culture as 'humming with life' (Phipps & Gonzalez, 2004). These students were critical of the way their culture has been 'Othered', and in joining an international community of storytellers wanted to 'be allowed room to express themselves in resistance to the dominant cosmopolitan imagination' (Holliday, 2011: 12).

Vignette from Shkolo Vasil Levski (a Bulgarian complementary school in London)

The Bulgarian-English digital story *Question Mark Movie* is striking in the way in which the young people have the confidence and courage to interrogate the concept of belonging. The ten young people involved in making this film in 2017 were different ages (10–14 years old) and included nine girls and one boy. In an interview I carried out at the Bulgarian School in 2018, the students reflected upon the process and how they looked 'deep into the word' and what it actually meant to belong here and to belong to yourself. Milena, the head teacher, explained how the students discussed belonging from different angles and points of view and that in Bulgarian a person would say: 'I am Bulgarian, not I belong to Bulgaria'. The students believed the hardest challenge in making the digital story was to get the main point across to the audience and show the audience what they were thinking. Iva, one of the older students, talks about the title of the film *Question Mark Movie* and the main question: 'who are we?' She thinks they took a risk in framing the main message as a question and they were 'scared in a way ... to get the point out'. The main message that they wanted to present to the audience was that young people should not be labelled for what they like and what they are good at; they do not have to be in different groups because of their interests and hobbies. Mirela and Stefani, the two sisters, explained how in the making of the digital story the students learned about other people's talents and thought about how they bonded together in the same group: 'as we're all friends and even ages don't matter to us, we get everyone's ideas and then mix them together to make the best cake ever' (Figure 12.2).

The digital story opens in silence with a large question mark that fills the screen. The next shot is of a 12-year-old girl, Alexandra, pacing around a backyard on her own and being introduced by the numbers that define her and then hanging about with a friend throwing small pebbles into a river. The Bulgarian voiceover and subtitles in English continue with the narrative of numbers. As the film shifts inside, Alexandra is seen typing at a computer: 'Sometimes I think that I'm just a number surrounded by loads of other numbers ... Numbers, numbers, numbers. My head can't fit them all in'. The digital story has a strong pace and rhythm and it is full of movement and vibrancy. As well as critiquing the way children are divided and controlled, the students show their energy, skills and creativity. The film includes scenes of students playing music and

Figure 12.2 Students editing the Bulgarian-English digital story, *Question Mark Movie*

doing sport/gymnastics, dance and art. The students wanted to include a scene with dance steps from Bulgarian folk dancing 'as it shows what our country is about ... although it's a small country we still have a big heart'. They described why they included art: 'it really expresses our feelings when we're drawing' and in this scene they are drawing a typical Bulgarian house from a village.

The young people, in making this Bulgarian-English digital story, are learning how to frame and present their ideas. They talk about the importance for 'children to be free outside and play with their friends' and how movement is 'how your personality forms'. They understand how the different camera angles change the mood of a story and how to use space and movement to communicate the main message. The young people discussed their ideas in depth in Bulgarian, improvised the scenes, edited the film, wrote the final script in Bulgarian for the voiceover and translated the script into English for the subtitles, step by step and frame by frame, changing the words around to make meaning. The film ends with the powerful message: 'Adults, please remember!!! We are not numbers!! We are only kids'.

The narrative analysis of *Question Mark Movie* reveals how key decisions were made collaboratively, fostering an inclusive pedagogical approach to learning (hooks, 1994). The students reflected: 'we all gave in our ideas, even if someone didn't like something but someone else freely liked it, we tried to work with it so everyone gets an equal part in it. We worked well together and everyone was listening to everyone's ideas, so we didn't really argue, we tried to make compromises and all get what we wanted'. The analysis of critical events in the digital story demonstrates how these students wanted to counter the dominant school narrative of numbers, competition and test preparation (Sheehy, 2013). In making *Question Mark Movie* the students moved across borders of languages, spaces and friendships, cultivated an ideational fluency (Cremin & Maybin, 2013) and created a deeply collaborative perspective on inclusion.

Vignette from the Second Primary School of Liopetri, Cyprus

The Greek-English digital story *Irene – a refugee's story* is a strong example of how young children (aged 7–8 years old) can imagine, empathize and represent the complex emotions embodied in the stories of refugees. The name, Irene, means peace in Greek and the young children in making the digital story explore what it means to be constantly on the move and not to belong anywhere. The children came up with the idea that Irene was lost in the sculpture park and they would map out her journey through the landscape. The open air sculpture park has sculptures created by sculptors from around the world and it is located in a rocky landscape with the sea as a backdrop. The young children take their story outside to the Ayia Napa sculpture park and their interaction with the sculptures forms the backbone of their story.

In the making of this digital story, the children were learning how to tell a story from different viewpoints and perspectives and to understand more literary, poetic language. Sotia, the primary school teacher, had a research background in bidialectism and she opened up the space in the project to explore the concept of a refugee in the Cypriot Dialect and to translate and adapt the ideas into Modern Standard Greek in the filming process. In viewing the young children's language varieties as on a continuum, Sotia was able to use the Cypriot Dialect to deepen the children's understanding and their linguistic repertoire. Chryso, the project drama tutor with a research background in applied theatre and citizenship, worked in close collaboration with Sotia and the children to devise a way into the story of a refugee. In an interview in 2018, Sotia reflected: 'it was really impressive how 7-year-old students engaged so actively in the making of the story bringing constantly new ideas to the table. Students collaborated creatively and critically to produce their story using all of all their available linguistic resources'.

In thinking about how to explore the idea of belonging, Sotia discovered an educational resource designed for 5–8 year olds on the website of the UNHCR United Nations Refugee Agency for Cyprus. This was an animated Greek adaptation of a German children's story, *Karlinchen*, by Annegert Fuchshuber (1995). The children engaged in watching part of the animated story about a young girl who is a refugee, but not the ending. The poetic language is moving and sad and there are images and echoes from this story that emerge in the story the young children created in the sculpture park. The young girl in the original story wears a brown coat and a red scarf and encounters different characters along the way, including the Stone Eaters.

Irene – a refugee's story opens with a shot of a young girl's feet walking through the rocky landscape. The image of walking predominates the action in the digital story and the young girl's experience of not belonging anywhere. There were several students who wanted to play the young refugee, Irene, and this was resolved by the young children in an ingenious way. Almost seamlessly, the different girls interchanged in the role as the young refugee but always wore a signifying brown coat and pink scarf. This deepened their empathy and understanding of how anyone could be forced to go through these experiences. The children were aware of the obstacles and barriers that a young refugee would face and in the first encounter the sculpture acts as a gateway and you only see the hands of the boy as he asks: 'what does a child want here alone?' Irene enters the land of the Enchanted Sculptures and the story unfolds through the interaction with the sculptures that take on different voices and characters. This creates a powerful and moving story as Irene is overwhelmed at times by the size of the sculptures and the growing sense that she does not belong there: 'No one likes me because I came from another country and I'm different'. In the children's creation of the story, Irene is searching for her parents and she is told she will find them in the Land of the Frightened Refugees. The children decided to use a sculpture of two figures huddled in an embrace to represent the parents standing still and terrified (Figure 12.3). A hug, a hand reaching

Figure 12.3 Making the digital story, *Irene – a refugee's story*, in the Ayia Napa sculpture park

out, become symbols of hope but the fear remains. The story ends with the words: 'However, she never stopped being frightened'.

The narrative analysis of *Irene – A refugee's story* shows key decisions that students made in constructing their migration narrative. At the end of their story there is hope in the hand reaching out; however, in contrast with *Karlinchen*, written by an adult for children and having the typical happy ending, these young children in *Irene – A refugee's story* represent a deep empathy with the sadness and trauma embodied in the refugee experience. In a self-recorded review of the narrative, a student reflected upon this critical event: 'I would like to add that Irene was very sad and that fear never left her'. In making *Irene – a refugee's story*, the students have taken their story into the local landscape, walked in the footsteps of their character (Mackey, 2010) and developed a deeply empathetic perspective on inclusion.

Conclusion

This chapter explored how young people use digital storytelling to embody their languages, cultures, identities and interests. A narrative analysis of the digital stories demonstrated how young people wanted the space to express themselves in resistance to dominant narratives of 'Othering', competition and exclusion. Digital storytelling is connected with ideas of hope, justice and compassion, and in constructing alternative narratives 'perhaps digital storytelling is trying to call new communities into being' (Hartley, 2017: 221). This was reflected in the way these young people chose to become part of a multilingual community of digital storytellers. In making their digital stories, these students drew on their full linguistic repertoire and made key decisions about how their languages would be included and represented. Narrative analysis of critical events in their digital stories demonstrated how these students had repositioned themselves in relation to their own cultures and the culture of others (Phipps & Gonzalez, 2004). The analysis of key experiences represented in the digital stories demonstrated how these young people were pushing boundaries of themselves and others (Nyboe & Drotner, 2008) and developing 'competences of complexity' in relation to their identities, others' identities and belonging to a community.

This chapter also examined how multilingual digital storytelling extends notions of literacy and inclusion. Narrative and biographical analysis of the digital stories revealed that these young people constructed stories that mattered to them and that their collaborative narratives were not simply 'story for story's sake' (Hartley, 2017). The narrative analysis of key places in the digital stories showed how digital storytelling permeated school borders and how material spaces and places shaped the literate experiences of these young people (Mills & Comber, 2013). As well as engaging in the multiliteracies' process of transmediation (Mills, 2016) and learning to make meaning across multiple modes, these young people were making decisions about their languages and reflecting on the extent to which their languages are included in school settings.

Project-based experiential learning has the potential to open up spaces for young people's languages and cultures in school (Anderson et al., 2014). The students in Palestine presented their culture in an upbeat and creative way; the Bulgarian students in England began to understand what it means to belong in two languages and two cultures (Phipps & Gonzalez, 2004); the students in Cyprus used translanguaging in Cypriot Greek and Modern Standard Greek to enhance their meaning-making processes (García, 2009) and ideational fluency. In becoming more critically aware of how their languages and cultures are included in school contexts and wider society and more insightful of dominant narratives about education and migration, these young people were able to frame alternative narratives on what it means to belong in school classrooms and beyond.

Project website

https://goldsmithsmdst.com/

Multilingual digital stories in the three vignettes

Young Palestinian Talents: https://vimeo.com/138513881
Question Mark Movie: https://vimeo.com/220131613
Irene – A refugee's story: https://vimeo.com/219229870

Acknowledgements

I would like to express my sincere thanks to all the students and teachers involved for their commitment and hard work. I would also like to thank the Paul Hamlyn Foundation for supporting the Critical Connections project through two rounds of funding (2012–2014; 2015–2017).

References

Alrutz, M. (2015) *Digital Storytelling, Applied Theatre, & Youth: Performing Possibility*. Oxford: Routledge.
Anderson, J. (2016) The critical connections pedagogical framework. In J. Anderson and V. Macleroy (eds) *Multilingual Digital Storytelling: Engaging Creatively and Critically with Literacy* (pp. 226–247). Oxford: Routledge.
Anderson, J. and Macleroy Obied, V. (2011) Languages, literacies and learning: From monocultural to intercultural perspectives. *National Association for Language Development in the Curriculum (NALDIC) Quarterly* 8, 3.
Anderson, J. and Macleroy, V. (eds) (2016) *Multilingual Digital Storytelling: Engaging Creatively and Critically with Literacy*. Oxford: Routledge.

Anderson, J. and Macleroy, V. (2017) Connecting worlds: Interculturality, identity and multilingual digital stories in the making. *Language & Intercultural Communication* 17 (4), 1–24.

Anderson, J., Macleroy, V. and Chung, Y.-C. (2014) *Critical Connections: Multilingual Digital Storytelling Project. Handbook for Teachers*. London: Goldsmiths, University of London.

Cohen, L., Manion, L., Morrison, K. and Bell, R. (2018) *Research Methods in Education* (8th edn). London: Routledge.

Cremin, T. and Maybin, J. (2013) Children's and teachers' creativity in and through language. In K. Hall, T. Cremin, B. Comber and L. Moll (eds) *International Handbook of Research on Children's Literacy, Learning and Culture* (pp. 275–290). Oxford: Wiley-Blackwell.

Cummins, J. and Early, M. (eds) (2011) *Identity Texts: The Collaborative Creation of Power in Multilingual Schools*. Stoke-on-Trent: Trentham Books.

Darvin, R. and Norton, B. (2014) Transnational identity and migrant language learners: The promise of digital storytelling. *Education Matters* 2 (1), 55–66.

Fuchshuber, A. (1995) *Karlinchen*. Berlin: Annette Betz Verlag.

Ganley, B. (2013) Foreword. In J. Lambert (ed.) *Digital Storytelling: Capturing Lives, Creating Community* (4th edn). New York: Routledge.

García, O. (2009) *Bilingual Education in the 21st Century: A Global Perspective*. Oxford: Wiley-Blackledge.

García, O. (2017) *Translanguaging in the Crossroads of Civilization*. In R. Tsokalidou (ed.) *Beyond Bilingualism to Translanguaging* (pp. 15–19). Athens: Gutenberg.

Habib, S. (2017) *Learning and Teaching British Values: Policies and Perspectives on British Identities*. London: Palgrave MacMillan.

Hartley, J. (2017) Smiling or smiting? Selves, states and stories in the constitution of politics. In M. Dunford and T. Jenkins (eds) *Digital Storytelling: Form and Content* (pp. 167–182). London: Palgrave Macmillan.

Heath, S. (2013) *The Hand of Play in Literacy Learning*. In K. Hall, T. Cremin, B. Comber and L. Moll (eds) *International Handbook of Research on Children's Literacy, Learning and Culture* (pp. 184–189). Oxford: Wiley-Blackwell.

Holliday, A. (2011) *Intercultural Communication and Ideology*. London: Sage.

hooks, b. (1994) *Teaching to Transgress: Education as the Practice of Freedom*. London and New York: Routledge.

Kushnir, A. (2017) *Youth, Theatre, Radical Hope and the Ethical Imaginary: An Intercultural Investigation of Drama Pedagogy, Performance and Civic Engagement*. See https://www.oise.utoronto.ca/dr/youth-theatre-radical-hope/.

Lambert, J. (2013) *Digital Storytelling: Capturing Lives, Creating Community* (4th edn). New York: Routledge.

Leung, C. and Scarino, A. (2016) Reconceptualising the nature of goals and outcomes in language/s education. *The Modern Language Journal* 100 (S1), 81–95.

Mackey, M. (2010) Reading from the feet up: The local work of literacy. *Children's Literature in Education* 41, 323–339.

Mercer, S. (2016) Seeing the world through your eyes: Empathy in language learning and teaching. In P. MacIntyre, T. Gregersen and S. Mercer (eds) *Positive Psychology in SLA* (pp. 91–111). Bristol: Multilingual Matters.

Mills, K. (2016) *Literacy Theories for the Digital Age: Social, Critical, Multimodal, Spatial, Material and Sensory Lenses*. Bristol: Multilingual Matters.

Mills, K. and Comber, B. (2013) Space, place and power. In K. Hall, T. Cremin, B. Comber and L. Moll (eds) *International Handbook of Research on Children's Literacy, Learning and Culture* (pp. 412–423). Oxford: Wiley-Blackwell.

Nyboe, N. and Drotner, K. (2008) Identity, aesthetics, and digital narration. In K. Lundby (ed.) *Digital Storytelling, Mediatized Stories: Self-representations in New Media* (pp. 161–174). New York: Peter Lang.

Pahl, K. and Escott, H. (2019) Learning from Ninjas: Young people's films as a lens for an expanded view of literacy and language. *Discourse: Studies in the Cultural Politics of Education* 40 (6), 803–815.

Pahl, K. and Rowsell, J. (2010) *Artifactual Literacies: Every Object Tells a Story*. New York: Teachers College Press.

PHF & Innovation Unit (2012) *Learning Futures: A Vision for Engaging Schools*. London: Paul Hamlyn Foundation.

Phipps, A. and Gonzalez, M. (2004) *Modern Languages*. London: Sage.

Sefton-Green, J. and Brown, L. (2014) *Mapping Learner Progression into Digital Creativity*. Oxford: Nominet Trust.

Sheehy, M. (2013) What does human geography have to do with classrooms? In K. Hall, T. Cremin, B. Comber and L. Moll (eds) *International Handbook of Research on Children's Literacy, Learning and Culture* (pp. 400–411). Oxford: Wiley-Blackwell.

Wrigley, T. (2014) *The Politics of Curriculum in Schools*. London: Centre for Labour and Social Studies (Class).

A Non-Traditional Approach to Listening to Students' Voices

Marie-Paule Lory

Assistant Professor, University of Toronto Mississauga

In Canada, numerous researchers and teachers are working collaboratively to implement inclusive practices that conceptualize diversity as an asset in classrooms. Among the many projects that have been developed, storytelling practices represent a powerful pathway to support the identity development (and affirmation) of our pupils. Storytelling offers space to cultivate shared experiences and it has been proven to foster a sense of belonging among teachers, pupils and families.

My own research involving storytelling practices is largely arts-based: Plurilingual Drama-based activities (Armand *et al.*, 2013) and Plurilingual Kamishibai (Lory, 2018). In both projects, pupils' linguistic and cultural repertoires are at the heart of the pedagogical approaches. The Plurilingual Drama-based project engages pupils in play-based activities such as opening/closing rituals, breathing techniques and warm-up and acting exercises during which they express themselves in the languages of their choice while sharing personal, real or imaginary stories (examples of activities are available in French in the pedagogical guide, *Theatre Pluralité Élodil*: http://www.elodil.umontreal.ca/guides/theatre-pluralite-elodil/). The Plurilingual Kamishibai project is a storytelling practice inspired by a Japanese tradition. Students collaborate to create, write and illustrate a plurilingual story on a number of story boards. Afterwards, a storyteller uses a frame to showcase the illustrated boards in order to enact their story in front of an audience.

In the Canadian provinces of Quebec and Ontario, our research results have demonstrated that leveraging linguistic and cultural diversity enables teachers to establish a more equitable class atmosphere conducive to learning as pupils' voices are truly heard. For example, in the Plurilingual Drama-based project implemented in 2018 in Ontario for pupils with immigrant backgrounds, the teachers involved in this innovative project underlined that the unconventional and informal space fostered by the Plurilingual Drama-based sessions allowed pupils and teachers to get to know each other better. They noticed that this new space represented an opportunity to better comprehend pupils' experiences during their journey to Canada. This project led to the creation of strong bonds among all participants (pupils and teachers alike). The results also showed that these newly established relationships had a positive impact when the learners returned to a more conventional class setting: they were more focused and their willingness to learn academic content increased. In addition, through their shared experiences and stories, teachers noticed how pupils develop a sense of belonging to a new community when their linguistic and cultural repertoires are seen as an asset by their teachers and peers.

References

Armand, F., Lory, M.-P. and Rousseau, C. (2013) 'Les histoires, ça montre les personnes dedans, les feelings: Pas possible si pas de théâtre' (Tahina). *Revue de linguistique et de didactique des langues* 48, 37–55.

Lory, M.-P. (2018) Le Kamishibaï plurilingue: Une pratique orale créative qui valorise la diversité linguistique et culturelle. *Vivre le primaire*, Autumn, 69–70. See https://aqep.org/wp-content/uploads/2018/09/10-lekamishibai.pdf.

13 Inclusion Strategies for Emergent Bilingual Pupils in Pre-School in France: The Importance of the Home-School Relationship

Ann-Birte Krüger and Nathalie Thamin

Introduction

In many parts of Europe and the rest of the world, school populations are characterized by plurilingualism and multiculturalism. Many publications emphasize the importance of welcoming and recognizing linguistic and cultural diversity in an inclusive way in schools in general (García, 2009a; García *et al.*, 2006; Moro, 2012) and in pre-school in particular (Birot, 2016; Hélot & Rubio, 2013; Krüger *et al.*, 2016; Rayna & Brougère, 2016; Thomauske, 2017), as pre-school represents one of the most important milestones in the various stages contributing to pupils' success in education (Bauthier, 2005).

This is all the more true in a migration context, because at this age children's identities are developing, each of them with their own particularities. As Kàdas-Pickel (this volume) points out in her chapter on identity negotiation, children's home environments and schools are places of paramount importance for the construction of the self, a process in which 'being perceived' plays an important part. Therefore, teachers' positive attitudes towards children's languages and cultures play a particularly important role in identity construction (Komur-Thilloy & Paprocka-Piotrowska, 2016; Leclaire & Perregaux, 2016). Like Mary and Young (2017: 108), we consider 'a child whose language differs from the language of the school to be an emergent bilingual from the very first day s/he sets foot in the school'. Teachers' lack of knowledge about language acquisition and bilingualism, combined with erroneous notions about languages and their speakers in the educational context in France (Hélot, 2007), give rise to situations where pupils are perceived as deficient in the school language (Thamin, 2015) rather than being emergent bilinguals. This lack of knowledge among teachers was the starting point for our six-year research project and teacher education program concerning the education of emergent bilingual pupils in pre-school and primary school in the Franche-Comté region (a region situated in the east of France bordering on Alsace, Burgundy and Switzerland). Most of the migrants in Franche-Comté are from North Africa, Turkey and the Balkans. The number of immigrants in this part of France is below the national average (7% of the population, compared with the national average of 10%; INSEE, 2012). With the exception of some economic hotspots (Besançon, Montbéliard/ Belfort) and some small cities close to the Swiss border (Saint-Claude, Pontarlier, Morteau), the area is relatively rural. Pre-school and primary school teachers working in the Franche-Comté region in urban areas with low socioeconomic status (SES) reported a lack of teacher training focused on the needs of their specific multicultural and non-French speaking populations. Their pivotal question concerned how to work with very young pupils who do not speak the language of the school, especially when this was the case of the majority of the children in their classrooms. Our response to these teachers consisted of setting up conferences, work groups, exchanges and observations of pedagogical practices, as well as asking them to participate in research projects put into place by some of their colleagues (Gillot, 2017; Simonin, 2018). The project enabled us to work collaboratively with professionals and to analyze their experiences and methods (Simonin & Thamin, 2018). On the basis of our model of inclusion and welcoming pupils in schools in general, and in pre-school in particular, we decided to concentrate specifically both on the role of children's home languages in school and on home-school relationships, the two being closely connected.

On the basis of our experience with and observation of very young children (two to six years old) with a migration background in pre-school, this chapter sets out to examine the complex relationship between families and schools, and looks for a way to transform the classroom into a space that is welcoming to all. Our research questions were: how does an innovative home-school relationship contribute to the inclusion of emergent bilingual pupils in pre-school and what strategies are needed in order to empower parents? After presenting the French pre-school context in which the study took place, we describe our use of the model of the home-school relationship as a theoretical framework and an analytical tool. The main section then explores the innovative classroom practices we developed over the course of our project concerning emergent bilingual pupils in pre-school. We then detail, within the project, how researchers and teachers explored different ways of empowering children and parents through various pedagogical practices and how teachers' positive attitudes and skills were developed.

Context of the Study: The Pre-school System in France and the 'Traditional' Way of Dealing with Emergent Bilingual Pupils

The term 'pre-school' as used in this chapter denotes pre-primary education (*école maternelle*), which in France is public and free, and starts at the age of two/three years old. Up to now this part of the school system has been optional, but this changed in September 2019 when it became compulsory. It should be emphasized that pre-school enjoys wide social acceptance in France, with some 97.6% of three-year-olds and almost 100% of four- and five-year-olds voluntarily attending pre-school,[1] even when teaching and learning conditions are not always ideal with class sizes of up to 30 pupils with only one teacher. In schools located in officially designated high-priority areas (*réseau d'éducation prioritaire*), where the children attending school come from predominantly low SES families, classes are smaller, with about 20 pupils per class. This was the case in most of the schools we worked with in our project.

Pre-primary education in France is governed by a national curriculum. The latest version, entitled *L'école maternelle: un cycle unique, fondamental pour la réussite de tous* (Pre-primary education: a single cycle, fundamental to the success of all), dates back to 2015. It sets out the objectives for, and the foundations of, pre-primary education including its general orientation and expectations regarding the subjects and skills to be taught in pre-school by the end of *Cycle 1*, that is by the age of five/six, after three years of schooling (MEN, 2015; OECD, 2016). These goals include 'the development of the French language in all its dimensions', 'moving, expressing oneself and understanding through physical and artistic expression', 'becoming a pupil' and 'living together'. The most important aspect seems to be the first, which implies a solid mastery of the school language and raises, in our context, the question of how to reach this goal with non-native children when they arrive at school. In primary and secondary schools in France, newly arrived children who do not speak the language in which education takes place can claim additional language support in French as a second language, taught by a specialized teacher when available (Frisa, 2014; Goï, 2015; MEN, 2012). This does not, however, apply in the case of children under six. The 2002 curriculum states the following about these young pupils:

> It is not necessary to provide lessons in French as a second language for the very youngest pupils. The communication situations arising in day-to-day school life are usually very effective (…). (MEN, 2007: 88–89, our translation)

This recommendation assumes that immersion in the French language throughout the school week (24 hours per week) is enough to master the school language. This could be true if the teacher actively guided the process of learning French with all the specialized techniques of second language teaching (Birot, 2016; Goï, 2015; Klein, 2014). We will deal with the subject of classroom practices in more detail in the third part of this chapter. The study by Carol *et al.* (2016) has demonstrated how little one-to-one communication takes place between teachers and emergent bilingual pre-school pupils each day. When teachers lack knowledge and awareness of plurilingualism because they have never undergone training in this area, they clearly do not have the tools and strategies needed to support their pupils (Young & Mary, 2016). Where this is the case, the classroom policy has been, and frequently still is, a 'French only' language policy (Mary & Young, 2017), and children without French as a mother tongue are stigmatized as being deficient in language skills. Their home languages are considered by teachers to be of little or no importance for the learning of French (MEN, 2007; Young, 2012). The result of such language policies in school or classrooms is that children who have not yet acquired the language of the school fall silent (Birot, 2016; Thomauske, 2017). The children's home languages and their natural translanguaging practices are disregarded in school, and as a result they are not able to base their second language acquisition on these helpful competences (Cummins, 2000).

Regarding the new curriculum (MEN, 2015), several interesting innovations for emergent bilingual pupils in pre-school in France are worth highlighting. For the first time, the new curriculum recognizes the importance of the interaction between oral and writing skills (Cadet & Pegaz-Paquet, 2016), up to now frequently seen by the Ministry of Education as two quite separate abilities. Teaching oral language skills in pre-school is a persistently weak point, as a 2011 report on pre-schooling in France has pointed out (Bouysse *et al.*, 2011). How can the building of oral skills be supported in concrete terms? How can the oral production time of emergent bilingual pupils be promoted and multiplied (Simonin, 2018)? These questions are frequently raised by the teachers taking part in our professional development sessions, and constitute a real challenge, even though a number of studies offer appropriate and interesting answers as to how to teach oral language skills in pre-school (Péroz, 2013). From a second language acquisition perspective, the interaction between children's oral and writing skills is central to preparing children for literacy.

One sub-section on oral skills included in the curriculum for the first time in 2015 concerns awareness of language diversity as a new teaching objective. Even though this is an important step forward in comparison with earlier curricula, there is cause for skepticism since the languages discussed are not specifically the languages of the pupils but 'regional languages, foreign languages and sign language' (MEN, 2015: 7). We also find it regrettable that there is no continuity of this type of practice through primary school and that it can only start in the second year of pre-school, even though some studies (Audras & Leclaire, 2016; Birot, 2016), as well as our own classroom observations, have demonstrated the benefit of language awareness practices in welcoming very young children at the start of pre-school in France.

The new curriculum also considers home-school relationships to be of great importance, as one of the first points on the first page of the curriculum is entitled 'A school that welcomes children and their parents' (MEN, 2015: 1, our translation). In referring to this relationship, the official discourse uses terms such as 'regular dialogue', 'confidence' and 'two-way information', while adding that it is for the educational practitioners in schools to define the ways in which the relationship between home and school is handled. The objective of fostering home-school relationships is to promote successful schooling for each and every pupil, while taking into consideration the diversity of families. The curriculum also states that this relationship enables parents to understand the specific characteristics of the French pre-school system. To sum up, the curriculum seems to offer a real starting point for positive home-school relationships, but the shape of this relationship needs to be better defined to ensure that parents have an equally important role. Up to now schools have seemed to be content with merely explaining to parents how the school works, rather than establishing a real exchange between the partners about education and striving for a genuine inclusion of parents in their children's schooling. We will elaborate on our model of inclusion in the context of the home-school relationship in the next section.

Literature Review

Why collaborate with parents?

The transition from the world of home to the school environment involves an emotional, cultural and linguistic separation for the child. Before entering the school system, the child's life has been dominated by the use of the mother tongue or mixed bilingual practices – depending on specific family backgrounds and histories. Upon entry into pre-school, the children's socialization soon places them in relationships which can be either conflictual or consensual. The child inhabits different worlds, more or less harmoniously: his/her home, with its language, music, food, smells and ways of interacting with his/her parents; and school with its standards, language and ideals. Migrant parents may feel that they are being dispossessed of their child. Professionals must keep in mind the need to support parents in their role as parents, to reassure them and help them to be legitimate interlocutors (Goï, 2008, 2015; Mestre, 2015), even when their relationship to school is very different from that of non-migrant parents. The family language can constitute a bridge between school and home and help the child in this transition (Leclaire & Perregaux, 2016: 283). In Moro's (2010, 2012) analysis, the school needs to have a positive view of migrant families and the languages spoken at home in order to provide caring and stress-free support in relation to the language of the school, which mobilizes a new set of functions, particularly cognitive and reflexive ones (Wallon *et al.*, 2008). Schools also need to enable the child to understand the school environment, with its standards, codes and rules. Fostering collaboration between parents and teachers helps families to feel included, and increases their confidence. In addition, the involvement and inclusion of parents often allows teachers to change their perception of both parents and child (Simonin, 2018), and increases pupil participation in the classroom thanks to the atmosphere it creates (Flecha, 2015).

'Co-éducation' or collaborative spaces?

In the French school context, the term 'co-education'[2] implies that the family is in a partnership with teachers designed to foster cooperation between parents/guardians and professionals for the benefit of pupils and the relationships between them. Progress is being made in the institutional discourse on school-family relationships which can been seen in the following official documents: the 2006 official text on the role and place of parents in school (MEN, 2006); the 2008 circular entitled 'A school open to parents' (MEN, 2008); the 2012 circular on 'Schooling for newly arrived non-French speaking pupils' (MEN, 2012); the 2015 Pre-school Curriculum (MEN, 2015); and the circular for the 2019 school year (MEN, 2019).

However, educational professionals often remain reluctant to collaborate with parents, especially migrants, and vice versa. Migrant families of diverse and multiple cultures often remain invisible in the school culture, which is governed by ethnocentric and rigid normative functions. A lack of mutual understanding between teaching staff and parents, as well as the often negative and segregated attitudes of schools towards families with a migrant background, can be observed (Changkakoti & Akkari, 2008) and are detrimental to the dynamics of academic achievement and to the psychological development of pupils, who are often caught up in conflicts of loyalty (Goï, 2015). In Mestre's (2015: 186) view, we need to invent ways of creating spaces where children are not subjected to comments that belittle their parents. Likewise, in the words of Leclaire and Perregaux:

> If we wish to give back to parents their role as co-educators, we must create spaces where these contradictions can be mutually experienced, thought about, reflected on, so as to enable the parents, and hence their children, not to abandon their vision of the world, but to think about putting the contradictions into words and transforming them into a precious asset. (Leclaire & Perregaux, 2016: 274, our translation)

But what are these spaces, exactly?

Concepts of space and place

> Space is a doubt: I constantly have to mark it, to designate it: it is never mine, I am never given it, I have to conquer it. (Perec, 1974: 140, our translation)

The word 'space' has long conveyed a certain neutrality, but the way in which geography has evolved and has brought to the fore the relationship between space and those who act within it has made it part of a process. In *La production de l'espace*, Lefèbvre (1974: 40, our translation) highlights the importance of space as an eminently political product of society: '[...] Every society (hence every mode of production, with the diversities it encompasses, the discrete societies that reflect the general concept) produces a space, its own space'. Social space refers to the spatial dimension of society and its representations. Social space is constructed as it is put into practice not only by the social actors involved, but also by the individual and collective imagination and ideologies that condition social life (Senegal, 1992). In the words of the anthropologist Augé, 'If a place can be defined as identity, relationship and history, a space that can be defined as neither identity, nor relationship nor history is a non-place (...)'. A place would therefore be 'a spatial and temporal construct that expresses the identity of a group and determines by its organization the collective and individual practices of that group' (Augé, 1992: 100, our translation).

Individual and collective concepts and shared ideologies are both the components and the result of discourses that take place in multidimensional social groups. Despite the difficulty experienced by school staff in implementing collaboration, schools offer spaces for collaboration with families that are shared with the child and work in his/her favor. Mary and Young (2017), basing themselves on the work of Conteh and Brock (2011), emphasize the importance of developing *safe spaces* that can be symbolic as well as physical, which allow the emergent bilingual child (García, 2009b) to optimize his/her learning. By accepting and promoting the language and culture of the child, we make possible the connection between his/her experiences at home and at school. The work of Flecha (2015: 49) shows that schools studied in his project were not 'places where social inequalities are reproduced and perpetuated, but [places] that promote the image of schools as spaces for social transformation and overcoming inequality'.

Spaces for collaboration, safe spaces and transversal symbolic spaces

What kinds of space have we identified as fostering collaboration between teachers and families, thus enabling parents to become legitimate partners (Leclaire & Perregaux, 2016)? Relationships between families and educational staff can exist within different spaces: physical, symbolic and collaborative.

The opportunities for informal and formal contacts between families and the school are particularly abundant in the French pre-school context (as compared with subsequent school years), particularly in urban and low socioeconomic contexts.[3] They offer real spaces for collaboration. One example of an informal contact opportunity is the time designated for parents to bring their children to the classroom at the beginning of the school day and pick them up at the end of each day. Other opportunities occur when parents participate in school outings (trips to the ice rink, visits to the library and so on), school events, etc. Formal contacts can also take place in the form of meetings between teachers and parents, for example, when the child is enrolled for the next school year, parent-teacher meetings at the beginning of the school year and collective and individual parent meetings.

Flecha (2015) commented recently on a European research project called *INCLUD-ED*. Researchers conducted a longitudinal case study over four years in schools with low SES families and strong community involvement in several European countries (Malta, Finland, Lithuania, the UK and Spain). The project highlighted five types of family and community involvement – informative, consultative, decisive, evaluative and educative – and their individual effects on academic achievement. Results showed that community participation is especially important for pupils from minority cultures, as it contributes to greater coordination between home and school activities, and revealed that the decisive, evaluative and educational types of participation contribute most to academic success. The data emphasize the transformative capacity of the schools involved in the project (Flecha, 2015: 49). Children were also given more opportunities for interaction with adults in various spaces, which in turn accelerated the learning process. In the next section we will analyze the types of family and community participation in schools that exist in our context.

Data Collection and Analysis: Specific Family Collaboration Activities in Pre-school

Data collection

Our research and training program focuses on the schooling of emergent bilingual pupils and the training of pre-school teachers in a context of plurality. Recent studies (García & Sánchez, 2015; Krüger *et al.*, 2016; Panagiotopoulou, 2016) show the importance for researchers and teacher trainers of working more closely with professionals in the field, allowing and encouraging mutual exchange and the sharing of knowledge and practices among all the actors involved in education. It was within this framework that we collaborated with the local education authority for

Traveler and Newly Arrived Emergent Bilingual Pupils support service (CASNAV Besançon, see Adam-Maillet, this volume) and with teachers in several pre-schools in the Franche-Comté region. The data collection methodology adopted was ethnographic and qualitative. It is based on eight semi-structured interviews, recorded and/or filmed class observations at two nursery schools (one class of 24 learners in Besançon and two classes comprising a total of 45 learners in Béthoncourt) as well as exchanges and meetings with the teaching staff at the nursery school in Besançon, and two formal individual teacher-parent meetings at the school in Béthoncourt. We will also refer to a protocol for conversations with the pupils' parents, devised and tested by the teaching staff at the Besançon school, which focused on languages and the relationship between the school and families (Simonin, 2018).

Data analysis

Taking Flecha's (2015) typology as our basis, our experience in the French context shows that families and the members of the community communicate mainly within an informative, and maybe sometimes consultative, space. However, the implementation of a set of practices makes it possible to develop an innovative home-school relationship, where parents are involved and take a decisive role in their children's education. We aimed to answer the question: 'How can we involve parents and what methods can we consider and test?' To answer the question, we present several methods used by teachers working in our 'French as a second language' project in pre-school.

From our analysis of the data we extracted several formal and informal situations and activities that are specifically linked to the home-school relationship. The interview data were transcribed and translated into English by the authors for the purposes of this chapter. We propose a classification according to three categories: (1) formal contact with teachers and head teachers in pre-school – personal meetings with teachers and head teachers from registration to later occasions during the three years of pre-school; (2) informal contact with teachers and head teachers – informal day-to-day conversations, accompanying children on school excursions, festivities in school, 'café parents' (coffee mornings held for parents to exchange on a given subject related to their children's education such as food, sleep, language use); (3) classroom activities – language awareness activities for different age groups and with different objectives

Formal contact: Improving communication with parents

> For me, a school works ... the basis of everything is the relationship with the parent. (Pre-school head teacher, Besançon REP+, 2016, our translation)

The role of the head teacher and the dynamic cohesion of the team are essential (Rigolot & Thamin, 2019). They influence the relationship with parents, the dynamics of innovative, pedagogical, inclusive practices and positive attitudes to linguistic and cultural diversity (McAndrew & Audet, 2013). This school dynamic is based on the engagement of teachers, and their ability to experiment, to reflect on their methods with regard to individual pupils and to question more standardized methods. Formal support in the French context can take the form, for example, of a school project where pupils' languages and the place given to their families in school are central (Simonin, 2018). This type of support also includes collaboration with local associations and a differentiated pedagogical approach that reinforces the autonomy of children.

Welcoming families when children enter school means being present for (a) immediate communication, (b) explaining the objectives and functioning of school and (c) putting in place useful linguistic mediation. Teachers and families have access to useful resources on the Ministry of Education website to assist with home-school communication, such as a welcome booklet translated into 13 languages, with audio versions, explaining to families the role and functioning of school.[4] The presence of interpreters during meetings may occasionally be necessary, especially when parents have only recently arrived in France. It is also important to translate written communications into the family's language, maybe with the help of pictures.

In terms of formal contacts, Simonin and her team experimented with an interview protocol for parents with children new to the school, implemented at the start of the school year (Simonin, 2018). These data form part of the collaborative research.[5] Such meetings allow teachers to reach out to parents and to foster genuine cooperation between the families and the school in the interests of the children's education. The exchanges enable teachers to understand factors that may have an impact on learning (family languages, relationship to literacy, attitudes towards school). The aim of the interviews is to gain a better understanding of pupils' bilingualism, which language(s) are spoken and understood, the nature of the children's linguistic resources and their relationship to their mother tongue, with a view to adapting the way French is taught in the classroom in the light of this deeper understanding. Our research shows that these interviews have an influence on parents' confidence and give families a sense that they are being listened to. In the following extract, for example, a Turkish speaking mother expresses her regret that her (five-year-old) daughter stopped speaking Turkish with her at the end of the last year of pre-school. The mother's stepbrother accompanied her to the interview to interpret.

(T = teacher; I = stepbrother and interpreter)
T: So at the very beginning of the year I remember she wasn't at all in the learning mindset / she was very into playing / her cousin: / she

wasn't thinking about what she was learning at school / whereas now her behaviour has changed completely / she really applies herself now
I: (TRANSLATES INTO TURKISH FOR THE MOTHER)
T: So, yes, that's very good // acquiring the language is going much better too / so there there's still / I'll show you
I: She (THE MOTHER) says she's stopped speaking Turkish at home / the little girl
T: At home?
I: Yes, she doesn't speak it any more //
(MOTHER SPEAKS IN TURKISH)
I: Yes, so XXX doesn't speak any more, as I said / it's taken over, it's even easier for them to speak French now // they're getting a bigger and bigger vocabulary
T: So what do they do with their mother, then?
I: They speak French, but she understands, and even if she doesn't understand they can translate too / they can convey the message
T: They translate what they've just said in French for their mother?
I: That's right.

During the interview, in observing the mother's facial expressions, the researcher could sense that the mother was experiencing feelings of regret. The fact that the interview was being conducted at school, in an institutional context, may well have influenced the mother's report and the way she spoke of valuing and using French in the home context. It is not likely that the daughter used no Turkish when she spoke to her mother given her mother's low proficiency in French, but it is possible that her use of French had increased since the beginning of her enrollment in pre-school. This increased use of French is what the mother regrets.

It is worth mentioning that the teachers we worked with conducted this kind of individual meeting with parents on average four times a year throughout the three years of pre-school.

Informal contact with the teacher and head teacher

Informal contact consists of small talk in day-to-day encounters, exchanges during companionship on school excursions, festivities in school and the *'café parents'*.

Some schools hold regular *'café parents'* in order to create a different context for conversations about parenting issues such as languages, cultures, children's personal development and education, parenthood and the role of pre-school. The aim is (a) to meet for coffee in school time with family, staff and local people from outside school, (b) to exchange views with families, especially those that have found it difficult to participate in school life and (c) to take on board the families' requests, concerns and needs. This process helps to create an egalitarian relationship between teachers and families. In order to encourage the families to participate, interpretation into several languages may have to be provided.

Some teams also create blogs in order to share day-to-day classroom activities with families, and these are visited frequently, even by families with low literacy skills. An example of a school blog can be found here: http://mat-cologne-besancon.ac-besancon.fr/category/infos-parents/. This blog builds the languages of the families into the home page and reflects the school's many multilingual activities (multilingual digital picture books, nursery rhymes in French and in the children's languages).

Raising awareness about languages and including home languages in the classroom for different age groups and with different objectives

On the basis of observations, informal talks and one formal interview with a teacher, we will describe the various strategies and practices linked to language awareness (LA) activities with the different age groups at preschool and with specific reference to the home-school relationship.

The *Handbook of Language Awareness* (Garrett & Cots, 2018) and the work of Michel Candelier on the didactics of plurilingualism (Troncy, 2014) demonstrate that LA now encompasses a large field, with many different definitions and applications. We agree with the definition of the Association for Language Awareness (ALA): LA is '**explicit knowledge about language, and conscious perception and sensitivity in language learning, language teaching and language use**'.[6] It was already noted by Hawkins (1987) that LA could unlock the language knowledge and skills brought by children from home to school. 'Being aware of the otherness on our doorstep, embodied by the presence of children of diverse cultural backgrounds in our classrooms, is the first step in raising language and cultural awareness at school' (Young, 2018: 27). These precepts concerning an LA pedagogy based on the children in the classroom, their languages and their families are in line with the LA practices of the teacher with whom we worked in close collaboration throughout our research and training program. Her activities involved linking the children's home lives with their school lives, providing an additional dimension to the LA approach.

In the case of very young children (two- to three-year-olds starting formal schooling), we observed that the act of bringing the children's home lives into school is clearly an affective one. One example of this was that our teacher asked families to take a picture of themselves with their child and then used these photographs throughout the school year for different purposes in the classroom: to point to the parents' picture at the beginning of the year, to explain that the parents would be back later, to learn to say 'Mum' and 'Dad' in the languages of the children in the class, to point to when the teacher wanted to know how to say something in the home language and, finally, as a kind of security blanket.

The teacher stressed that at the beginning of the year the home languages were used in a more individual approach to calm and reassure the young children. Often it underpinned a one-on-one exchange with a single child, or one child with his/her parents, about how to express something in the child's home language, in order then to express it in French. In these situations, the teacher spontaneously used the little knowledge she had acquired of the home languages to help a pupil in her class feel better. The role of the parents in the photo project is essential even when their involvement is only sporadic and mainly virtual, showing how the presence of the parents and their home languages is necessary for the well-being of every child at school. This practice of using the home languages with very young children in the first year of pre-school is a rather innovative approach in French schools and does not feature in the school curriculum as previously described. Nevertheless, the positive results of these methods are in line with the thinking and findings of several studies in the French pre-school context with children of the same age group, such as those of Barrateau and Dompmartin-Normand (2015) and Audras and Leclaire (2016), and endorse the findings of an interesting study by Leclaire and Lemattre (2015) on the outcomes of the use of home languages with very young children as transcultural mediation in a therapeutic context.

The use of home languages by the same teacher with another class of children aged four to five years old (a mixed class of second- and third-year pre-schoolers) was different, with more frequent and consequential involvement of parents and their home languages. The activities for this age group correspond more closely to the typical LA activities such as reading children's books in different languages. Taking inspiration from the book *Les langues du monde au quotidien* (Languages of the World Everyday, Kervran, 2013) the teacher engaged in LA activities at intervals throughout the school year (for example, by using a mascot who travelled through different countries and to the children's homes). She had taken over the class in September 2015, with about 20 pupils, all of whom (with the exception of two or three) had a migrant background, even though most of them were born in France. She realized at the beginning of the school year that some of these emergent bilingual pupils had difficulty communicating in French even though they were in their last year of pre-school and some of them also displayed behavioral difficulties. She decided to start a multimodal LA project in the 2015/2016 school year with the aim of finding a solution to these problems and including and valuing the cultures and languages of all the children in her class. The parents in the project participated by translating, interpreting and reading children's picture books, and also intervened when the teacher invited them to talk individually about language use in their families. At the beginning of the year the objectives of the project and how it would evolve were left open; it focused on the children and on their desire to take part in and develop the project.

The pupils brought examples of the languages of their cousins and other family members living in other countries into school. They chose to create a globe displaying different objects such as sheets of paper with

Figure 13.1 The multilingual globe

words in different languages and some objects linked to these languages (Figure 13.1). Progressively, the classroom became a multilingual space, with notices in different languages, and the relationship with the children's families became increasingly relaxed because they were part of the project. We observed how parents came in and talked to the teacher without any shyness and how, in informal interviews, they praised the inclusion of their languages in school as well as the teacher's classroom language policy. With reference to the difficulties encountered at the beginning of the year, the teacher described in a formal interview how things had developed and the central point of her classroom language policy:

> I stopped saying to the children 'We have to speak French' because I realised that not being able to speak their language at all made them clam up completely. They didn't even speak French any more. They didn't speak at all. So now I've completely changed the way we do things. I haven't got any silent children any more. Even when we're speaking French, I ask them how you say it in their language. Yes, they feel comfortable. They know where they fit in at school. They feel that they have a right to speak. It's a question of personality too. Even though they make mistakes in French, they communicate with each other. And when they don't know how, then words come out in other languages, or they ask each other. (Pre-school teacher, Bethoncourt REP+, 2015)

Here the teacher pointed to the different impacts of making space for home languages at school at various levels: behavior, performance in the language of the school and emotional aspects. Benefits were observed in the form of metalinguistic insights about languages and language practices. An example of languages being compared occurred when a Turkish mother read aloud in Turkish the same book as the class had read in French. The teacher asked the class to compare the book titles, and the young pupils aged four and five realized that the Turkish title had fewer words because there were no articles. This discovery helped the teacher and the other pupils understand why choosing the correct article in French could be a challenge for the Turkish pupils in the class.

Finally, these experiences in including home languages at school illustrate how the school has benefitted from opening up to welcome all children and their parents and how this has led to diversifying family participation. The teacher showed us that children must first feel comfortable at school before they can start to learn, and that this is only possible when parents are included.

Conclusion

This chapter has discussed how an innovative home-school relationship contributes to the inclusion of emergent bilingual pupils in pre-school, and what strategies are needed in order to empower parents. Our main aim was to highlight the fact that the well-being of children at school depends on their sense of being included in the school, together with their languages, their cultures and their families (Armand, 2014). We have linked our theoretical discussion about involving families and creating spaces in school where families can be included with the pedagogical practices and classroom language policies of two teachers with whom we have worked closely over the course of several years. This collaboration between researchers and pre-school teachers was extremely productive and opened the way to further collaboration on teacher training between the team and to joint publications (Simonin, 2018; Simonin & Thamin, 2018). Our data show that the home-school relationship assumes different shapes, depending on the context, and that more specific categorization than the simple dichotomy of formal or informal contact needs to be found. So we can see that involving parents in pre-school should take different forms and must go further than merely explaining to parents how school works. It even goes beyond simply inviting parents to participate: we need specific, concrete activities where families can be involved and discussions held with and for parents in order to encourage their participation in school life. Our results corroborate the findings of international studies on the positive impact of involving families in school (Flecha, 2015). It is important to point out that this positive impact applies equally to children, parents and teachers. We have tried to provide some transferable examples of these activities and teaching strategies from our data. The approaches adopted have physical, collaborative and symbolic transversal dimensions which create safe spaces, such as the translanguaging practices and meeting points along the lines of the *'café parents'* that we have described.[7]

Notes

(1) *Libération*, 27 March 2018. See http://www.liberation.fr/france/2018/03/27/scolarisation-obligatoire-a-3-ans-le-cadeau-discret-de-macron-au-prive_1639324.
(2) It is interesting to note that, while this term exists in English language research, it refers to mixed-sex education. It is for this reason that we have opted for the English terms 'home-school relationship' and 'family involvement'.
(3) Called REP+ (schools situated in an officially designated high-priority area). Ministry of Education. See http://eduscol.education.fr/cid52780/la-politique-refondee-de-l-education-prioritaire-les-reseaux-d-education-prioritaire-plus-ou-rep.html.
(4) Eduscol. See http://eduscol.education.fr/cid59114/ressources-pour-les-eana.html#lien0 (accessed 5 October 2019).
(5) In the context of her dissertation, supervised by N. Thamin, M.-C. Simonin (2018) analyzed these conversations with the parents of children in her class. She also carried out additional interviews for research purposes with six parents of pupils, used as case studies in her work. This needs to be referenced and included in the bibliography.
(6) Association for Language Awareness. See https://www.languageawareness.org.
(7) The BILEM (Bilinguisme en maternelle) project website on bilingualism in pre-school, providing information on three topics, welcoming pupils and their families, teaching, and research, can be found at http://bilem.ac-besancon.fr.

References

Armand, F. (2014) Pourquoi l'éducation inclusive en maternelle? Les jeunes enfants sont-ils 'racistes'? *Revue Préscolaire* 52 (3), 21–23.
Audras, I. and Leclaire, F. (2016) Accueillir dans sa langue l'enfant et sa famille: S'appuyer sur les langues des enfants pour la réussite de tous dès l'école maternelle. In A.-B. Krüger, N. Thamin and S. Cambrone-Lasnes (eds) *Diversité linguistique et culturelle à l'école: Accueil des élèves et formation des acteurs* (pp. 93–112). Paris: L'Harmattan.
Augé, M. (1992) *Non-Lieux: Introduction à une anthropologie de la surmodernité*. Paris: Le Seuil.
Barrateau, M. and Dompmartin-Normand, C. (2015) Éveil aux langues en maternelle: Accueillir les élèves et leurs parents dans leur diversité linguistique et culturelle. In D.-L. Simon, C. Dompmartin-Normand, S. Galligani and M.-O. Maire-Sandoz (eds) *Accueillir l'enfant et ses langues: Rencontres pluridisciplinaires sur le terrain de l'école* (pp. 167–188). Paris: Riveneuve éditions.
Bauthier, E. (ed.) (2005) *Apprendre à l'école, apprendre l'école*. Lyon: Chronique sociale.
Birot, S. (2016) Témoignage: Quelle prise en charge des enfants allophones en classe ordinaire? In G. Komur-Thilloy and U. Paprocka-Piotrowska (eds) *Education Plurilingue: Contextes, Représentations, Pratiques* (pp. 273–280). Paris: Orizons.
Bouysse, V., Claus, P. and Szymankiewicz, C. (2011) *L'école maternelle*. Rapport no. 2011–108. See http://media.education.gouv.fr/file/2011/54/5/2011-108-IGEN-IGAENR_215545.pdf (accessed July 2018).
Cadet, L. and Pegaz-Paquet, A. (2016) Prendre/apprendre la parole: L'oral à l'école primaire dans les textes officiels. *Le français aujourd'hui* 4 (195), 9–22.

Carol, R., Behra, S. and Macaire, D. (2016) Les élèves allophones à l'école maternelle: Interactions langagières et appropriation du français. In A.-B. Krüger, N. Thamin and S. Cambrone-Lasnes (eds) *Diversité linguistique et culturelle à l'école: Accueil des élèves et formation des acteurs* (pp. 47–68). Paris: L'Harmattan.

Changkakoti, N. and Akkari, A. (2008) Familles et écoles dans un monde de diversité: Au-delà des malentendus. *Revue des sciences de l'éducation: Écoles et familles de minorités ethnoculturelles* 34 (2), 419–441. See https://www.erudit.org/fr/revues/rse/2008-v34-n2-rse2553/019688ar/.

Conteh, J. and Brock, A. (2011) 'Safe spaces'? Sites of bilingualism for young learners in home, school and community. *International Journal of Bilingual Education and Bilingualism* 14 (3), 347–360.

Cummins, J. (2000) *Language, Power and Pedagogy: Bilingual Children in the Crossfire.* Clevedon: Multilingual Matters.

Flecha, R. (2015) Successful educational actions through family involvement. In R. Flecha (ed.) *Successful Educational Actions for Inclusion and Social Cohesion in Europe* (pp. 47–65). Cham: Springer. See https://www.schooleducationgateway.eu/files/esl/downloads/13_INCLUD-ED_Book_on_SEA.pdf (accessed 3 July 2018).

Frisa, J.-M. (2014) *Accueillir un élève allophone à l'école élémentaire.* Besançon: Canopé.

García, O. (2009a) Education, multilingualism and translanguaging in the 21st century. In T. Skutnabb-Kangas, R. Phillipson, A.K. Mohanty and M. Panda (eds) *Social Justice Through Multilingual Education* (pp. 140–158). Bristol: Multilingual Matters.

García, O. (2009b) Emergent bilinguals and TESOL: What's in a name? *TESOL Quarterly* 43, 322–326.

García, O. and Sanchez, M. (2015) Transforming schools with emergent bilinguals: The CUNY-NYSIEB Project. In I. Dirim, I. Gogolin, D. Knorr, M. Krüger-Potratz, D. Lengyel, H. Reich and W. Weiße (eds) *Intercultural Education: Festschrift for Ulla Neumann* (pp. 80–94). Berlin: Waxmann.

García, O., Skutnabb-Kangas, T. and Torres-Guzmán, M.E. (eds) (2006) *Imagining Multilingual Schools: Languages in Education and Globalization.* Clevedon: Multilingual Matters.

Garrett, P. and Cots, J.M. (eds) (2018) *The Routledge Handbook of Language Awareness.* New York: Routledge.

Gillot, C. (2017) Les relations école-famille au prisme du bilinguisme émergent: L'exemple des écoles maternelles du secteur REP+ de Montbéliard. Masters thesis in educational research, ESPE de Besançon.

Goï, C. (2008) *Élèves nouvellement arrivés en France et parents allophones: Construire le lien entre l'école et la famille.* Les Cahiers pédagogiques no. 465. See http://www.cahiers-pedagogiques.com/Eleves-nouvellement-arrives-en (accessed November 2018).

Goï, C. (2015) *Des élèves venus d'ailleurs.* Futuroscope: Canopé Editions Eclairer.

Hawkins, E.W. (1987) *Awareness of Language: An Introduction.* Cambridge: Cambridge University Press.

Hélot, C. (2007) *Du bilinguisme en famille au plurilinguisme à l'école.* Paris: L'Harmattan.

Hélot, C. and Rubio, M.N. (eds) (2013) *Développement du langage et plurilinguisme chez le jeune enfant.* Toulouse: Érès.

INSEE Franche-Comté (2012) *Immigrés en Franche-Comté*, Info web, N° 93, octobre 2012.

Kervran, M. (ed.) (2013) *Les langues du monde au quotidien: Une approche interculturelle. Cycle 1.* Rennes: Canopé éditions.

Klein, C. (dir.) (2014) *Les premiers apprentissages quand le français est langue seconde. Maternelle et début du cycle 2.* Paris: CRDP: Canopé-CNDP.

Komur-Thilloy, G. and Paprocka-Piotrowska, U. (eds) (2016) *Éducation plurilingue: Contextes, représentations, pratiques.* Paris: Orizons.

Krüger, A.-B., Thamin, N. and Cambrone-Lasnes, S. (eds) (2016) *Diversité linguistique et culturelle à l'école: Accueil des élèves et formation des acteurs.* Paris: L'Harmattan.
Leclaire, F. and Lemattre, B. (2015) Dépasser les frontières pour re-tisser les liens: L'éveil aux langues en contexte thérapeuthique. In D.-L. Simon, C. Dompmartin-Normand, S. Galligani and M.-O. Maire-Sandoz (eds) *Accueillir l'enfant et ses langues: Rencontres pluridisciplinaires sur le terrain de l'école* (pp. 45–72). Paris: Riveneuve éditions.
Leclaire, F. and Perregaux, C. (2016) Répertoires langagières: Une base pour un travail d'aide. In T. Auzou-Caillemet and M. Loret (eds) *Prendre en compte le corps et l'origine socioculturelle dans les apprentissages* (pp. 273–293). Paris: Retz.
Lefèbvre, H. (1974) *La Production de l'espace.* Paris: Anthropos.
Mary, L. and Young, A.S. (2017) From silencing to translanguaging: Turning the tide to support emergent bilinguals in transition from home to pre-school. In B. Paulsrud, J. Rosén, B. Straszer and Å. Wedin (eds) *New Perspectives on Translanguaging and Education* (pp. 108–128). Bristol: Multilingual Matters.
McAndrew, M. and Audet, G. (2013) *La réussite scolaire des élèves issus de l'immigration: Les écoles et les enseignants font une différence!* Montreal: CEETUM. See https://www.cipcd.ca/wp-content/uploads/2014/10/mcandrew-audet-enjeux-2013.pdf (accessed February 2021).
MEN (2006) B.O. no. 31 du 31 aout 2006. *Le rôle et la place des parents à l'école*, no. 2006-137 du 25-8-2006. See http://www.education.gouv.fr/bo/2006/31/MENE0602215C.htm (accessed November 2019).
MEN (2007) *Qu'apprend-on à l'école maternelle: 2007–2008. Les programmes.* Paris: CNDP.
MEN (2008) Circulaire no. 2008-102 DU 25-7-2008. *Ecole-famille.* Opération expérimentale, 'Ouvrir l'école aux parents pour réussir l'intégration'. B.O. no. 31 du 31 juillet 2008. See https://www.education.gouv.fr/bo/2008/31/MENE0800648C.htm (accessed November 2019).
MEN (2012) Circulaire no. 2012-141 du 2 octobre 2012. *Organisation de la scolarité des élèves allophones nouvellement arrivés.* See http://www.education.gouv.fr/pid285/bulletin_officiel.html?cid_bo=61536 (accessed July 2018).
MEN (2015) Bulletin spécial du 26 mars 2015. *Programme d'enseignement de l'école maternelle.* See http://www.education.gouv.fr/cid87300/rentree-2015-le-nouveau-programme-de-l-ecole-maternelle.html (accessed July 2018).
MEN (2019) B.O. no. 22 du 29 mai 2019. *Recommandations pédagogiques, les langues vivantes étrangères à l'école maternelle.* Note de service no. 2019-086 du 28-5-2019. See https://www.education.gouv.fr/pid285/bulletin_officiel.html?cid_bo=142292 (accessed January 2020).
Mestre, C. (2015) Les parents migrants et l'école. *Spirale* 3 (75), 186–187.
Moro, M.R. (2010) *Grandir en situation transculturelle.* Paris: Editions Fabert.
Moro, M.R. (2012) *Enfants de l'immigration, une chance pour l'école.* Montrouge: Bayard.
OECD (2016) *Starting Strong – Early Childhood Education and Care – France.* See http://www.oecd.org/education/school/ECECMN-France.pdf (accessed July 2018).
Panagiotopoulou, A. (2016) *Mehrsprachigkeit in der Kindheit: Perspektiven für die frühpädagogische Praxis.* WiFF-Expertise 46. Munich: Deutsches Jugendinstitut. See https://www.nifbe.de/images/nifbe/Fachbeiträge/2017/Exp_Panagiotopoulou_web.pdf (accessed February 2021).
Perec, G. (1974) *Espèces d'espaces.* Paris: Editions Galilée.
Péroz, P. (2013) *Apprentissage du langage oral à l'école maternelle. Quel modèle? Les enjeux de l'oral dans nos classes.* Marseille: Conférence en ligne. See https://halshs.archives-ouvertes.fr/halshs-00922667/document (accessed July 2020).
Rayna, S. and Brougère, G. (eds) (2016) *Petites enfances, migrations et diversités.* Brussels: Peter Lang.

Rigolot, M. and Thamin, N. (2019) 'Pratiques professionnelles inclusives à l'école maternelle en contexte de diversité: Quelle approche interventionniste?' In I. Lorincz (ed.) *Pour une éducation langagière plurilingue, inclusive et éthique* (pp. 25–35). Györ: Universitas-Györ Nonprofit Kft.

Senegal, G. (1992) Aspects de l'imaginaire spatial: Identité ou fin des territoires? *Annales de géographie* 563, 28–42.

Simonin, M.-C. (2018) Apprendre le français comme langue seconde à l'école maternelle. Masters 2 thesis in educational research, ESPE de Besançon.

Simonin, M.-C. and Thamin, N. (2018) Recherche collaborative à l'école maternelle et socialisation plurilingue. *Revue Diversité, La recherche en éducation. Vers de nouvelles interfaces* 192, 131–136.

Thamin, N. (2015) Quand des enfants allophones sont perçus comme des élèves 'en difficulté de langage' dès la maternelle: Pistes de réflexion à partir d'une recherche en Franche-Comté. In D.-L. Simon, C. Dompmartin-Normand, S. Galligani and M.-O. Maire-Sandoz (eds) *Accueillir l'enfant et ses langues: Rencontres pluridisciplinaires sur le terrain de l'école* (pp. 141–166). Paris: Riveneuve éditions.

Thomauske, N. (2017) *Sprachlos gemacht in Kita und Familie: Ein deutsch-französischer Vergleich von Sprachpolitiken und -praktiken*. Wiesbaden: Springer VS.

Troncy, C. (ed.) (2014) *Didactique du plurilinguisme: Approches plurielles des langues et des cultures. Autour de Michel Candelier*. Rennes: Presses Universitaires de Rennes.

Wallon, E., Rezzoug, D., Bennabi-Bensekhar, M., Sanson, C., Serre, G., Yapo, M., Drain, E. and Moro, M.-R. (2008) Évaluation langagière en langue maternelle pour les enfants allophones et les primo-arrivants. Un nouvel instrument: l'ELAL d'Avicenne. *La psychiatrie et l'enfant* 51, 597–635.

Young, A. (2012) Teacher training within the context of linguistic competences of pupils with migrant background: The French context. In E. Winters-Ohle, B. Seipp and B. Ralle (eds) *Lehrer für Schüler mit Migrationsgeschichte: Sprachliche Kompetenz im Kontext internationaler Konzepte der Lehrerbildung* (pp. 117–129). Münster: Waxmann.

Young, A. (2018) Language awareness, language diversity and migrant languages in the primary school. In P. Garrett and J.M. Cots (eds) *The Routledge Handbook of Language Awareness* (pp. 23–39). New York: Routledge.

Young, A. and Mary, L. (2016) Dix ans d'expérimentation dans la formation pour une meilleure prise en compte de la diversité linguistique et culturelle des élèves: Enjeux, défis et réussites. In A.-B. Krüger, N. Thamin and S. Cambrone-Lasnes (eds) *Diversité linguistique et culturelle à l'école: Accueil des élèves et formation des acteurs* (pp. 169–190). Paris: L'Harmattan.

Funds of Knowledge in Home, School and Research

Jean Conteh

Senior Lecturer, School of Education, University of Leeds (Retired)

Many years ago, when I returned to England from Sierra Leone, my two children, then aged seven and ten, began attending the local primary school in the city where we settled. My daughter's teacher found a book of stories from Sierra Leone in the city library and she invited me to read one to the class. All the children seemed to enjoy the story and, using words that appeared in it, my daughter and I taught them how to say 'hello' in Mende, one of Sierra Leone's languages. Afterwards, another child put her hand up and told us that her father was teaching her to write Arabic at home. With a huge smile on her face, she offered to show us what she could do and the teacher agreed. Afterwards, she told me that this was the first time, to her knowledge, that the child had shared anything of her home language and learning in school.

As a parent, I felt reassured by the teacher's positive attitude towards diversity and was impressed by her open-mindedness. It made her classroom a safe space and encouraged all the children, not just my daughter, to feel confident about the language and cultural resources they brought to the classroom. Years later, as a teacher and researcher, I understood how this illustrated the 'Funds of Knowledge' philosophy (González et al., 2005). The original Funds of Knowledge research was carried out among Mexican heritage families in the Unites States of America from the 1980s. González et al. (2011: 485) argue that it differs crucially from other approaches to so-called 'parent/family involvement' in that it aims at mutual transformation, not only of students' and families' relationships with the school, but also of teachers' relationships with students and families. For me, this is the essence of empowerment.

References

González, N., Moll, L. and Amanti, C. (eds) (2005) *Funds of Knowledge: Theorizing Practices in Households, Communities and Classrooms*. New York: Routledge.

González, N., Wyman, L. and O'Connor, B. (2011) The past, present and future of 'funds of knowledge'. In M. Pollock and B. Levinson (eds) *A Companion to the Anthropology of Education* (pp. 481–494). Malden, MA: Wiley-Blackwell.

14 Teacher Language Awareness: A Personal and Pedagogical Journey

Ondine Gage

Chapter Overview

Policies in language education can be quite complex and driven by competing ideologies (García, 2009). Populist fears can impact decision making in language education as a way of appeasing constituents. The language education policy in the US context from 1968 to this day reflects this pendulum sway of competing ideologies. Teachers, in their day-to-day contact with students, must navigate these competing ideologies for the betterment of their students. This chapter is a case study illustrating how a teacher's language awareness can foster an inclusive classroom, engaging students in language awareness while enduring a restrictive language education policy context. The research design is inspired by an ecological view of language awareness (van Lier, 2004), recognizing that the classroom and its participants may be situated within competing language ecologies, which affect both teaching practices and students' learning in schools. This case study examines three data points: (1) a macro level description of the policy context at the time of the study; (2) a chronological narrative of the teacher's language training and her pedagogical perspectives on classroom practice; and (3) a micro level study of classroom data of students and their teacher engaging in language awareness. These data points reveal the ways in which a teacher's formative experiences impact her Teacher Language Awareness (TLA), and the choices she makes in response to a policy context focused on monolingualism. Finally, it considers some essential characteristics for creating an inclusive environment and how these characteristics might be understood within the current literature on TLA (Andrews & Lin, 2018; Andrews & Svalberg, 2017).

Caught between competing language ideologies

The data for this chapter were collected in 2010, nine years into the Bush administration's No Child Left Behind (NCLB) federal education policy, which mandated that States assess and monitor the English language proficiency of children growing up in families where languages other than English were spoken (Poza & Valdéz, 2016). Although a new president had just been elected in 2008, the language education policy under NCLB of the former administration was being fully implemented. The country was deep in a recession and the US Congress continued to stall any review of NCLB policy (Klein, 2015). Ignoring research on the social, emotional, cognitive and linguistic benefits of offering developmental bilingual education (Cummins, 1980; Wong Fillmore, 1991), NCLB's policies placed undue emphasis on the speed of English language acquisition. A primary goal of the Bush administration's 2001 NCLB educational policy had been that all students gain English language proficiency within three years or less of entering school (Evans & Hornberger, 2005). Illustrating the administration's ideological force, the language of the public record had changed abruptly in 2001. The Bilingual Education Act of 1968, which had offered federal funding for bilingual programs, was revoked in 2001 (Evans & Hornberger, 2005) and the word 'bilingual' was expunged from the public record (Crawford, 2002). The name of the Federal Office of Bilingual Education and Minority Languages was changed to the Office of English Language Acquisition, Language Enhancement and Academic Proficiency for Limited English Proficient Students (Gándara & Baca, 2008). Within this constrained policy context focused on English language acquisition, schools were under pressure to provide evidence of economically disadvantaged groups' achievement as determined by Annual Yearly Progress (AYP) measured through assessment (Evans & Hornberger, 2005).

Moreover, the school in this study, located in a rural California community, exemplified the problems of the convergence of both State and Federal NCLB policies [author's interpretation], where criteria for measuring the achievement of AYP goals labeled schools and students as failing, despite having shown growth (Darling-Hammond, 2004; Pease-Alvarez *et al.*, 2010). The State of California had passed the controversial Proposition 227 (Prop 227) in 1997, which effectively eliminated the existing bilingual education programs serving 29% of English learners and provided no clear alternative for the other 71% of designated English learners not enrolled in bilingual education (Gándara & Baca, 2008). The language in the Proposition required that teachers conduct instruction 'overwhelmingly' in English using an approach labeled 'Structured English Immersion', without clear guidelines as to what this meant. Moreover, it allowed parents to sue teachers who were not conducting instruction 'overwhelmingly' in English, although this was never enforced (Gándara & Baca, 2008). While Prop 227 created confusion about how English learners were to be instructed and fear around using a language other than English in the classroom, the convergence of Federal NCLB funding three years later created the 'perfect storm' (Gándara & Baca, 2008), where the State decided to interpret the NCLB assessment mandate by testing students only in English. The convergence of the Federal NCLB and State Prop 227 policies created a hostile environment for bilingual education, as academic instruction and assessment were conducted in English, regardless of students' proficiency in the language.

The school in this study served 79% low-income students (as determined by the number of students who qualified for government-sponsored free and reduced food services). The school community was composed of 93% non-European immigrants; 33% came from multilingual homes and were assessed as not needing English language support and 35% were identified as needing English language support. In fact, the school demographics are characteristic [author's comparison] of the schools in the United States that suffered the most under NCLB (Darling-Hammond & Banks, 2010). Because the school had not met NCLB's specified AYP goals for five years, the district governance faced a State takeover of the school or restructuring; the district opted to restructure the school. Although the NCLB penalty may appear to offer the school a 'clean slate' to start over, the reality presents many challenges to schools and the communities they serve.

The restructuring of the school included several measures, which disrupted the community. The school was disbanded and restructured into two new schools – a kindergarten to fifth grade school (serving 5–11 year-olds), and the middle school where this study was conducted (serving 12–15 year-olds). This means that children were moved to different schools and parents had to reregister children in the new school. All but 30% of the teachers were removed which meant that the teachers were mostly new to this teaching context; therefore, the continuity of instruction and prior relationships between and among students and their teachers were fractured. Additionally, the administrators reapplied for jobs in the new school. Therefore, at the beginning of the data collection for this study, the school had a new name, new faculty and new students.

The teacher profiled in this case study was among the retained instructors, who were also transitioning to new teaching assignments. She had begun employment eight years earlier as an English as a second language (ESL) teacher. However, in the restructuring of the school, the school district had adopted a scripted ESL program, to comply with NCLB, that required adhering to a pre-packaged, publisher-authored, scripted curriculum. These programs ensure pacing guidelines to move students quickly through the materials. Desiring an assignment that allowed her more autonomy to exercise her expertise and professional judgement, she requested a reassignment to English language arts (ELA). This curriculum consisted of a more flexible literature anthology. Having worked with ESL students for most of her career, she requested the ELA transitional-level class geared at students who were more than two years behind grade level in ELA and students who still needed English language support as determined by State testing. Grade 8 transitional-level ELA students are also at a critical juncture in their academic development because successful completion of this course allows students to enter high school eligible for college preparation courses (which in the United States generally serves 15–18 year-old students).

The policy context of this study illustrates how the ideological shift in language education, under NCLB and aimed at accelerating growth, penalized underperforming schools such as the one in this study. Moreover, the convergence of the Federal policy with the State policy under Prop 227 created an environment in language education that was hostile to bilingual instruction.

Research Design and Methods

This case study examines the links within the data (Duff, 2008) to consider the primary research question: What characteristics might a multilingual teacher bring to a linguistically diverse classroom in a policy context focused on monolingualism? To answer the primary research question, interview data are used to explore the instructor's language education and migrant work experience and to answer the secondary research question: How might a teacher's formative experiences impact her teacher language awareness, including beliefs and practices as well as perspectives on her students' learning? After addressing the teacher, the interview data are triangulated with classroom language exchanges to consider: How might the instructor's teacher language awareness impact pedagogical choices to create a more inclusive classroom? In answering the secondary and tertiary research questions, this chapter returns to the primary research question to examine how the language-learning experiences of a multilingual teacher contribute to creating an inclusive classroom space for linguistically **diverse** students within a monolingual policy context.

The data sources for this study include open-ended, semi-structured interviews with the teacher and six case study students participating in the transitional English language arts class. As a participant-observer, the researcher made audio recordings of classroom language exchanges over a six-month period, as well as maintaining field notes and reflective memos during nine months of classroom observations. These data have been evaluated to create a portrait of the instructor in order to explore how her educational and career experiences shaped the ways in which she engaged with her students.

Developing a Praxis of Language Learning and Teaching

Like many Anglo-Americans, the instructor in this study grew up in a monolingual English speaking social context. She had chosen French as a foreign language in school. While working her way through college, she continued studying French and worked during the summers as an au pair in a French speaking country. Returning home, she completed her college studies with a degree in applied linguistics and two minors, one in English and one in French.

In her final year of college, she was recognized as an outstanding student in linguistics and offered an English grammar teaching position within an intensive English language program, a position generally reserved only for graduate students. Having observed her classes at that time, the author notes two unique characteristics about her teaching: (1) working mostly with Arabic and Japanese students, she playfully embedded Arabic and Japanese learned from her students into classroom exchanges; and (2) she conducted a playful grammar class, employing communicatively oriented grammar activities. In essence, her grammar class did not demand that students drill, memorize forms or label parts, but instead the students made a meaningful connection between the form and function within the grammar lesson.

After completing a bachelor's degree, she launched her overseas teaching career, which began with a one-year English as a foreign language (EFL) teaching post in a French speaking country and was followed by a seven-year period teaching in Japan. During that period, she achieved the Japanese language exam for foreigners, an unusual distinction for English speaking foreigners hired to teach EFL, and a master's degree in TESOL. Reflecting on her overseas teaching experience, she has said that the host countries she worked in as a migrant teacher respected her language-learning abilities; however, she ultimately returned to the United States to reside near family.

Returning to the United States, she was hired to teach ESL in a public middle school context (11–15 year-olds) not long after the passage of Prop 227, where the instructional context was, in her words, 'like night and day … it is NOT the same job …'. In Japan, she had 60 college students who had shared the same heritage language and had been highly educated in their home language. In the US context, her students were younger, but they had also had very different learning experiences and had been identified by reading level in English as two years behind their academic ranking, which placed them in the transitional ELA classes. Few of the 29 bilingual students in this case study had any formal schooling in their heritage languages and the two monolingual English speakers received additional assistance. All attended school in English only, while their home languages were Spanish (80%), Tagalog (6%), Hindi (3%) and Samoan (3%). Moreover, the State identified 70% of the case study class as needing English language support. Keeping her students' focus was a huge challenge as the class's attention was divided by the almost daily power struggle between the personalities of the 13 to 15-year-old students and their instructor. Her students' latent academic abilities and identities as learners had been a huge concern when she began teaching in the United States. As she lamented, 'When I lose control of the class, I feel terribly guilty for the students who want to learn. It only takes one or two students to throw everyone off track. I feel responsible when I lose them'. It was this conundrum that had motivated her to learn a fourth language, Spanish, when she had returned to the United States 12 years earlier.

'Being put in your students' shoes'

Although she was not teaching in a bilingual program, her masters in TESOL program had emphasized the importance of 'constantly being put in your students' shoes', she said. She felt strongly as well that '... every teacher should learn another language'. Working predominantly with Spanish speakers in the United States, she saw learning Spanish as an essential tool for her profession. Living with host families and participating in intensive Spanish language programs, she spent her holidays studying Spanish abroad. Eventually, she became a recognized translator at her school.

Using multiple languages for multiple purposes

In observing her class over a nine-month period, it was clear that she was not able to fully use her multiple language abilities within the current policy context, although she ran Japanese and French clubs for interested students at lunchtime. However, she frequently used Spanish to translate for other faculty and to speak with the parents. Moreover, she decided that drawing on students' knowledge of Spanish fulfilled the California Standards requirement to teach Latin and Greek cognates. In this way, she cloaked her use of Spanish as instruction in academic English.

Cognitive support

When asked about how she used Spanish with her students, she was not particularly aware of using Spanish. Over the course of interviews and observing her in class, the researcher noted that the teacher used Spanish both for academic purposes and also for emotional and social purposes. She used Spanish to establish shared understanding with her students and to draw out cognate relationships between English and Spanish. 'For lower levels, there I might use it [Spanish] more often as a hook to get them back into a shared understanding – something recognizable, as a tool to reel them in'. In essence, Spanish was used as cognitive support to stimulate noticing and making connections between languages. When letters were sent home to parents with the English translation on one side and Spanish on the other, I noticed that she took care to explain the Spanish letter in Spanish. For example, in a field trip permission letter, she emphasized the purpose of the letter and where the parents' signatures should be so that students could participate in the field trip. In both cases, she demonstrated an awareness of the potential disconnect between the parents' knowledge of Spanish and the children's undeveloped knowledge of Spanish; therefore, she made sure to explain the meaning of the letter carefully and to elicit explanations of particular words from students who had more developed Spanish. In essence, these examples show that she was aware of the need for and use of both languages to support cognitive comprehension and development.

Nurturing

She also admitted that she used Spanish as a means of nurturing and mentoring students. 'I use Spanish in a nurturing role. I use Spanish to express affection and concern for them. I sometimes ask them in Spanish, "Is that why your parents sent you to school?" when they misbehave'. In this sense, Spanish was used as a way of appealing emotionally to her students to bring their focus back to their schoolwork.

Connecting with parents

Moreover, she complained that the parents of her students only hear from the school when the children get into trouble. Her goal was to turn that paradigm around: 'I sell students with the fact that I want to make good news calls home'. She kept a list on the board of children's positive contributions to the class, such as showing kindness to classmates, making connections to curricular concepts and willingly participating in class dialog. In this way, she recorded points to make 'good news calls'. As she said, 'When I call parents, I offer Spanish', although many answered her in English. Regardless, offering their language shifted the dynamic in her mind: 'I think they see me as someone who has made an effort to be there for them and their children'. Moreover, she empathized with the parents. As part of a group of teachers who conducted neighborhood walks to meet families in their homes and discuss preparation for college, she indicated, 'We [the teachers] go door-to-door in the neighbourhoods to talk with families about the program. It is a real eye-opener to realize that a fair number of kids live with so little. For those who have more, it is because of a great sacrifice on the parents' part'. In sum, she empathized with the parents who, like many parents, long to provide for their child and may sacrifice so their children do not appear impoverished in school. Together, this teacher used Spanish as a tool to engage cognitively, emotionally and socially with her students and their parents. Moreover, she also used it as a tool to promote the academic status of their heritage languages and to support immigrant families.

Building learner identities

One of the motivations for inviting my research into her classroom was her concern for the students' academic development and her search for ways to help build the students' confidence and identities as learners.

She sought to encourage the students to see the value of their home language and bilingual ability. In her words, 'I sell bilingualism as a tool. I value the same thing. I want them to see the legitimacy of bilingualism as a tool. I'm constantly campaigning for "building their bilingual biceps"'. Noticing metalinguistic connections between languages may not come naturally to bilingual students. In order to build metalinguistic awareness, she actively promoted these connections in her pedagogy and rewarded children when they made connections.

> I like languages and I want to know, I want them [the students] to know that I'm curious. The students I work with are at varying levels [of Spanish]. Some came here in the third, fourth, or fifth grades. Some were born and raised here. Few honour that [their language ability]. I don't get the sense that kids have a lot of academic Spanish. I wouldn't say they speak only 'kitchen Spanish', but most do not read in Spanish, and they aren't as aware of using Spanish as a tool. Spanish is a social thing for them. Yes, a solidarity tool. It is a language of comfort; it is easy. But I'm trying to sell it as academic.

Although this instructor was teaching in a context where English was the medium of instruction, she used her multilingual resources as a means of prompting metalinguistic awareness.

In summary, this instructor profile illustrates the teacher's formative experiences. While her academic achievements and language-learning experiences would appear to have informed her knowledge about language, she also recognized that metalinguistic awareness, play with language and connections between languages supported her students' language and cognitive development. Moreover, in the US public school context, her particular sensitivity to her students' academic struggle is noteworthy. At this point in her career, she becomes much more concerned with her students' identities as learners and ways in which to engage them in school. Her desire to learn a fourth language is evidence of her commitment to mediate academically but also socially and emotionally with her students and their families. I now turn to the classroom language data.

Classroom Practices: Affordances for Language Awareness

The classroom language data capture spontaneous language exchanges in order to understand Affordances for Language Awareness or opportunities for making meaning. My goal was to examine the 'totality of meaning making' (van Lier, 2000: 251) within the classroom. Classroom language exchanges, participants, topics being discussed and the situational contexts were recorded, transcribed and coded. The unit of analysis, codified as *Language Awareness Related Episodes* (LAREs), builds upon the work of Swain and Lapkin's (1995) *language related episodes* (LREs), but follows van Lier's (2000) recommendation that in an ecological account 'the unit of analysis is activity itself' (van Lier, 2000: 253).

Therefore, LAREs represent episodes which are: (a) related to the clarification of understanding in conversations that might contribute to the possibility for language awareness or an *affordance*, and (b) are bound by an idea being discussed in a language-classroom setting.

Context of classroom exchanges

The classroom exchanges were observed while text was either being read to students or being reviewed as a follow-up to reading. The students used consumable textbooks (which they kept and wrote in) and the instructor projected the text on a computer (SMART) board in front of the class. This allowed the instructor to: (a) shift between the text and images; (b) zoom into specific paragraphs, sentences, words or morphemes; (c) write, circle, underline or draw on the text and make margin notes as a model for the students; and (d) save the images and modeled text so that the class could return to a discussion. The instructor frequently de-centered herself, explicitly exposing her own thoughts and questions about the text, but also elicited assistance from students as is common in formative think-aloud assessment of learning (Valencia & Hebard, 2013).

Student contributions to classroom exchanges were encouraged provided they were respectful of all students. This created a safe space for all students to contribute. Student contributions were documented by fellow students in the class and governed equitably. The students could direct the class's attention to the text to ask questions or offer thoughts. The students also rotated leadership roles in the class, including keeping track of points given to students: (1) who offered interesting questions; (2) who contributed translanguaging connections; and (3) who wondered by asking questions that connected the text to issues beyond the text. Each month, the instructor rotated the cooperative structure, taking into consideration students' preferences by requesting a private letter explaining who they felt they could work well with. The instructor consulted the students' letters as they provided student inclusion in the decision process, but also held students accountable contractually for their decisions. The instructor gave a great deal of thought to assigning 'shoulder partners' for the month, as these were the partners students collaborated with during class activities. Although the instructor was summarily in charge, there was a strong classroom ethos of respect for one another. When the social activity disrupted the class focus, the instructor would bring the students back to the issue of respect for one another and their own learning.

Language Awareness Related Episodes

The four LAREs categories identified in this study are exemplified in Tables 14.1–14.4. The examples of the LAREs categories illustrate classroom practices in which affordances for language awareness occurred.

Teacher Language Awareness 251

Table 14.1 Affordances for metalinguistic awareness: Verbal exchanges exploring meaningful parts of words and phrases, including morphemes, synonyms, translanguaging, polysemy, etc.

Example 1
Student 1: Why didn't slaves kill their owners?
Teacher: 'kill'? Or in some way 'rebel'?
Student 2: Like tie him up and make him suffer?
Teacher: oh, ok. (*recasting*) Why didn't the slave 'rebel'?

Example 2
Teacher: 'Vivid' sounds like a Latin word, what is it?
Student 3: vivir
Teacher: vivir – living. So if it is alive it must be very ... colourful ... lively?

Example 3
Teacher: So *primordial* has to do with something that has been around since earliest times ... Spanish speakers you have the advantage ... use those bilingual biceps. What is the root?
Student 3: Ohhh (*expressing his epiphany*) primo!
Teacher: There you go! Sounds like *primero,* which means?
Student 3: One
Teacher: So even if the second part is not familiar, the first part has something to do with ... (*pausing as if figuring it out herself*).
Student 3: Since the first day!

Table 14.2 Affordances for analeptic awareness: Verbal exchanges that drew on shared experience/understanding as a reference in meaning-making

Examples from data	
Student 1:	fased?
Teacher (*zooming in on the word*):	façade ... looks like it should be 'fased' you are right, if there is an –e at the end. But see this c with a tail on it? It is called a Cedilla. In French, it is pronounced..
Student 2:	Like an -s
Teacher:	So if I say façade, what does it sound like?
Student 2:	a face.
Students 2 & 3:	the front of the building
Teacher:	What does our school building look like?
Students:	dirty
Teacher:	Oh, you think it is dirty. What is a painting on the outside?
Students:	a mural
Teacher (*pointing to an image on the screen*):	This is the façade of the building.

Table 14.3 Affordances for proleptic awareness: Verbal exchanges prompting inference where participants explore unknown examples prompted by hints, questions, etc., which concluded in deduced or inferred meaning-making

Teacher:	She told them stories of her own first flight ... hmm ... Like an airline flight?
Student 1 (*correcting teacher*):	Like a voyage.
Student 2:	Her first experience.
Teacher:	What kind of experience?
Student 3:	She escaped
Teacher (*reading a line from the text*):	'It was born on the wind'. You can barely hear it but it was ... (*pause*)
Student 3: soft	

252 Part 2 'Actuality Implies Possibility': New Practices of Inclusion

Table 14.4 Affordances for awareness of register shifts: Verbal exchanges in which register shift prompted awareness, using alternative social norms for achieving meaning-making among interlocutors

Example 1 (discussing the events of a short story)	
Student 1:	She wanted to go to Harvard.
Teacher:	True, but all through the story?
Student 2 (whispering an answer to Student 1):	She wants to get out of Brooklyn. She wants to get out of Brooklyn. Está bien
Student 1:	She wanted to get out of Brooklyn throughout the story.
Example 2 (correcting homework together, student struggles with the word *leisure*)	
Teacher (reassuring him):	You can pronounce it [li ʒər] or [le ʒər] … we don't know much about his plans. Leisure would be down time? Time to relax?
Student 1:	Time that is not used.
Teacher:	Yeah, on vacation you have plenty of time to relax.
Student 2:	Time to chill.
Teacher:	Ah, so if I say, 'At your leisure' it means take your time.

Affordances for metalinguistic awareness

The first LAREs category is affordances for metalinguistic awareness. These examples illustrate conversations between the students and their teacher exploring meaningful parts of words and phrases, including morphemes, synonyms, translanguaging, polysemy, etc. In the data sample in Table 14.1, an affordance for metalinguistic awareness is illustrated by two examples. In Example 1, students are asking questions about a historical fiction text describing the Underground Railroad, which metaphorically represented the migration of escaping slaves fleeing bondage before the US Civil War, 1861–1865. In this example, the student offers several comments: *Why didn't slaves kill their owners? Like tie him up and make him suffer?* The instructor directs the students' attention to *rebel*, which provides a superordinate category to the student's examples. By focusing the students on the more abstract concept *to rebel*, the instructor spontaneously draws on her TLA to offer an opportunity for the students to connect the meaning to a topic that they are engaged in thinking about. In the second example, the instructor draws on her knowledge of cognates to elicit translanguaging knowledge, but shaping the word *living* as *alive, colourful, lively* to connect students to the word in question, *vivid*.

Moreover, the second and third examples also illustrate how the instructor drew on her awareness of cognates to draw out the participation of Student 3. Student 3 was a case study student who was one of the most recent migrant students in the class. He was a student who was not happy being in the United States and had complained that he wanted to return to Mexico. Although he was placed in the transitional ELA class, he was mostly a receptive participant in class discussions unless the instructor asked for cognate comparisons. In this context, he demonstrated sophisticated translanguaging and engaged actively in the class discussions. The samples from the data show the classroom language practices in which the instructor drew on her TLA to engage in conversations and explore thought processes with her students, which provide affordances for metalinguistic awareness.

Affordances for analeptic awareness

The LAREs category, affordances for analeptic awareness, was drawn from van Lier's (2004) discussion of *analepsis* or relying on the intersubjectivity of shared experiences between interlocutors to gain an affordance. The examples in Table 14.2 illustrate the ways in which the instructor and her students drew on shared knowledge or the intersubjectivity of the outside of their school building to offer a connection to the meaning of *façade* which provide an *affordance for analeptic awareness*.

In the example in Table 14.2, the instructor could have simply provided students with a definition; however, instead she elicits students to puzzle through the strange spelling and the sound of the word which is like 'face', drawing students to notice the elements of curiosity. She then builds on their shared experience of the mural on the outside of the school building to co-construct the meaning of *façade*.

Affordances for proleptic awareness

Table 14.3 provides data examples of the third LAREs category, *affordances for proleptic awareness*. Prolepsis 'involves leaving things out and inviting the speaker to step into the enlarged common space' (van Lier, 2004: 161). As prolepsis often involves ellipsis, it requires that the listener/reader construct the same implication as the speaker/writer is suggesting. Therefore, constructing the necessary inference to fill in the space may require content, context or culture knowledge that a listener/reader may not have. In the examples, the instructor provides hints or puzzling suggestions to lead the listener/readers down the path of the speaker/author to create the imagery of the text.

In affordances for proleptic awareness, both the students and the teacher fill in the missing inferred information. The teacher, in fact, led the students to a wrong inference, checking the students' understanding. Student 1 corrects the teacher. Affordances for proleptic awareness allow for co-constructed interpretation of contexts not explicitly provided in the text but requiring a process of deduction to achieve comprehension.

Affordances for awareness of register shifts

The fourth LAREs category is *affordances for awareness of register shifts*, which are exchanges in which alternative social norms are used for achieving meaning-making. Note that in Example 1 in Table 14.4, a student translanguages in solidarity to assure his classmate that he is offering the additional information. This exchange was collected on a day when Student 1 had been out of class and missed some of the review of the text. Student 1 was a little timid and the instructor was prompting her to participate. Student 2 offers assistance but adds assurance by whispering *está bien* 'it is right'. While this example of translanguaging may not appear significant, it establishes the truth value of the affordance, by offering the language of home, which symbolically shows solidarity with the student's struggle.

In Example 2 from Table 14.4, the class is reviewing questions to a reading assignment when one student struggles with the meaning of the word 'leisure'. The word leisure became a point of focus as the students and teacher examined the context clues and made comparisons to their own understanding. Students and the teacher produced several synonyms drawing on different registers to co-construct meaning, including time that is not used, on vacation you have plenty of time to relax, and time to chill. The last example, time to chill, reflects an example of the informal register of North American English. All definitions are offered to construct the more formal usage of leisure. In these examples, students co-construct knowledge through variations in register and language to establish both truth-value and meaning of an utterance.

Tables 14.1–14.4 represent samples of the data collected in the study to illustrate the LAREs captured in the classroom data. These data present ways in which this instructor drew on her TLA to engage students in affordances for language awareness. I now turn to a discussion of the teacher profile and data to consider the characteristics in her praxis of inclusive practices in TLA.

Discussion

In returning to the research questions outlined at the beginning of this chapter, I examine the triangulated data to consider characteristics that a multilingual teacher might bring to a linguistically diverse classroom in a policy context focused on monolingualism. In examining the evidence from the data, I note characteristics of the teacher's TLA, which shaped classroom inclusion and identified legitimate opportunities to navigate policy that did not support inclusion. These characteristics include *empathetic perspective-taking, supporting learner identity* and *affordances for language awareness*.

Empathetic perspective-taking: Building a home-to-school connection

One characteristic shown in the data is her *empathetic perspective-taking*. Her empathy and concern for the families' perspectives would appear to reflect her own experiences of having been a migrant worker with only incipient language abilities in a host country. Her empathy, which is evidenced in the interview data and the classroom observation data, appears to guide her very thoughtful interactions with parents and students. In the interview data, she described home visits where she noted how parents made great sacrifices in order to provide for their children. Moreover, she committed to learning Spanish, her fourth language, in order to communicate directly with children and their parents, despite the Prop 227 restrictive language teaching environment. She sensed that parents appreciated that she 'made an effort to be there for them and their children' in using their heritage language. In the classroom observation data, she tallied children's accolades for 'good news' calls daily to counter the general narrative that teachers only call home to parents when children are in trouble at school. In the classroom, she also took care to teach the children the content of the field trip permission letters in Spanish in order to ensure that the children understood the Spanish of the letter and could mediate essential information to their busy parents. These examples illustrate the characteristic of *empathetic perspective-taking* in building a home-to-school relationship, which showed the families that they were central to her teaching practice.

Supporting learner identity

Another characteristic evidenced in the data is her sense of *supporting learner identity*. The instructor chose to circumvent the restrictive language policy under Prop 227 to promote multilingualism and the children's heritage language status in her classroom. Her support of multilingual learner identity is evidenced by the interview data where she very publically admits that she values 'learning languages', volunteers to advise the Japanese and French club at lunch hour and 'sells bilingualism' to her students. In other words, she actively strives to support the children's curiosity about languages and culture as well as their own multilingual ability. Moreover, her desire for her students to see their 'Spanish as academic' and take pride in their heritage language is evidence of her concern that ignoring students' multilingual abilities was not benefiting her students' identities as learners. In fact, her ability to draw out Student 3, referenced in Table 14.1, Examples 2 and 3 through *affordances for metalinguistic awareness* by engaging Student 3's translanguaging to make metalinguistic observations, shows the ways in which she adapted the task to build on a learner's identity. As Fought (2006) describes, youth language use may appear stochastic as they navigate language use, which symbolically associates or marginalizes them from social communities in the school context. By privileging the ability to draw on translanguaging skills, the instructor supports students' multilingual identities as learners.

Affordances for language awareness

Furthermore, the LAREs classroom data illustrate affordances for language awareness as evidenced by the many ways in which the students and their teacher co-constructed language in her class. The examples of *affordances for metalinguistic, analeptic, proleptic* and *register shifts awareness* illustrate not only her knowledge about language but the sensitivity with which she listens to her students' meaning-making in applying this knowledge. For example, the class co-constructed the meaning of the text through metalinguistic discussions. They drew on analepsis or shared knowledge. In cases where schematic knowledge was implied or inferred, they co-constructed the proleptic frameworks for bridging the inferred or implied information. Moreover, register shifts, contributing to meaning-making, were a part of this inclusive classroom practice. Not only is the instructor observant of her students' knowledge, she is also aware of the need to support their identities as learners by adapting instruction accordingly. Taking great care to support an environment where students feel respected, the instructor created an inclusive environment. In fact, the findings in this case study of (1) *empathetic perspective-taking in building home-to-school connections*, (2) *supporting learner identity* and (3) building *affordances for language awareness* appear to be valuable characteristics in TLA.

Adding to a definition of teacher language awareness

Andrews and Svalberg (2017) define TLA by focusing their work on language teacher cognition. While they acknowledge that 'teacher education needs to develop teachers' awareness of language as a social practice' (Andrews & Svalberg, 2017: 228), they look to future research to examine the social dimensions of TLA. In Andrews and Lin's (2018) discussion of *Language Awareness and Teacher Development*, the definition of TLA revolves centrally around teacher knowledge *of* and *about* the language as well as *knowledge of the learners*. In fact, Andrews and Svalberg (2017), in examining the problems and challenges within TLA research, acknowledge that TLA is a new area of research which lacks a unifying conceptual framework. While knowledge of and about language is important, the current ecologically inspired study aims to illustrate the complexity of macro-ecological policy, which impacts classroom learning. Moreover, these issues are especially important when considering the language and identity development of youth.

Since this case study describes one teacher, it cannot make general claims about best practices and pedagogy. However, it does provide implications for language teacher education. This work suggests that a teacher's empathetic perspective-taking in building home-to-school relationships may be equal to knowledge about language, especially in the context of primary education when children's identities as learners are developing. More research is needed to clarify whether the teacher's language-learning experiences were critical to the development of empathetic perspective-taking in building home-to-school relationships and whether these experiences might foster these sensitivities in others. This study demonstrated that a teacher's knowledge about language applied to her own language-learning experiences also provided her with tools for circumnavigating a policy climate that was not grounded in research or best practices. As Young (2018: 23) asserts, 'Tensions associated with prejudice and negative attitudes towards difference, more often than not fueled by fear, may spill over from the wider society into schools and classrooms'. In a policy climate that openly ignores students' primary languages and assesses and ranks students by their ability to use the dominant language, the practitioner's day-to-day commitment to students is not enough to counter policies that divide citizenry. Yet in this climate, characteristics of TLA as described in this study may be the best alternative. These characteristics created the inclusive classroom practices that gave rise to affordances for language awareness in the classroom. Moreover, these characteristics shaped classroom inclusion, offering 'ways to legitimize interaction between language' (Young, 2018: 25) and offer legitimate opportunities to circumnavigate the policy that did not support inclusion.

Towards a plurilingual community

This chapter has illustrated a teacher's characteristics and classroom data to show the ways in which a teacher's multilingual language awareness offered affordances for language awareness that mediate and mentor language awareness between her students. Moreover, her sensitivity to the students' needs and respect for the value of engaging the student perspective contribute to a linguistically positive environment where competing language ecologies are brought together to foster an inclusive classroom environment, despite a policy context favoring monolingualism. Yet, as Young (2018) asserts, the onus should not rest exclusively on the teachers. In an ideal setting, one teacher would not need work against the seemingly insurmountable effects of policies driven by populist fear. A teacher like the one in this study might be part of a larger school culture of inclusion.

Little and Kirwan (2018) describe one such context in which the entire school culture promotes plurilingualism. Students starting school at age four begin to engage in plurilingual exploration of their own and others' language use. By sixth grade, the school environment allows for students to develop not only their own and the official school languages but to explore and dabble in the other languages of their classmates. In essence, some students begin to learn other students' languages and are free to work at translating, creatively using or concurrently narrating their messages in several languages. This example illustrates what might be possible in a truly inclusive school culture. Little and Kirwan (2018) offer a model of schooling that is an optimal environment for building both a plurilingual and language-aware community.

References

Andrews, S.J. and Lin, A.M.Y. (2018) Language awareness and teacher development. In P. Garrett and J.M. Cots (eds) *The Routledge Handbook of Language Awareness* (pp. 57–74). New York: Routledge.
Andrews, S.J. and Svalberg, A.M.-L. (2017) Teacher language awareness. In J. Cenoz, D. Gorter and S. May (eds) *Language Awareness and Multilingualism* (pp. 219–231). New York: Springer.
Crawford, J. (2002) Obituary: The Bilingual Education Act, 1968–2002. In J. Crawford (ed.) *Advocating for English Learners: Selected Essays by James Crawford*. Clevedon: Multilingual Matters. See http://www.languagepolicy.net/books/AEL/Crawford_BEA_Obituary.pdf (accessed May 2019).
Cummins, J. (1980) The cross-lingual dimensions of language proficiency: Implications for bilingual education and the optimal age issue. *TESOL Quarterly* 14 (2), 175–187.
Darling-Hammond, L. (2004) From 'separate but equal' to 'No Child Left Behind': The collision of new standards and old inequalities. In D.M.G. Wood (ed.) *Many Children Left Behind: How the No Child Left Behind Act is Damaging Our Children and our Schools* (pp. 3–32). Boston, MA: Beacon Press.
Darling-Hammond, L. and Banks, J.A. (2010) *The Flat World and Education: How American's Commitment to Equity will Determine our Future*. New York: Teachers College Press.
Duff, P.A. (2008) *Case Study Research in Applied Linguistics*. New York: Lawrence Erlbaum.
Evans, B. and Hornberger, N. (2005) No Child Left Behind: Repealing and unpeeling federal language education policy in the United States. *Language Policy* 4, 87–106.
Fought, C. (2006) *Language and Ethnicity*. Cambridge, MA: Cambridge University Press.
Gándara, P. and Baca, G. (2008) NCLB and California's English language learners: The perfect storm. *Language Policy* 7, 201–216. doi:10.1007/s10993-008-9097-4
García, O. (2009) *Bilingual Education in the 21st Century: A Global Perspective*. Malden, MA: Wiley-Blackwell.
Klein, A. (2015) The nation's main K-12 law: A timeline of the ESEA. *Education Week*, 1 April. See https://www.edweek.org/ew/section/multimedia/the-nations-main-k-12-law-a-timeline.html (accessed February 2019).
Little, D. and Kirwan, D. (2018) From plurilingual repertoires to language awareness: Developing primary pupils' proficiency in the language of schooling. In C. Hélot, C. Frijins, K. Van Gorp and S. Sierens (eds) *Language Awareness in Multilingual Classrooms in Europe* (pp. 169–206). Boston, MA and Berlin: Walter de Gruyter.
Pease-Alvarez, L., Davies Samway, K. and Cifka-Herrera, C. (2010) Working with the system: Teachers of English learners negotiating a literacy instruction mandate. *Language Policy* 9, 313–334.
Pozá, L. and Valdéz, G. (2016) Assessing English language proficiency in the United States: From No Child Left Behind to the Common Core. In E. Shohamy (ed.) *Language Testing and Assessment*. Dordrecht: Springer.
Swain, M. and Lapkin, S. (1995) Problems in output and the cognitive processes they generate: A step towards second language learning. *Applied Linguistics* 16, 371–391.

Valencia, S.W. and Hebard, H. (2013) Classroom literacy assessment strategies for informing instruction and monitoring student progress. In B.M. Taylor and N.K. Duke (eds) *Handbook of Effective Literacy Instruction: Research-Based Practice K-8* (pp. 106–136). New York: Guilford Press.
van Lier, L. (2000) From input to affordance: Social-interactive learning from an ecological perspective. In J. Lantolf (ed.) *Sociocultural Theory and Second Language Acquisition* (pp. 245–259). Oxford: Oxford University Press.
van Lier, L. (2004) *The Ecology and Semiotics of Language Learning: A Sociocultural Perspective*. Dordrecht: Kluwer Academic.
Wong Fillmore, L. (1991) Second language learning in children: A model of language learning in social context. In E. Bialystok (ed.) *Language Processing in Bilingual Children* (pp. 49–69). Cambridge: Cambridge University Press.
Young, A. (2018) Language awareness, language diversity, and migrant languages in primary school. In P. Garrett and J.M. Cots (eds) *The Routledge Handbook of Language Awareness* (pp. 23–39). New York: Routledge.

Awakening to Languages for Japanese Primary Schools

Mayo Oyama

Part-time lecturer, Ritsumeikan University, Japan

Japan has the lowest immigration rate among OECD countries, and is characterized by double monolingualism: only Japanese and English are regarded as important, and ability in other languages is hardly recognized in educational systems.

I began my research on language teaching for young learners when English courses were first imposed by the government twice a week in elementary schools. I focused on awakening to languages activities. It is a teaching method that incorporates multiple language varieties simultaneously, facilitating metalinguistic learning rather than the acquisition of a specific language, while offering possibilities to include minority languages in classroom activities. Most importantly, the activities seemed to meet the intellectual level of children much more than dry drills.

The majority of the children were initially reluctant to work on unknown languages, but as they continued their activities, we could observe their increasing interest in different languages which may have positively influenced their openness to classmates' minority languages. For their minority language classmates, there were children who were eager to speak their home languages when opportunities were provided, but also children rather reluctant to do so. But bringing minority pupils' linguistic repertoire to classroom activities was possible not only through having children utter the languages but also through children sharing knowledge of their home languages in Japanese. I think this approach, one that provides a space in which one can talk about language, if not actually speaking the languages, was a key to meeting those children's needs.

One teacher practicing this pedagogy reported to me that when the children visited Hiroshima on a school excursion, they spontaneously began to discuss the word 'life' as used by one of the Atomic bomb survivors, and that the meaning was different from the word 'life' as they understood it. She connected this to what they had learned through the awakening to languages practices implemented in the classroom.

Reference

Pearce, D.R., Oyama, M., Moore, D. and Irisawa, K. (2020) Plurilingualism and STEAM: Unfolding the paper crane of peace at an elementary school in Japan. *Journal of Multilingual Theories and Practices* 1 (2), 243–265.

15 Fostering More Inclusive Linguistic Practices in Portuguese Classrooms: Is Teacher Education the Key for Integrating Heritage Languages?

Rosa Maria Faneca, Maria Helena Araújo e Sá and Sílvia Melo-Pfeifer

Introduction

This study analyses an in-service teacher education programme oriented towards the linguistic and educational integration of students with migrant histories in a Portuguese context. Portugal, a country that has received young people from different cultural and linguistic origins (SEF, 2016), is called upon to integrate them into the educational system, through constructing opportunities for success that do not 'monolingualize' these students but rather stimulate their bilingual development. In a context where teachers are increasingly encouraged to rethink and reorganize syllabi, it is important to consider a pedagogy that is differentiated and intentional regarding linguistic and cultural diversity, as well as capable of including new school populations (not only from communities with a longer history of permanence in the country, such as those originating from Portuguese-speaking countries, but also from communities with a more recent contact with Portugal, such as refugees). Thus, it is necessary to rethink the homogenizing mindset and the monolingual habitus (Gogolin, 2008) that still characterize the teaching profession and the classroom practices in the Portuguese context. In our view, this has implications for both pre-service and in-service teacher education in all subject areas.

After briefly framing the study within language education policies directed towards the integration of linguistic and cultural diversity and teacher education, we present the state of the art of diversity inclusion in Portuguese schools. Following this, we describe the continuing professional development (CPD) programme we put into practice, in terms of objectives and methodological options, structure, content and assessment tools. Then, we present the didactic proposals developed by ten teachers who attended the course, highlighting the way these actors reinterpreted and transposed the principles of the first phase of the programme to their practices (the languages they worked with, the concepts they taught, the objectives they defined). Finally, we systematize the programme's potential from the perspective of the teacher-actors, in order to understand the possibilities of including diversity in the classroom, and particularly heritage languages (HLs)[1], which the teachers discovered in their practice (i.e. benefits of their inclusion for both plurilingual and monolingual students). We answer the following questions:

- What educational practices were constructed and implemented by a group of teachers in an in-service teacher education context with the purpose of promoting the inclusion of languages and cultures?
- How did the teachers assess the practices they implemented and how did they reflect on them?

The answers to these questions will allow us to understand the short-term impact of the CPD on the teachers' didactic repertoire, while simultaneously revealing what aspects of working with linguistic and cultural diversity the teachers most favoured by the end of a structured CPD.

Linguistic and Cultural Diversity in the Classroom: Questions for Teacher Education

Language education policies and principles of teacher education

As a result of constant migratory flows and demands for mobility, the linguistic policy of the European institutions explicitly promotes plurilingualism, notably through the Common European Framework of Reference for Languages (Council of Europe, 2001) and the more recent Framework of Reference for Pluralistic Approaches (Candelier *et al.*, 2012). The latter document promotes pedagogical and didactic methodologies centred on the mobilization of more than one language, linguistic variety or culture through an integrated didactic of languages, language awareness, intercomprehension and an intercultural approach.

Even if a citizen's plurilingualism acquired in the school context is promoted, the structuring role that HLs and cultures can acquire, from a cognitive, affective and identity perspective, is relatively downplayed (with the exception of the proposals in Candelier *et al.*, 2012; see also Castellotti & Moore, 2010). HLs, absent in curricular landscapes, are often considered obstacles to learning, which block participation in socialization, integration and the exercise of citizenship processes (Hélot & Ó Laoire, 2011; Little, 2010; Young, 2011).

This hierarchical perception of languages that compose students' repertoires is often accompanied by an equally hierarchized perception of the speakers' competences. Additionally, if linguistic repertoires are hierarchized, it should be stated that, depending on the perception of their value, languages are also frequently belittled or ignored: 'teachers in the multilingual classroom may continue to underestimate the competence of plurilingual students and to silence their voices, rather than using crosslinguistic learning strategies and learners' metalinguistic awareness as learning resources across languages and even across school disciplines' (Hélot & Ó Laoire, 2011: xi).

In this context marked by paradox and tension, in which linguistic and school ideologies have a determining role (Armand, 2017; Blanchet & Clerc Conan, 2015; Galligani, 2009), teacher education has taken on an undeniable importance for the development of professional awareness of the issues at stake and of a pedagogical practice that is consequently more substantiated, informed and engaged. As stated by Meier and Conteh (2014):

> Some teachers are already embracing the possibilities of developing multilingual pedagogies. (…) Even if sympathetic to the idea, they often do not feel empowered or qualified to bring a more multilingually informed approach to their classrooms. (Meier & Conteh, 2014: 296)

Mary and Young (2010) showed that quality teacher education in the area of language didactics can have positive effects on the more complex representations regarding language teaching. Thus, teacher education that is conceived in order to address these themes promotes an awareness of the phenomena of linguistic transfer and of the importance of considering the prior knowledge of students with migratory histories, as well as the development and construction of a more engaged professional identity that does not respond to diversity in a negative or excluding way (Mary & Young, 2010). This professional identity is revealed in the way the teacher is capable of responding 'to all possibilities and potentialities at the classroom level, thus forging one's own policies that are locally effective and empowering' (Hélot & Ó Laoire, 2011: xvii).

To respond to these needs in terms of professional development, De Mejía and Hélot (2017) consider that it is necessary to abandon a traditional disciplinary perspective, a monolingual view of the classroom and a monoglossic understanding of the plurilingual competence of learners. Considering that CPD should be designed for the context in which trainees will be acting, the authors argue that such programmes should be 'situated in practice, linked to actual classroom practice in local settings' (De Mejía & Hélot, 2017: 272), and should provide integrated support for linguistic development in all languages that compose students' repertoires, be they school languages, HLs or foreign languages (FLs) (De Mejía & Hélot, 2017: 273).

In the same vein, Helmchen and Melo-Pfeifer (2018: 12) synthesize three principles that may inform teacher education practices for linguistic and cultural diversity, namely that practices should be:

- *anchored in the context, i.e. teacher and student-centred*, regarding their attitudes, motivations, experiences, knowledge and abilities, aims and goals, in order to achieve meaningful and sustainable learning experiences, implying the co-responsibility of the trainee in the formative process;
- *collaborative*, implying a socioconstructivist approach to teaching and professional development, highlighting the importance of learning from and with each other in order to develop a collective and shared pool of multilingual knowledge and pedagogical repertoires;
- *inquiry-based*, suggesting that teachers, as well as their students, are multilingual detectives engaged in multilingual practice and discoveries, driven by specific questions and pedagogical needs.

Despite the existence of a few ongoing CPD, at the European level (Lourenço & Andrade, 2018), De Mejía and Hélot highlight teachers' resistance towards the development and implementation of practices that are welcoming of diversity, resistances that we also have encountered in the Portuguese context (Faneca *et al.*, 2018). De Mejía and Hélot conclude by observing a

> degree of resistance on the part of the teacher trainees to attempt to get them to reflect critically on aspects of multilingualism and multiculturalism in the classroom and their insistence on clinging to transmission-oriented pedagogy, with its emphasis on solutions to 'problems' involving 'correct training'. (De Mejía & Hélot, 2017: 275)

As we shall see in the empirical section of this chapter, the aforementioned formative principles (anchored in practices and contexts, concomitantly developing all languages, centring on the teacher, ...) may help to analyse the conceptualization and implementation of action research projects, making it easier to assess the impact of CPD.

The Portuguese context: Diversity in schools, language education policy and teacher education

In Portugal, the migratory flows of the last decade (SEF, 2016) have introduced 'a multilingual and multicultural dimension' into schools (Mateus, 2011: 14), precipitating two diagnostic state-led studies of the languages spoken by the students. The first, involving 30,000 students and published in 2003, was coordinated by the Department for Basic Education (DEB/ME, 2003); the second was coordinated by the Institute for Social and Economic Studies and was conducted in 1150 primary schools with 15,397 students (DGE/ME, 2005). These two studies focused on the linguistic diversity present in Portuguese public schools and identified around 80 different languages spoken in the family context, frequently associated with the use of Portuguese, and 36 languages spoken with friends at school. A third study took place between 2003 and 2007, coordinated by the Institute of Computational Linguistics and Theory, directed at the first and second cycles of basic education in the Lisbon area, with 410 schools participating and reaching 74,595 students. This study identified around 58 languages spoken by these students in the family context. The three studies confirmed the presence of a large variety of spoken languages in the Portuguese school context, the main ones being Portuguese Creole languages (from Cape Verde, Guinea-Bissau and Sao Tome and Principe), German, Spanish, French, Gujarati, Hindi, English, Mandarin, Moldovan, Romanian, Russian and Ukrainian.

During the school year 2014/2015, from a total of 1,641,003 students (aged 5–18) enrolled in public schools, 49,743 presented with migratory backgrounds (DGEEC, 2016). These students came from more than 30 countries (with the most significant, in descending order, being: Brazil, 11,476; Cape Verde, 6275; Angola, 3534; Ukraine, 3512; Guinea-Bissau, 3350; Romania, 3044; Sao Tome and Principe, 2467; France, 1846; China, 1745; Spain, 1618; Moldova, 1473; United Kingdom, 1200). These students are either first generation (meaning they were born outside Portugal and moved at some point during their lifetime) or second or third generation (born in Portugal but from families, either parents or grandparents, who moved from other countries). Regarding the presence of HLs in Portuguese public schools, the same study concludes that these are the languages of the same countries mentioned above, most notably Brazilian Portuguese.

This diversity brings with it educational challenges at various levels, in particular concerning curricular management and organization, education for diversity, and teacher education. Portugal, it should be noted, has yet to include in its official curricula any sort of cross-curricular conception of integrated didactics of the language of schooling, in order to facilitate the integration and success at school of students with migratory backgrounds. Having said that, the assumption seems to be that HLs are not usable in the classroom and might even get in the way of the acquisition of the language of schooling (regardless of whether or not the languages are close to or even variants of the same language). Thus, students' languages, even when thematized in the classroom, and despite the affective and identity value assigned to them, are not considered as a valuable didactic project *per se* and, therefore, are not mobilized in the classroom.

Under these circumstances, efforts in terms of language education policy have been directed towards offering programmes of Portuguese as a non-native language (PNNL)[2] and/or support to PNNL in the basic schooling years (students aged 6–15) and in specialized secondary education (students aged 16–18) in the sciences, humanities or the arts. The intention behind such programmes/support is to provide more equitable conditions for curricular access and educational success, namely with respect to learning and mastering the Portuguese language (PL), as a vehicle for the acquisition of formal, scholarly knowledge. In practical terms, students who speak another native language are placed in a regular classroom and given a PNNL diagnostic test to assess their knowledge of the PL. Based on the results, they are categorized in their PNNL proficiency level. From then on, they attend PNNL classes all the time, if the school meets the conditions for a PNNL class (minimum 10 students). Otherwise, they attend regular classrooms and are pulled out for PNNL classes from time to time or they attend regular PL classes but follow the PNNL curriculum for their assessed proficiency level (A1, A2 or B1), and may receive extra PNNL-support classes (DGIDC/ME, 2005).

Two studies have attempted to assess the school results of students attending PNNL: DGE (2009) and Madeira *et al.* (2014). Both studies conclude that there is a generalized absence of resources and support. It was observed that most students with identified needs at this level did not benefit from specific PL support. For Madeira *et al.* (2014), this absence is due to: (i) the limited offer of PNNL classes; (ii) the lack of specialized teachers; (iii) the minimum number of students required to organize groups by levels of proficiency; and (iv) its absence from technical and private schools.

On the other hand, the growing cultural and linguistic plurality in schools, recognized by teachers, points to the need for continuing teacher professional development oriented towards the promotion of plurilingual and intercultural approaches that are integrative, flexible and reflexive in the classroom. The need and urgency for these programmes is equally demonstrated by research that shows that schools and teachers have a tendency to neither consider HLs nor consider students' plurilingual repertoires in their daily practices and planning. The results of the study by Faneca *et al.* (2016), for instance, show that the inclusion of an education with HLs is not one of the priorities of the teaching staff even if, somewhat paradoxically, they recognize themselves as being ill prepared to manage plurality and variation. It is therefore interesting to question whether it is lack of priority that influences lack of preparation or if, as is often repeated by a certain dominant discourse in the teaching profession, it is lack of preparation that causes teachers to relegate linguistic and cultural diversity to a position of inferiority (or even invisibility).

The reader is reminded that both the profile of PNNL teachers and policies oriented towards plurilingualism are yet to be defined (Madeira *et al.*, 2014). Pre-service teacher education does not include, in a sufficient, consistent and sustainable way, topics related to plurilingual and pluricultural education (Moreira & Vieira, 2014). Since 2007, the certification system for student-teachers enrolled in professional master's courses in education has been established (Ministério da Educação, 2007), but it does not contain a profile for PNNL teachers. Specific training for PNNL teachers is therefore relegated to CPD, where the offer is insufficient to cover all schools at the national level (Seabra et al., 2018).

An Innovative Teacher Education Programme: Objectives, Participants, Structure and Methodological Options

The CPD programme analysed in this chapter, with a duration of 50 hours, had the following objectives:

- to promote teachers' reflection on the possibilities of including HLs in their practice;
- to contribute to the development of teachers' pedagogical, didactic and research competences; and
- to foster the development of didactic materials that allow the teacher to act in this area, in a perspective of emancipation and transformation of the work context.

The CPD programme was developed based on the results of a previous project called 'The role of heritage languages in the development of plurilingual competence by young people with a migratory background: A case study in schools of Central Portugal', which took place between 2013 and 2015 and showed that schools and teachers do not mobilize students' HLs and do not practice a holistic language education. The CPD programme was accredited (i.e. recognized by the Ministry of Education in order to allow progression in the teaching career), and took place in a school in Coimbra, central Portugal, between January and June 2017.

With these objectives and within this context, the CPD programme comprised 25 hours of face-to-face sessions, organized in three stages, as systematized in Table 15.1, and 25 hours of individual work in teachers' own classrooms.

The CPD was aimed at all school teachers of both linguistic and non-linguistic subjects in the Coimbra district (a total of 136 teachers); only 10 teachers enrolled. These ten participants were all women, language teachers and born in Portugal, who declared Portuguese as their mother tongue. In terms of subject distribution, seven were teachers of English, one was a teacher of Spanish, one was a teacher of French and one was a teacher of Portuguese (as mother tongue). All were teaching during the school year 2016/2017 in basic education (second and third cycles) with students aged 10–15 and secondary education (students aged 16–18) in the Coimbra district. The participants enrolled in the programme because they wanted to deepen their knowledge of the proposed theme.

Table 15.1 Structure, calendar and training contents

Phases	Sessions	Dates	Contents
First stage	1st	25 January 2017	Discovering the CPD, the language biographies and other assessment instruments.
Second stage	2nd	22 February 2017	Pedagogical and didactic challenges and training needs. Assistance in constructing a project.
	3rd	15 March 2017	Syllabus and linguistic diversity (educational objectives, contents and practices).
	4th	29 March 2017	Representations of languages, cultures, peoples and countries.
	5th	26 April 2017	Language status and HL teaching contexts.
Third stage	6th	10 May 2017	Didactic strategies focused on awareness of diversity and plurilingual and intercultural development.
	7th	24 May 2017	Analysis and discussion of didactic resources.
	8th	28 June 2017	Sharing the didactic projects developed by the trainees: assessing the relevance of the programme for teachers' professional development and its pedagogical and didactic implications.

The first two stages of the programme focused on theoretical reflections at a macro level (syllabus and linguistic diversity, language status, representations of languages, cultures, peoples and countries). Several moments were dedicated to the discussion and sharing of professional experiences related to the theme. The second stage also addressed teachers' actual educational practices, at a more micro level (pedagogical and didactic challenges, didactic strategies and didactic materials). More concretely, participants were invited to elaborate and implement, in their own educational contexts, an action research project involving the possibility of including diversity in the classroom. For this purpose, trainees were invited to: (i) reflect on practices that favour the inclusion of linguistic and cultural diversity in their subject areas; and (ii) discover the tensions and contradictions that emerge from a more inclusive process of teaching/learning. It was suggested that all teachers initiate their projects with a common activity, a language biography of the students (as a didactic strategy), in order to get to know their histories and life stories, as well as their attitudes towards languages (real and declared practices), their functions and statuses. The choice of action research as a formative pathway was due to its praxeological and reflexive dimensions: action research is thought to have a positive impact in dealing with dilemmas and uncertainties related to the profession, namely by fostering teachers' reflexivity on their contexts and pedagogical habitus.

The third stage was dedicated to sharing and discussing the action research projects developed by the teachers. This last stage of the programme also allowed teachers to share explicit knowledge about what had been acquired, to assess the gaps between the current situation and the desired situation, to design and plan new actions, to act again and to reflect upon new inclusive dynamics.

In Search of Signs of Development of Pedagogical Practices that Promote Plurality

In this section the projects conceived and implemented by the teachers are analysed, as well as their reflections on the whole process, collected at the end of the programme through individual written testimonies. Content analysis of the action research projects was carried out in terms of aims, materials, strategies, languages and content. Discourse analysis of teachers' statements about project implementation and assessment was carried out.

We shall start by presenting the 10 pedagogical projects, referring to a synopsis containing elements taken from each project (see Appendix 15.1).

It can be noted that the projects were implemented: in mixed-aged classrooms (involving six different levels from years 5–12); in different subjects (four language subjects – Portuguese, English, Spanish and French), but more often in English language classes (seven out of the 10 projects) as a result of the teachers' professional profiles; and lasting an average of four 90-minute lessons. The teachers involved several languages in the proposed activities, namely: the language of schooling (Portuguese); three curricular FLs (English, French and Spanish); HLs and linguistic varieties (from Colombia and Venezuela for Spanish, from Angola and Brazil for Portuguese, from Australia and the United States for English), and other languages – Cape-Verdean Creole, Umbundu, Romanian, Guinea-Bissau Creole and Nepalese are included in the projects. These languages and linguistic varieties were selected because they were part of the students' linguistic repertoires.

The activities' objectives were essentially directed towards the socio-affective dimension of plurilingual and intercultural competence (Coste *et al.*, 1997), considering teachers' desire to: (i) increase sensitivity, curiosity and respect towards diversity; (ii) develop awareness of different languages with different statuses and functions; and (iii) recognize languages as an opportunity for learning and developing students' verbal and communicative competences. Teachers also sought to orchestrate moments of questioning (of stereotypes, preconceived attitudes, etc.) and address principles of human relationships. Their aim was to promote a greater awareness of the multilingual and multicultural dimension of contemporary societies, developing critical thinking, awareness of diverse perspectives and points of view as a way of building more plural, cohesive and inclusive societies. It should be noted that some projects focus on objectives that are strictly related to the development of students' linguistic competences, articulating them with a broader concept of language as a hybrid and plural space serving interpersonal relationships and human communication.

In the following section, we shall analyse these pedagogical experiences in greater detail, focusing on the three principles previously referred to (De Mejía & Hélot, 2017; Helmchen & Melo-Pfeifer, 2018):

- Practices anchored in the context.
- Work culture and collaborative practices.
- Inquiry-based pedagogy.

Anchoring in the context

The nuclear role held by context (including, in particular, actors and how they interrelate as well as the syllabus) is highlighted in the way the ten projects were conceived and staged.

Contextual anchoring is apparent, firstly, in the selection of content or objects to be worked on (languages and cultures and their varieties, but also themes and topics) that the teachers articulate with the students' biographies, collected in the initial activity. In this activity, the students were led to reflect on languages (all those present in the classroom and in their verbal repertoires) and associated cultures. This allowed teachers to get to know students' life stories and identify students with migratory backgrounds, building pedagogical proposals articulated with the complexity of the concrete educational situations, exploring them from the perspective of whole-classroom learning (see, for example, Projects 2 and 7).

The 'written curriculum' (Glatthorn, 2000), with the various elements it contains (learning profiles and target competences, didactic units, content, assessment, time, etc.), is another central element of the anchoring of these projects. Teachers were concerned about articulating their projects with the subjects' syllabi, selecting didactic units and teaching times, thereby experimenting with possibilities of curricular flexibility. A brief parenthesis should be opened to note that, frequently, the institutionalized curriculum is used by teachers as an argument to justify the difficulty of implementing educational practices that are innovative and more adapted to the characteristics of the context. In the situation under analysis, although this perception of the institutionalized curriculum as a constraint is also quite present, the activities proposed afforded a different (i.e. more autonomous, more flexible, more significant) understanding of it, as can be seen in the following excerpt, highlighted by the use of verbal forms such as *'it is possible'* or *'I can'*:

> **Prof_6**: It is possible to integrate activities that promote reflection upon languages and cultures, including HLs, into my subject's syllabus

[Spanish] and I can develop activities that foster an awareness of linguistic and cultural diversity among students. I can implement diverse plurilingual didactic practices in my classes, treating grammatical and lexical content, as well as content of a social, cultural, religious and even political nature[3].

Thus, teachers explore the syllabi of language courses in search of curricular elements (competences, objectives, content, didactic units, etc.) that they can re-contextualize in innovative pedagogical practices:

> Prof_3: within the scope of the Multiculturalism unit, the students were faced with the need to understand that differences of others also include the languages they speak and/understand.

> Prof_9: With respect to the activities included in the French language programme, (…) they served as motivation to learn new languages, which leads me to affirm that linguistic diversity is an opportunity and not a problem.

At the end of the programme, teachers' voices reveal that, despite the innovative proposals they were able to develop and implement, this articulation is an aspect that remains a dilemma in terms of their professional activity, which warrants reflection when designing CPD in this domain:

> Prof_1: The truth is that we struggle with a certain lack of articulation between 'good intentions' and political correctness and the classroom reality, with complying with programmes and plans, exams, continuous assessment tests and everything that is part of our teaching practice and which can hardly be matched with the flexibility that the management of linguistic and cultural issues requires.

Work culture and collaborative practices

Another aspect that should be highlighted in these teachers' projects is the fact that they are based on a collaborative work culture in the classroom, pointing to socioconstructivist perspectives in the construction of knowledge. This collaborative work involves different actors with different roles according to their profiles, in a logic of differentiated pedagogy that mobilizes a variety of interactional formats: pair-work (Projects 1, 2, 6 and 9), group work (Projects 1, 3, 7 and 9), family involvement (Projects 1, 2, 6, 7, 9 and 10), and teacher and students (Projects 1, 2, 3, 6, 9 and 10). The students with HL histories take on an active role in several activities, for example by using their HL orally or in written form, in readings, songs, games or linguistic exercises (Projects 1, 2, 6, 7, 9 and 10) or by making oral presentations about their families' cultures and their regions of origin (Projects 1, 2, 6, 7, 9 and 10). In this way, many activities included the classroom's cultural and linguistic diversity, affording meaningful and inclusive learning experiences that the classroom felt a part of, and contributing to 'questioning stereotyped attitudes', 'developing critical attitudes about the world' or 'relating cultures' and 'relativizing cultures and viewpoints' (see the projects' objectives in Appendix 1). It should be noted that the word 'new' often recurs in teachers' projects: 'new learnings', 'new languages', 'new cultures', 'new experiences', 'new ideas'. These 'new' elements are generally brought in by the HL students (see, for example, Project 6), assigning them a 'new' role of protagonists which, surely, they are not used to in formal academic day-to-day life.

These culturally and linguistically inclusive, collaborative practices allowed students not only to learn from each other and from the teacher, sharing and developing experiences, linguistic and cultural knowledge and pedagogical repertoires, but also to grow together towards co-existence with otherness and intercultural dialogue. As the teachers themselves write, 'The students managed to work with each other' (Prof_6), which is considered a fundamental skill to be integrated into school pedagogy:

> Prof_6: Sometimes we notice communication problems among students, between students and teachers, or even problems that arise from culture shock between pupils in the class. For this reason, it is very important that the teacher is attentive (…) avoiding conflict arising from social, ethnic, linguistic, cultural, religious, etc., differences. Only in this way is it possible to promote plurilingualism and multiculturality in the classroom.

Inquiry-based pedagogy

To approach the diversity present in classrooms and amplified by the projects' activities, the teachers adopted a discovery-centred pedagogy (of the self and the other, of their languages, cultures and interactions) and encouraged the questioning of dilemmas and concrete daily problems, frequently related to intercultural interaction (see, for example, the materials selected for analysis in Projects 3 and 4, or the activities in Project 8). To this end, teachers found inspiration in the pluralistic approaches (Candelier *et al.*, 2012) discussed during the programme sessions, namely the intercultural approach (in all 10 projects), intercomprehension (e.g. exploring similarities between Romance languages and varieties such as Portuguese, Spanish, Romanian, French, Cape-Verdean or Guinea-Bissau Creoles – Projects 1, 2, 6, 9, 10) and integrated didactics of HLs (Projects 1, 2, 6, 7, 9, 10). Involving the whole class, the staging of these activities was based, at various moments, on the asymmetry of knowledge and competences between all actors, an essential assumption for pluralistic approaches. Thus, for instance, in Project 10, the linguistic and cultural knowledge of a Romanian-speaking student was a key element to understanding a Romanian fairy tale, just as in Project 2 the Cape Verde student took on a nuclear role in exemplifying marriage traditions in Cape Verde, bringing testimonies from his family, photographs and other traditional objects used in this ceremony. The teacher thus took on a new role: he/she became a partner in the search for and discovery of answers and solutions (for example, describing different wedding traditions in Cape Verde and Cape Verdean Creole language evolution). By providing more space for students' voices, biographies and experiences, teachers dismantled the traditional hierarchical roles in the classroom.

The pedagogical situations in which these projects were implemented served to foster diversity by taking into account the levels of learning, student ages and the subjects involved. It can also be observed that all the didactic proposals have a common denominator related to the intention of educating for active and critical participation in plural societies. Teachers seem to recognize that this intention implies an integrated mobilization of all the components of plurilingual and intercultural competence (knowledge, attitudes and skills) around a key dimension that Byram, in the model first presented in 1997, called 'critical cultural awareness'.

To sum up, all the activities were anchored in the linguistic and cultural diversity of the depicted phenomena and situations, aiming at understanding linguistic processes (e.g. intercomprehension between Portuguese and Romanian in Project 10) and cultural differences (such as the activities involving Cape Verdean culture, history and geography in Project 2, or the carnival traditions in Cape Verde, Guinea-Bissau and Venezuela in Project 6), and thus leading students to compare and establish bridges between the languages and cultures involved.

This discovery-oriented pedagogy, built on students' curiosity and their desire to know and learn about themselves and others (cf. objectives and activities, Appendix 1) is, according to the teachers, 'a great exercise, to try to put ourselves in "the place of the other"' (Prof_1), especially when this other is the classmate next to you, leading to 'trying to understand what are the difficulties and expectations of a student with a HL that is different from Portuguese' (Prof_1). It is a pedagogy in which everyone is a winner, students and teachers, as Prof_3 recognizes:

> Prof_3: the Project led me to reflect upon what HLs represent in terms of personal knowledge, and to value as much as possible the enrichment it means to all those with whom these languages are shared.

Linguistic and Cultural Diversity in the Classroom: Benefits, Opportunities and Constraints

The analysis of the projects shows the teachers' ability to combine, explicitly, their students' diversity and HLs with the curricular content. Even if, in some cases, the teachers had still not developed plurilingual learning strategies, at the end of the CPD programme they could project themselves in a professional didactic future that was plurilingual, giving differentiated answers to situations that they are frequently faced with and that constitute true challenges to curricular innovation and flexibility.

Throughout the process, the teachers showed a double evolution: on the one hand, they exemplified possibilities of transition from a monolingual/monocultural education to a bi-/plurilingual/cultural mode of communication in the classroom, with the creation of spaces of contact – in both speaking and writing – with other languages. On the other hand, teachers also reflected upon the benefits for students (all students, not just HL students) in terms of plurilingual and intercultural development. Equally, the teachers showed greater awareness about the issues at stake and a capacity to reflect on them in the scope of their professional practices, thinking of ways to improve them, especially from the perspective of the integration and well-being of HL students, but with evident educational benefits for all students. Thus, it is possible to state that this CPD programme played a fundamental role in the process of professional knowledge construction.

However, the analysis of their projects and reflections underlines the fact that teachers' positioning towards the curricular integration of questions related to linguistic and cultural diversity varies between the opportunities they sense (such as the promotion of socio-affective relations with languages, development of attitudes of respect towards otherness, opening of spaces for contact, and intercultural development) and the constraints they feel (lack of time for individual support, curricular design, subjects' syllabi, exams). For example, one teacher said:

> **Prof_3**: The negative aspect refers to the impossibility of assessing the staging of the activities set out in the plan, given the approaching end of the school year.

The words of Prof_6 are especially revealing of these tensions:

> **Prof_6**: Linguistic diversity (…) is mostly an opportunity for my subject (…). However, linguistic diversity can also be a problem, the allocated time for teaching Spanish sometimes doesn't allow teachers to provide the individual support to HL speakers.

Teachers also highlight constraints imposed by the absence of specific educational policies for integrating HL students (particularly in terms of the offer of PNNL and support for differentiated assessment), which could make it easier for teachers who have little experience in implementing plurilingual dynamics in the classroom.

Through analysing the teachers' projects we found a lack of articulation between the specific curricular languages and the HLs. In this context, we observed that diversity was rarely viewed as an advantage in teaching/learning a particular language, and that teachers, in the objectives they set out for activities, essentially focused on transversal socio-affective aspects.

The absence of a collaborative work culture in schools, related to a professional identity that is very contingent on a single language (Portuguese teacher, French teacher, etc.), which is also borne out by other studies on curricular innovation in this area, can also be highlighted in these projects. In line with this, even though all the trainees were language teachers, they rarely created bridges between the subjects, reflecting a culture of isolation in teaching (except in Project 1, Portuguese and Spanish, and Project 9, French, Spanish and Portuguese).

Nonetheless, after the programme, teachers' discourses became noticeably more objective, with the verbalization of concrete possibilities for curricular integration of linguistic and cultural diversity, highlighting the benefits arising for all the school actors. As stated, the benefits mentioned are mainly socio-affective, focusing on the development of positive attitudes towards diversity and its presence in the school context. However, it should be noted that such benefits do not pertain solely to students, but to the global school community, including the teachers:

> **Prof_3**: the Project had positive aspects, leading me to reflect on what the HL represent in terms of personal knowledge, and to value as much as possible the enrichment it represents to all of those who share it.

Final Reflection

The objective of the CPD programme was to reflect on the possibilities of including diversity and HLs in teachers' daily practices, and to contribute to the development of pedagogical, didactic and research competences through the implementation of self-tailored projects. To reflect on the programme's contribution, we analysed the ten projects developed by the participating teachers and their final reflections.

The data collected at the beginning of the programme show that teachers did not build a learning path from the knowledge already acquired by the student, meaning that inclusion of students' HLs was not initially equated. This does not mean that the teachers did not recognize the importance of valuing these languages (due, mostly, to their affective and identity value), but that they found insufficient anchors (at an educational level, but also at the level of the school culture and their own professional knowledge) for working systematically with the HLs.

However, throughout the development of the projects, there was a progressive dialogue between HLs, curricular languages and the language of schooling. The small experiments were successful, judging by the teachers' voices, and they showed a possible renewal of materials and practices, making them more suitable to the heterogeneity of the classroom and fostering processes of meaningful learning. These experiences showed the possibilities of a differentiated management of the curriculum, attentive to differences and, therefore, contextualized.

Globally, the CPD programme enabled us to recognize that teachers need theoretical knowledge regarding the inclusion of diversity, but also to experience pedagogical strategies that allow them: (i) to mobilize the linguistic and cultural diversity of students with migratory backgrounds strategically and as a pedagogical tool, going beyond an affective asset; and (ii) to support all their students' plurilingual development through systematic activation and exploration of their repertoires. Of paramount importance is the acknowledgement that it is possible to integrate linguistic and cultural diversity into teaching practices, by purposely redesigning content and classroom practices to use students' linguistic resources without giving up on disciplinary content.

Nevertheless, the programme showed that, in order to mobilize the students' HLs, teachers need training that is oriented towards the development of professional knowledge, as well as skills and attitudes that encourage them to mobilize linguistic and cultural resources for affective but also for cognitive purposes. However, as has also been shown in other studies (Billiez & Moro, 2011; Young & Mary, 2016), this does not automatically produce change in pedagogical practices.

Finally, if the results do reveal that the implementation of HL inclusion projects in their subjects gave teachers a meaningful opportunity to reconstruct their professional knowledge and pedagogical practices, which they assessed as relevant, the lasting, long-term impact, in respect of teacher development and learning outcomes, remains to be assessed in terms of the implementation of new practices of pedagogical change.

Appendix 15.1 Faneca et al.

Title	Subject	Students	Duration	Linguistic development			Objectives	Activities
				Of the language of schooling	Of heritage languages	Of foreign languages		
1. *Twelve Pilgrim Tales*, Gabriel García Marquez	Portuguese	Year 8 (ages 13–14)	4 sessions x 90 min	Portuguese	Spanish (Colombian variety)		Fostering awareness of linguistic and intercultural diversity (orality)	Reading (silent and out loud, in Portuguese and Spanish) of the text (chosen by the Colombian student). Quiz (oral comprehension). Discussion on linguistic and cultural diversity (of Spanish and Colombian culture).
2. The Role of HLs in the English Classroom	English	Year 8 (ages 13–14)	5 sessions x 45 min	Portuguese	Cape-Verdean Creole	English	Developing respect for linguistic and cultural diversity. Raising awareness of the existence of minority languages. Learning about the evolution of those languages.	Discussion about Cape Verde (culture, history, geography,...). Listening to, analysing and translating the song 'Sodade' (Cesária Évora). Pair work: comparing marriage traditions in Cape Verde, Portugal and Anglophone countries. Vocabulary matching exercise: Cape-Verdean Creole/English. Translation (into English) of a Cape-Verdean recipe. Analysis of documents (texts, pictures, film) and project work on several cultural aspects (history, geography, architecture, gastronomy, symbols and traditions) from Cape Verde and in Anglophone countries.
3. The Multiculturalism We Live In	English	Year 11 (ages 17–18)	4 sessions x 90 min	Portuguese		English (American English, Australian English)	Reflecting on cultural and linguistic differences of the people/communities that share the planet. Questioning stereotyped attitudes. Developing a critical attitude.	Analysis of the film *Crash* (P. Haggis, 2004). Reading and analysing the poem 'The British' (B. Zephaniah). Writing a poem from the title: 'The Portuguese' (group work).

	Language	Year/ages	Sessions	Language of instruction	Target languages	Objectives	Activities
4. From a Language Biography to the Multicultural and Multilingual World	English	Year 12 (ages 16–17)	4 sessions x 90 min	Portuguese	English (American English, Australian English)	Developing the capacity to question stereotyped attitudes. Relating cultures and confronting points of view. Developing attitudes of openness towards new experiences, ideas, societies and cultures.	Analysing the poem 'Two Worlds' (S. Mirza) around the following questions: 'What is Culture?'; 'What do people mean when they talk about cultural identity?'. Making students' language biographies. Guessing game: 'Whose language biography is this?'
5. Language Biographies	English	Years 5 and 6 (ages 10–12)	4 sessions x 90 min	Portuguese	English	Getting to know, share and develop the students' linguistic repertoires.	Survey of students' language biographies. Presentation and discussion of results (by the teacher). Discussion about the cultures mentioned in the students' answers and oral and written activities of comparison between different cultures and languages. From the song 'Countries of the World': locating the countries mentioned and exploring cultural aspects.
6. El carnaval en el mundo tradiciones y curiosidades	Spanish	Year 11 (ages 17–18)	4 sessions x 90 min	Portuguese	Cape-Verdean and Guinea-Bissau Creole, Spanish (Venezuelan variety)	Raising awareness of linguistic and cultural diversity. Fostering curiosity towards other languages. Broadening linguistic awareness. Facilitating contact with new languages. Developing attitudes of respect, tolerance and acceptance towards others and their languages and cultures.	Searching for informative texts on carnival celebrations in different countries. Investigation with the families of students with HLs on carnival traditions in their countries of origin. Writing texts about carnival celebrations in different countries, and presenting them orally.
7. Interculturality in the Classroom	English	Year 8 (ages 13–14)	3 sessions x 90 min	Portuguese and PNNL	Nepalese, Umbundu	Building citizenship that is active, critical and aware of the value of diversity. Recognizing diversity as an opportunity for learning for all. Respecting and preserving linguistic and cultural diversity. Promoting multilingualism and multiculturalism. Mobilizing the Nepalese and Angolan students' linguistic competences. Promoting the academic achievement of all students.	From the didactic unit 'Identifying environmental problems and possible solutions – description of a typical house': oral descriptions of a typical house in the countries of origin of the students in the classroom (Portugal, Nepal, Angola). Analysing the film *Dashain Festival – Nepal Travel Guide* about a festival in Nepal. Group work: oral descriptions of a festivity/national tradition of the students' choosing. Presentations and debate around linguistic and cultural diversity.

8. Multiculturalism in the English Classroom	English	Year 11 (ages 17–18)	4 sessions x 45 min	Portuguese	English and varieties of English	Reflecting on the theme. Developing critical thinking. Developing communication competences in English.	From the didactic unit 'Multicultural society – immigration, demographic, ethnicity': exploring the song 'Imagine' (J. Lennon). Writing a text: 'Won't you be my neighbour'. Debate: 'Do you think that people of different ethnic backgrounds can live together in harmony?'
9. 'Mon toit, tu tejado, seu telhado'	French	Year 8 (ages 13–14)	4 sessions x 90 min	Portuguese	Spanish (Columbian variety) French	Raising awareness of diversity. Comparing three languages (Spanish, French and Portuguese) and the cultures associated with them.	Analysis of the song: 'Le rap des langues de ma classe'. Identifying the languages present. Analysis of the film L'Auberge Espagnole. Creating an advertisement for renting a house. Comparing adverts from three countries: Portugal, Colombia, France.
10. For a Good Language Learner, Heritage Languages are a Wealth of Opportunities	English	Year 7 (ages 12–13)	3 sessions x 45m	Portuguese	Romanian English	Understanding that language serves interpersonal relations and interaction.	From the didactic unit 'Going home for Easter': Reading a blog on Easter in Romania. Testimony of a student with Romanian HL on her experiences of Easter in Romania. Producing a text about students' Easter experiences (in Portugal and Romania). Oral reading and analysis of the fairy tale 'The tortoise and the hare' (in Romanian, English and Portuguese). Analysing an informative text on aspects of Romanian language and culture. Filling in a worksheet with words in the three languages.

Acknowledgements

This work is financially supported by National Funds through FCT – Fundação para a Ciência e a Tecnologia, I.P., under the project UID/CED/00194/2019. We would also like to thank the teachers who participated in this training programme.

Notes

(1) 'Heritage language', the most commonly used term in Anglophone literature (Brinton *et al.*, 2008), was adopted here, even if it could be recognized as a translation that does not cover the concepts used in Portuguese. In Portugal, neither '*língua de herança*' nor '*língua de origem*' are widely used, but rather '*línguas da emigração*' (migrant languages), a term that we do not gladly use because of the amalgamation with the perceived status of the speakers. Furthermore, this concept does not convey the relationship the speaker has with his resources. Heritage language, despite criticism, is a concept with a more positive emotional charge that puts the speaker at the centre (as someone with a heritage).
(2) It is not our intention to discuss the official terminology adopted by these programmes; we can nonetheless note that the students are defined in terms of what they are not (not natives, not speakers of Portuguese), which can be perceived as a disempowering designation.
(3) All teachers' excerpts were translated from Portuguese by the authors of this chapter.

References

Armand, F. (2017) L'enseignement du français en contexte de diversité linguistique au Québec: Idéologies linguistiques et exemples de pratique en salle de classe. In M. Potvin, M.-O. Magnan and J. Larochelle-Audet (eds) *La diversité ethnoculturelle, religieuse et linguistique en éducation* (pp. 172–182). Montreal: Fides Éducation.
Billiez, J. and Moro, M.-R. (eds) (2011) L'enfant plurilingue à l'école. *Revue transculturelle L'Autre* 35 (12), 2.
Blanchet, P. and Clerc Conan, S. (2015) Passer de l'exclusion à l'inclusion: Des expériences réussies d'éducation à et par la diversité linguistique à l'école. *Migrations Société* 162 (6), 49–70.
Brinton, D., Kagan, O. and Baukus, S. (eds) (2008) *Heritage Language Education: A New Field Emerging*. New York: Routledge.
Byram, M. (1997) *Teaching and Assessing Intercultural Communicative Competence* (1st edn). Clevedon: Multilingual Matters.
Candelier, M., Grima, A.C., Castellotti, V. *et al.* (2012) *A Framework of Reference for Pluralistic Approaches to Languages and Cultures: Competences and Resources*. Strasbourg: European Centre for Modern Languages, Council of Europe.
Castellotti, V. and Moore, D. (2010) Valoriser, mobiliser et développer les répertoires plurilingues et pluriculturels pour une meilleure intégration scolaire. In D. Little (ed.) *L'intégration linguistique et éducative des enfants et des adolescents issus de l'immigration études et ressources no. 4*. Strasbourg: Council of Europe. See https://www.coe.int/t/dg4/linguistic/Source/Source2010_ForumGeneva/4ValoriserCastellottiMoore_FR.pdf (accessed September 2019).
Coste, D., Moore, D. and Zarate, G. (1997) *Plurilingual and Pluricultural Competence*. Strasbourg: Council of Europe. See https://www.coe.int/t/dg4/linguistic/Source/SourcePublications/ (accessed September 2019).
Council of Europe (2001) *Common European Framework of Reference for Languages: Learning, Teaching, Assessment*. Strasbourg: Council of Europe.

DEB/ME (2003) *Caracterização nacional dos alunos com língua portuguesa como língua não Materna*. See https://www.om.acm.gov.pt/documents/58428/280091/235201. pdf/c40d5d32-f765-4757-ac15-69cadc2a209f (accessed September 2019).

De Mejía, A.-M. and Hélot, C. (2017) Teacher education and support. In W. Wright, S. Boun and O. García (eds) *The Handbook of Bilingual and Multilingual Education* (pp. 270–281). Oxford: Wiley Blackwell.

DGE (2009) *Relatório de Português Língua Não Materna (PLNM) – 2006/07 e 2007/08*. Lisbon: Ministério da Educação – Direção Geral de Inovação e Desenvolvimento Curricular.

DGEEC (2016) *Educação em Números – Portugal 2016*. Lisbon: Direção-Geral de Estatísticas da Educação e Ciência. See http://www.dgeec.mec.pt/np4/17/ (accessed September 2019).

DGE/ME (2005) *Análise do inquérito no âmbito do conhecimento da situação escolar a dos alunos cuja Língua Materna não é o Português*. Lisbon: Instituto de Estudos Sociais e Económicos.

DGIDC/ME (2005) *Português língua não materna no currículo nacional: Documento orientador*. Lisbon: DireçãoGeral de Inovação e de Desenvolvimento Curricular.

Faneca, R., Araújo e Sá, M.H. and Melo-Pfeifer, S. (2016) Is there a place for heritage languages in the promotion of an intercultural and multilingual education in the Portuguese schools? *Language & Intercultural Communication* 16 (1), 44–68.

Faneca, R., Araújo e Sá, M.H. and Melo-Pfeifer, S. (2018) Les langues et cultures d'origine vues par les enseignants au Portugal. *Recherches en didactique des langues et des cultures, Les Cahiers de l'ACEDLE* 15 (3). See http://journals.openedition.org/rdlc/3727 (accessed September 2019).

Galligani, S. (2009) La langue de l'école comme facteur d'intégration des nouveaux arrivants: Cas des enfants de travailleurs migrants temporaires. In J. Archibald and S. Galligani (ed.) *Langue(s) et Immigration(s): Société, École, Travail* (pp. 149–166). Paris: L'Harmattan.

Glatthorn, A.A. (2000) *The Principal as Curriculum Leader: Shaping What Is Taught and Tested* (2nd edn). Thousand Oaks, CA: Corwin Press.

Gogolin, I. (2008) *Der monolinguale Habitus der multilingualen Schule*. Münster and New York: Waxmann.

Helmchen, C. and Melo-Pfeifer, S. (2018) Introduction: Multilingual literacy practices at school and in teacher education. In C. Helmchen and S. Melo-Pfeifer (eds) *Plurilingual Literacy Practices at School and in Teacher Education* (pp. 9–15). Berlin: Peter Lang.

Hélot, C. and Ó Laoire, M. (2011) Introduction: From language education policy to a pedagogy of the possible. In C. Hélot and M. Ó Laoire (eds) *Language Policy for the Multilingual Classroom: Pedagogy of the Possible* (pp. xi–xxv). Bristol: Multilingual Matters.

Little, D. (2010) *The Linguistic and Educational Integration of Children and Adolescents from Migrant Backgrounds*. Brussels: Council of Europe.

Lourenço, M. and Andrade, A.I. (2018) Embracing diversity in early years' settings: Challenges and opportunities for teacher professional development. In S. Blackman and D. Conrad (eds) *Responding to Learner Diversity and Difficulties* (pp. 3–23). Charlotte, NA: Information Age.

Madeira, A., Teixeira, J., Botelho, F., et al. (eds) (2014) *Avaliação de Impacto e Medidas Prospectivas para a Oferta do Português Língua Não Materna (PLNM) no Sistema Educativo Português*. Lisbon: DGE/MEC. See https://www.dge.mec.pt/sites/default/files/Curriculo/EBasico/PLNM/estudo_plnm.pdf (accessed September 2019).

Mary, L. and Young, A. (2010) Preparing teachers for the multilingual classroom: Nurturing reflective, critical awareness. In S. Ehrhart, C. Hélot and A. Le Nevez (eds) *Plurilinguisme et formation des enseignants* (pp. 195–219). Frankfurt: Peter Lang.

Mateus, M. H. (2011) Diversidade linguística na escola Portuguesa. *Revista Lusófona de Educação* 18 (18), 13–24.

Meier, G. and Conteh, J. (2014) Conclusion: The multilingual turn in languages education. In J. Conteh and G. Meier (eds) *The Multilingual Turn in Languages Education: Opportunities and Challenges* (pp. 292–299). Bristol: Multilingual Matters.

Ministério da Educação (2007) Decree-Law no. 43/2007, of 22 February. Diário da República,1ª série no. 38. See https://dre.pt/application/dir/pdf1sdip/2007/02/03800/13201328.PDF.

Moreira, M.A. and Vieira, F. (2014) Formar professores para a diversidade linguística nas escolas portuguesas. In M.A. Moreira and K. Zeichner (eds) *Filhos de um Deus Menor: Diversidade linguística e justiça social na formação de professores* (pp. 215–236). Ramada: Pedago.

Seabra, T., Mateus, S., Matias, A.R. and Roldão, C. (2018) Imigração e escolaridade: Trajetos e condições de integração. In R.M. Carmo, J. Sebastião, J. Azevedo, S. da Cruz Martins and A. Firmino da Costa (eds) *Desigualdades Sociais: Portugal e a Europa* (pp. 301–314). Lisbon: Editora Mundos Sociais, ISCTE.

SEF (2016) *Relatório de imigração, fronteiras e asilo [Immigration, Borders and Asylum Report]*. Lisbon: Serviço de Estrangeiros e Fronteiras. See https://sefstat.sef.pt/Docs/Rifa2016.pdf (accessed September 2019).

Young, A. (2011) La diversité linguistique à l'école: Handicap ou ressource? La formation de tous les enseignants à la diversité. *La Nouvelle Revue de l'Adaptation et de la Scolarisation* 55 (3), 93–110.

Young, A. and Mary, L. (2016) Autoriser l'emploi des langues des enfants pour faciliter l'entrée dans la langue de scolarisation: Vers un accueil inclusif et des apprentissages porteurs de sens. *La Nouvelle Revue de l'Adaptation et de la Scolarisation* 73 (1), 75–94.

Suitably Equipped: Towards Confidently Handling a Multicultural Class

Kathelijne Jordens

Adult education teacher, Ligo – Centres of Basic Education, Belgium

As a teacher (currently I teach Dutch and mathematics to people who speak Dutch as a second language), I try to incorporate elements of students' home languages as well as aspects of their cultures into my lessons. This approach is rewarding on a socio-affective level because people with different backgrounds learn to appreciate and respect each other. Moreover, welcoming home languages in class can serve as an asset for learning (through short translations, or a moment to discuss something complicated in a shared language other than Dutch). After a few years, the multicultural flow in class feels very natural.

In retrospect, I would never have been capable of handling my class in this way without the hands-on training I gained carrying out the 'Validiv' project. This project focused on home language use in class. Through trial and error, we explored strategies to incorporate the home languages of children in learning processes during group work. It proved that it is possible to purposely use the linguistic repertoires of children to obtain socio-affective and cognitive benefits (Jordens *et al.*, 2018).

It is reassuring that, given the proper training, incorporating the linguistic and cultural repertoires of students in learning processes is achievable. However, to obtain long-term effects, training should meet certain requirements. Teachers need theoretical knowledge centered around the inclusion of diversity and, importantly, they must also be given the opportunity to try out the insights they have gained. In this way, teachers experience how the initial investment of including home languages and cultural elements can eventually save them time and energy in class and foster an atmosphere in which students can make progress.

Reference

Jordens, K., Van den Branden, K. and Van Gorp, K. (2018) Multilingual islands in a monolingual sea: Language choice patterns during group work. *International Journal of Bilingual Education and Bilingualism* 21 (8), 943–955.

16 Pedagogies of Powerful Communication: Enabling Minoritized Students to Express, Expand and Project Identities of Competence

Jim Cummins

The preceding chapters present vivid descriptions of long-standing and ongoing processes of exclusion that *constrict* the educational possibilities of minoritized students and communities. They also present inspirational accounts of pedagogical initiatives undertaken by teachers, often collaborating with university-based researchers, that *construct* interpersonal spaces of reciprocal empowerment between teachers and students. The construct of *educator agency* is key to understanding how exclusionary structures and ideologies can be transformed into spaces of inclusion, affirmation and belonging that fuel academic engagement and attainment. I am using the term 'agency' to refer to the power of educators to make choices and to act in ways that express and define their identities.

Fundamental to understanding the challenge to exclusionary structures and ideologies documented by many chapters in this volume is the fact that individual educators are never powerless. Although they frequently work in conditions that are oppressive both for them and their students, educators *do* have choices in the way they orchestrate the interactions that take place in their classrooms. They determine for themselves the social and educational goals they want to achieve with their students. Educators always have options with respect to their orientation to students' languages and cultures, in the forms of parental and community participation they encourage and in the ways they implement pedagogy and assessment.

Teachers' instructional choices within the classroom are crucial in determining the extent to which minoritized students will emerge from an identity cocoon defined by their assumed limitations in the language of instruction into an interpersonal space defined by their talents and accomplishments – linguistic, artistic and intellectual. For this to happen, teachers must see through the institutional labels and societal stereotypes to the potential within. They must also be prepared, through their instruction, to challenge the broader societal power structures that devalue student and community identities.

In this concluding chapter, my goal is to try to pull together the interlocking themes that run through the preceding chapters. Collectively, what are these accounts of teachers, students, parents and communities working together actually saying? I see this task as an urgent practical endeavour rather than an intellectual exercise. What kind of tapestry emerges from the threads that weave themselves through this volume? How can we enable our sceptical colleagues, our school administrators and/or inspectors, our pre-service teachers and our policymakers to *see* what is so obvious to all the contributors to this volume?

The title of this chapter 'borrows' two concepts that capture a significant part of the narrative articulated in the voices of teachers, students and researchers who speak to us from these pages. The essence of the pedagogical approaches described in this narrative is reflected in the phrase 'pedagogies of powerful communication', which derives from Dana Walker's (2014) book entitled *A Pedagogy of Powerful Communication: Youth Radio and Radio Arts in the Multilingual Classroom*. The book describes a year-long participatory study of Latinx high school students in the United States who created radio programmes and wrote poetry and prose that was broadcast to an audience of peers and adults. This term is equally apt to describe the practices of inclusion documented in this volume which enabled minoritized students to express and expand their identities in the context of multilingual classroom interactions as well as creative and intellectually challenging projects.

The term 'pedagogies of powerful communication' also references the construct of *power* which is fundamental to everything that goes on in schools. When we talk about 'powerful communication', we are highlighting characteristics of the instructional interactions orchestrated by classroom teachers. These interactions open up spaces where power is generated both for students and for teachers. The pedagogy communicates powerful messages to students about who they are, who they can become and what they can achieve. But the term also references the *outcomes* of these pedagogies for students. Pedagogies of powerful communication enable students to do powerful things with language, art and other semiotic tools. The affirmation of identities that is a by-product of students' powerful communication results in what Patrick Manyak (2004) called *identities of competence*. Minoritized students develop the deep conviction that they have the ability to succeed academically and, as a result, they engage academically to a much greater extent than when their identities are implicitly or explicitly devalued.

In order to bring coherence and meaning to research findings such as those discussed in this book, scientists construct models or theoretical frameworks. In most scientific disciplines, knowledge is generated not by evaluating the effects of particular treatments under strictly controlled conditions, but by observing phenomena, forming hypotheses to account for the observed phenomena, testing these hypotheses against additional data, and gradually refining the hypotheses into more comprehensive theories or models that have broader explanatory and predictive power. Theoretical claims or propositions are, by definition, applicable across contexts. The validity of any theoretical principle is assessed precisely by how well it can account for all the relevant research findings in a variety of contexts. If a theory cannot account for a particular set of research findings, then it is an inadequate or incomplete theory and must be modified or qualified.

Thus, one way of presenting the 'big picture' sketched by the contributions to this volume is to view the findings and claims advanced in the various chapters through the lens of one or more theoretical frameworks that address similar phenomena. We can ask to what extent the theoretical propositions within these frameworks are consistent with and can account for the findings discussed throughout the volume. When we bring theoretical claims and empirical findings into dialogue with each other, we can potentially identify gaps in the extent to which existing frameworks can account for the empirical data. We can also potentially identify other considerations specified in these theoretical frameworks that are not represented within the focus of the present volume.

In the following sections, I outline two overlapping theoretical frameworks that were proposed both to identify sources of potential underachievement among minoritized students and also to point towards empirically supported instructional directions for reversing patterns of underachievement. I illustrate the various theoretical claims that collectively constitute these frameworks with reference to the observations and findings described in the preceding chapters.

The Empowerment Framework

The central tenet of this framework was expressed as follows:

Minority students are disabled or disempowered by schools in very much the same way that their communities are disempowered by interactions with societal institutions. ... This analysis implies that minority students will succeed educationally to the extent that the patterns of interaction in school reverse those that prevail in the society at large. (Cummins, 1986: 23–24)

SOCIETAL POWER RELATIONS
influence
the ways in which educators define their roles (teacher identity)
and
the structures of schooling (curriculum, funding, assessment, etc.)

which, in turn, influence
the ways in which educators interact
with linguistically- and culturally-diverse students.

These interactions form
an
INTERPERSONAL SPACE
within which
learning happens
and
identities are negotiated.

These IDENTITY NEGOTIATIONS
either
Reinforce coercive relations of power
or
Promote collaborative relations of power

Figure 16.1 Societal power relations, identity negotiation and academic achievement
Source: Adapted from Cummins (2001).

It follows from this theoretical proposition that effective education for students from minoritized communities *requires* educators to challenge coercive relations of power as they are manifested in the structures and processes of schooling. At the time that this framework was initially proposed, issues related to societal power relations and teacher–student identity negotiation were largely absent from mainstream discussions of educational effectiveness.

Variations of this framework (Figure 16.1) have been proposed for more than 30 years (Cummins, 1986, 1989, 1996, 2001, 2021). The framework argues that relations of power in the wider society, ranging from coercive to collaborative in varying degrees, influence both the ways in which educators define their roles and the types of structures that are established in the educational system. Coercive relations of power refer to the exercise of power by a dominant individual, group or country to the detriment of a subordinated individual, group or country. The assumption is that there is a fixed quantity of power that operates according to a zero-sum or subtractive logic; in other words, the more power one group has, the less is left for other groups.

Collaborative relations of power, by contrast, reflect the sense of the term *power* that refers to *being enabled*, or *empowered* to achieve more. Within collaborative relations of power, power is not a fixed quantity but is generated through interaction with others. The more empowered one individual or group becomes, the more is generated for others to share. The process is additive rather than subtractive. Within this context, empowerment can be defined as *the collaborative creation of power.* Schooling amplifies rather than silences minoritized students' power of *self*-expression regardless of their current level of proficiency in the dominant school language.

Educator role definitions refer to the mindset of expectations, assumptions and goals that educators, individually and collectively, bring to the task of educating linguistically and culturally diverse students. As educators, we are constantly sketching a triangular set of images reflecting our identity choices or role definitions:

- an image of our own identities as educators;
- an image of the identity options we highlight for our students;
- an image of the society we hope our students will help form.

The concept of *educator role definitions* highlights a similar reality to what García *et al.* (2016) later termed *stance* with specific reference to educators' philosophical orientation to translanguaging in the classroom. According to García and colleagues (2016: 50), the translanguaging stance 'is a necessary mindset or framework for educating bilingual students that informs everything from the way we view students and their dynamic bilingual performances and cultural practices to the way we plan instruction and assessment'.

There is ample evidence that students who have been failed by schools predominantly come from communities whose languages, cultures and identities have been devalued in the wider society. In the past, schools have reinforced this pattern of disempowerment by punishing students for speaking their home language, or stigmatized varieties of those languages, in the school and ignoring or dismissing the knowledge and cultural values of minoritized communities, often termed *funds of knowledge* (e.g. Mary & Young, this volume). Schools typically viewed minoritized students as inherently inferior, a judgement frequently legitimated by culturally biased IQ tests (Cummins, 1984). Not surprisingly, students often disengaged themselves from school learning under these conditions.

Educational structures refer to the organization of schooling in a broad sense that includes policies, programmes, curriculum and assessment. While these structures will generally reflect the values and priorities of dominant groups in society, they are not by any means fixed or static and can be contested by individuals and groups.

Educational structures, together with educator role definitions, determine the patterns of interactions between educators, students and communities. These interactions form an interpersonal space within which the acquisition of knowledge and formation of identity is negotiated. Power is created and shared within this interpersonal space where minds and identities meet. Thus, these teacher-student interactions constitute the most immediate determinant of students' academic success or failure. The interactions between educators, students and communities are never neutral; in varying degrees, they either reinforce coercive relations of power or promote collaborative relations of power. Canadian First Nations scholar, Marie Battiste (2013: 175), expressed this reality very clearly: 'Every school is either a site of reproduction or site of change. In other words, education can be liberating, or it can domesticate and maintain domination. It can sustain colonization in neo-colonial ways or it can decolonize'.

Congruence of the Empowerment Framework with Research Themes and Findings

The salience of power relations in the education of minoritized students and communities is reflected in the fact that the terms 'empower' and 'empowerment' occur multiple times throughout this book. Majima and Sakurai (this volume), for example, point to the central role of the Chinese-Japanese bilingual teacher in a primary school in Osaka in enabling Chinese speaking students to acquire not only cultural and linguistic knowledge but also to become empowered in the development of their identities. In a very different context, Galligani and Simon (this volume) highlight the empowering impact of an innovative university diploma course at Grenoble Alpes University designed to promote inclusion among adult refugee students. They also note the importance assigned to the construct of 'empowerment' in an influential UNESCO (2005) report on the role of education in enabling adults from socially marginalized communities to participate fully in their societies.

The opposite of 'empowerment' is obviously 'disempowerment', and several chapters in this volume highlight the ways in which societal ideologies and exclusionary educational structures create contexts of exclusion and disempowerment for minoritized students and communities. The preschool teacher, Sylvie, whose innovative transformative teaching was documented by Mary and Young (this volume), noted that 'to make headway, you have to go against the flow'. The 'flow' in this case is the set of normalized assumptions throughout the French school system that French is the only language that is legitimate for teachers or students to use within the school. Mary and Young point out that these monolingual ideologies and French-only policies undermine the ability of emergent bilingual pupils to use their home languages as resources for learning. Obviously, these policies also ensure that most bilingual pupils will have few opportunities to develop literacy in their home languages, and consequently will not experience the full range of personal, linguistic and cognitive benefits associated with bilingualism and biliteracy.

Several other chapters highlight similar evidence-free assimilationist policies operating within particular societies and educational systems. Ideologies of linguistic repression reflecting coercive relations of power are clearly documented in Germany (Panagiotopoulou et al., this volume; Thomauske, this volume), Belgium (Rosiers, this volume), Japan (Majima & Sakurai, this volume) and the United States (Gage, this volume). These ideologies are often reinforced by societal structures such as teacher education pre-service and in-service programmes that seldom include any sustained focus on issues related to linguistic diversity or plurilingual and pluricultural education. Faneca et al. (this volume), for example, document this pattern in the Portuguese context. Similarly, curricula rarely, if ever, connect with the lives of minoritized students and assessment practices are invariably monolingual in the dominant language.

Despite the prevalence of coercive relations of power operating in the wider society and in most schools that reflect the values and ideologies of the societies that fund them, several chapters highlight the power of teacher agency to disrupt these exclusionary policies and practices. For example, Kitsiou et al. (this volume) and Sánchez and Espinet (this volume) highlight how translanguaging pedagogy that engages learners' plurilingual resources can scaffold instruction and affirm learners' identities. Some of the chapters focus on the agency of individual teachers (e.g. Gage, this volume; Pickel, this volume), while others document the collective pedagogical transformation that results when an entire school embraces ideologies and practices of inclusion and empowerment (e.g. Krüger & Thamin, this volume; Majima & Sakurai, this volume).

The complexities of developing whole-school multilingual education policies are illustrated in Purkarthofer's chapter (this volume), which describes the efforts of two highly diverse schools in Austria to include and reinforce students' languages. One of these schools, which had a long-standing bilingual education policy, focused on German and Croatian, but other languages spoken by significant numbers of students such as Turkish, Kurdish, Hungarian or Slovak were left out of the school's language policies and occupied lower status in the operational language hierarchy of the school. In the other school discussed by Purkarthofer, a variety of languages were valued and incorporated in instruction in addition to German. In the context of this more open orientation to multiple languages, the status of mother tongue teachers was elevated so that they were valued within their schools for the expertise they brought to teaching and learning generally. Interestingly, according to Purkarthofer, this model has spread to a network of schools across Vienna, illustrating the willingness of educators and school administrators to question normalized assumptions when they see more enlightened alternatives that appear to work well.

The significance of educator role definitions and the ways in which teacher-student interactions can promote processes of identity negotiation that promote collaborative relations of power is vividly illustrated in Pickel's chapter. Rather than viewing her newcomer students as deficient in French and needing remediation, Pickel focused on giving voice to her students through multimodal and multilingual literacy projects that involved autobiographical writing, photography, and correspondence with students of similar ages in New York who were also newcomers and learning the language of instruction. Students typically wrote their initial autobiographical drafts in their home language and later selected or summarized part of their story and translated it into French to share with their peers and teacher.

The 'identity texts' created by students were displayed in a public exhibition in one of the prominent art galleries in the students' home town of Mulhouse in the region of Alsace. The reflections of students on this entire process illustrates how their identity texts not only *expressed* their current identities but also actively *expanded* their sense of who they were and who they could become, and enabled them to *project* this expanded and enhanced identity into new social spheres (transatlantic communication, art gallery exhibition). Through this process, their identity texts held a mirror up to these newcomer students in which their identities were reflected back in a positive light. They experienced a profound transformation from identities of incompetence defined by their inability to express themselves fully in French to identities of competence (Manyak, 2004) defined by their intellectual and creative accomplishments. The definition of *empowerment* as *the collaborative creation of power* (Cummins, 2001) is captured well by the students' reflections reported in Pickel's chapter.

Macleroy's chapter (this volume) documents the outcomes of a similar five-year multilingual digital storytelling project (2012–2017) carried out in the United Kingdom. The larger project from which Macleroy's data are derived (Anderson & Macleroy, 2016) involved seven community-operated complementary schools, six mainstream schools and three overseas schools in Algeria, Palestine and Taiwan. The project included both primary and secondary level students who were studying a variety of languages: Arabic, Chinese, Croatian, English, English as an additional or foreign language, French, German and Greek. Critical ethnography, linked to ecological, collaborative and multimodal perspectives, was chosen as the central methodological approach to data gathering and interpretation. Macleroy (this volume) documents how the shared multilingual interpersonal spaces created by digital storytelling enabled the students to push the boundaries of themselves and others and to reposition themselves in relation to their own languages and cultures and those of others with whom they communicated. They developed what Macleroy terms 'competences of complexity' in relation to their own identities, the identities of others and the communities to which they belonged.

In summary, despite the range of sociolinguistic and sociopolitical contexts reflected in the preceding chapters, the educational ideologies and innovations they document are readily interpretable within the theoretical constructs identified in the empowerment framework. We see the operation of societal power structures reflected in educational structures and dominant ideologies that actively 'minoritize' and exclude multilingual students. We also see the power of educators, students and communities to challenge these coercive power structures and toxic ideologies, and in the process create patterns of identity negotiation that generate empowerment for students and educators alike.

It is important to ask, however, if this framework and the instructional directions it proposes, many of which are exemplified and documented in this volume, tell us the whole story or give us the full picture of what schools need to do to reverse pervasive patterns of underachievement among immigrant-background and marginalized students. The second framework I discuss (Table 16.1) cautions against viewing any one set of interventions or initiatives (e.g. 'translanguaging') as a panacea and suggests broadening the analytic lens to include evidence-based instructional responses to the major sources of potential underachievement.

Beyond Empowerment: Evidence-Based Instructional Responses to Reverse Underachievement

I have argued (Cummins, 2018, 2021) that a first step in thinking about educational policies and pedagogical practices that might be effective in reversing patterns of underachievement among minoritized students is to examine the research evidence regarding causes of underachievement (see Table 16.1). Three sources of potential educational disadvantage can be identified (excluding special education needs):

- home–school language switch requiring students to learn academic content through a new language;
- social disadvantage associated with low family income and/or low levels of parental education;
- marginalized group status deriving from societal discrimination and/or racism in the wider society.

Some 'minority' communities are characterized by all three risk factors, e.g. many Latinx students in the United States. In other cases, only one risk factor may be operating, e.g. high socioeconomic status (SES) white European-background students learning the school language as an additional language. These three risk factors become realized as *actual* educational disadvantage only when the school fails to respond appropriately or reinforces the negative impact of the broader social factors.

Table 16.1 Evidence-based instructional responses to sources of potential underachievement

Student background	Linguistically diverse	Low-SES	Marginalized status
Sources of potential disadvantage	• Failure to understand instruction due to home–school language differences.	• Inadequate health care and/or nutrition; • Housing segregation; • Lack of cultural and material resources in the home due to poverty; • Limited access to print in home and school.	• Societal discrimination; • Low teacher expectations; • Stereotype threat; • Stigmatization of L1/L2 language varieties; • Identity devaluation.
Evidence-based instruction response	• Scaffold comprehension and production of language across the curriculum; • Engage students' multilingual repertoires; • Reinforce academic language across the curriculum.	• Maximize print access and literacy engagement; • Reinforce academic language across the curriculum.	• Connect instruction to students' lives; • Decolonize curriculum and instruction through culturally sustaining pedagogy; • Valorize and build on L1/L2 language varieties; • Affirm student identities in association with academic engagement.

These three 'risk factors' for underachievement can be aligned with evidence-based instructional responses that respond specifically to (a) the challenges multilingual students experience in learning a new language and catching up with 'mainstream' students in academic achievement across the curriculum, (b) the effects of poverty and other forms of social disadvantage and (c) the effects of social and educational discrimination faced by minoritized students.

Supporting students in learning the school language and the language of schooling

With respect to supporting multilingual students in catching up academically, *all teachers* need to be prepared (in both senses of the term) to scaffold their instruction in ways that enable students to participate academically. As illustrated by the research documented in the present volume, 'translanguaging pedagogy' can operate as a powerful scaffold to support academic language learning (e.g. Sánchez & Espinet, this volume). However, 'scaffolding' entails a considerably wider range of instructional strategies than simply engaging students' plurilingual repertoires. The Reversing Underachievement framework also highlights the need for teachers to provide sustained instructional support to enable students to gain access to and actively use the academic registers that are characteristic of literacy and subject matter content across the curriculum.

In the current volume, there is ample documentation of the importance of engaging students' multilingual repertoires and enabling them to use their languages as powerful tools for learning and communication. Several chapters also focus on the ways in which a focus on language awareness can reinforce students' insights into how language operates in academic contexts (e.g. Gage, this volume). However, the instructional responses referenced by the constructs of 'scaffolding instruction' and 'reinforcing academic language across the curriculum' go far beyond what is typically included in translanguaging pedagogy and promoting cross-linguistic language awareness. In any comprehensive account of evidence-based instructional strategies to reverse underachievement, scaffolding strategies and an explicit focus on demystifying how academic language works must share the stage with translanguaging pedagogy and other initiatives to promote identities of competence among minoritized students (see Wong Fillmore, 2014, for the importance of an explicit instructional focus on reinforcing students' knowledge of how academic language works).

This is not in any way a critique of the present volume. It is simply a reminder that translanguaging pedagogy is not a panacea by itself, and not the whole story in helping minoritized multilingual students to catch up academically.

Enabling students to become actively engaged with literacy

Similar considerations can be invoked in relation to the impact of social disadvantage. Some of the sources of potential underachievement associated with social disadvantage are beyond the capacity of individual schools to address (e.g. housing segregation and overcrowding), but the potential negative effects of other factors can be partially reversed by school policies and instructional practices. In this regard, extensive research suggests that *the role of literacy engagement is crucial*. Students from socially and economically disadvantaged backgrounds experience significantly less access to print and opportunities to engage with literacy in their homes, schools and neighbourhoods than students from more advantaged backgrounds (e.g. Duke, 2000). An obvious reason for limited print access in children's homes is that parents who are experiencing economic difficulties do not have the money to buy books and other cultural resources (e.g. smartphones, tablets, computers) and some may not have had opportunities to become literate in their own languages. Research from around the world has demonstrated a *causal* relationship between literacy engagement and literacy achievement (Krashen, 2004). In fact, the extensive research of the Organisation for Economic Cooperation and Development (OECD, 2010) suggests that schools could 'push back' about one-third of the negative effects of social disadvantage by ensuring that students from low socioeconomic backgrounds become actively engaged with reading and other literacy activities from an early age.

Several of the chapters in the current volume address the importance of literacy engagement (e.g. Macleroy, this volume; Pickel, this volume). However, the focus of these chapters is primarily on the affordances that multilingual or translanguaging pedagogy offers to enable minoritized students to engage in powerful and identity-affirming forms of literate self-expression. Chapters focusing on pre-school environments have also highlighted the multiple benefits that are generated when parents are invited to read stories in their home languages to students (e.g. Mary & Young, this volume). However, the significance of print access and literacy engagement for long-term student achievement goes beyond the multilingual dimensions of this process. For example, longitudinal research carried out in Aotearoa/New Zealand from pre-school through age 16 has shown that the extent to which 'literacy saturation' characterized the pre-school programmes attended by students in the early years significantly predicted later reading comprehension at ages 14 and 16 (Wylie & Thompson, 2003; Wylie *et al.*, 2006).

Nurturing identities of competence among students from marginalized communities

The empowerment framework (Figure 16.1) directly addresses the ways in which societal institutions such as schools have devalued the cultures, languages and identities of marginalized or minoritized communities and it highlights the need for educators, individually and collectively, to challenge disempowering structures and ideologies by orchestrating patterns of interaction that affirm students' identities. A major way in which schools contribute to reversing underachievement is by enabling students to mobilize their entire linguistic repertoire to engage in powerful communication involving the creation of identity texts (e.g. Macleroy, this volume; Pickel, this volume). This process nurtures the development of identities of confidence and competence.

Conclusion

The chapters in this volume demonstrate clearly that teachers have the power to transform the interpersonal spaces within which identities are negotiated. They can challenge rather than remain complicit with coercive relations of power. In doing so, they generate power for both their students and themselves. Students' identities are affirmed by virtue of seeing what they are capable of creating when given the opportunity, and teachers' own identities as *educators* who can make a difference in the lives of students and their communities are also affirmed as a result of seeing what their students have achieved.

The dialogue in this chapter between, on the one hand, two theoretical frameworks designed to identify pedagogical directions for reversing underachievement and, on the other hand, the detailed analyses of ideologies and instructional initiatives contained in this volume, reinforces the need to place societal power relations and teacher–student identity negotiation at the centre of any discussion of educational effectiveness. The relevance of power relations and identity negotiation is widely acknowledged in scholarly discourse associated with the disciplines of applied linguistics and sociology (e.g. Darvin & Norton, 2014). However, these constructs are largely absent from 'mainstream' scholarly discourse associated with educational reform, and not at all prominent in official policies or curriculum documents or in the pre-service or in-service education of teachers.

Thus, it is important for a book such as this to vigorously assert its 'mainstream' credentials. This book is not just about supporting 'second language learners' in learning the dominant language of school and society. On the contrary, it speaks powerfully to the need to fundamentally rethink the problematic ideologies and instructional practices that are infused and normalized within 'mainstream' educational systems.

In asserting their 'mainstream' credentials, books such as this should also acknowledge the need for educators to integrate in their instruction the overlapping, but conceptually distinct, strategies outlined in Table 16.1. In order to effectively challenge disempowering educational structures and ideologies, instructional strategies such as scaffolding access to meaning, reinforcing academic language across the curriculum, maximizing literacy engagement and connecting to students' lives must be integrated on an equal basis with strategies that engage students' multilingual repertoires (i.e. translanguaging pedagogy) and affirm their identities. These instructional strategies overlap and reinforce each other. They are not in competition. They all contribute to the rich and complex 'mental tapestry', mindset, 'stance' or role definition that effective and empowered educators bring to the classroom every day.

References

Anderson, J. and Macleroy, V. (2016) *Multilingual Digital Storytelling: Engaging Creatively and Critically with Literacy*. London and New York: Routledge.
Battiste, M. (2013) *Decolonizing Education: Nourishing the Learning Spirit*. Saskatoon, Canada: Purich Publishing.
Cummins, J. (1984) *Bilingualism and Special Education: Issues in Assessment and Pedagogy*. Clevedon: Multilingual Matters
Cummins, J. (1986) Empowering minority students: A framework for intervention. *Harvard Educational Review* 56, 18–36.
Cummins, J. (1989) *Empowering Minority Students*. Sacramento, CA: California Association for Bilingual Education.
Cummins, J. (1996) *Negotiating Identities: Education for Empowerment in a Diverse Society* (1st edn). Los Angeles, CA: California Association for Bilingual Education.
Cummins, J. (2001) *Negotiating Identities: Education for Empowerment in a Diverse Society* (2nd edn). Los Angeles, CA: California Association for Bilingual Education.

Cummins, J. (2018) Urban multilingualism and educational achievement: Identifying and implementing evidence-based strategies for school improvement. In P. Van Avermaet, S. Slembrouck, K. Van Gorp, S. Sierens and K. Maryns (eds) *The Multilingual Edge of Education* (pp. 67–90). London: Palgrave Macmillan.

Cummins, J. (2021) *Rethinking the Education of Multilingual Learners: A Critical Analysis of Theoretical Concepts*. Bristol: Multilingual Matters.

Darvin, R. and Norton, B. (2014) Transnational identity and migrant language learners: The promise of digital storytelling. *Education Matters* 2 (1), 55–66.

Duke, N. (2000) For the rich it's richer: Print experiences and environments offered to children in very low and very high-socioeconomic status first-grade classrooms. *American Educational Research Journal* 37 (2), 441–478.

García, O., Ibarra Johnson, S. and Seltzer, K. (2016) *The Translanguaging Classroom: Leveraging Student Bilingualism for Learning*. Philadelphia, PA: Caslon.

Krashen, S.D. (2004) *The Power of Reading: Insights from the Research* (2nd edn). Portsmouth, NH: Heinemann.

Manyak, P.C. (2004) 'What did she say?': Translation in a primary-grade English immersion class. *Multicultural Perspectives* 6, 12–18.

OECD (2010a) *PISA 2009 Results: Learning to Learn – Student Engagement, Strategies and Practices (Vol. III)*. Paris: OECD. See http://www.oecd.org/dataoecd/11/17/48852630.pdf.

UNESCO (2005) *Guidelines for Inclusion: Ensuring Access for Education for All*. Paris: UNESCO. Retrieved from https://unesdoc.unesco.org/ark:/48223/pf0000140224

Walker, D. (2014) *A Pedagogy of Powerful Communication: Youth Radio and Radio Arts in the Multilingual Classroom*. New York: Peter Lang.

Wong Fillmore, L. (2014) English language learners at the crossroads of educational reform. *TESOL Quarterly* 48 (3), 624–632.

Wylie, C. and Thompson, J. (2003) The long-term contribution of early childhood education to children's performance – evidence from New Zealand. *International Journal of Early Years Education* 11 (1), 69–78. doi:10.1080/0966976032000066109

Wylie, C., Hodgen, E., Ferral, H. and Thompson, J. (2006) *Contributions of Early Childhood Education to Age-14 Performance: Evidence from the Longitudinal 'Competent Children, Competent Learners' Study*. Wellington: Ministry of Education.

Glossary

dominant language: A language occupying a more powerful position in society which may differ from the language(s) used by many of its members, but which is dominant due to its status in society, the resources available and how it is recognized and valued in language policies.

emergent bilinguals: Individuals who are beginning to learn an additional language and developing their bilingualism, and whose ability in one or more of these languages is said to be emerging. The term emphasizes the learner's potential to become bilingual, rather than solely focusing on the development of the dominant language within their context.

empowerment: Providing individuals and/or groups with the opportunities, knowledge and tools to realize their strengths and potential, make informed choices and take charge of their lives.

family language(s): Language(s) or varieties of languages most commonly spoken at home with parents and family/community for daily interactions. There is an emphasis on ties of filiation and the fact that this language differs from the language(s) used by those outside the family sphere, in education, for example. *See also* home and heritage language.

heritage language(s): This is the preferred term for minority languages in the United States and Canada and is usually defined as all the languages used in society, other than the dominant language (i.e. English) that a speaker has a personal desire to (re)connect with. *See also* family language and home language.

home language(s): Language(s) or varieties of languages spoken at home with parents and family/community. There is an emphasis on the social space, the home, and the fact that this language differs from the language(s) used in other social spaces such as schools. *See also* heritage language and family language.

inclusion: Inclusion implies that institutions should address the diverse needs of all learners, taking into account their specific backgrounds. Although the term inclusion has been associated with the notion of handicap in some contexts, its use in this volume is in line with the definition provided by UNESCO as 'a dynamic approach of responding positively to pupil diversity and of seeing individual differences not as problems, but as opportunities for enriching learning' (UNESCO, 2005: 12).

integration: Incorporation of an individual or minority group into a majority group. Some authors in this volume use the term integration to refer to a state of social cohesion while others view integration as a form of imposed assimilation.

language awareness: Language awareness, as defined by the Association for Language Awareness, refers to 'explicit knowledge about language, and conscious perception and sensitivity in language learning, language teaching and language use'. See https://www.languageawareness.org/?page_id=48.

language policy: Language policy involves the explicit and implicit regulations for the use of languages and their distribution. It is a multifaceted phenomenon (Spolsky, 2004) that requires an investigation of language management, language ideologies and beliefs and language practices.

minoritized language(s): The language(s) spoken by a minoritized and/or marginalized group. A language that has been attributed a less powerful position by society/a dominant group.

multilingual: A term used to refer to the presence and/or use of multiple languages by a person and/or within a specific context. Within the framework of research and policy documents published by the Council of Europe, the term is used to describe a context (territorial, political, etc.), as opposed to personal linguistic competences. *See* plurilingual.

plurilingual: Within the framework of research and policy documents published by the Council of Europe, the term plurilingual refers to a person, or persons, whose language repertoire is composed of a variety of linguistic skills (speaking, understanding, interacting, reading, writing), varying in degrees of competence, in several languages.

(language/linguistic) repertoire: The complex, dynamic construct of resources available to an individual, following trajectories, affects and experiences that a particular speaker can access at different times in order to communicate with others.

translanguaging: The practice of using all the languages an individual has at his/her disposal as a resource for meaning-making and negotiating in communicative contexts. It also represents an approach to pedagogy that affirms and leverages students' dynamic language practices in teaching and learning.

References

Spolsky, B. (2004) *Language Policy*. Cambridge, MA: Cambridge University Press.
UNESCO (2005) *Guidelines for Inclusion: Ensuring Access to Education for All*. Paris: United Nations Educational, Scientific and Cultural Organization. https://unesdoc.unesco.org/ark:/48223/pf0000140224?posInSet=1&queryId=43ff467a-18c6-4fdd-90d7-c0984baebef0.

Index

academic language, explicit instruction of 247, 293–4
action-research methodology 191, 268
adult students 131–45, 149–68, 282–3
Affordances for Language Awareness 249–54, 255, 256, 295
agency
　educator agency 284, 290
　learners' 166, 202, 203, 206–7, 211
　teachers' 71, 113, 114, 118, 124–7, 141, 284, 290
Alim, H.S. 173, 180, 181
Alrutz, M. 208
analeptic awareness 251, 253, 256
Anders, Y. 63
Anderson, J. 203, 206, 207, 209, 210, 218, 291
Andrews, S.J. 242, 256
anthropology 135, 151, 157, 228
Aotearoa/New Zealand 295
applied theatre 208, 215
Arabic
　Brussels 75, 78
　Critical Connections: Multilingual Digital Storytelling 210, 211–13
　Germany 42–6
　Greece 162, 164, 165
　New York City 178
　and 'plebian' multilingualism 75
Armand, F. 220, 236, 263
Arndt, S. 59
artifactual literacies 208
assimilation 44, 45, 61, 63, 64, 94–6, 118, 290
Association for Language Awareness (ALA) 233
attrition, language 92
Audet, G. 231
Audras, I. 234

Augé, M. 228
Austria 16–33, 290
"authentic chroniclers" 188
autobiography 185–200, 291

Baca, G. 243
Backus, A. 153
Baker, C. 95, 98, 120, 172
balanced bilingualism 31
Ball, S. 72
'Ballet Dancers' painting 155
Banks, J.A. 18, 243, 244
Barcelona European Council (European Commission, 2002) 16
Barrateau, M. 234
Battiste, M. 289
Baudelet, C. 122
Baumert, J. 54, 63
Bauthier, E. 222
Beacco, J.C. 9, 135
Behrensen, B. 39
Belgium 70–91, 282–3, 290
belonging 202–20
Berliner Bildungsprogramm 57
'Between the devil and the deep blue sea' 71
Betz, T. 57
bi-dimensional objectives 157
Biesta, G. 118
Bilingual Education Act 1968 (US) 243
bilingual picture books 69, 124–5, 176
biliteracy 105, 106–7
Billiez, J. 276
biographic approaches to research 20
biographical analysis 209, 217
Birot, S. 225
Blackledge, A. 17, 40, 58, 186, 187
Blanchet, P. 263
Block, D. 186, 187

blogs 233
Blommaert, J. 5–6, 59, 70, 75, 153
Bonacina Pugh, F. 6, 71, 72, 79, 80, 87, 115
books
　digital multilingual picture books 69
　multilingual books 234
　multilingual picture books 124–5, 176
　and socioeconomic disadvantage 294
　translations of 125, 179
Boos-Nünning, U. 37
borderlands 205
bottom-up discourses 86–7, 144
Bourdieu, P. 61, 122, 186, 187, 189, 196
Brazilian Portuguese 265
Brock, A. 228
'broken' language 62
Bronfenbrenner, U. 200
Brown, L. 206
Brussels 70–91
builder roles 136, 146
Bulgarian 210, 213–15
Burgenland-Croatian 18–19, 22–3, 25, 28–9, 30
Burris, M.A. 191, 197
Busch, B. 16, 20
Bush, George W. 242–3
Butler, J. 44
Byram, M. 273

café parents 232–3, 237
Canada 91–2, 96, 220–1
Canagarajah, S. 17, 27, 158
Candelier, M. 233, 262, 263, 272
Carol, R. 225
Carrasquillo, A. 171
Carvajal, F. 21
Celic, C.M. 172, 173
Cenoz, J. 16
censorship of home languages 5
Chagnon, G. 123
Charmaz, K. 58
Children Crossing Borders (CCB) study 57–8
Chinese 93–111, 169, 171, 176, 289
Christopoulos, D. 149
citizenship 106, 166, 206, 263
civic engagement 206

Clerc Conan, S. 263
co-construction 156, 254, 256
co-education 227–8
cognitive abilities 196, 198, 247, 276
Cohen, L. 210
co-learners 136, 140, 146
co-learning 157
collaborative creation 191–6, 205, 214–15
collaborative meaning-making 158–9, 205, 218
collaborative power relations 288, 291
collaborative practices 271–2
collaborative spaces 227
collaborative teaching practices 264
collective action 143–4
colonialism 58, 59, 172, 289
Comber, B. 208, 217
Common European Framework of Reference for Languages 262
comparative case study approaches 174
competences of complexity 207, 217, 292
complementary languages 158–9
complementary schools 111
computer-mediated communication 150, 164–5
consent 138–9, 210
constant comparative method 117–18
Conteh, J. 5, 189, 228, 263
content and language integrated learning (CLIL) 75, 84–5
content-based learning 97
contextual anchoring 270–1
continuing professional development (CPD) 261–82
Copland, F. 72
cosmopolitanism 213
Coste, D. 135, 269
Cots, J.M. 233
Council of Europe 115, 134, 262
Creese, A. 18, 40, 71, 72, 80, 84, 86, 87
Cremin, T. 205, 215
Crevits, H. 75–6
critical applied linguistics 59
Critical Connections: Multilingual Digital Storytelling 202–20
critical consciousness 121–2
critical cultural awareness 273
critical ethnography 209–10, 291
critical multilingual identities 181

critical pedagogy 156, 162–3, 164
critical reflection 125
critical teacher language awareness 114
critical theory frameworks 121–2
critical thinking 164, 180, 269
critical whiteness studies 58
Croatian 26–7 *see also* Burgenland-Croatian
Crookes, G.V. 114, 121
cultural capital 61, 196
cultural diversity 126, 221, 222, 231, 262–7, 273–5
cultural integration 133, 141
cultural sensitivity 153, 162–4
culturally and linguistically diverse (CLD) pupils 94, 95–108
culturally sustaining pedagogy 173, 180, 181
Cummins, J. 52, 81, 94, 96, 98, 104, 105, 107, 110, 114, 125, 140, 141, 185, 188, 189, 191, 192, 195, 196, 197, 207, 243, 286, 287, 291, 292
CUNY-NYSIEB 173–81
curricula 77, 97, 225–6, 234, 265, 270–1, 290
Cypriot Dialect 215
Cyprus 202–20
Czech Heritage Language School in Iceland 33–4

Damasio, A.R. 186–7, 193, 194
Darling-Hammond, L. 243, 244
Darvin, R. 206, 296
Daskalaki, I. 150, 151, 157, 161
day-care 46, 56
De Korne, H. 20
De Mejía, A.-M. 263, 264, 270
Declaration of Human Rights 134
decolonialization 289
decontextualized mode 162
deficit perspectives
 devaluing home languages 288
 France 124, 190, 222–3, 225
 Germany 40, 47, 56, 63
 Iceland 34
 parents 62
 teachers 81
Dei, G.S.N. 14
Delpit, L.D. 188
Derry, S.J. 117
detectives 136, 139, 146, 264

Dewey, J. 18
Dewitz, N.v. 38
Dialogic Language Assessment (DLA) 97, 101–2
dictionaries 64
didactics of plurilingualism 233
Diehm, I. 38
digital multilingual picture books 69
digital multilingual stories 202–20, 291
digital translingual spaces 161–5
diglossic ideologies 14
Dirim, İ. 37, 47, 59
discipline 36, 42–3, 61
discourse analysis 269
discourse maps 29
discrimination 5, 6, 126, 292
discursive practices 58
disempowerment 4, 286, 288, 289
Dolby, N. 126
Dompmartin-Normand, C. 234
Donlevy, V. 35
Drotner, K. 205, 207, 217
Duff, P.A. 245
Duke, N. 294
Durkheim, E. 132, 186
Dutch 70–91, 282–3

Early, M. 140, 185, 188, 189, 191, 195, 196, 197, 207
early childhood education 54–69, 112–29, 244 *see also* pre-school education
ecological perspectives 25, 118, 209–10, 242, 249–50, 291
education as a political act 162–3
educational framework of literacy attainment 106–7
educator role definitions 288–9, 291
Ek, L.D. 59
elite multilingualism 27, 86
ellipsis 253
emergent bilingualism 47, 93–110, 116, 118, 124–5, 190, 222–40
emergent biliteracy 105, 116
empathy 120, 123, 126, 142, 153, 180, 206, 208, 254–6
empowerment
 acquiring the 'Norm' language as empowerment 60–1
 framework of 286–92, 295
 and identity texts 189, 191, 195–7

empowerment (*Continued*)
   mutual empowerment 165–6
   refugee students in France 133, 141
   refugee women in Greece 150, 155, 165–6
   teachers' role 146, 163, 170, 174, 181
England 202–20
English
   Critical Connections: Multilingual Digital Storytelling 210
   English as a Second Language (ESL) 91–2, 244
   English-as-a-New Language (ENL) programs 171
   as language of instruction in US 170, 173–4, 181
   as a mediation language 162, 166
   peripheral varieties of 27
   TESOL 246
English as a Foreign Language (EFL)
   Austria 19–20, 22, 23, 24, 26
   Belgium 75, 84
   Germany 42
   teacher qualifications in 246
enriched learning 134
equality, versus equity 4
equity 4, 21, 80, 122, 126, 173
Escott, H. 208
Escudé, P. 4
Espinet, I. 173
ethnocentricity 119, 135, 227
ethnography
   critical ethnography 209–10, 291
   ethnographies of multilingualism 40
   language policies in Brussels 71–3, 87
   of language policy and planning research 20
   newcomer students in Germany 40–7
   polyphonic video-ethnographic methods 55
   pre-school education in France 230
   refugee women in Greece 151, 155, 157
   video ethnography 55, 57
   young people's multilingual digital stories 209–10
European Commission 35, 112
European Parliament 13, 134
European Union (EU) multilingualism goals 16

Evans, B. 243
exclusionary chains 21
experiential learning 218

fairness 202–20
Faneca, R. 264, 266, 277–9
Farsi 162, 164, 165
feminist theory 191
Ferreira, A. 6
fields of exclusion, schools as 21
film 55, 57, 202–20
Flecha, R. 14, 227, 228, 229, 230, 236
Flemish language policies 73–6
Flores, N. 5
focus groups 57, 58
foot knowledge 208
forbidden languages 43–4, 45, 75
forced migration 42, 46, 110
Foucault, M. 45, 186, 187, 194, 195
Fought, C. 255
Framework of Reference for Pluralistic Approaches 262
France
   early childhood education 68–9
   home-school relationships in pre-school 222–40
   migrants 52–3
   monolingual ideologies 6, 112, 115–16, 118–21, 289
   multilingual pre-school in 112–29
   newcomer immigrants' identity negotiation 185–200, 291
   pre-school education 222–40
   university diploma programme for refugee students 131–45
Freinet, C. 122
Freire, P. 121, 156, 191
French
   Brussels 70, 75, 77, 79–80, 82, 83, 84, 87
   Canada 220–1
   France 115, 124, 185, 190, 224
   French as a second language (FSL) 52–3, 224, 230, 245
   French for Academic Purposes 140
   migrants in France 137, 192
Frenzel, B. 39, 41
Frieters-Reermann, N. 39
Frimberger, K. 155
fringes of lessons, multilingualism at the 42–3

Frühe Chancen. Schwerpunkt-Kitas: Sprache und Integration (Early Chances: Language and Integration) 55–6
Fuchshuber, A. 215
funds of knowledge 121, 241, 288

Gal, S. 76, 113
Galligani, S. 263
Gándara, P. 243
Ganley, B. 203
García, O. 5, 9, 47, 59, 95, 114, 120, 126, 135, 139, 146, 156, 170, 171, 172, 173, 174, 176, 178, 179, 180, 181, 190, 205, 218, 222, 228, 229, 242, 288
Garett, P. 233
Gee, J.P. 29
Georgi, V.B. 36, 37
German
  Austria 19, 22–4, 25–6, 27, 28–9
  early childhood education in Germany 55–68
  German as a second language (GaSL) 40, 41, 47
  Germany 36, 43–6
  plurilingualism 54
Germany 35–52, 290
Gibson, S. 21–2
Gillot, C. 223
Giroux, H. 22, 150, 187–8
giving-receiving-reciprocating principle 138, 143
Glatthorn, A.A. 270
Global Englishes 27
globalization 70, 93, 107
glocalisation 149–50
Gogolin, I. 71, 87, 261
Gonzalez, M. 205, 207, 209, 213, 217, 218
González, N. 121, 241
grammar teaching 246
Gramsci, A. 59
Greece 149–68
Greek 161–2, 165–6, 210, 215
Grenoble Alpes University (UGA) 131–45
Grosjean, F. 46
grounded theory methodology (GTM) 58
group work by language 177
Gudat, M. 40

Habib, S. 207
Hancock, A. 110
Hartley, J. 217
Hawkins, E.W. 233
head teachers/senior leaders 52, 116, 119, 213, 230–1
Heath, S. 208
Hebard, H. 250
Heckmann, F. 35
hegemony 22, 45, 59, 61
Heller, M. 40
Helmchen, C. 264, 270
Hélot, C. 4, 52, 71, 87, 113, 189, 190, 222, 263, 264, 270
heritage languages *see* home languages
Hersi, A.A. 126
hidden curricula 18
hierarchies, language 16, 28, 30–1, 181, 263
high expectations 124, 293
Hillmert, S. 21
Hinton, L. 31
Holliday, A. 24, 59, 213
home languages *see also* repertoires, linguistic
  adult students 131–45, 149–68, 282–3
  awareness raising 233
  'benign neglect' 96
  Brussels 75–6
  censorship of home languages 5
  considered obstacles to further language learning 46, 65, 66, 75, 91–2, 121, 263
  Czech Heritage Language School in Iceland 33–4
  devaluing 58, 286, 288
  for discipline purposes 36, 42–3, 61
  empathetic perspective-taking 254–5
  for group work 84–5
  home-school relationship 223
  and identity 189
  legitimacy 196
  literacy 105, 176, 289
  loss of 105
  measuring L1 proficiency 104–5
  multilingualism-as-norm lessons 179–80
  to nurture students 233–4, 248
  parental collaboration 60–5, 68–9
  parents' use of at home 118

home languages (*Continued*)
  partnering same language-speaking students 84–5, 175, 177–8
  as resource 118, 120–1
  respecting 123
  scaffolding with 173
  social status 21
  teachers learning 121, 175, 233, 247–8, 255
  teachers' recognition of 80–1, 225
  translanguaging pedagogy 169–83
  used to calm/reassure children 233–4
  visibilizing 64–5, 196
  whole-school multilingual education 16–33, 290
home visits 111, 255
home-school relationship 222–40
  see also parents
homogenization 46–7, 71
hooks, b. 18, 204, 214
Horan, D.A. 126
Hornberger, N. 16, 17–18, 20, 29, 30, 71, 72, 87, 243
Huber, J. 123
Hungarian 19, 23, 30
hybrid identities 106

Iceland 33–4, 146
ideational fluency 205, 215, 218
identity
  affirmation of 173, 206, 290
  construction through discourse 187
  crises of 97
  critical theories of 186
  fluidity of 207
  hybrid identities 106
  identities of competence 284–97
  identity negotiation 101, 106–7, 185–200, 222, 287, 289, 292, 296
  identity texts 140, 185, 189, 197, 207, 291
  interrogation of 207
  learner identities 246, 248–9, 255–6
  multidimensionality of 187
  in multilingual digital storytelling spaces 206–7
  multilingual identity 22, 255
  multiple identities 155, 157–8
  narrative identity 186, 188, 193–4, 208
  and otherness 194–5
  teachers' professional 263, 275

ideologies, language *see also* monolingual ideologies
  assimilation 44, 45, 61, 63, 64, 94–6, 118, 290
  Austria 22–4, 26–7, 29–31
  competing language ideologies 242–59
  critical awareness of emergent bilingualism 124–5
  definition 113
  Germany 37, 59
  homogenization 71, 87
  intercultural competences 123
  language policies 17
  multilingual education 17
  social justice 121–2
  Spolsky's framework 40
  teachers' 135–6, 139–41
  US 242–5
illegal status (migrants) 39
imagined experience 205
imagined groups 21
immersion 116, 121, 224–5
imperialism 59
INCLUD-ED 229
inclusive education
  as a dynamic system 143–4
  inclusion as collective social responsibility 134–5
  inclusion versus integration 56
  UNESCO 3, 21, 56, 77, 133, 134
informal school situations 43, 229, 230
inquiry-based pedagogy 272–3
inquiry-based teacher education 264
inscription 135, 144
in-service teacher training 261–82
Inside Out and Back Again (Lai, 2011) 179
integration
  cultural integration 133, 141
  de facto language policies 60–5
  versus inscription 135
  monoglossic ideologies 3
  national plans for 55, 56
  semi-integrative schooling 39
  sociological perspectives 132–5
  structural integration 133, 141
intercultural being 205
intercultural communicative skills 165, 203
intercultural competences 123, 150, 266, 269, 272

intercultural literacy 203–4
interdisciplinary perspectives 59, 151, 157
international remedial classes 41
Irene – a refugee's story 215–17
Irvine, J. 76

Jankowicz-Pytel, D. 165
Janssens, R. 70, 83
Japan 93–110, 259–60, 290
Japanese 95, 96–7, 246
Jaspers, J. 5, 71, 75, 83, 86
Johnson, D. 72, 87
Jordens, J. 115–16
Jordens, K. 283
Ju, C. 155

Kádas Pickel, T. 190, 191
Kanouté, F. 187
Karakaşoğlu, Y. 37, 38
Karlinchen (Fuschshuber, 1995) 215, 217
Kassis, M. 47
Katholiek onderwijs 75
Kaufmann, J.C. 138
Kemper, T. 39
Kervran, M. 234
Kimhag, K. 200
Kinloch, V. 188
Kirwan, D. 257–8
Kitas (German early language education) 54–68
Kiyota, J. 98
Kleifgen, J.A. 47, 95, 171, 181, 190
Kleyn, T. 170, 172, 173
Knappik, M. 47
knowledge
    cognitive abilities 196, 198, 247, 276
    foot knowledge 208
    funds of knowledge 121, 241, 288
    knowledge-based society 14
    metalinguistic knowledge 40, 236, 249, 252–3, 255, 256, 259–60, 263
    shared knowledge 253
Korntheuer, A. 39
Kramsch, C. 150
Krashen, S.D. 294
Kremnitz, G. 116
Kroskrity, P.V. 17, 113
Krüger, A.-B. 229
Krumm, H.-J. 46
Kurdish 28, 30

Kurita, Y. 96
Kushnir, A. 206

Lahire, B. 4, 135
Lai, T. 179
Lambert, J. 203, 207
language awareness approaches 37, 233, 242–59
Language Awareness Related Episodes (LAREs) 249–58
language markets 61
language of instruction
    Austrian school policies 25
    Dutch-medium schools 71, 73, 74, 76–7
    English in USA 170, 173–4, 181
    scaffolding 173
    students' commitment to learn 190
language tickets 77, 78–9, 86
language transmission 31
languages other than English (LOTE) 171
Languages Without Borders 152–60
languaging 5 *see also* translanguaging
Langues du monde au quotidien (Languages of the World Everyday, Kervran, 2013) 234
Lapkin, S. 249
layering 72, 84
learner agency 166, 202, 203, 206–7, 211
learning success, promises of 44–7, 75
Leclaire, F. 222, 226, 227, 228, 234
Lefèbvre, H. 228
Lemattre, B. 234
Lengyel, D. 37
Leung, C. 80, 86, 87, 206
Li Wei 59, 156, 173, 174, 176, 178, 179, 181
life story work 185–200
'limited bilingualism' 30
Lin, A.M.Y. 242
Lin, G. 176
lingua francas 70, 83
linguicism 37
linguistic capital 196
linguistic diversity *see also* home languages
    as advantage to all students 273–4
    as an asset 220–1
    critical engagement with 114

linguistic diversity (*Continued*)
  inclusive education 222
  mobilizing to reverse underachievement 295–6
  and social justice 14
  and teacher education 126, 262–7, 273–4, 290
  as tool for learning 80
linguistic landscapes 20, 23
linguistic transfer 263
linguistic virtuosity 173
literacy
  artifactual literacies 208
  biliteracy 105, 106–7
  deficit perspectives 40
  educational framework of literacy attainment 106–7
  enabling active engagement in 294
  home languages 105, 176, 289
  illusion of fixed 205
  importance of literacy engagement 294–5
  intercultural literacy 203–4
  L1 proficiency linked to L2 literacy 105
  linked to oral skills 225
  multilingual digital stories 202–20
  multiliteracies 217–18
  parents' 294
  and physical movement 208
  reading skills 103–4, 105
  solitary literacy 197
  trilingual literacy in Austria 20, 29, 30
Little, D. 257–8
long-term support for language learners 104
Lory, M.-P. 220
Luhmann, N. 21

Maak, D. 39
Mackey, M. 208, 217
Macleroy, V. 203, 206, 207, 209, 210, 291
Macnaghten, P. 58
Madeira, A. 266
Majima, J. 94, 95, 100, 105
Manyak, P. 285
Martinez, R.A. 114, 126, 171, 181
Martin-Jones, M. 114, 192, 197
Martin-Rojo, L. 5
Mary, L. 4, 71, 72, 87, 97, 113, 115, 116, 121, 126, 222, 225, 228, 263, 276

Mascareño, A. 21
Massumi, M. 39, 41, 47
Mateus, M.H. 264
mathematics 85, 97, 282–3
Mauss, M. 138, 143
May, S. 5
Maybin, J. 205, 215
McAndrew, M. 231
McCarty, T. 72
Mead, G.H. 186
Mecheril, P. 46, 47, 59, 60
mediation languages 153, 161, 162
mediation skills 53, 140, 142
Meier, G. 5, 263
Melo-Pfeifer, S. 264, 270
Menken, K. 173
messy cultures 205
Mestre, C. 227
metalinguistic knowledge 40, 236, 249, 252–3, 255, 256, 259–60, 263
meta-working awareness 164–5, 166
Mignolo, W.D. 58
Miller, J. 188
Mills, K. 208, 209, 217
Moll, L. 172, 173, 181
monoglossic ideologies 3–15, 41, 95
monolingual ideologies
  all students benefit from moving away from 274
  Austria 22, 30
  Belgium 74–5, 87
  disrupting 173
  France 6, 112, 115–16, 118–21, 289
  Germany 37, 38
  Japan 94
  and multilingual realities 71
  national linguistic policies 161
  and nation-building 59
  Netherlands 130
  New York City 171
  Portugal 261
  separated classes 62
  and speech and language pathology 184
  and teacher education 263–4
  USA 245
Moreira, M.A. 267
Moro, M.R. 135, 222, 226, 276
Morrell, E. 188
mother tongue at home only 61–2
mother tongue education 19, 30, 62
  see also home languages

multiculturalism 77, 176, 223, 264, 269, 272, 282–3
multilingual books 234
multilingual digital stories 202–20
multilingual education, definition 17–18
multilingual globe project 234–5
multilingual identity 22, 255
Multilingual Language Learner/English Language Learner (MLL/ELL) 171, 178
multilingual picture books 124–5, 176
multilingual repertoires *see* repertoires, linguistic
multilingual turn 5
multilingual word walls 179
multilingualism-as-norm lessons 179
multiliteracies 217–18
multimodality 155, 158, 173, 198, 209, 234, 291
Murakami, C. 116
Musk, N. 18
mutual empowerment 165–6
Myers, G. 58

Nakajima, K. 94, 97, 98, 101
narrative approaches to data analysis 209–10
narrative identity 186, 188, 193–4, 208
national curricula 224
nation-states 5, 58, 116, 172
'native speaker' teachers 19, 24, 26
native-speakerism 24, 47, 59, 62
neo-colonialism 289
neolinguicism 37
Netherlands 130
neuroscience 186
New York City 169–83
New Zealand 295
newscasts, multilingual 180
No Child Left Behind (NCLB) 242–4
non-verbal communication 232
normalizing multilingualism 29–31
Norton, B. 21, 186, 187, 206, 296
Nyboe, N. 205, 207, 217

Ó Laoire, M. 4, 263
OECD (Organisation for Economic Cooperation and Development) 54, 63, 294
official status languages 22, 26, 116
Ohta, Y. 96
open classroom policy 119–20

oral skills 103–4, 225
Otheguy, R. 172
Othering
  banning of Other languages 63
  of culture 213
  and identity negotiation 192, 194–5
  languages mark people as 'Other' 21
  Othered languages in Austria 30
  Othered languages in Germany 55, 56, 58–9, 60, 62
  resistance acts 217
  visibilizing Other languages 64–5

Pachler, N. 72, 84
Pahl, K. 208
Palestine 202–20
Palmer, D. 114, 126, 171, 181
Panagiotopoulou, A. 37, 38, 40, 46, 47, 48, 229
Papastergiadis, N. 187
parents
  collaboration with 56–7, 111
  and early childhood education 54–68
  empathetic perspective-taking 254–5
  funds of knowledge 241
  good news calls to 248
  home-school relationship 222–40
  informal contact with 229, 230, 232–3, 235
  involvement in research 20
  language agreements 76
  legitimate interlocutors 226
  parental education programs 63
  parent-teacher communication 82, 119
  partnerships with 57, 61–4, 65–6, 119, 227–8
  as resources for teacher 119
  responsibility for mother tongue education 62
  skill in majority language 76, 106
  skills in minority languages 23, 25–6, 106
  trust relationship with 68–9
  using home languages with 248–9
  welcoming to classroom 118, 119–20
Paris, D. 173, 180, 181
participant observation studies 20, 245
participatory methodologies 149–68
participatory social cohesion 141–2
paternalism 62, 63
Paul Hamlyn Foundation 202–3

Pavlenko, A. 17, 186, 187
pedagogies of powerful
 communication 284–97
'pedagogies of the possible' 4
peer groups 60–1
Pennycook, A. 59
People of Color 58–9
Perec, G. 228
Perregaux, C. 222, 226, 227, 228
perspective-taking 254–5, 256–7
Phipps, A. 205, 207, 209, 213, 217, 218
photography 185, 191–2, 203, 206, 234
Photovoice 191, 197
physicality of learning 208
Pietsch, S. 63
Piller, I. 14
PISA 54, 63
playgrounds and corridors 76–7, 84
pluridialectal repertoires 5
Plurilingual Drama-based activities 220
Plurilingual Kamishibai 220
plurilingual repertoires 5
plurilingualism
 elite versus refugee integration 54
 language policies 262
 plurilingual communities 257–8
 plurilingual repertoires 61
 plurilingual resources 64
 supporting via professional
  education networks 52–3
poetry 179, 192, 203, 285
policies, language
 acquiring the 'Norm' language 60–1
 Austrian schools 24–6, 30–1
 bilingual education 98, 171, 174
 competing language ideologies
  242–59
 de facto 55, 60–5
 declared policies at school level
  76–7, 86
 Flanders' multilingual policies 75
 'French only' 112, 225
 German early childhood
  education 58
 governmental level 73–6, 77–8, 86,
  95–100, 134, 161, 189, 242–3,
  257, 262
 implicit 77, 86
 and inclusion/exclusion 21, 133–5
 language policy research 72
 link to language practices 72

policy documents as data source 73
 prohibitions on minority language
  use 37, 43–4, 97
 Spolsky's framework 40, 72
polyphonic video-ethnographic
 methods 55, 57
Portugal 261–82, 290
Portuguese 265–6, 269
Portuguese as a non-native language
 (PNNL) 266
postcolonialism 58, 172
posters 23
poststructuralism 5, 186–7
power
 assimilation 45
 coercive 290, 292
 collaborative power relations 288
 culture of power 188
 hegemony 22, 45, 59, 61
 and identity 187
 language ideologies 17, 59
 Other languages 55
 parent-practitioner imbalance 63–4
 pedagogies of powerful
  communication 284–97
 power to act 189
 in preparatory classes 43
 racialized hierarchies 58
 teacher lanaguage ideologies 114
preparatory classes 39, 40–7, 52–3
pre-school education 54–68, 112–29,
 222–40, 295 *see also* early
 childhood education
preservation of languages 64
prestige languages 28, 75, 83, 86–7
prestige multilingualism 75
Prévert, Jacques 192
professional education networks 52–3
proficiency
 Chinese pupils in Japan 100–8
 common underlying proficiency 110
 English for LOTE students in New
  York 171
 English Proficient (EP) status 171
 L1 proficiency linked to L2 105, 110,
  197–8
 language hierarchies 263
 and learning success 75
 to participate in research 139
 plurilingual proficiency 101
 preparatory classes 47

prohibitions on minority language use 37, 43–4, 97
Project PRESS 149–68
project-based experiential learning 218
proleptic awareness 251, 253, 256
Pulinx, R. 75, 76, 113, 124
pull-out classes 103 *see also* separated classes
punishment 43–4, 45, 77, 78
Purkarthofer, J. 20, 25

Quehl, T. 46, 47
Question Mark Movie 213–15

race 58, 188
racialized hierarchies 58
racism 6, 78, 292
Radtke, F.-O. 38
Ramaut, G. 85, 86, 87
Rampton, B. 70, 72
Rawls, J. 21
reading skills 103–4, 105
reciprocity principle 143–4
reflective practice 125, 152–3
refugees
  Austria 26–7
  Germany 36, 38–40
  refugee students in France 131–45
  refugee women in Greece 149–68
register shifts 253–4, 256
repertoires, linguistic *see also* home languages; translanguaging
  complementary languages 158–9
  and identity 189
  importance of engaging 294
  instructional design 173
  legitimacy 196
  multilingual digital stories 202–20
  and multilingual education 31
  in refugee contexts 153
  as resource 34, 37, 38, 80, 118, 120–1
research ethics 102
resistance, acts of 44
Reversing Underachievement 293–4
revitalization 22, 23
Reynolds, C. 123
Ricento, T. 72, 87
Ricoeur, P. 186, 188, 193
right to education 38–9, 134
Rigolot, M. 231
Rios, F. 126

Robert Bosch Foundation 36, 39
Roma communities 52–3
Rosen, L. 37, 38, 40
Rosiers, K. 83, 87
Roßbach, H.-G. 56, 63
Rowsell, J. 208
Ruiz, R. 189, 195

safe spaces 22, 228–9, 241, 250
Sakurai, C. 96, 97, 98, 100, 101
Sánchez, M.T. 173, 174, 176, 179, 181, 229
sanctions for non-use of main classroom language 37, 43–4, 77, 78, 86
Saxena, M. 114
scaffolding 56, 76, 84, 120, 173, 181, 293, 294
Scarino, A. 206
Schnapper, D. 132, 133, 141
school environment, understanding 227
school language profiles (SLP) 20
science 85, 97
Scotland 110–11
second language acquisition, understanding of 115, 116, 126, 222–3, 225
second language learners, migrants automatically seen as 43
Sefton-Green, J. 206
self, concepts of 186 *see also* identity
self-empowerment 61
self-esteem 64, 97
self-knowledge 187
self-recognition 106
semi-integrative schooling 39
semilingualism 62
semiotic resources 17, 198, 209, 285
sensitizing concepts 58–9
separated classes
  Germany 39, 40–7, 52–3, 56, 61–2
  Japan 103
  newcomer immigrants' identity negotiation 190
  pre-school education in France 224
  for refugees in Germany 39
shared knowledge 253
Sheehy, M. 204–5, 215
shift, language 23
Shohamy, E. 55, 59, 71, 72, 86, 87
Sierens, S. 85, 86, 87

Sierra Leone 241
signage 23, 130
silenced dialogue 188
silencing 63, 188, 225, 235, 263
Silverstein, M. 113
Simon, D.L. 135
Simonin, M.-C. 223, 225, 227, 230, 231, 236
situated experience 209
Skutnabb-Kangas, T. 98
Skype 152, 165, 212
Slovak 19, 27, 30
Slovene 23
Smet, P. 75
social capital 30, 31
social cohesion 4, 14, 21, 75, 138–44
social determinism 141
social justice 6, 13, 14, 110, 121–2, 126, 156, 209–10, 217
social space 228
socialization 56, 61, 195, 226
socioconstructivist approaches 172, 264, 271
sociocultural contexts 156
socioeconomic disadvantage 223, 224, 229, 244, 292, 293, 294
sociopolitical contexts 40, 162–3
solidarity 136, 254
solitary literacy 197
space, concepts of 157, 161–5, 227–8
Spanish
    Austria 20, 23, 24, 29
    USA 178, 246–7, 249, 255
specialist instruction 99, 116, 171, 190, 200, 224, 244, 293
speech and language pathology 184
spiral development of material 162–3
Spitzberg, B.H. 123
Spolsky, B. 40, 72, 113
Sprach-Kitas (Language Day-care Centers) 56
Spyropoulou, A. 149
stances 172, 288, 296
stereotypes 156, 162, 269, 285
stigma 56, 76, 288
storytelling 64, 202–21, 291 *see also* autobiography
Strobbe, L. 85, 87
structural integration 133, 141
Strzykala, J. 40, 42
Suarez, D. 126

Suárez-Orozco, C. 171, 181
submersion education 95
subtitles 209
Svalberg, A.M.-L. 242, 256
Swain, M. 249
Sweden 200–1
symbolic capital 61, 189, 196
symbolic multilingualism 23
symbolic spaces 229
symbolic violence 5, 6

Tagg, C. 165
teacher education
    continuing professional development (CPD) 261–82
    Critical Connections: Multilingual Digital Storytelling 204
    inquiry-based teacher education 264
    and integration of heritage languages 261–82
    Japan 97
    and linguistic diversity 126, 262–7, 273–4, 290
    multilingual populations 223
    for multilingualism 126
    plurilingualism 225, 266–7
    pre-service teacher education 266–7
    professional education networks 52–3
    in-service teacher training 261–82
    theoretical training 283
teachers
    acceptance of other languages 80–1
    agency 71, 113, 114, 118, 124–7, 141, 284, 290
    all teachers need training 293
    awareness of multilingualism 82–5, 86–7
    classroom management 85
    critical awareness of language acquisition 124–5
    critical teacher language awareness 114
    deliberate use of multilingualism 36–7
    early childhood education 56
    educator agency 284
    educator role definitions 288–9, 291
    empowering role of 146
    fear of lack of control 85, 86
    going against the flow 125

ideal multilingual education 23–4
imposing language policies 78–9
interpretation of policies 71, 77–85, 86
knowledge of language acquisition 222–3
language ideologies 135–6, 139–41
learning students' home languages 121, 175, 233, 247–8, 255
mainstream versus specialist 116
mediation skills 53
migrant teachers 35, 36–8
minority language teachers 22, 25
multilingual teachers 41, 82, 84
'native speaker' teachers 19, 24, 26
as partners in inquiry-based pedagogy 272–3
perceived and practiced language policies in Brussels classrooms 77–85
policing the use of non-classroom languages 44–6
professional education networks 52–3
role in multilingual groups 21–2
role in teaching migrants new 'Norm' language 61–4
and social inclusion 139–41
specialist instruction 99, 116, 171, 200
teacher attitudes and an inclusive approach 133
teacher cognition 113
teacher lanaguage ideologies 113
Teacher Language Awareness (TLA) 242–59
teacher-learner relationship 142
teacher-student role exchange 166
use of multilingual resources in classroom 42
techniques of the self 187
technology
  computer-mediated communication 150, 164–5
  digital multilingual picture books 69
  digital multilingual stories 202–20, 291
  digital translingual spaces 161–5
  Skype 152, 165, 212
TESOL 246
Thamin, N. 223, 231, 236
thematic analysis 73
think-alouds 250

Thomauske, N. 55, 56, 57, 58, 59, 61, 63, 64–5, 124, 222, 225
Thompson, J. 295
Thordardottir, E. 184
Tobin, J. 55, 57
tom Dieck, F. 40
Tomozawa, A. 94, 95
transcultural mediation 234
transdisciplinary approaches 205, 206
transformation 136
transformative pedagogy 170, 173, 178, 181, 202, 207
translanguaging
  affordances 252
  and the borderlands 205
  in the classroom 120–1, 169–83, 290, 293, 296
  Critical Connections: Multilingual Digital Storytelling 218
  digital translingual spaces 165
  home language teachers with specialized training 99
  in language policies 17
  and linguistic competence 59
  metalinguistic awareness 255
  multilingual identity 255
  multimodal resources 158–60
  Project PRESS 158–60, 161–5, 166
  refugee women in Greece 156
  register shifts 254
  safe spaces 250
  speech and language pathology 184
  stances 288
  teacher ideologies 135–6
  translanguaging pedagogy 169–83, 290, 293, 296
  versus translation 158–9, 161–2
  translingual learning strategies 40
  translingual spaces 161–5
translations
  autobiography 192
  of books 125, 179
  in the classroom 177, 178
  multilingual digital stories 209
  by parents 64, 234
  versus translanguaging 158–9, 161–2
  using school communities for 179
transmediation 209, 217–18
Traveler and Newly Arrived Emergent Bilingual Pupils support service 230

Travellers 68–9
trilingualism 20, 29, 30
Troncy, C. 233
Tsioli, S. 157
Tsokalidou, R. 166
Turkish
   Austria 19, 28, 29, 30, 31
   France 231–2, 236
   Germany 37, 42
   and 'plebian' multilingualism 75

UGA (Grenoble Alpes University) 131–45
Ugly Vegetables, The (Lin) 176
underachievement, reversing 292–5
UNESCO 3, 21, 56, 77, 80, 133, 134, 289
UNHCR 149, 150, 215
unintended consequences 91–2
university diploma programme for refugee students 131–45
USA 170, 173–4, 178, 181, 242–59, 290

Valencia, S.W. 250
Valenzuela, A. 171, 172, 181
Van Avermaet, P. 3, 5
Van den Branden, K. 85, 87
van Lier, L. 242, 249, 253
varieties of languages 26–7
Verhelst, M. 85, 87
Verschueren, J. 59

Vertovec, S. 156
video ethnography 55, 57
Vieira, F. 267
Vietnamese 179
Villa Correa, B.E. 143
voice 141–2, 180, 187–8, 220–1, 263

Walker, D. 285
Wang, C. 191, 197
Welsh 172
Westphal, M. 39
whispering 43–4
whole-body learning 208
whole-school multilingual education 16–33, 290
Williams, C. 172
Wong Fillmore, L. 243, 294
Woolard, K.A. 59, 114
word walls, multilingual 179
work cultures 271–2
World Summit for Children 55
Wrigley, T. 206
Wylie, C. 295

Yoshimura, M. 95
Young, A. 4, 46, 71, 72, 87, 97, 113, 115, 116, 121, 124, 126, 189, 222, 225, 228, 233, 257, 263, 276
Young Palestinian Talents 211–13

Zimmermann, P. 56